international
review of
social history

Supplement 13

Marriage Choices and
Class Boundaries:
Social Endogamy in History

Edited by Marco H.D. van Leeuwen, Ineke Maas, and Andrew Miles

T0345468

CAMBRIDGE
UNIVERSITY PRESS

University Printing House, Cambridge CB2 8BS, United Kingdom

Cambridge University Press is part of the University of Cambridge.

It furthers the University's mission by disseminating knowledge in the pursuit of education, learning and research at the highest international levels of excellence.

www.cambridge.org
Information on this title: www.cambridge.org/9780521685467

© Internationaal Instituut voor Sociale Geschiedenis

First published 2005

A catalogue record for this publication is available from the British Library

ISBN 978-0-521-68546-7 Paperback

CONTENTS

Marriage Choices and Class Boundaries:
Social Endogamy in History

Edited by
Marco H.D. van Leeuwen, Ineke Maas, and Andrew Miles

NOTES ON CONTRIBUTORS

Marie-Pierre Arrizabalaga, Université de Cergy-Pontoise, UFR de Langues, 33 Boulevard du Port, 95011 Cergy-Pontoise Cedex, France; e-mail: marie-pierre.arrizabalaga@lang.u-cergfy.fr

Hilde Bras, Department of Social Cultural Sciences, Faculty of Social Sciences, Vrije Universiteit Amsterdam, Buitenveldertselaan 3–7, 1081 HV Amsterdam, The Netherlands; e-mail: haj.bras@fsw.vu.nl

Hans Henrik Bull, Department of Archaeology, Conservation and Historical Studies, University of Oslo, Box 1008 Blindern, N-0315 Oslo, Norway; e-mail: h.h.bull@iakh.uio.no

Martin Dribe, Department of Economic History, Lund University, PO Box 7083, SE-220 07 Lund, Sweden; e-mail: Martin.Dribe@ekh.lu.se

Katherine Holt, Department of History, Kauke Hall, College of Wooster, Wooster, OH 44691, USA; e-mail: kholt@wooster.edu

Jan Kok, Internationaal Instituut voor Sociale Geschiedenis, Cruquiusweg 31, 1019 AT Amsterdam, The Netherlands; e-mail: jko@iisg.nl

Margareth Lanzinger, Institut für Geschichte, Universität Wien, Dr Karl Lueger-Ring 1, 1010 Wien, Austria; e-mail: margareth.lanzinger@univie.ac.at

Marco H.D. van Leeuwen, Internationaal Instituut voor Sociale Geschiedenis, Cruquiusweg 31, 1019 AT Amsterdam, The Netherlands; e-mail: mle@iisg.nl

Luigi Lorenzetti, Istituto di Storia delle Alpi (ISAlp), Università della Svizzera italiana, Via Lambertenghi 10, CH-6900 Lugano, Switzerland; e-mail: luigi.lorenzetti@lu.unisi.ch

Christer Lundh, Department of Economic History, Lund University, PO Box 7083, SE-220 07 Lund, Sweden; e-mail: christer.lundh@ekh.lu.se

Ineke Maas, Department of Sociology, Utrecht University, Heidelberglaan 2, 3584 CS Utrecht, The Netherlands; e-mail: w.a.f.maas@fss.uu.nl

Koen Matthijs, Centre for Population and Family Research, Department of Sociology, Catholic University of Leuven, Van Evenstraat 2B, B-3000 Leuven, Belgium; e-mail: Koen.matthijs@soc.kuleuven.be

Andrew Miles, ESRC Centre for Research on Socio-Cultural Change (CRESC), University of Manchester, 178 Waterloo Place, Oxford Road, Manchester M13 9PL, UK; e-mail: andrew.miles@manchester.ac.uk

Muriel Neven, Archives of the City of Verviers, Thier Mère-Dieu 18, B-4800 Verviers, Belgium; e-mail: Muriel.Neven@ulg.ac.be

Michel Oris, Département d'histoire économique, Université de Genève, 40, Boulevard du Pont-d'Arve, CH-1211 Genève, Switzerland; e-mail: Michel.Oris@histec.unige.ch

Jean-Pierre Pélissier, INRA – Unité Mona, 65 Boulevard de Brandebourg, 94200 Ivry, France; e-mail: Jean-Pierre.Pelissier@ivry.inra.fr

Danièle Rébaudo, Enquête 3000 Familles, 1 place Aristide Briand, 92195 – Meudon cedex France; e-mail: rebaudo@bellevue.cnrs-bellevue.fr

Reto Schumacher, Département d'économétrie, Université de Genève, 40, Boulevard du Pont-d'Arve, CH-1211 Genève, Switzerland; e-mail: reto.schumacher@metri.unige.ch

Bart Van de Putte, Centre for Population and Family Research, Department of Sociology, Catholic University of Leuven, Van Evenstraat 2B, B-3000 Leuven, Belgium; e-mail: Bart.vandeputte@soc.kuleuven.be

IRSH 50 (2005), Supplement, pp. 1–23 DOI: 10.1017/S002085900500204x
© 2005 Internationaal Instituut voor Sociale Geschiedenis

Endogamy and Social Class in History: An Overview*

MARCO H.D. VAN LEEUWEN AND INEKE MAAS

INTRODUCTION

The social identities of marriage partners [...] are among the most sensitive and acute indicators of community or class feelings. Who marries whom, without courting alienation or rejection from a social set, is an acid test of the horizons and boundaries of what each particular social set regards as tolerable and acceptable, and a sure indication of where that set draws the line of membership.[1]

It took a marriage to reproduce a class structure, or to alter it, as Thompson claimed for England in the nineteenth century. Kocka too, in his study of class formation in Germany, noted that the essence of class formation is the process of simultaneous closure of marital barriers between certain social groups and the blurring of barriers between others.[2]

Given the importance for social history of marriage patterns by social class, it is remarkable that historians have studied endogamy by region and age much more than endogamy by social class.[3] Endogamy by social class is also known as social endogamy or social homogamy (we use the terms interchangeably here, although, strictly speaking, social endogamy refers to marrying within the same class – and thus assumes the existence of a limited number of discrete classes – while social homogamy refers to marrying someone of approximately the same status – and thus assumes the existence of a continuous status scale). Scholars from other disciplines, notably sociology, have written more on social endogamy. Sociologists

* We are grateful to Jos Dessens, Chris Gordon, Wim Jansen, Jan Kok, Frank van Tubergen, Lex Heerma van Voss, Richard Zijdeman, and members of the editorial committee of this journal for their comments.

1. F.M.L. Thompson, *The Rise of Respectable Society: A Social History of Victorian Britain, 1830–1900* (London 1988), p. 93.
2. J. Kocka, "Family and Class Formation: Intergenerational Mobility and Marriage Patterns in Nineteenth-Century Westphalian Towns", *Journal of Social History*, 17 (1984), pp. 411–433; *idem*, "Problems of Working-Class Formation in Germany: The Early Years 1800–1875", in I. Katznelson and A.R. Zolberg (eds), *Working-Class Formation: Nineteenth-Century Patterns in Western Europe and the United States* (Princeton, NJ, 1986), pp. 279–351.
3. See for example Guy Brunet, Antoinette Fauve-Chamoux, and Michel Oris (eds), *Le choix du conjoint* (Paris, 1996); Christophe Duhamelle and Jürgen Schlumbohm (eds), *Eheschließungen im Europa des 18. und 19. Jahrhunderts. Muster und Strategien* (Göttingen, 2003); R. Gehrmann (ed.), *Determinanten und Muster des Heiratsverhaltens in Europa in der Neuzeit: Ausgewählte Fallstudien*, special issue, *Historische Sozialforschung*, 28 (2003).

have dealt with contemporary patterns and their determinants to a greater degree than with the long-term historical trends that escape survey data. Nonetheless, their valuable work – notably on the determinants of social endogamy – can be usefully consulted, since it yields insights that can be tested against the historical record, thus furthering our understanding of processes of class formation in the past and also establishing, or questioning, the validity of theoretical notions.

By and large, a few groups of key questions recur in the literature on marriage and social class, and, for that matter, in much of the literature dealing with social inequality. One set of questions in the literature on endogamy by social class focuses on geographical and temporal variations in patterns of endogamy. Were there regional differences in who married whom, and did these change over time? If so, did these regional patterns converge or diverge? A second set of questions focuses on determinants of endogamy. What factors determine who marries whom? And has the relative importance of these factors changed over time? A third set of questions relates to the durability of social inequality, as measured by the mobility a society allows it members.

Stratification sociologists often look at the degree of intergenerational class mobility, or indeed of marital mobility, to judge the "social fluidity" or "openness" of a society.[4] Equipped with such information, it is possible to look at a fourth and final set of questions on the consequences of differences in processes of class formation for social and political relationships. One can speculate, for example, to what extent major differences between countries in patterns of inequality, labour relations,

---

4. P. Sorokin, *Social and Cultural Mobility* (New York, 1959), pp. 138–141; D.V. Glass, *Social Mobility in Britain* (London, 1954); S.M. Lipset and R. Bendix (eds), *Social Mobility in Industrial Society* (Berkeley, CA, 1959); C. Tilly, *The Vendée* (Cambridge, MA, 1964), pp. 93–99; P.M. Blau and O.D. Duncan, *The American Occupational Structure* (New York, 1967); A. Sharlin, "From the Study of Social Mobility to the Study of Society", *American Journal of Sociology*, 85 (1979), pp. 338–360; M. Hout, "The Association Between Husbands' and Wives' Occupations in Two-Earner Families", *American Journal of Sociology*, 88 (1982), pp. 397–409; H. Sixma and W. Ultee, "Marriage Patterns and the Openness of Society: Educational Heterogamy in the Netherlands in 1959, 1971 and 1977", in B.F.M. Bakker, J. Dronkers, and H.B.G. Ganzeboom (eds), *Social Stratification and Mobility in the Netherlands* (Amsterdam, 1984), pp. 91–108; P.M. Horan, "Occupational Mobility and Historical Social Structure", *Social Science History*, 9 (1985), pp. 25–47; F.L. Jones, "Marriage Patterns and the Stratification System: Trends in Educational Homogamy since the 1930s", *Australian and New Zealand Journal of Sociology*, 23 (1987), pp. 185–193; Robert D. Mare, "Five Decades of Educational Assortative Mating", *American Sociological Review*, 56 (1991), pp. 15–32; I.K. Fukumoto and D.B. Grusky, "Social Mobility and Class Structure in Early Industrial France", in A. Miles and D. Vincent (eds), *Building European Society: Occupational Change and Social Mobility in Europe 1840–1940* (Manchester, 1993); A. Miles, "How 'Open' Was Nineteenth Century British Society? Social Mobility and Equality of Opportunity", in *ibid.*; W. Uunk, *Who Marries Whom? The Role of Social Origin, Education and High Culture in Mate Selection of Industrial Societies during the Twentieth Century* (Nijmegen, 1996).

and social unrest can be explained by differences in social stratification and class mobility. This type of question has been posed notably with regard to intergenerational mobility, but it can also be asked with regard to marriage patterns according to social class. For example, from Karl Marx and Werner Sombart onward, scholars have attributed the absence of a large socialist party in the United States – in contrast to many European countries – to the greater permeability of social class boundaries there.[5]

Given the importance of social endogamy for social and labour history, it is fortunate that so many scholars have contributed to the present volume. Each contribution is a case study that sheds light on a number of key questions. The findings are much more comparable than was previously the case in this type of research, since all the contributors have used the same social-class scheme. This also makes it possible to undertake a comparative analysis of the data underlying these case studies (see the conclusion to this volume). Is it a permissible exaggeration to claim that these studies mark the commencement in earnest of the global comparative study of partner choice according to social class in the past?[6]

A prime reason why no comparative study on this central theme in social history has hitherto appeared is the fact that until recently it was impossible to allocate the same occupations in different regions and

---

5. Karl Marx, *The Eighteenth Brumaire of Louis Napoleon* (New York, 1852); W. Sombart, *Why Is There No Socialism in America?* (New York, 1976), first published in German in 1906, esp. p. 115; S. Thernstrom, *The Other Bostonians: Poverty and Progress in the American Metropolis 1880–1970* (Cambridge, MA, 1973), esp. pp. 258–259. The question of how to explain American exceptionalism has continued to arouse interest. See for example K. Voss, *The Making of American Exceptionalism: The Knights of Labor and Class Formation in the Nineteenth Century* (Ithaca, NY [etc.], 1993), and the special supplement to *Historical Materialism*, 11 (2003). It remains to be seen, of course, whether the social fluidity in the USA during the nineteenth and early twentieth centuries was indeed greater than that in Europe. See J. Long and J. Ferrie, "A Tale of Two Labor Markets: Intergenerational Occupational Mobility in Britain and the US since 1850", NBER Working Paper No. 11253 (April 2005).

6. Of course, valuable historical single case studies of marriage patterns according to social class do exist. See for example A. Daumard, "Les relations sociales l'époque de la Monarchie Constitutionelle d'après les registres paroissaux des mariages", *Population*, 12 (1957), pp. 445–466; A. Daumard, "Structures et relations sociales: Paris au milieu de XVIIIe siècle", *Cahier des Annales*, 18 (1961); R.D. Penn, *Skilled Workers in the Class Structure* (Cambridge, 1985), pp. 158–182; P. Borscheid, "Romantic Love or Material Interest: Choosing Partners in Nineteenth-Century Germany", *Journal of Family History*, 11 (1986), pp. 157–168; D. Mitch, " 'Inequalities Which Everyone May Remove': Occupational Recruitment, Endogamy, and the Homogeneity of Social Origins in Victorian England", in Miles and Vincent, *Building European Society*, pp. 140–164; A. Miles, *Social Mobility in Nineteenth- and Early Twentieth-Century England* (Basingstoke, 1999). For a study comparing mobility patterns in several German regions using the same social-class scheme see R. Schüren, *Soziale Mobilität: Muster, Veränderungen und Bedingungen im 19. und 20. Jahrhundert* (St Katharinen, 1989). As far as we are aware, no studies comparing patterns of homogamy among historical populations in different countries have ever appeared before.

languages to the same classes.[7] This problem has recently been tackled by developing two comparative tools: HISCO and HISCLASS. Both HISCO, the standard occupational coding scheme, and HISCLASS, the social-class scheme based upon HISCO, were conceived to meet the need to find a way to undertake international social mobility analysis.[8] Both the coding and the social-class scheme can, however, be used for many other purposes. Occupations form the heart of the world of work, and the world of work is central to social and labour history.

All the contributions to this volume have used the same social-class scheme – more information on HISCLASS is presented in the various contributions as well as in the conclusion to this volume – and as a result their findings can be compared. These contributions cover the past three centuries, with a focus on the nineteenth century, and they take in large or small parts of Austria, Belgium, Brazil, France, the Netherlands, Norway, Sweden, and Switzerland. While this coverage is heavily biased towards Europe, one of the essays in this volume thus deals with a Latin American society.

Social homogamy in the past can be studied using historical sources, notably censuses and vital registration data, including marriage certificates, which are available not just in Europe but also in other parts of the world. Both HISCO and HISCLASS can be used as instruments of global history and have already been tested and applied in different parts of the globe.[9] We hope, therefore, that this volume will be seen as an invitation to historians and other scholars around the world. Even as it is, these essays cover a wide range in terms of chronology and subject: Belgium, the

7. The issue of the non-comparability of the various historical studies on social mobility has been raised, for example, in H. Kaelble, *Historical Research on Social Mobility: Western Europe and the USA in the Nineteenth and Twentieth Centuries* (London, 1981), and *idem, Social Mobility in the 19th and 20th Centuries: Europe and America in Comparative Perspective* (Leamington Spa, 1985).

8. Marco H.D. van Leeuwen, Ineke Maas, and Andrew Miles, *HISCO: Historical International Standard Classification of Occupations* (Leuven, 2002); *idem,* "Creating an Historical International Standard Classification of Occupations (HISCO): An Exercise in Multi-National, Interdisciplinary Co-Operation", *Historical Methods,* 37 (2004), pp. 186–197; M.H.D. van Leeuwen and I. Maas, "HISCLASS", paper presented at the 5th European Social Science History Conference (Berlin, 24–27 March 2004). See too the individual contributions and the conclusion to this volume for more information on HISCO and HISCLASS, as well as the History of Work Website mentioned below. These three projects originate with the long-established research project HISMA (Historical International Social Mobility Analysis).

9. The History of Work website of the International Institute of Social History (see http://historyofwork.iisg.nl) contains occupational titles coded into HISCO from the following countries: Belgium, Brazil, Canada (Quebec), Finland, France, Germany, Greece, The Netherlands, Norway, Portugal, Spain, Sweden, UK, and Switzerland. Work on coding occupations in other countries, such as India, Italy, Russia, and the Philippines is currently underway. See, for example, V. Vladimirov (ed.), *Istoricheskor professiovedenie. Sbornik nauchnikh statie* (Barnaul, 2004).

leading industrial nation outside Britain; France, which has experienced many major social and economic transformations over the past two centuries; traditional Nordic farming communities; a mountain community (in Austria); and a slave-owning society (Brazil). This wide variety may provide a window on regional and temporal variations in social endogamy and a testing ground for theories on its determinants.

DETERMINANTS OF SOCIAL ENDOGAMY

Determinants of social-class endogamy can be clustered in various ways. A threefold division between individual preferences, third party influences, and the structural constraints imposed by the marriage market is often used.[10] We will use the same framework, although we distinguish a total of five clusters. The first and second group of determinants deals with the marriage market. A distinction is made between factors influencing the likelihood of encountering marriage candidates in a given locality, at least long enough to have some sense of whether they would be suitable spouses, and factors dealing with the degree to which geographical marriage horizons shrank or expanded. A third cluster relates to the social pressure from parents, peers, and the community favouring partners from some social classes and rejecting others. The fourth group concerns personal autonomy – the degree to which one can resist such pressure. And, finally, there is a fifth group, that of personal preferences.

Likelihood of meeting on the marriage market

The opportunity to meet a potential spouse is often seen as an important factor explaining why people marry individuals similar to themselves.[11] The marriage market is limited to certain contexts, for example to the neighbourhood where one lives, and these contexts are to some extent already socially homogenous. Thus people end up marrying people similar to themselves even if they have no special desire to do so. The likelihood of meeting may be dissociated into two components: the likelihood of meeting within a certain geographical region, and the likelihood as a function of the size of that region – in other words the "marriage horizon". We begin with a discussion of the first component.

10. M. Kalmijn, "Status Endogamy in the United States", *American Journal of Sociology*, 97 (1991), pp. 496–523, and M. Kalmijn, "Intermarriage and Endogamy: Causes, Patterns, Trends", *Annual Review of Sociology*, 24 (1998), pp. 395–421.
11. See, for example, P.M. Blau, T.C. Blum, and J.E. Schwartz, "Heterogeneity and Intermarriage", *American Sociological Review*, 47 (1982), pp. 45–62; M. Kalmijn and H. Flap, "Assortative Meeting and Mating: Unintended Consequences of Organized Settings for Partner Choices", *Social Forces*, 79 (2001), pp. 1289–1312; Kalmijn, "Intermarriage and Endogamy".

Mating requires meeting. In the contemporary world, young people might meet at kindergarten, at family gatherings, at school, in the neighbourhood, at church, through sports clubs and other associations, during public celebrations, leisure activities, work, and on the Internet – to list but a few of the more important meeting places that exist. It has been said that, today, school and work are more important in producing socially homogamous marriages than family networks are, and that neighbour-hoods do not seem to have this effect.[12]

Young people spend a large part of their youth at school, and thus the people they meet at school form an important pool of those they get to know well enough to consider forming a relationship.[13] Schooling has of course increased dramatically in virtually all countries in the world over the past two centuries. Primary education has become compulsory in many countries, raising participation rates to extremely high levels. More importantly for endogamy, access to secondary and tertiary education – where participants might begin to look for a partner – has generally increased and in many countries become more universal, covering the whole spectrum of society to a larger degree than was formerly the case. One would expect this to lead to higher rates of exogamous marriage, the more so the older the age at which children are stratified into different school levels.[14] Furthermore, many leisure activities are in some way connected with school,[15] either because schools organize them – compulsory swimming classes for example – or, for example, because children from the same school support the same football team (perhaps more so today than in the past). Even if they are not organized by schools, leisure activities are important meeting places for adolescents – all the more so if both boys and girls are actively involved.

The effect of educational expansion has actually been even greater than one might suppose. Whereas schools in Europe in the eighteenth and nineteenth centuries instructed children in the virtues of class im-mobility,[16] they did so to a lesser extent in the twentieth century. It has been argued that pupils who were taught non-conservative values were

12. Kalmijn and Flap, "Assortative Meeting and Mating".

13. At least in the case of co-educational schools.

14. See Jutta Allmendinger, *Career Mobility Dynamics: A Comparative Analysis of the United States, Norway, and West Germany* (Berlin, 1989).

15. See, for instance, M.P. Atkinson and B.L. Glass, "Marital Age Heterogamy and Homogamy, 1900 to 1980", *Journal of Marriage and the Family*, 49 (1985), pp. 685–691; F. van Poppel and A.C. Liefbroer, "Leeftijdsverschillen tussen huwelijkspartners. Een interpretatie van verander-ingen en verschillen in de negentiende en twintigste eeuw", *Tijdschrift voor Sociale Geschiedenis*, 2 (2001), pp. 129–152.

16. H. Chisick, *The Limits of Reform in the Enlightenment: Attitudes Towards the Education of the Lower Classes in the Eighteenth Century* (London, 1991); M.H.D. van Leeuwen, *Logic of Charity: A Simple Model Applied to Amsterdam 1800–1850* (London, 2000).

more likely to develop an appetite for non-traditional marriages.[17] However, important differences might have existed between countries such as Britain – with a higher degree of class-specific education, due to the existence of expensive "public" schools – and the Netherlands – where education was less influenced by class and more influenced by religious-based divisions.

Many people find their spouse at work, and in this respect the varying and historically changing forms of the labour market will have had an impact on endogamy patterns, although as yet we know very little about how this worked. A young man employed at a small workplace will meet fewer women than one working in a large factory or a modern institution such as a post office or a bank, where not only are the "birds" more numerous, they are also of a different feather. The rise of industry and of other large, meritocratic internal labour markets from the mid-nineteenth century onwards led thus, *ceteris paribus*, to a higher likelihood of marrying outside one's social class.[18] Other developments in the labour market, such as changes in labour-related migration patterns, might also have influenced social homogamy.[19]

In cities, the social composition of neighbourhoods is another factor influencing marriage patterns by social class, because many people marry someone living close by. So even if they have no intention of marrying within their own class, many will nonetheless do so if their neighbourhood consists of people working in the same trade or type of factory, for

17. D.J. Treiman, "Industrialization and Social Stratification", in E.O. Laumann (ed.), *Social Stratification: Research and Theory for the 1970s* (Indianapolis, IN, 1970), pp. 207–234; E. Shorter, "Illegitimacy, Sexual Revolution, and Social Change in Modern Europe", *Journal of Interdisciplinary History*, 6 (1971), pp. 237–272; idem, "Female Emancipation, Birth Control, and Fertility in European History", *American Historical Review*, 78 (1973), pp. 605–640.

18. Treiman, "Industrialization and Social Stratification"; C. Kerr, J.T. Dunlop, F.H. Harbison, and C.A. Myers, *Industrialism and Industrial Man* (Cambridge, MA, 1960); Miles and Vincent, *Building European Society*. The studies by Shorter cited in the previous footnote offer a similar argument: increasing market contacts. A recent survey is offered by John C. Brown, Marco H.D. van Leeuwen, and David Mitch, "The History of the Modern Career: An Introduction", in David Mitch, John C. Brown, and Marco H.D. van Leeuwen (eds), *Origins of the Modern Career* (Ashgate, 2004), pp. 3–41.

19. In the case of an increase in seasonal migration, for example, one would expect a decrease in homogamy according to social class. For a survey of migration in Europe, see Leslie Page Moch, *Moving Europeans: Migration in Western Europe since 1650* (Bloomington, IN, 1992). In societies where it was common for girls to seek employment elsewhere as a servant before marriage, such service could broaden the marriage horizon, not just geographically but also socially, as the girls acquired the social and other skills valued in the social circles of their employers; perhaps the girls also developed a taste for another way of life. See L. Broom and J.H. Smith, "Bridging Occupations", *British Journal of Sociology*, 14 (1963), pp. 321–334; T. McBride, "Social Mobility for the Lower Classes: Domestic Servants in France", *Journal of Social History* (1974), pp. 63–78; H. Bras, *Zeeuwse meiden. Dienen in de levensloop van vrouwen, ca. 1850–1950* (Amsterdam 2002). A decrease in service over time would, in that case, mean an increase in social homogamy, while an increase in service would mean the opposite.

example.[20] Over the past two centuries, a growing share of the world's population has lived in cities; currently, for the first time in history, more people now live in urban areas than rural areas. The social composition of urban districts might thus have had a considerable impact on social endogamy worldwide.

We know very little about long-term changes in spatial social segregation in cities, however. It is thus possible, for example, that in some cities neighbourhoods were more alike two centuries ago (with spatial segregation within wards being more prevalent than between wards, with, for instance, the upper classes living on the main streets, the middle classes on side streets, and the poor on side streets of side streets) than today (with a few rich neighbourhoods, a large number of mixed neighbourhoods, and mostly poor neighbourhoods). If so, then for those cities the changes in spatial social segregation will have increasingly favoured social endogamy, all other things being equal. We cannot tell, however, in which cities such a process has occurred.

The likelihood of meeting a partner from a particular social group also depends on the size of the various social groups and on their degree of geographical isolation.[21] If meeting is a random phenomenon, the chances of meeting someone from a particular social class are the product of the relative size of one's own group and the relative size of the other social class. The more heterogeneous a population, the lower the chances of meeting someone from the same social class. If meeting implies mating – which of course it does not invariably – a higher degree of social heterogeneity would imply more exogamy. It is not just the sizes of the various social groups that matter; so too does the degree to which they live in geographical isolation. The chances of marrying a coastal fisherman are obviously less for a woman living inland than for one living on the coast, and the likelihood of marrying a farmer is greater for farmers' daughters (since they too live in the countryside) than it is for either coastal inhabitants or urban dwellers.

Further, a population that is religiously (or ethnically) heterogeneous is more likely to be socially exogamous because prospective marriage candidates are selected first on the basis of religion (or ethnicity), thus leaving fewer, if any, marriage partners in the same social group. This

20. P.M. Blau and J.E. Schwartz, *Crosscutting Social Circles* (New York, 1984); William R. Catton, Jr and R.J. Smirich, "A Comparison of Mathematical Models for the Effect of Residential Propinquity on Mate Selection", *American Sociological Review*, 29 (1964), pp. 522–529; Gillian Stevens, "Propinquity and Educational Homogamy", *Sociological Forum*, 6 (1991), pp. 715–726.

21. Blau and Schwartz, *Crosscutting Social Circles*; Peter M. Blau, Terry C. Blum, and Joseph E. Schwartz, "Heterogeneity and Intermarriage", *American Sociological Review*, 47 (1982), pp. 45–62; T.C. Blum, "Structural Constraints on Interpersonal Relations: A Test of Blau's Macrosociological Theory", *American Journal of Sociology*, 91 (1985), pp. 607–617.

would lead one to expect that a country that is more religiously (or ethnically) diverse would have higher exogamy than a country that is less diverse, and that a country that becomes more diverse in the course of time will witness an increase in the proportion of exogamous marriages.

Geographical marriage horizons

The likelihood of finding a suitable marriage partner depends not only on the degree to which one becomes acquainted with the possible marriage partners in a region but also on the changing boundaries of what constitutes a region. A great many studies, on all parts of the globe, have demonstrated that most people tend to marry someone living close by.[22] On foot in accessible terrain – that is, no mud, rivers, mountains, and gorges – one can perhaps walk 20 kilometres to another village and walk the same distance back on the same day. This distance comes close to the limit of trust that separated the known universe from the "unsafe" world beyond. If marriage "horizons" expanded, young suitors would be able to meet more potential marriage partners. The increase in the means and speed of transportation brought about by new and improved roads and canals, and by new means of transport such as the train, the bicycle, the tram, and the motorcar brought a wider range of potential spouses within reach. These new means of transport increased the distance one could travel during the same day, and thus expanded the geographical marriage horizon.[23]

In the course of the past two centuries, the average unmarried citizen

22. See, for example, Alice Bee Kasakoff and John W. Adams, "Spatial Location and Social Organisation: An Analysis of Tikopian Patterns", *Man*, New Series, 12 (1977), pp. 48–64; Wesley Andrew Fisher, *The Soviet Marriage Market: Mate-Selection in Russia and the USSR* (New York, 1980), pp. 200–203; Barrie S. Morgan, "A Contribution to the Debate on Homogamy, Propinquity, and Segregation", *Journal of Marriage and the Family*, 43 (1981), pp. 909–921; Thomas W. Pullum and Andres Peri, "A Multivariate Analysis of Homogamy in Montevideo, Uruguay", *Population Studies*, 53 (1999), pp. 361–377; Stevens, "Propinquity and Educational Homogamy".

23. J. Millard, "A New Approach to the Study of Marriage Horizons", *Local Population Studies*, 28 (1982), pp. 10–31. Rosental sets the limit at 25 km; see Paul-André Rosental, "La migration des femmes (et des hommes) en France au XIXᵉ siècle", *Annales de Démographie Historique*, 1 (2004), pp. 107–136, esp. p. 109. Frans van Poppel and Peter Ekamper suggest a lower limit of 20 km in "De Goudse horizon verruimd. Veranderingen in de herkomst van Goudse bruiden en bruidegoms", in J. Kok and M.H.D. van Leeuwen (eds), *Genegenheid en gelegenheid. Twee eeuwen partnerkeuze en huwelijk* (Amsterdam, 2005). Kok and Mandemakers found that the degree to which a town or village was isolated had an effect on the degree of social homogamy; see Jan Kok and Kees Mandemakers, "Vrije keuze uit een beperkt aanbod. De huwelijksmarkt in Utrecht en Zeeland, 1840–1940", in Kok and van Leeuwen, *Genegenheid en gelegenheid*. For a discussion of the effect of changes in transport on migration, see, for example, Collin Pooley and Jean Turnbull, *Migration and Mobility in Britain since the 18ᵗʰ Century* (London, 1988), pp. 64–71 and 303–306.

will have met more marriage partners from his own social class and from other classes than previously. He or she will also have engaged more frequently in the gentle art of writing love letters. In the past two centuries the number of letters and postcards written per head of the population increased greatly.[24] In a more recent phenomenon, millions of people – even in geographically remote villages – are contacting one another on the Internet. Dating sites, where men and women specify their wishes and present what they have to offer in a favourable light, abound, but these are by no means the only way contacts are established using the Internet. Friends and potential marriage partners, however remote, are just a mouse click away, and their number seems almost unlimited. In the past, another important factor in bringing together young adults from different regions was the army. Conscription broadened the marriage horizon of the young men of a region by bringing them into contact with young women from elsewhere, and from other classes, notably when farmers' sons were barracked near the city. This geographical expansion of the marriage market could well have increased contacts between social classes, and so led to more exogamy.

While this might well have been the general rule, the broadening of the marriage horizon could also have had the opposite effect. Members of small social groups – or groups fair in size but dispersed over the country – could have been able to travel far enough to meet potential marriage partners from their own class, whereas previously they would have been prepared to settle for someone from another class. This scenario implies a strong desire to marry within one's own class, a desire frustrated by the lack of suitable candidates. While one can imagine various kinds of groups for which this was perhaps true – notably religious and ethnic minorities[25] – it is more difficult to imagine it being the case for social classes, except for the elite, and wealthier farmers, where the desire to preserve the family's property or social status was an overriding issue.[26]

Social pressure

Parents, peers and other individuals or community institutions all play a part in the marriage process. In every country, past and present, the permission of parents has been required if children wanted to marry before

---

24. D. Vincent, *The Rise of Mass Literacy: Reading and Writing in Modern Europe* (Cambridge, 2002).

25. This can be seen as evidence of the fact that social-class relations were complicated and sometimes overridden by other allegiances. See Lex Heerma van Voss and Marcel van der Linden (eds), *Class and Other Identities: Gender, Religion and Ethnicity in the Writing of European Labour History* (New York [etc.], 2002).

26. One wonders to what extent it was also true for social groups with a modest amount of property, such as shopkeepers.

they came of age, and this age has varied between countries and over time. Indeed, there have been societies, such as Imperial China, where children were legally subject to parental power until their parents had died.[27] Apart from this formal power granted to them by law, parents usually have power by force of custom, or because they control the resources of the family. The parents might refuse to meet, host or house a potential spouse; they might shame him (or her) or otherwise attempt to deter the couple from marrying – by not contributing to the costs incurred by the newly-weds in setting up a household of their own (as was common practice for newly-weds in Europe), or by the threat of disinheritance for instance.

Parents from propertied classes could exert more pressure than those from the labouring classes. The customary way to become a farmer, for example, was to be born into a farming family, learn by helping one's father, and later on to inherit the farm; alternatively, one could marry the daughter of a farmer who had no son as heir.[28] Similarly, a merchant's son would work at his father's office to learn the trade, and gradually take over more of his father's work until his father ultimately withdrew from the business. Assuming that parents normally prefer their offspring to marry someone from their own class, parental authority should lead to social endogamy, and the weakening of the legal and material bonds between parents and children over the course of the past two centuries should have led to greater exogamy.[29]

If parents wanted to influence their children's choice of partner, they could do so most effectively if they were both still alive. If either or both of the parents died before the child reached marriageable age, their influence would be lessened or rendered nonexistent. By the same token, however, with one or both parents deceased, pressure on the child to marry might have increased (one less mouth to feed), even if that meant marrying into a less desirable class. In fact, several studies have suggested that endogamy

---

27. Arthur P. Wolf and Chieh-shan Huang, *Marriage and Adoption in China, 1845–1945* (Stanford, CA, 1980); see also R.S. Watson and P. Buckley Ebrey (eds), *Marriage and Inequality in Chinese Society* (Berkeley, CA, 1991). In addition to parents, other kin might also have helped or hindered. See, for example, the role of grandparents and other kin in intergenerational mobility in nineteenth-century China, as described in Cameron Campbell and James Lee, "Social Mobility from a Kinship Perspective: Rural Liaoning, 1789–1909", *International Review of Social History*, 48 (2003), pp. 1–26.

28. Well-to-do farmers could supply the non-inheriting child with a farm or another livelihood during their life. See Dirk Damsma and Jan Kok, " 'Ingedroogde harten?' Partnerkeuze en sociale reproductie van de Noord-Hollandse boerenstand in de negentiende en vroeg-twintigste eeuw, 1940", in Kok and van Leeuwen, *Genegenheid en gelegenheid*.

29. If, on the other hand, parents prefer a degree of upward mobility for at least one of their children, for example their firstborn son, one would expect them to try to retain a greater grip on the eldest son than on his siblings. A decrease in parental authority over time would mean that the difference in endogamy practices between the firstborn son and the others would have slowly declined in the course of time.

rates for children with two surviving parents were higher than those for orphans or semi-orphans.[30] Perhaps the effect of missing one's parents varied according to gender. Granted that widowers remarried more often than widows, orphans whose mothers had died were more likely to have a step-parent than orphans whose father had died. If this created tensions (notably, as is sometimes claimed, between daughters and stepmothers), these would have been a reason to marry in order to leave the parental home as soon as possible, even if the marriage partner was not entirely socially desirable.

In some societies, parents exercised different powers over daughters than they did over sons. In Sweden, for example, in the nineteenth century, an unmarried woman never came of age; whatever her age, by law she had to ask a male relative (usually her father) for permission to marry. It was far from being a global rule, however, that daughters were subject to greater parental authority than sons. If the transmission of family status or property was an overriding issue, and if this took place down the male line – for example, where farms were handed over to the eldest son – then one can imagine that parents would have wanted a considerable influence over whom this son married, and have been content with less influence over whom their other children married. The effect of parental power on social endogamy may thus have differed according to gender and inheritance system.

Even if a young couple were lucky enough not to experience the constraints of parental power, they were still subject to the scrutiny of their peers. These peers might approve of a potential union with one of their own; but when marriages were considered unacceptable, due to large age differences or differences in region of origin, religion, or social class, they might disapprove and shame the boy or girl in question, and perhaps even beat them up, as happened in some regions.[31]

Work evenings – sometimes referred to by the French term *veillées* – were common throughout Europe.[32] In the long winter evenings, the

---

30. F. van Poppel, J. de Jong, and A.C. Liefbroer, "The Effects of Paternal Mortality on Sons' Social Mobility: A Nineteenth Century Example", *Historical Methods*, 31 (1998), pp. 101–112; M.H.D. van Leeuwen and I. Maas, "Partner Choice and Endogamy in the Nineteenth Century: Was There a Sexual Revolution in Europe?", *Journal of Social History*, 36 (2002), pp. 101–123.
31. On *charivari* see J.L. Flandrin, *Les amours paysannes XVI–XIX siècles* (Paris, 1975); Jacques Le Goff and Jean-Claude Schmitt (eds), *Le charivari* (Paris, 1981), and M. Segalen, *Love and Power in the Peasant Family: Rural France in the Nineteenth Century* (Oxford, 1983). One intriguing question, however, is whether *charivari* were usually related to social exogamy. Most seem to be about girls becoming romantically attached to boys from another village or town, about inappropriate age differences between lovers, and about extramarital relations. Were *charivari* perhaps rural phenomena, and thus a feature of populations that were socially rather homogamous?
32. M. Mitterauer, *A History of Youth* (Oxford, 1990), pp. 178–184; Edward Shorter, *The Making of the Modern Family* (New York, 1975), pp. 124–127; Louise Tilly and Joan Scott, *Women, Work and Family* (New York, 1978), pp. 38, 58, and 187.

unmarried girls of the village would join their mothers and potential suitors in a communal barn to work, mostly to spin, sing, and talk, perhaps dance, and to eat and drink. What the ballroom was for the urban *jeunesse dorée*, the *veillée* was for rural populations, except that the former had leisure, while the latter also had to work. It is often said that marriages were made in the *veillée*.

In large parts of Europe a tradition of "bundling" or night-courting existed, whereby groups of young men went off to visit young unmarried women with the intention of getting to know them, and ultimately of sleeping with them as a prelude to marriage.[33] This practice was restricted to rural areas. There was pressure to marry the child of a farmer from the same village rather than someone from another village, or a travelling woodcutter from a completely different region. Farmers' sons were allowed to join a rural fraternity of older boys who assembled in the village, chiefly to organize courtship. On Saturday night, they assembled and went off together to call on the girls.

The fact that schooling has become both more universal and longer implies that the duration of peer pressure in school will have increased. Its *extent*, however, might well have decreased since schooling now encompasses all social groups to a greater degree than before, and most schools no longer instruct pupils on the wholesome virtues of rigid class boundaries. The *duration* of peer pressure in general has increased even more than the expansion in the educational system would suggest though, due to the growth in the nineteenth and twentieth centuries of an institutionalized youth culture, with sports clubs and the like.[34]

Another form of communal pressure was formed by the sermons heard at church. The priest, or other religious minister, might take a more liberal view of endogamy, or warn against the dangers of marrying above one's station. In extreme cases he might even name the culprit. His opinions reflected not just his personal convictions; they also reflected the teachings of his Church. And some religions might have been more restrictive than others when it came to marriage. It has been argued, for instance, that Catholicism has tended to be more conservative than Protestantism, particularly with regard to marriage, although both religions have presumably become less conservative over time.[35]

---

33. See the literature cited above, as well as K.R.V. Wikman, "Die Einleitung der Ehe. Eine vergleichende Ethno-soziologische Untersuchung über die Vorstufe der Ehe in den Sitten des Schwedischen Volkstums", *Acta Academiae Aboensis Humaniora*, XI (1937), pp. 1–384; Van Leeuwen and Maas, "Was There a Sexual Revolution in Europe?"; Yochi Fischer Yonin, "The Original Bundlers: Boaz and Ruth, and Seventeenth-Century English Courtship Practices", *Journal of Social History*, 35 (2001/02), pp. 683–705.

34. Mitterauer *A History of Youth*, pp. 226–240.

35. J. Smits, W. Ultee, and J. Lammers, "Educational Homogamy in 65 Countries", *American Sociological Review*, 63 (1998), pp. 264–285.

One might expect the size and homogeneity of a community to have influenced the degree to which it could exert pressure on non-conformists. In a small community which is homogenous with regard to norms on partner choice, the pressure to conform would have been greater than in a larger community, where one could escape social control or where several sets of norms co-existed.

Some scholars have argued that the power of parents, peers and the community has declined over the past few centuries. Segalen writes:

> In traditional society, problems that would today be considered personal, whether to do with the intimacies of the heart or of the body, were the responsibility of the community. The formation of the couple, as well as concerning the young people themselves, involved the two families and the entire social group. [...]. Family considerations weigh heavily on the individuals, who tend to disappear in the face of the wider aims of economic and social improvement of the family line. In these terms the couple is merely a link in the chain leading to the growth of patrimony or resisting the fragmentation of landholdings through inheritance. The individuality of the couple, or rather, its tendency towards individuality, is crushed by the family institution, and also by the social pressure exercised by the village community as a whole.[36]

Shorter claimed that

> There was a preference for custom over spontaneity and creativity. These little collectivities, be it the guild, the family lineage, or the village as a whole, correctly recognized that too much innovation would ring their death bell; and so they insisted [on] [...] the old ways of proposing marriage [...]. Once the heart began to speak, it would give instructions often entirely incompatible with the rational principles of family interest and material survival on which the small community was ordered. Marry the woman you love, the heart might say, even though your parents disapprove.[37]

Shorter's sexual-revolution thesis belongs to a school of thought denoted as modernization theory. This school has long dominated sociological research into social mobility, including marital mobility and endogamy. In the field of endogamy Goode was probably the most eloquent spokesman of modernization theory. He wrote:

> With industrialization, the traditional family systems are breaking down [...]. Elders no longer control the major new economic or political opportunities, so that family authority slips from the hands of such family leaders. The young groom can obtain his bride on his own, and need not obey anyone outside their family unit, since only the performance on the job is relevant for their advancement. They need not rely on family elders for job instruction, since schools, the factory, or the plantation or mine will teach them the new skills [...]. Nor do they even need to continue working on the land, still in the possession of

36. Segalen, *Love and Power in the Peasant Family*, pp. 38, 41.
37. Shorter, *The Making of the Modern Family*, pp. 19–20.

the elders, since the jobs and the political opportunity are in the city. Thus industrialization is likely to undermine gradually the traditional systems of family control and exchange.[38]

Personal autonomy

From this outline, it might seem as if in their choice of partner young men and women were but clay in the hands of others. Of course this was not true. While social pressure could make it more difficult to marry outside one's social class, it was rarely impossible. Rather than imprisoning, starving, or killing non-conformists, they were forced to pay a price in the form of gossip, vile looks, nasty remarks, lost friendships, the denial of assistance, and being disinherited; those determined enough might decide that this was a price worth paying. Whether they paid was not entirely a decision of the heart; it also depended on their personal resources to withstand such communal pressure.

One such resource was the possibility of finding work at an early age on wages allowing one to escape the parental household and set up a place of one's own – or at least to remain with one's parents but with greater independence. It has, for example, been noted that the availability of factory work for young men and women with wages that peaked early in the life course gave them considerable leeway to do what they wanted.[39] These personal resources might have differed according to social class, region, and period. The existence of factory work in some regions and not in others, and the general rise in the availability of such work over time, will have favoured those born later and those born in industrial areas.

One factor so far missing from the discussion is the possible influence of social security schemes, with benefits being granted either on a means-tested basis or an insurance basis by the state or insurers. While some parts of Europe were characterized by poor relief provided by private and public agencies as well as insurance, especially on a mutual basis, from as early as the late Middle Ages, marked variations existed between regions, and great changes have taken place over time. Even today, when the marketing of social security is much stronger than it has been for decades, almost everyone in Europe turns to the state for financial support when they become seriously ill or reach old age, and, when truly in need, most of them will receive assistance.

While help by family, friends and neighbours is still very important in certain respects – as regards the time, love and care given to the ill and the elderly for example – the rise of state schemes has left people less dependent on their family (and on the Church for that matter: in

---

38. W. Goode, *The Family* (Englewood Cliffs, NJ, 1964), pp. 108–109.
39. Shorter, "Female Emancipation"; Treiman, "Industrialization and Social Stratification"; Tilly and Scott, *Women, Work and Family.*

continental Europe poor relief tended to be regulated to an important degree by the Church until well into the twentieth century). One might speculate then that there was an inverse correspondence between the degree to which such schemes existed[40] and the need to comply with parental and communal pressure in such important matters as the choice of spouse. Furthermore, parents could afford to let children marry whomever they wanted to if they no longer regarded their children as necessary for their own future well-being.[41] This might have been a factor contributing to differences between countries and to a gradual loosening over time of the grip of the collectivity in matters of marriage.[42]

Personal preferences

One can certainly be forgiven a degree of scepticism regarding our list of factors determining the choice of spouse. Surely, one might argue, personal preferences play a major role, and perhaps a larger role than any of the other factors usually mentioned.[43] And surely one would be right in

---

40. An overview can be found in J. Alber, *Von Armenhaus zum Wohlfartsstaat* (Frankfurt, 1982).

41. Smits, Ultee, and Lammers, "Educational Homogamy".

42. We have suggested that, since they needed to inherit the farm, farmers' sons were at the mercy of their fathers. This is only one side of the coin, however. Older farmers also needed heirs to take over their farms and provide for them in old age. "Retirement contracts" could be drawn up for this purpose, in which the owner of a farm yielded the usufruct of his farm to another person in return for food and shelter. This person was usually one of his sons, who promised to house his father – and mother – in either the farmhouse or in an annexe, and provide food, such as milk, beer, grains, meat, but also fuel and other necessities. The relative freedom on the part of the farmer to choose his heir encouraged high rates of endogamy. A farmer's son had an interest in pleasing his father by marrying a potentially good farmer's wife, i.e. a farmer's daughter. Marrying outside the farming class could harm his chances of taking over the farm. These contracts fell into disuse from the end of the nineteenth century onwards. One reason given for this is the rise of banks, which were willing to offer credit to buy a farm, and, indeed, of savings banks, where older farmers could deposit the proceeds from the sale of their farm (with the farmers then moving to live in the town). One could thus argue that in the heyday of the retirement contract, farmers with property had the sort of pension protection that other social groups lacked until the rise of the welfare state. Farmers with property lost that protection when retirement contracts fell out of use.

43. Compare the debate conducted in this journal by Wall, King, and Gillis: J.R. Gillis, "'A Triumph of Hope over Experience': Chance and Choice in the History of Marriage", *International Review of Social History*, 44 (1999), pp. 47–54; S. King, "Chance Encounters? Paths to Household Formation in Early Modern England", *International Review of Social History*, 44 (1999), pp. 23–46; *idem*, "Chance, Choice and Calculation in the Process of 'Getting Married': A Reply to John R. Gillis and Richard Wall", *International Review of Social History*, 44 (1999), pp. 69–76; R. Wall, "Beyond the Household: Marriage, Household Formation and the Role of Kin and Neighbours", *International Review of Social History*, 44 (1999), pp. 55–67. Wall stresses structural factors, notably of a social and economic nature, whereas King and Gillis emphasize chance and cultural factors. Our introduction discusses social, economic, as well as

attributing importance to matters of the heart and other intimate desires. However, many such intimate forces of attraction are not just difficult to measure, they might also vary widely between individuals from the same social class. Historians and sociologists have seldom, if ever, studied beauty, kindness, humour, or good-naturedness as determinants of marriage patterns. Nor will we be doing so here either. This would be a grave omission only if such characteristics differed from one social class to another.

Almost any study of endogamy will show that people were more likely to marry others from the same social class, and that this cannot simply be explained by class sizes and random chance.[44] A large number of other factors played a role. What concerns us here is the question of whether, in the absence of these other factors, young men and women would still prefer socially endogamous marriages. To answer this question, one has to consider what distinguishes an enduring intimate endogamous relationship from an exogenous one. One significant point is that individuals from the same social class are more familiar with the work that characterizes their class. Furthermore, these individuals are more likely to share a similar understanding of one another and the world, which might make a marriage easier (others, in contrast, prefer a partner with different tastes in order to make their marriage more "exciting"). Not only does a socially homogenous marriage increase the likelihood of the couple having the same tastes, it also makes it easier to undertake things together, to run a household jointly, to raise children (and to have the same attitude towards their partner). And, finally, it might be easier to trust someone from one's own social circle – to trust his or her tastes, character, and future earning capacity – than someone alien to it.

While it is not easy to formulate and test hypotheses on such preferences in the past, two such hypotheses do present themselves. Following Bourdieu, Kalmijn has argued that, *ceteris paribus*, most people prefer a partner who shares one's values and tastes, one's cultural background – though many would not mind having a wealthier partner, i.e. someone from an economically higher class.[45] The other notion we can research is

cultural factors. It notes that even "chance" meetings between certain individuals are influenced by structural factors such as group size and class differences in the likelihood of meeting, and that cultural factors could include the wish for a partner with the same values and tastes, which in turn is associated with social background.

44. See for example Hout, "The Association Between Husbands' And Wives' Occupations in Two-Earner Families"; Jerry A. Jacobs and Frank F. Furstenberg, "Changing Places: Conjugal Careers and Women's Marital Mobility", *Social Forces*, 64 (1986), pp. 714–732; Kalmijn, "Status Endogamy in the United States".

45. M. Kalmijn, "Assortative Mating by Cultural and Economic Occupational Status", *American Journal of Sociology*, 100 (1994), pp. 422–452; Pierre Bourdieu, *Distinction: A Social Critique of the Judgement of Taste* (London, 1984).

that individuals from propertied classes are inclined to marry one another. Having land and cattle made men and women from farming backgrounds attractive marriage candidates. Marriage among farmers was especially important since, to run a farm, a wife was needed to do the cooking, milking, and haymaking, while the husband did the other farm work.[46] Endogamy among farmers was also important because it sometimes provided them with a means to enlarge the farm, or to keep it within the family.[47]

The same can be said for the urban propertied classes.[48] From letters, diaries, and the like we know that in the nineteenth century the Dutch elite, for example, thought of marriage in the most exalted and romantic terms, but considerations of status and property were never far away either.[49] The issue of the commensurability of love and property is an interesting one. The Dutch elite thought that to marry for the sake of money was vulgar, while marrying for love without money was foolish. Ideally one would have both, and parents took great care to create a circle of potential marriage candidates that would match their status; one of these candidates, it was hoped, would be "lovable".

According to some theories, the importance of personal preferences in the choice of marriage partner changed over time. Shorter claimed that after the end of the eighteenth century romantic love gained ground in the Western world: "the most important change in nineteenth- and twentieth-century courtship has been the surge of sentiment [...]. People started to place affection and personal compatibility at the top of the list of criteria in choosing marriage partners. These new standards became articulated as romantic love."[50] If so, one would expect class homogamy in relation to

---

46. Mitterauer, *A History of Youth*; Segalen, *Love and Power in the Peasant Family*.
47. See Orvar Löfgren, "Family and Household among Scandinavian Peasants: An Exploratory Essay", *Ethnologica Scandinavia* (1974), pp. 17–52, esp. p. 33; L.F. Saugstad and Ö. Ödegard, "Marriage Pattern and Kinship in Pre-industrial and Present-Day Norway", in S. Åkerman *et al.* (eds), *Chance and Change: Social and Economic Studies in Historical Demography in the Baltic Area* (Odense, 1978), pp. 84–94. Tilly and Scott, *Women, Work and Family*, p. 33.
48. "Curieusement le modèle bourgeois se rapproche du modèle paysan, dans la mesure où l'institution matrimoniale coïncide avec un 'établissement'. Au mariage, les parents transmettent une partie de leurs biens à leurs enfants; ils doivent donc en contrôler soigneusement la formation"; Martine Segalen, *De l'amour et du mariage autrefois* (Paris, 1981), pp. 68, 85. See too George Alter, *Family and the Female Life Course: The Women of Verviers, Belgium, 1849–1880* (Madison, WI, 1988), pp. 148–150, on the town of Verviers.
49. Thimo de Nijs, "Partnerkeuze in de hoge Rotterdamse burgerij 1815–1890", in Kok and Van Leeuwen, *Genegenheid en gelegenheid*.
50. Shorter, *The Making of the Modern Family*, p. 148. Stone too argues that this trend commenced in the late eighteenth century. See Lawrence Stone, *The Family, Sex and Marriage in England 1500–1800* (New York, 1977). Macfarlane, however, dates its beginnings much earlier: Alan Macfarlane, *Marriage and Love in England: Modes of Reproduction, 1300–1840* (Oxford, 1986).

Figure 1. "It's Love". Part of a series of five illustrated cards called "The Dream",written by Mathilde Janssens and sent to her fiancé, Félix Van Sweevelt, Antwerp, 1913.
Source: E. Van Driessche (ed.), Des accordailles aux épousailles. Galerie CGER, Bruxelles, 19 février–1 mai 1988 (Brussels, 1988), p. 322.

economic characteristics to have declined, but not perhaps in relation to cultural characteristics.[51]

CONCLUSION

Much of the literature on social endogamy is about patterns and their determinants; relatively little is about its consequences, and even less focuses on long-term changes. This is perhaps not surprising. Much of the theory originates with sociology, and the data that sociologists often use – survey data – do not cover very long time spans. But long-term data do exist in the historical domain. Marriage records, census data, and other material are available in many countries across the globe for long stretches of time, and these can be used to test and refine theories on social endogamy.

In theory, there were evidently several groups of factors determining endogamy. Their relative strength over time can be discerned by relating endogamy patterns in countries and periods to the strength of the indicators of these determinants, which also varied by country and over time. It is worthwhile distilling the hypotheses on changes in social endogamy over time which have emerged from our review of the literature – if only because the literature deals more with structures and their determinants than with processes over time and their causes. Table 1 presents these hypotheses in a stylized way. Though this presentation shows a certain lack of regard for complicating factors, it serves a useful purpose and, we hope, will help others to identify simple ideas that can be tested against the historical data.[52]

Class formation is a central theme for social history. While the centrality of the theme and the availability of the sources are old, the articles in this volume are truly children of their time, firstlings of the twenty-first century. This is because only now has it become possible to classify historical individuals across regions and cultures into social classes in a similar way, using occupations as an indicator of social class.

Each of these articles addresses some of the issues raised here. Bras and Kok, using a large Dutch database covering the nineteenth century, test various hypotheses, including notions on the possible effect of being an orphan, being geographically endogamous, the career history of men and women, and the social relations and property structures of the various agrarian regions they study. They devote much attention to rural labourers, a social group sometimes overlooked in studies of class

51. In order, however, to participate in certain cultural activities – such as attending classical concerts or expensive dance parties, or dining in chic restaurants – one does need economic resources. In other words, there is some association between cultural participation and economic position.
52. The body of this review article, though necessarily global, does differentiate according to possession of property, inheritance system, gender, group size, and type of religion.

Table 1. *Hypotheses on changes in social endogamy over time.*

Macro characteristics		Effect on social endogamy	Global changes in macro characteristics over time	Resulting changes in social endogamy over time
Likelihood of meeting someone from another class	Universal education	−	+	−
	Associational life	+	+	+
	Ethnic/religious diversity	−	?	?
	Modern labour market	−	+	−
	Spatial social segregation	+	?	?
Marriage horizons	Means of transport	−	+	−
	Means of communication	−	+	−
	Conscription	−	+	−
Social pressure	Parental control	+	−	−
	Communal traditions	+	−	−
	Peer group control	+	?	?
	Adult mortality	−	−	+
Personal autonomy	Economic independence at early age	−	+	−
	Social security schemes	−	+	−
Personal preferences	Notions of romantic love	−	+	−

formation. So, too, do Dribe and Lundh, Arrizabalaga, and Bull. Dribe and Lundh note the existence of rural retirement contracts as well as bundling or night-courting in their Swedish parishes in the nineteenth century, as does Bull for the Norwegian valley he studies in the period 1750–1900.

Interestingly, Bull suggests that "the introduction of the ideal of romantic love led parents to control the mating process even more firmly. If children risked losing their way in the process of night-courting, falling in love with the wrong person, parents would take action to prevent this from happening." Dribe and Lundh look at the effect of property on social homogamy, as does Arrizabalaga. Arrizabalaga also looks at the various options available to men and women in the French Basque country in the nineteenth century to improve their fate – and at the differences between these men and women: marrying someone from the same class (heirs of propertied families and the landless); migrating to America (men of all classes); migrating to the city and remaining single, or marrying a cotter locally (daughters of propertied farmers).

Lanzinger looks at a small conservative Austrian market town, in what is now part of Italy, in the period 1700–1900. Marriage in this society was regulated through settlement policies, which barred undesirables from moving to the community. By law, only citizens with property could marry. Every couple had to prove that they could financially support a family – otherwise they would not be allowed to marry. This law was introduced in 1820 and in some areas remained in effect until as late as 1923.

The four Belgian authors – Van de Putte, Oris, Neven, and Matthijs – test various assumptions on a large database covering both rural and urban areas in both the French- and the Dutch-speaking parts of Belgium in the nineteenth century. They analyse the effect of migration, occupational identity, and ethnicity (in the form of language barriers) on social homogamy. The effect of both short- and long-term migration on marriage patterns according to social class forms the core of the article by Pélissier, Rébaudo, Van Leeuwen, and Maas. They study a large nationwide sample covering France in the nineteenth and twentieth centuries. They address such questions as: Did migrants constitute a permanent proletariat? Does the direction (rural–urban or urban–rural) of migration matter? Do wars make a difference? What is the effect of social pressure, notably that exerted by parents? Did the expansion in marriage horizons matter?

Schumacher and Lorenzetti, in their contribution on the Swiss town of Winterthur, are particularly interested in the association between social structure, social endogamy, and class relations. They derive a social-stratification scale from marriage patterns and, on the basis of these patterns, investigate whether the great national strike of 1918 increased class consciousness.

Holt looks at both formal Catholic marriages and informal, consensual unions of enslaved and free Brazilians in a plantation society during the nineteenth century. How did Brazilians cope with the rather rigid class and racial hierarchies that characterized plantation life? Could a free or freed woman marry a wealthy planter, and if so could their child pass for white? What were the benefits of formal marriage, and at what cost did they come? Which layers of society entered consensual unions and why did they do so? Were there differences between men and women in the costs and benefits associated with these two types of marriage?

There are many insights to be derived from comparative historical studies of class formation; insights, we believe, that are central to social and labour history. Many more, indeed, than can be dealt with in this volume, and also more than is at present possible. But this volume can perhaps help to give the topic the prominence it deserves. Furthermore, the conclusion to this volume presents the first truly comparative – in the sense of using the same social-class scheme – study of social endogamy in the past. Were there significant territorial differences, and if so what were they? Did they change over time, and if so how quickly and in what direction? Were temporal changes a mere reflection of changes in class structure, in particular the decline of the endogamous class of farmers, or were these temporal changes still evident even after the influence of changes in class structure had been filtered out? In short, was society becoming more open as well? And what do the marriage patterns observed tell us about the social distance between classes?

IRSH 50 (2005), Supplement, pp. 25–41 DOI: 10.1017/S0020859005002051
© 2005 Internationaal Instituut voor Sociale Geschiedenis

Marriage Choices in a Plantation Society: Bahia, Brazil*

KATHERINE HOLT

SUMMARY: This article examines the evolving significance of formal marriage and of partner selection in nineteenth-century Santiago do Iguape Brazil. Across social divides, racial and class endogamy were the norm for marriage partners, but consensual unions were far more likely to unite couples of different races. The information about enslaved couples was more sporadic, but I found that most slaves married partners who shared their country of origin, and that there was a higher slave-marriage rate on larger plantations. My research suggests that free and enslaved people constantly violated the borders separating them within a stratified plantation society, but that formal marriage retained a special significance and was reserved for unions between social equals.

The exigencies of export production dominated every aspect of daily life on the sugar plantations of Santiago do Iguape, Bahia. Located along the large bay surrounding the provincial capital of Salvador in northeastern Brazil, the parish combined the ideal climatic and soil conditions for sugar production, which had provided its primary economic activity for nearly three centuries. Nearly every household owed its livelihood to sugar, from the powerful mill owners at the pinnacle (HISCLASS 1+2), the overseers and clerks who managed sugar production (HISCLASS 3+4+5), the free skilled workers who transformed cane juice into refined sugar (HISCLASS 6+7), the smaller cane growers dependent on mill owners to process their crops (HISCLASS 8), to the households headed by less-skilled workers and subsistence farmers (HISCLASS 9, 10+12, and 11). As Table 1 demonstrates, Iguape was a highly stratified society. At the base of the region's wealth were the enslaved majority who performed the arduous physical labor of clearing the fields, planting sugar cane, weeding, cutting,

* I would like to thank Professor Jeremy Adelman as well as the staff of Arquivo Público do Estado da Bahia (APEB) and the Family History Center of Princeton. My research was supported by the Fellowship of Woodrow Wilson Scholars at Princeton University and a Fulbright-Hays Grant from the US Department of Education.

Table 1. *Head of Household HISCLASS Distribution, Santiago do Iguape, Bahia 1835*

	HISCLASS	N	%
1+2	Higher managers and professionals	25	2.6
3+4+5	Lower managers and professionals, clerical & sales	74	7.7
6+7	Skilled workers	98	10.2
8	Farmers and fishermen	83	8.7
9	Lower skilled workers	227	23.7
11	Unskilled workers	118	12.3
10+12	Farm workers	334	34.8
	Total	**959**	**100.0**

Source: "*Relação do Numero de fogos, e moradores no Districto da Freguezia de Sant Iago Maior de Iguape[...]1835*", Arquivo Público do Estado da Bahia (APEB), Sec. Colonial e Provincial, maço 6175-1. Occupations coded according to M.H.D. van Leeuwen and I. Maas, *HISCLASS*. Paper presented at the 5th European Social Science History Conference (Berlin, 24–27 March 2004) and I. Maas and M.H.D. van Leeuwen, "SPSS Recode Job from HISCO into HISCLASS", May 2004.
Note: Heads of households were always free or freed.

and bundling the ripe cane at harvest, and the dangerous task of feeding it through the mill's powerful rollers.[1]

Throughout the Atlantic world, sugar plantations were notorious for their high human toll. A constant stream of African slave imports provided most of the labor for Iguape's sugar growth and processing. In 1835, 54 per cent of Iguape's population was enslaved, and most of these slaves had been born in Africa. Of the remaining population, 8 per cent was *branco* (of European descent), 27 per cent *pardo* (combined African/European), and 11 per cent *preto* (of African descent). Slavery remained the predominant form of labor on Iguape's sugar plantations until its abolition in 1888. Slavery was widespread, and its influences permeated all other social relationships.

Despite the rigid racial and class hierarchies that typified plantation life, free people of color were the largest population group in Iguape by 1872, suggesting that even within such a stratified slave society, social norms regulating partner selection did not always hold. Iguape's position as such a quintessentially Brazilian plantation society makes it a valuable case study.

1. On the region's economic and social base, see Stuart Schwartz, *Sugar Plantations in the Formation of Brazilian Society: Bahia, 1550–1835* (New York, 1985), B.J. Barickman, *A Bahian Counterpoint: Sugar, Tobacco, Cassava, and Slavery in the Recôncavo, 1780–1860* (Stanford, CA, 1998); and Arlene Díaz and Jeff Stewart, "Occupational Class and Female-Headed Households in Santiago Maior do Iguape, Brazil, 1835", *Journal of Family History*, 16 (1991), pp. 299–313.

This article examines how Bahians across color, class, and legal divides selected their marital and sexual partners, and traces the evolving significance of formal marriage during the nineteenth century. Notwithstanding the high value placed on legitimacy within nineteenth-century accounts, and a subsequent historiographical emphasis on the patriarchal family as the model for all other households, recent studies reveal a diverse array of family types and ensuing domestic arrangements in nineteenth-century Brazil.[2] Households, even in plantation regions, were both smaller and less complex than previously assumed.[3] However, to some extent this research has focused on the *outcome* rather than the *process* of family formation. More investigation is needed of individual strategies in partner selection and family formation, and especially how local economic and demographic structures shaped norms surrounding partner selection. A closer examination of partner selection in Iguape both emphasizes the diversity present in slave societies within Brazil, and the links between Iguape and other Atlantic slave societies dominated by plantation production.

I use three sets of sources for this study. The first is the manuscript census compiled for Santiago do Iguape parish in 1835. Household by household, this census listed the name, race, age, marital status, and occupation of each inhabitant, along with a description of their relationship to the household head. Enslaved and free dependents were included as part of their master's household – even in the cases of large plantations with hundreds of slaves – reflecting their subservient place within local society. The living arrangements recorded by census takers reveal tangible clues of how individuals in a slave society organized their domestic relationships. The demographic information from the 1835 census is complimented by the aggregate data from the less detailed 1872 national census.

Iguape's parish records provide a second source of quantitative information about partner selection during the nineteenth century. Local parish priests routinely recorded the names, parentage, and legitimacy of birth for prospective spouses, as well as the owners of enslaved partners; information on their ages, occupations, and races was recorded far more

---

2. Eni de Mesquita Samara, *A família brasileira* (São Paulo, 1983); Dain Borges, *The Family in Bahia, Brazil, 1870–1945* (Stanford, CA, 1992); Mariza Corrêa, "Repensando a família patriarcal brasileira", *Cadernos de Pesquisa*, 37 (1981), pp. 5–16; Elizabeth Anne Kuznesof, "Sexual Politics, Race, and Bastard-Bearing in Nineteenth-Century Brazil: A Question of Culture or Power?", *Journal of Family History*, 16 (1991), pp. 241–260; Donald Ramos, "Single and Married Women in Vila Rica, Brazil, 1754–1838", *Journal of Family History*, 16 (1991), pp. 261–282.

3. B.J. Barickman, "Revisiting the *Casa-Grande*: Plantation and Cane Farming Households in Early Nineteenth-Century Bahia", *Hispanic American Historical Review*, 84 (2004), pp. 619–661.

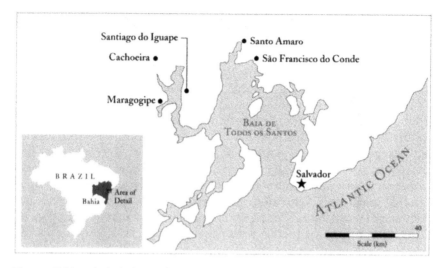

Figure 1. Bahia: principal nineteenth-century *recôncavo* population centers.

sporadically, making longitudinal analysis of these factors difficult. These records only record formal Catholic marriages rather than consensual unions. These quantitative sources are supplemented by written accounts from travelers, advice manuals, and journals. Such written sources privilege the experiences of elites, but still provide important insight into the discourse surrounding marriage and sexual partnerships.

My research suggests that although the formal marriages contracted between elites on the sugar plantations presented a highly visible example of domestic organization aspired to by many members of the middle and lower classes, the influence of this patriarchal model was not absolute.[4] Consensual unions – couples living together without being legally married – provided a widespread and widely tolerated alternative to formal marriage, even within the fervently Catholic culture. Households consisting of unmarried women and their children were also quite common. Especially among farm laborers, artisans, and slaves, affective ties and family formation rarely required official sanction. Even the sons of plantation owners frequently founded consensual families before, and sometimes alongside, their legitimate households. Conversely, numerous enslaved couples fought to have their unions legitimized by the church,

---

4. I define patriarchy as a hierarchal relationship of power that privileges masculinity and age. It is not limited to men, as women can borrow its privileges and act patriarchally, but it implies an assumption of masculine prerogatives and activities. The exercise of this type of power often involves the formulation of a large household with a married man presiding over children, *agregados*, and slaves, but my use of "patriarchal" as a relationship of power does not mean that all who acted patriarchally necessarily lived in households of this type.

suggesting that even members of the most marginalized social groups saw a concrete value in legal marriage. It is important to uncover how individuals from different social, racial, and economic groups weighed these considerations in deciding whether formally to marry, and how to select a partner.

PARTNER SELECTION IN 1835 SANTIAGO DO IGUAPE

"When two individuals of different sexes agree to live together, they can not do this, my Cora, except by a solemn contract that gives each party reciprocal rights and duties."[5] In this 1849 letter to his daughter Cora, Bahian statesman José Linho Coutinho placed great emphasis on legitimate – that is, church-sanctified – marriage as the primary bond uniting men and women in nineteenth-century Bahia. Officially sanctioned Catholic unions were the only legally recognized form of marriage in Brazil until the creation of civil marriage in 1890. Catholic marriage was the vehicle for producing legitimate heirs, and its contract the basis for elite social and economic continuity within Bahia's traditional plantation society. Formal marriage also conveyed social prestige, emphasizing a family's stability and respectability within the community.

Weighing against the social benefits of legitimate marriage were considerable economic costs. Fulfilling the ecclesiastical requirements for legal marriages could be quite cumbersome – posting the banns in each parish where the couple had resided, compiling genealogies – as well as expensive. Even more trouble resulted for couples who required religious dispensations to marry. Marriage between cousins, in-laws, couples suspected of prior sexual intimacy, or even those linked by the bonds of spiritual kinship as godparents required costly appeals to dissolve their impediments. In the face of such obstacles, it was no wonder that so many couples eschewed formal marriage.[6] The considerable percentage (11.4 per cent) of Iguape marriages that took place despite the economic burden of ecclesiastical dispensations reflected the higher economic status of most free couples who contracted formal marriage.[7]

Ironically, despite his laudatory view of marriage, José Linho Coutinho himself never married Cora's mother. Instead, after the couple's informal

---

5. José Lino Coutinho, *Cartas sobre a educação de Cora* (Salvador, 1849), Carta XXX, p. 107.
6. Linda Lewin's exhaustive study of Brazilian marriage and inheritance law argues that "by declining to facilitate access to the sacrament of matrimony, through simplified procedures and lower fees, the church insured that *mancebia* [consensual unions] would thrive"; Lewin, *Surprise Heirs* (Stanford, CA, 2003): vol. 2, p. 87.
7. A survey of all marriages recorded at five-year intervals found that 7.5 per cent of free marriages required dispensations for consanguinity and 3.9 per cent for "illicit affinity"; Family History Center, Princeton (FHC), *Livros de matrimonios*, Santiago do Iguape, 1774–1805; 1806–1857; 1857–1902.

relationship ended, Coutinho married another elite woman and started a second, legitimate family. This type of successive family formation was fairly common among elite men in nineteenth-century Brazil. Brazilian law allowed recognized "natural" children, conceived by parents with no impediments to their marriage, to inherit alongside any successive legitimate half-siblings; legislative reform in 1847 restricted these children's rights somewhat by requiring that they be notarily recognized before either of their parents married in order to inherit. Natural children could also be legitimized by their parents' subsequent marriage. Consensual unions represented greater flexibility for men than formal marriage which – even in the rare case of divorce – was dissoluble only by death.[8]

In contrast, formal marriage to another partner was rarely an option for women who formed consensual unions. Virginity formed an essential component of female honor, and in most cases a prerequisite for marriage. To this end, unmarried elite daughters were strictly guarded within their parents' homes. European travelers frequently commented on the degree of isolation of elite Brazilian women: writing in 1846, George Gardner commented that "I have lived for a week at a time in houses where I was well aware there were ladies, without ever seeing more of them than their dark eyes peering through chinks about the doors of the inner apartments."[9] By the end of the century, however, the norms surrounding the socialization of elite women underwent a dramatic shift. Carefully chaperoned family gatherings became a venue where young women could talk, dance, and flirt with men who met with their parents' approval. However, most of Iguape's elites still regarded female virginity as a requirement for formal marriage.

Two main exceptions existed to the emphasis on female virginity for brides. The first came in the cases of long-time consensual couples who formalized their relationships in a deathbed marriage. For example, Manoel Paulo dos Santos married Eusebia Maria as she lay dying in 1845 "to benefit her soul"; the couple had lived together for years, but the religious benefits of church marriage only became overwhelming when faced with the possibility of her eternal damnation.[10] The other exceptions were women of color whose elite lovers provided them with dowries upon dissolving the relationship. Traveler Henry Koster wrote that this capital allowed such women to marry a man "of her own rank, who regards her rather as a widow than as one whose conduct has been incorrect".[11] These

---

8. Linda Lewin, "Natural and Spurious Children in Brazilian Inheritance Law from Colony to Empire: A Methodological Essay", *Americas*, 48 (1992), pp. 351–396.
9. George Gardener, *Travels in the Interior of Brazil* (New York, 1970 [1846]), p. 14.
10. Marriage of Manoel Paulo dos Santos and Eusebia Maria (27 September 1845), FHC, *Livros de matrimonios*, Santiago do Iguape, 1806–1847, p. 164.
11. Henry Koster, *Travels in Brazil* (Carbondale, IL, 1966 [1817]), p. 175.

Table 2. *Marital status of free and enslaved adults by race and sex, Santiago do Iguape, Bahia 1835*

	Men				Women			
	Ever married		Single		Ever married		Single	
	N	%	N	%	N	%	N	%
Free *branco*	106	50.0	106	50.0	102	51.8	95	48.2
Free/freed *pardo*	256	48.6	271	51.4	276	45.5	330	54.5
Enslaved *pardo*	2	3.4	56	96.6	1	1.9	52	98.1
Free/freed *preto*	76	33.6	150	66.4	107	33.9	209	66.1
Enslaved *preto*	103	5.7	1720	94.3	86	8.0	991	92.0
Total free	438	45.4	527	54.6	485	43.3	634	56.7
Total enslaved	105	5.6	1776	94.4	87	7.7	1043	92.3

Source: See Table 1.
Note: Adult is defined as age sixteen or older to facilitate comparisons with the 1872 census. Ever-married totals include currently married as well as widowed individuals. *Branco* referred to individuals of European descent, *preto* to those of African descent, and *pardo* to those whose color suggested European and African parentage.

exceptions emphasized that in nineteenth-century Brazil both the decision to marry formally and the selection of a suitable partner depended on a careful calculation of the religious, economic, and social costs and benefits. Marriage was neither the only nor even always the most popular alternative for Iguape's couples.

The pictures of domestic arrangements that emerge from the 1835 Iguape parish census provide further evidence for the widespread coexistence of legal and natural unions. Iguape's parish priest preserved an unusually detailed account of the legal and affective ties that bound parish households together. The census enumerates legitimate families headed by married couples, families consisting of male household heads listed with single female "domestics" and their natural children, as well as single mothers heading independent households.

The information recorded about marital status was immediately striking: as Table 2 demonstrates, in 1835 the majority of Iguape's adults had never married. Even when the enslaved population was omitted, only 45.4 per cent of adult men and 43.3 per cent of adult women were married or widowed. In the sixteenth and seventeenth centuries, the scarcity of elite women contributed to a low formal marriage rate in Bahia; however by 1835 the free sex ratio was 91, meaning that free women slightly outnumbered free men. The low rate of formal marriage could thus no longer be ascribed to a dearth of *branca* women. The census suggests a link between an individual's decision to contract formal marriage and their ascribed social status; confined by their African ancestry to the bottom of

Table 3. *Marital status of Santiago do Iguape household heads by HISCLASS, 1835*

HISCLASS	Household head's marital status								
	Ever married		Never married		Consensual union		Single parent		Total
	N	%	N	%	N	%	N	%	N
1+2	18	72.0	4	16.0	3	12.0	0	0.0	25
3+4+5	42	56.8	22	29.7	7	9.5	3	4.1	74
6+7	58	59.2	26	26.5	12	12.2	2	2.0	98
8	53	63.9	19	22.9	8	9.6	3	3.6	83
9	72	31.7	75	33.0	6	2.6	74	32.6	227
11	54	45.8	46	39.0	5	4.2	13	11.0	118
10+12	197	59.0	72	21.6	49	14.7	16	4.8	334
Total	494	51.5	264	27.5	90	9.4	111	11.6	959

Source: See Table 1.

Iguape's social ladder, *pretos* were the least likely of any racial group to form legal unions. A high proportion of free adults either could not afford the high ecclesiastical fees for legal marriage or found other family strategies more attractive.

Occupational class too played an important role in determining the likelihood of household heads selecting legal or consensual unions. Table 3 records the marital status of Iguape's heads of household by HISCLASS. For this calculation, I first divided households according to whether or not their members formed a legally married family. I then further examined the details recorded about unmarried heads' relationship with other members of their households, and separated them into cases presenting evidence of current consensual unions, single parents living with their children, and unmarried people showing no evidence of current sexual relationships.[12]

Not surprisingly, a slightly higher percentage (51.5 per cent) of Iguape's household heads had been married than the general population. The formation of a sexual partnership – whether through legal marriage or a consensual union – frequently provided the impetus for young couples to found an independent household. In Iguape, it was not unusual for unmarried children to remain living with their parents well into adulthood. Household heads identifiable as involved in consensual unions represented a further 9.4 per cent of households; slightly more numerous (11.6 per cent) were households like that of the freed *preta* slave Rita Delfina,

12. I would like to thank Elizabeth Anne Kuznesof for her helpful comments on my use of these categories at the 2004 Latin American Studies Association Conference.

comprised of single parents and their children. Nearly all of these families (96.1 per cent) were headed by the mother rather than the father.

One of the limitations of censuses is that they give a picture of a community at an isolated moment in time, rather than reflecting the more dynamic long-term interactions between members. If anything, my calculations probably under-report the number of household heads involved in extramarital sexual relationships, as the absence of offspring or a live-in sexual partner does not provide conclusive evidence of celibacy.[13] If households headed by individuals involved in current consensual unions and single parents are combined, a minimum of 21 per cent of Iguape's household heads engaged in sexual relationships outside marriage.

Table 3 further suggests a correlation between the decision to contract legal marriage and social class. Sugar-mill owners and heads of plantations had a higher marriage rate than lower-class household heads. Correspondingly, farm workers and lower skilled workers presented more evidence of consensual unions. The majority of heads in the lower-skilled worker category (HISCLASS 9) were women identified as spinners, seamstresses, and washerwomen – single mothers working in acceptable feminized occupations to support their children. Nearly 95 per cent of these single mothers were free women of color, placed at the bottom of the social hierarchy by the compounded liabilities of their race and sex.

Iguape's manuscript census permits another interesting insight into partner selection. Table 4 overleaf examines the racial endogamy among couples with both members present in a household. Henry Koster, an Englishman who ran a sugar plantation in the 1810s, remarked that although "Brazilians of high birth and large property do not like to intermarry with persons whose mixture of blood is very apparent", marriages between *branco* men and *parda* women were fairly common. Neighbors only gossiped when "the person is a planter of any importance, and the woman is decidedly of dark color, for even a considerable tinge will pass for white".[14] Still, the Iguape household census implied that race was a fundamental consideration when selecting a spouse. Among HISCLASS 1+2 formal marriages were fully endogamous. Even members of the lower echelons of Iguape society overwhelmingly contracted marriage with members of the same racial groups. In no social class did racially exogamous partnerships represent more than 8 per cent of formal marriages.

In contrast, the composition of consensual couples suggests that sexual boundaries were not nearly so rigid outside the bonds of legal marriage;

13. Katia M. de Queirós Mattoso, "Slave, Free, and Freed Family Structures in Nineteenth-Century Salvador, Bahia", *Luso-Brazilian Review*, 25 (1988), pp. 69–84. Mattoso calculated that 53 per cent of free couples in 1855 Salvador were living in consensual unions.
14. Koster, *Travels in Brazil*, p. 175.

Katherine Holt

Table 4. *Head of household partner selection by HISCLASS, Santiago do Iguape 1835*

HISCLASS	Legal marriages			Consensual unions			Total
	Same race	Different races	% racially endogamous	Same race	Different races	% racially endogamous	
1+2	10	0	100.0	2	1	66.7	13
3+4+5	30	2	93.8	4	3	57.1	39
6+7	41	1	97.6	7	5	58.3	54
8	32	1	97.0	2	6	25.0	41
9	27	1	96.4	5	1	83.3	34
11	12	1	92.3	3	2	60.0	18
10+12	145	9	94.2	37	12	75.5	203
Total	297	15	95.2	60	30	66.7	402

Source: See Table 1.
Note: Includes only couples with both members present.

fully one-third of all co-resident consensual relationship occurred between members of different racial groups. Across the boundaries of class, individuals employed different criteria in selecting partners for formal versus consensual partnerships. This finding in many ways explains the historical paradox raised by the high incidence of consensual unions despite a widespread contemporary discourse emphasizing the value of legal marriage: legal marriage was reserved primarily for unions regarded as desirable and socially respectable. In a society where race was a crucial part of assigning social status, it is not surprising that most legally married couples – and especially those of sugar plantation owners – were racially endogamous.

SLAVE PARTNER SELECTION

As early as 1719 the Brazilian prelacy affirmed the desirability of legal marriage for slaves. Church doctrine permitted Catholic slaves to marry other slaves or free people, admonished slaveholders not to impede slave marriages or separate married enslaved couples.[15] Questions concerning legal marriage between enslaved individuals were always polemic because they involved disputes over the individual rights of slaves as Catholic communicants and the property rights of slaveholders. Married enslaved couples enjoyed religious rights that limited their masters' power to sell

15. Sebastião Monteiro da Vide, *Constituições Primeiras do Arcebispado da Bahia* (São Paulo, 1853 [1719]), Livro I, Titulo LXXI, no. 303.

them in times of economic hardship, or even to split them up during an estate settlement. Married slaves facing separation could appeal to local clergy to intervene on their behalf.

Carlos Augusto Taunay, author of an influential Brazilian agricultural manual, typified slaveholders' ambiguous view of legal marriages for slaves in his discussion of encouraging reproduction by enslaved couples: "Should the unions be legitimate or transitory? Religion and good order ask that they be legitimate, but on the other hand, it seems unjust and harsh to impose a new captivity on the slaves, and especially on the women, who find themselves with two masters".[16] Although Tuanay's characterization of legal marriage as a form of servitude for women was revealing, his attitude against marriage for slaves was not so much benevolent as self-serving. Slaveholders sought to use legal marriage between their slaves to their personal advantage, encouraging it in some cases, as a way to foster reproduction of their labor force or reward amenable individuals, and discouraging it when the additional protections legal marriage offered enslaved families came into conflict with owners' desires to maximize their financial flexibility. Enslaved couples and families not united by legal marriage were even more vulnerable to separation through sale or testamentary bequest.

Information about nineteenth-century slave family formation, whether through formal marriage or consensual unions, is sporadic at best, but several excellent recent works have risen to the challenge.[17] In 1835, more than half the slaves living in Iguape were African-born. The grueling labor demands of sugar resulted in a very high slave mortality rate, fueling the demand for a constant stream of African slave imports.[18] The high predominance of men among slaves imported from Africa reinforced the obstacles placed in the way of natural increase; a slave sex ratio of 146 meant that men far outnumbered women among potential enslaved mates. Only after the effective cessation of the Atlantic trade in 1850 did the enslaved sex ratio on regional sugar plantations become more balanced. By

---

16. Carlos Augusto Taunay, *Manual do agricultor brasileiro* (São Paulo, 2001 [1830]), 78.

17. Recent works on slave families in Brazil include Robert Slenes, *Na senzala, uma flor: esperanças e recordações na formação da família escrava* (Rio de Janeiro, 1999); Isabel Cristina Ferreira dos Reis, *Histórias de vida familiar e afetiva de escravos na Bahia do século XIX* (Salvador, 2001); Anna Gicelle García Alaniz, *Ingênuos e libertos: estratégias de sobrevivência familiar em épocas de transição, 1871–1895* (Campinas, São Paulo, 1997); and Tarcísio Rodrigues Botelho, "Famílias e escravarias: demografia e família escrava no norte de Minas Gerais no século XIX", *População e família*, 1 (1998), pp. 211–234. For a detailed study of a slave woman who eschewed marriage despite her owner's initial insistence, see Sandra Lauderdale Graham, *Caetana Says No* (Cambridge, 2002).

18. See for example Michael Tadman, "The Demographic Cost of Sugar: Debates on Slave Societies and Natural Increase in the Americas", *American Historical Review*, 105 (2000), pp. 1534–1575.

1872, the enslaved sex ratio was 132, and only 5 per cent of the sugar *recôncavo's* slaves were of African birth.[19]

The 1835 census identifies 84 married slave women and 16 widows. Only 43 per cent of female slaves were African born, but they represented 72 per cent of the ever-married slave women, suggesting that the African women were more likely to contract marriage. This over-representation of Africans held for the ever-married male slaves as well; 86.7 per cent of ever-married men were African versus 60.1 per cent of all enslaved men. This higher marriage rate was even more striking considering the greater obstacles facing prospective African spouses. Priests verbally examined slaves on Catholic doctrine before they could marry. Although some slaves may have been exposed to Christianity in Africa, participation in the church ceremony would further require proficiency in Portuguese.

Unfortunately, the census does not provide detailed information about these enslaved Africans' ethnic identities; nearly all are identified merely as "da Costa" – "from the coast" of Africa, a label that served more to differentiate them from Brazilian-born slaves than to provide real information about their place of origin. Still, whether they were born in Africa or Brazil, most slaves chose marriage partners who shared their birthplace. The census identified 47 slave couples, 44 (93.6 per cent) of whom married partners sharing their national origin. The parish records recording each marriage celebrated in Iguape supported this preference for marital partners with the same region of origin: of 97 slave marriages sampled between 1800 and 1885, nearly 80 per cent were between spouses with the same place of birth.[20]

The economic status of their owners further influenced slaves' chances of contracting formal marriage. As Table 5 demonstrates, although the percentage of ever-married slaves did not uniformly increase with the size of holding, slaves living on extensive sugar plantations experienced the highest marriage rates. In 1835, only 11.5 per cent of the adult slaves on Iguape's largest sugar plantations had ever married. Nevertheless, the marriage rate was even lower for slaves living on Iguape's smallest holdings: 2.4 per cent. In a society where slaveholders were reluctant to make any concessions that might diminish their control over their slaves, slaves on large plantations could select from a larger pool of potential mates. Slaveholders feared that cross-plantation marriages encouraged absenteeism and flight, as well as concentrating the economic benefit from any future enslaved children in the hands of the holder of the female slave. The parish marriage records I sampled found no marriages between slaves held by different owners.[21]

19. See Table 6.
20. FHC, *Livros de matrimonios*, Santiago do Iguape, 1774–1805; 1806–1857; 1857–1902. Sample of every five years from 1800–1885; 1820 and 1825 could not be found.
21. *Ibid.*

Table 5. *Distribution of ever-married slaves by size of slave holding, Santiago do Iguape 1835*

Holding size (adults & children)	Number of ever-married slaves	Number of adult slaves on this size holding	% adult slaves ever-married on this size holding
20 or less	15	626	2.4
21–50	34	449	7.6
51–100	23	396	5.8
101–200	31	720	4.3
200+	102	884	11.5
Total	205	3,075	6.7

Source: See Table 1.
Note: Adult slaves defined as individuals aged fifteen and older; holding size is the number of slaves held within each household.

A low incidence of cross-plantation marriages seems to have characterized Brazilian slavery; Alida Metcalf's research on coffee plantations in Santana de Parnaíba and Linda Wimmer's on Bahian tobacco regions also suggest that slaveholders opposed these marriages whenever possible. In contrast, Emily West's study of antebellum South Carolina found that one-third of slave marriages were between spouses living on different plantations. The rates of cross-plantation marriages on the sugar plantations of the British Caribbean were also considerably higher than those found in Brazil. Historian B.W. Higman calculates that in St Kitts and Jamaica, nearly 30 per cent of slave marriages were cross-plantation. In Barbados, the rate was nearly one-half. Only on the isolated plantations of Dominica were the cross-plantation marriage rates anywhere close to those found in Brazil: no more than 6 per cent of Dominican slave marriages crossed plantation boundaries.[22]

Iguape's low rate of formal slave marriages did not signal the absence of family formation or affective ties within the enslaved community. Slaves

22. Alida Metcalf's study of a coffee plantation in Santana de Parnaíba Brazil in 1820 found that 94 per cent of slave marriages occurred between two slaves owned by the same master; Metcalf, "Searching for the Slave Family in Colonial Brazil: A Reconstruction from São Paulo", *Journal of Family History*, 16 (1991), pp. 283–297. Linda Wimmer's study of tobacco cultivation in eighteenth-century Bahia found 98 per cent of slave marriages between slaves held by the same owner; Wimmer, "Ethnicity and Family Formation among Slaves on Tobacco Farms in the Bahian Recôncavo, 1698–1820", in José C. Curto and Paul E. Lovejoy (eds), *Enslaving Connections: Changing Cultures of Africa and Brazil during the Era of Slavery* (Amherst, NY, 2004), pp. 149–162. Also, Emily West, "The Debate on the Strength of Slave Families: South Carolina and the Importance of Cross-Plantation Marriages", *Journal of American Studies*, 33 (1999), pp. 221–241; B.W. Higman, *Slave Populations of the British Caribbean, 1807–1834* (Baltimore, MD, 1984), p. 370.

Table 6. *Ever-married adults by race, civil status, and sex in selected sugar parishes, Bahia 1872*

	Sex ratio	Men		Women	
		N	% ever married	N	% ever married
Free *branco*	121	8,661	42.7	7,171	47.5
Free/freed *pardo*	115	10,357	49.7	8,986	51.7
Free/freed *preto*	113	6,115	46.5	5,431	35.7
Free *caboclo*	166	1,190	41.4	719	57.4
Total free	**118**	**26,323**	**46.3**	**22,307**	**46.6**
Enslaved *pardo*	132	1,276	40.2	964	57.5
Enslaved *preto*	132	2,369	43.6	1,794	41.6
Total enslaved	**132**	**3,645**	**42.4**	**2,758**	**47.2**

Source: Brazil, Directoria Geral de Estatística, *Recenseamento da população do Imperio do Brazil a que se procedeu no dia 1° de agosto de 1872* (Rio de Janeiro: 1873). The sample includes the sugar parishes of N.S. da Purificação, S. Pedro do Rio Fundo, N.S. do Oliveira, and S. Domingos in Santo Amaro; S. Gonçalo, Sant'Anna do Catú, N.S. do Monte, S. Sebastião, and N.S. do Soccoro in São Francisco do Conde; and Santiago do Iguape in Cachoeira.
Note: Adult defined as age sixteen or older; *caboclo* referred to individuals of mixed *branco* and Brazilian-Indian extraction.

who sought official sanction for their unions faced even greater impediments than impoverished free people. While ecclesiastical law stated that masters could not impede slave marriages, Iguape's parish records often included statements of owners' acquiescence, suggesting that their consent was a *de facto* requirement. Formal slave marriages represent a testimony to desirability of such unions, even in the face of extreme difficulty.

CHANGES OVER THE NINETEENTH CENTURY

The 1872 national census represented the next large-scale survey of Santiago do Iguape's population. Immediately striking was the dramatic decline in the absolute number, as well as the representation within the general population, of slaves. Over the course of thirty-seven years, Iguape's enslaved population fell from the absolute majority to less than one-third of the population. The end of the Atlantic trade had made its mark on the demographic composition of Brazil's sugar regions.

Table 6 presents the sex ratio, number, and percentage of adults in Bahia's sugar parishes identified in the 1872 census as ever married by sex, race, and legal status. Men significantly outnumbered women among both the free and enslaved populations. Still, 46.3 per cent of free men and 42.4

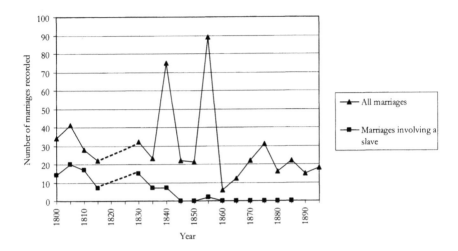

Figure 2. Annual number of marriages in five-year increments, Santiago do Iguape, 1800–1895. *Source:* FHC, *Livros de matrimonios*, Santiago do Iguape, 1774–1805; 1806–1857; 1857–1902. *Note:* Records for 1820 and 1825 could not be located.

per cent of enslaved men were identified as married or widowed. These numbers imply that while the marriage rate reported for free men remained about the same as in 1835 (when it was 45.5 per cent), the number of enslaved men classified as married or widowers rose dramatically from 5.6 per cent to 42.4 per cent.[23] If accurate, this would seem to suggest a remarkable change in slaveholders' willingness to permit their slaves to contract marriage and/or a greater estimation placed on legal marriage among Bahia's enslaved communities. However, the information recorded in Iguape's parish marriage records suggested an alternative explanation.

Figure 2 shows a slight decline in the annual number of marriages performed in nineteenth-century Iguape, with the exclusion of two large peaks mid-century. The year with the highest number of formal marriages was 1855. Significantly, this was the year a cholera epidemic ravaged the bay area, killing nearly 17,000 in the surrounding countryside. As the epidemic progressed, priests dispensed with the publication of marriage banns, allowing consensual couples to formalize their unions, and protect

23. I decided to use a sample from several nearby sugar parishes because the 1872 figures provided for Santiago do Iguape seem unreliable. For example, in the printed census for Iguape, the number of ever-married *branco* men was higher than the entire adult male *branco* population. It seems very unlikely that every *branco* man over age sixteen in the parish, as well as some even younger men, had legally married. Men rarely married before their mid-twenties. Second, Iguape's number of free ever-married (1,578) men outnumbered the free ever-married women (728) by more than two to one.

their immortal souls, without delay. Couples who had lived together for years, forming households and raising children, rushed to seek religious sanction of their unions in a time of crisis. The devastation of the epidemic was overwhelming; even in the 1872 census, Iguape had not recovered its 1835 population. Historian Johildo Lopes de Athayde found a parallel surge in marriage rates in Salvador, the nearby provincial capital.[24] Still, this mid-century surge in formal marriages appears to have been short-lived. The annual marriage rate for the final decade of the century was dramatically lower than that reported in the first.

The bottom line of Figure 2 represents the number of formal slave marriages each year. Despite the injunctions of local planters that "it is of absolute necessity that Masters, by some reward and other obvious and simple means, stimulate and invite slaves to marry", to preserve the region's labor force after the closure of the international slave trade in 1850, the number of formal slave marriages recorded instead declined, and ended completely after 1860.[25] Iguape's parish records suggest a greater slave reliance on informal unions over the course of the century, even in the face of greater sex-ratio equilibrium. This information contradicts the 1872 census's report that slave marriages increased. It seems probable that either the slave marriages reported in the census were not officiated and recorded in the same manner as those of free couples, or that the census estimates counted slaves living in consensual unions as effectively married. This explanation is further supported by historian Sheila de Castro Faria's findings that formal marriages among enslaved partners declined sharply after 1830 throughout Brazil.[26] Unfortunately, Iguape's parish records for the second half of the century did not include the race or legal condition of spouses, so it is impossible to assess the impact of abolition in 1888 on formal marriage strategies among former slaves.

Information about the contractants' ages was only recorded for 1885 and 1890. At the end of the century, the average age at marriage for women in Iguape was 26.1 with a median of 22; men averaged 30.7, with a median of 28. Grooms were an average of 4.3 years older than their brides. Spousal age differences thus contracted from an average of 7.9 years in 1835. The greater emphasis on mutual attraction between the young people involved, in contrast to pairings based entirely on men's economic prowess and women's sexual honor, contributed to a reduced age divide.

24. Johildo Lopes de Athayde, "La ville de Salvador au XIXe siècle" (Ph.D., Université de Paris X Nanterre, 1975), p. 252. On the cholera epidemic, see Donald B. Cooper, "The New 'Black Death': Cholera in Brazil, 1855–56", *Social Science History*, 10 (1986), pp. 467–488.
25. Miguel Calmon du Pin e Almeida, *Ensaio sobre o fabrico do açúcar* (Salvador, 2002 [1834]), p. 60.
26. Sheila de Castro Faria, "Família escrava e legitimidade: estratégias de preservação da autonomia", *Estudos afro-asiáticos*, 23 (1992), pp. 113–131.

The 1885 and 1890 parish records also provided details about twenty-nine couples' occupations. Not surprisingly in Iguape's plantation society, half of the men were farmers, and the remainder artisans, fishermen, and sailors. Only a handful of grooms were obviously elite: two businessmen and a man with a university degree. The difficulty of discerning a bride's class without information about her father's occupation makes suggestions about class homogamy unreliable; however, slightly more than half of the brides were identified as "domestics" – in this case, suggesting that the bride did not work outside her family home. Feminine reclusion remained an attractive characteristic for potential formal unions.

CONCLUSION

Writing in 1836, George Gardner observed that "marriage is less common in Brazil than in Europe", and credited the predominance of non-sacramental unions with "the greater laxity of morals which exists here among both sexes".[27] Formal marriage may have been less common in Brazil than in Gardner's native Great Britain, but his characterization of Brazilians as morally lax missed the point. Instead, Brazilians' choices to form alternative family and household arrangements were less proof of immorality than a reflection of different sets of community standards governing sexual relationships and partner selection. Formal marriage was not essential, but could be desirable under some circumstances. The dictates of race, class, and gender informed if and how Brazilians formally married.

In Iguape, consensual unions remained extremely common throughout the course of the nineteenth century. The trouble and expense of formal marriage contributed to its relative scarcity, along with the appealing flexibility of serial relationships. On the other hand, formal marriage conferred a greater degree of economic stability and social benefits. For members of the local elite, the social prestige of marriage and the formation of legitimate families outweighed the costs.

27. Gardener, *Travels in the Interior of Brazil*, p. 14.

IRSH 50 (2005), Supplement, pp. 43–63 DOI: 10.1017/S0020859005002063
© 2005 Internationaal Instituut voor Sociale Geschiedenis

Deciding Whom to Marry in a Rural Two-Class Society: Social Homogamy and Constraints in the Marriage Market in Rendalen, Norway, 1750–1900[*]

HANS HENRIK BULL

SUMMARY: This article presents the findings of a long-term study of social homogamy in the rural community of Rendalen, Norway, in the eighteenth and nineteenth centuries. Prior to 1870, the occupation of parents was not normally recorded in the Norwegian parish registers. It is therefore difficult to carry out historical studies of social homogamy in Norway over any length of time. The Rendalen database, however, provides this information from several other sources. Structural changes over time, which led to an increase in the number of farm workers, reduced the degree of homogamy among farmers as well as creating a larger marriage market for the farm workers, thereby increasing homogamy among these farm workers. Controlling for these structural changes, it is clear that social boundaries between farmers and farm workers prevailed at least until the end of the nineteenth century. Using a multivariate analysis, we are able to identify different family characteristics that led young men and woman to marry homogamously. The farmers, especially, exerted influence on their eldest sons to marry farmers' daughters, but the role of the father in the mating process also secured more economically viable partners for the other children too.

INTRODUCTION

In preindustrial rural society, a marriage did not involve simply forming a personal union; it also marked the start of a production unit. The choice of partner could have a great effect on economic outcome later in life. In this context, marriages could not be based solely on personal affection. This article presents the findings of a long-term study of social homogamy in the rural community of Rendalen, Norway, in the eighteenth and nineteenth centuries. It examines in what way social boundaries between the classes constrained the choice of marriage partner, and whether the role

* This article is part of my doctoral thesis. I am grateful to the Research Council of Norway for financial support. I am also grateful to the editorial committee of this journal for helpful comments and suggestions, and to Sølvi Sogner, Nico Keilman, George Alter, Mona Renate Ringvej, Svenn-Erik Mamelund, and Jennifer Høibråten.

of parents influenced their children's decision on whom to marry. Information is gathered and analysed using a population database based on family reconstitution methods. This makes it possible to identify the father's social position, information which is not obtainable directly from Norwegian marriage records.

BACKGROUND

In modern sociological research marriage patterns are regarded as the result of an interplay between three social forces: the preferences of the individual for a specific marriage candidate, influences from a person's own social group, and structural constraints in the marriage market.[1] An important structural constraint that can affect the degree of social homogamy is the relative number of individuals within each social group. The degree of homogamy is likely to be lower in a heterogeneous population. Especially within small social groups, the chance of marrying homogamously is relatively limited. Changes in the composition of these social groups can be controlled for to get a clearer view of the sort of boundaries that existed between classes.

Such boundaries between social groups in the marriage market could be enforced by third parties. In the Scandinavian peasant community parents are seen as influencing their children's marriage choices. It has been claimed that the degree of parental control was one effect of social stratification. The Swedish ethnologist, Orvar Löfgren, has emphasized that the large landless population that existed in the nineteenth century in the province of Scania in southern Sweden was an important explanation for the rigorous premarital parental supervision that was prevalent among farmers in the area.[2] Parents who feared that their children would marry downward went to great pains to organize a suitable marriage. The children were rather passive in this process. Löfgren states that the "parental control and strategic matchmaking functioned as important instruments for consolidating the social and economic position of well-to-do peasant families".[3]

The matchmaking process was quite different in the region of Dalecarlia in mid-western Sweden. Here, in a more egalitarian society dominated by smallholders, parental control was less prevalent. Young people played a

---

1. Matthijs Kalmijn, "Intermarriage and Homogamy: Causes, Patterns, Trends", *Annual Review of Sociology*, 24 (1998), pp. 395–421, 398 ff.
2. Orvar Löfgren, "Family and Household among Scandinavian Peasants", *Ethnologia Scandinavia*, 2 (1974), pp. 17–52, 30 ff. See also Martin Dribe and Christer Lundh, "Finding the Right Partner: Rural Homogamy in Nineteenth-Century Sweden", pp. 149–177 in this volume, for a discussion of homogamy in Scania.
3. Löfgren, "Family and Household among Scandinavian Peasants", pp. 30 ff.

more active part in searching for partners, in the form of so-called "night-courting". This was one way in which they could meet together in the sleeping quarters of young women on Saturday night, where they could develop and test their attraction to one another; eventually, this could lead to marriage. Löfgren explains this freedom from parental control in terms of parents being less afraid that their children would marry downward.

The institution of night-courting as part of the mating process was also of great interest to Eilert Sundt, the Norwegian pioneer of sociology and social anthropology, who studied the marriage patterns of the landed population in the 1850s. In the period 1848 to 1869 Sundt received several grants from the Norwegian government to study social conditions in Norway following the unrest among farm workers at the time. During these years he published a series of treatises covering such topics as mortality, marriage, sexual morality, cleanliness, temperance, domestic life, and the gypsies in Norway. He used a combination of quantitative and qualitative analysis, based on research methods such as questionnaires and interviews.[4]

Sundt explained night-courting as a way in which young people were able to get to know each other while at the same time allowing parents some control over the mating process.[5] Even though the courting happened in secret, parents had some idea about what was going on, and could give hints as to whether they approved of the connection or not. But Sundt also noted that this process made it more difficult for the parents seriously to disapprove of the marriage when the suitor announced himself. And as social stratification increased, the stakes became higher. In the Hedemarken region in the southeast of Norway, Sundt found that during the period of rural proletarianization in the mid-nineteenth century the traditional night-courting started to break down among affluent farmers. Instead of allowing night-courting, parents arranged small parties for their children where they could meet boys and girls from other farms in the area.[6] In this way, the meetings between young people could be more effectively controlled by the parents, and excessive socialization with social groups of lower status could be averted. Controlling the social networks of their children, the parents also managed to strengthen the group identification of their children and sustain firm social boundaries.

The idea of ever-increasing constraints on intersocial marriages during rural proletarianization in the nineteenth century is somewhat contrary to

---

4. Michael Drake, "Introduction", in Eilert Sundt, *On Marriage in Norway*, tr. and introduced by Michael Drake (Cambridge, 1980), p. xiv.
5. Eilert Sundt, *Sexual Customs in Rural Norway: A Nineteenth Century Study*, tr. Odin W. Anderson (Ames, IA, 1993), pp. 53 ff.
6. Sundt, *On Marriage in Norway*, pp. 164 ff., n.14; Sundt, *Sexual Customs in Rural Norway*, p. 66; Löfgren, "Family and Household among Scandinavian Peasants", pp. 30ff.

the changes in family life that Shorter and Stone claimed took place from the end of the eighteenth century. They argued that the selection of marriage partner was increasingly based on romantic love, with an ensuing reduction in parental authority and collective control.[7] Shorter and Stone's general theories have been much debated. While Macfarlane has stressed the importance of romantic love as a significant factor in matchmaking as early as the sixteenth century, others have claimed that great regional diversity persisted even within countries.[8] In the Norwegian context Kari Telste has argued, on the basis of court records, that there was a shift around 1800 whereby young people, influenced by the ideal of romantic love, demanded from their parents greater freedom to follow their own feelings. However, until the end of the nineteenth century parents could still exercise substantial influence on the marriage choices of their children.[9]

Perhaps the introduction of the ideal of romantic love led parents to control the mating process even more firmly. If children risked losing their way in the process of night-courting, falling in love with the wrong person, parents would take action to prevent this from happening. The idea that love was something of a mishap in the mating process among the rural population is also consistent with Sundt's impression at the time. He asserts that while romantic love flourished in the towns, the peasant youth searched for a partner in ways that can best be characterized as "looking for a marriage of convenience".

This was the case for the children of both the landowning and the landless population. According to Sundt, the sons of farmers sought a girl with an inheritance or a dowry that would help pay for a farm. In a time of extensive rural proletarianization, the sons of landowning farmers avoided choosing marriage partners who would cause them to experience down-ward social mobility.[10] In the quest for economic security, children did not necessarily resent parental control in the matchmaking process, as Löfgren has pointed out. At a time when a good farm was the main prerequisite for economic security and social prestige, parental counsel in the choice of marriage partner was often welcomed.[11]

Likewise the son of a cottar or worker would not even aspire to marry the daughter of a farmer, seeking instead a capable working mate with solid experiences as a farm servant. Sundt stressed that children from the lower

7. Edward Shorter, *The Making of the Modern Family* (London, 1976), and Lawrence Stone, *The Family, Sex and Marriage in England 1500–1800* (New York, 1977).

8. Alan Macfarlane, *Marriage and Love in England: Modes of Reproduction, 1300–1840* (Oxford, 1986). Martine Segalen, *Love and Power in the Peasant Family: Rural France in the Nineteenth Century* (Oxford, 1983).

9. Kari Telste, "Familien som kjenslefellesskap", in Sølvi Sogner (ed.), *I gode og vonde dagar. Familieliv i Noreg frå reformasjonen til vår tid* (Oslo, 2003), pp. 119–196, 134 ff.

10. Sundt, *On Marriage in Norway*, pp. 153 ff.

11. Löfgren, "Family and Household among Scandinavian Peasants", p. 31.

rural classes could not afford anything else because they recognized that it was the labour of the man himself and his wife that supported them.[12] Sundt emphasized that, among the rural classes, a potential partner's economic attributes took precedence over his or her cultural resources, even when individuals were free to choose independently. Basing the decision on whom to marry on romantic love was a freedom limited to the urban population. Here an educated young man who had built up an independent position was at greater liberty to consider "personal charm and attractiveness" when choosing his bride.[13] He had the economic freedom to choose a wife based on personal affection.

STUDYING SOCIAL HOMOGAMY IN NORWAY

Prior to 1870, the occupation of parents was not normally recorded in Norwegian parish registers. It is difficult therefore to carry out historical studies of social homogamy in Norway over any length of time. In addition, the strict privacy-protection law limits more extended research based on digitized sources after 1900. The few studies carried out have used data from family reconstitutions or other kinds of linked datasets. Using data from these kinds of sources, Dag Kristoffersen found that there were few mixed marriages between social groups, in his case between farmers and miners in the parish of Sandsvær in the eighteenth century.[14] The studies by Alf Steinar Kneppen and Ståle Dyrvik on social mobility in rural communities confirm this impression. They found that very few farm wives came from the cottar class, while Dyrvik's study also indicated that many cottar wives were the daughters of farmers. This is explained by the downward social mobility they experienced following their marriage to the younger sons of farmers, who were obliged to settle on a small cottar farm when the eldest brother took over the family farm.[15]

In a study of social mobility in the city of Bergen at the end of the nineteenth century, Yngve Torvanger demonstrated that women had a higher degree of upward mobility in marriage than men. He also showed that, even though intergenerational mobility for men declined over time, the possibility of upward mobility through marriage gradually increased.[16]

12. Sundt, *On Marriage in Norway*, p. 157.
13. *Ibid.*, p. 155.
14. Dag Kristoffersen, "'To bønder på en bergmann.' Befolkningsutviklingen i Sandsvær 1750–1801" (unpublished dissertation, University of Oslo, 1983), pp. 254 ff.
15. Alf Steinar Kneppen, "Giftermål og sosiale ulikheter i Ullensaker fra 1730-åra til 1840-åra" (unpublished dissertation, University of Oslo, 1976), p. 26; Ståle Dyrvik, "Om giftarmål og sosiale normer. Ein studie av Etne 1715–1801", *Artikler i etnologi*, Institutt for etnologi (Oslo, 1987), pp. 27–41, 36.
16. Yngve Torvanger, "Sosial mobilitet i Bergen 1850–1900: en kohortundersøkelse for rode 23 og 24" (unpublished dissertation, University of Bergen, 2000).

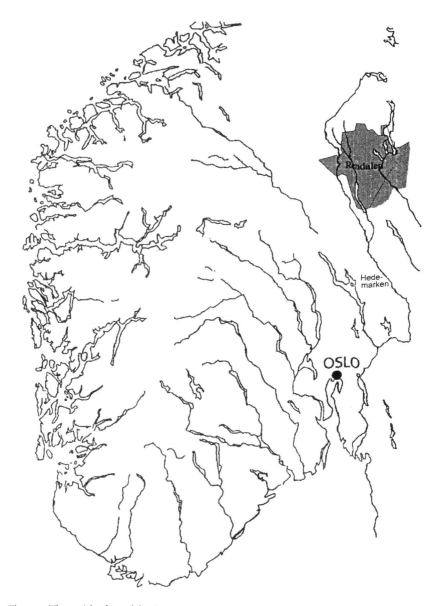

Figure 1. The parish of Rendalen in Norway.

Torvanger's findings point towards an increasingly more open urban society that was becoming less constrained by social boundaries. However, so far there has been no study of social homogamy covering a time span sufficiently long to verify and support Sundt's findings, 150 years ago, of a division between urban and rural areas concerning personal preferences in the choice of marriage partner.

AREA OF STUDY

Throughout the period covered in this study, Rendalen was an over-whelmingly rural area with a limited degree of occupational opportunities. This somewhat reflects the reality of Norway, where industrialization developed fairly slowly in the nineteenth century; only 16 per cent of the population lived in urban areas in 1865. Using the HISCLASS classification,[17] one sees that Rendalen was a two-class society of farmers (8) and farm workers (10+12). More than 95 per cent of those marrying were children of farmers or farm workers (Table 1, overleaf). Even at the end of the nineteenth century, less than 10 per cent came from a social group outside the farming community. Our analysis and discussion of homogamy will therefore revolve around the division between farmers and farm workers.

The farmers in Rendalen were mostly freeholders, who settled on a separate farmstead. Their production was largely organized as a subsistence economy based on agriculture and animal husbandry. By the middle of the nineteenth century, better access to cheap grain shifted farm production towards meat and dairy products for sale. This process was also supported by an upsurge in lumber prices, which created large incomes, especially for those farmers with forest property.

The group of farm workers was a relatively new social group in the eighteenth century. By the middle of the nineteenth century Norwegian peasant society had evolved from a relatively egalitarian peasant community to a more stratified society dominated by freeholders and cottars. The number of cottars rose substantially in the eighteenth and nineteenth centuries due to population growth and a relatively limited number of new farms. In reality, the cottages were small farmsteads, but formally they were integrated into the farm to which they belonged. The cottar was the farmer's tenant and had to pay him rent either in labour or in cash. The farmer could also request at any time the labour of the cottar or his wife at a fixed price.[18] The cottar institution ensured a stable and reliable workforce for the large farms. In the middle of the nineteenth century, the rise in the number of cottars abated and instead the group of day labourers expanded. The latter often rented sleeping quarters and worked on farms during the summer and as lumberjacks in wintertime. In this study, using HISCLASS, cottars and day labourers are taken as one social group (farm workers).

---

17. M.H.D. van Leeuwen and I. Maas, "HISCLASS", paper presented at the 5th European Social Science History Conference (Berlin, 24–27 March 2004), and I. Maas and M.H.D. van Leeuwen, "SPSS Recode job from HISCO into HISCLASS", May 2004.

18. Sølvi Sogner, "Freeholder and Cottar: Property Relationships and the Social Structure in the Peasant Community in Norway during the Eighteenth Century", *Scandinavian Journal of History*, 1 (1976), pp. 181–199, 181 ff.

Table 1. *Social origin of spouses in Rendalen 1750–1900*

Social origin of husband	Social origin of wife							Total	Missing
	(1–2)	(3–5)	(6–7)	Farmers and fishermen (8)	(9)	Farm workers (10+12)	(11)		
Higher managers and professionals (1–2)				3		2		5	3
Lower managers and professionals, clerical and sales (3–5)				4				4	1
Skilled workers (6–7)				10		11	1	22	4
Farmers and fishermen (8)	4	3	6	797 (76%) (79%)	8	185 (48%) (18%)	1	1,003	99 (9%)
Lower-skilled workers (9)				2	1	6		9	2
Farm workers (10+12)			10	232 (22%) (53%)	4	178 (46%) (41%)	10	434	64 (13%)
Unskilled workers (11)				4		5	2	11	
Total	4	3	16	1,052	13	387	13	1,488	173 (10%)
Missing			1	180 (15%)	1	133 (26%)		316 (18%)	61

Source: Rendalen database.
Note: Grouped by HISCLASS group. Absolute numbers and corresponding percentages for major social groups (for husband at the bottom of the cell and for wife above).

Figure 2. Farm workers on a small farm in Rendalen, c. 1900.

The work performed by farmers and farm workers was not particularly different. The farmer worked alongside his hired workers, and in the parish of Rendalen – unlike the Hedemarken region mentioned earlier – they would all eat together. They were all part of the same peasant culture. But the farm workers were subordinated to the farmers. The farmer was the manager both in his field and in his forest, while his wife supervised the work of female farm workers hired to help with domestic tasks. The wealth of a farm gave it an independent position in the community, and also determined its official position in the local community. This was especially the case after the 1814 constitution, when wealth became a prerequisite for the right to vote. As to night-courting, the practice seems to have persisted during the whole period despite fierce opposition from the local clergy.[19]

DATA

This article draws on the Rendalen database to study homogamy and the choice of marriage partners in the parish of Rendalen. The database covers

19. Tormod Rugsveen, "Om 'syndig nattløberi' i Rendalen", *Årbok for Nord-Østerdalen*, 11 (1992), p. 61.

about 2,200 marriages contracted in the parish over the period 1734–1900, and is linked by family reconstitution to birth and death records.[20] This makes it possible to trace the parents of the persons marrying. Several other sources, such as censuses, farm registers, and court journals, make it possible to determine the socio-economic position of the fathers close to the time of marriage. In cases where the father had died before the marriage, we used either his social position at the time of death or the position stated in the source closest to the time of death.

Because of the difficulty in identifying the family of origin in the earliest years, this study examines only those marriages that took place after 1750. Another problem which leads to the exclusion of certain marriages from the analysis is the difficulty in identifying the social status of fathers from other parishes. Fortunately for this analysis, Rendalen had a fairly stable population, and in 65 per cent of the marriages the families of both the wives and husbands were from Rendalen (Table 2). By studying the parents' occupations stated in the marriage register after 1874 and the data available from the national digitized censuses of 1801, 1865, and 1875,[21] it has proved possible to identify some of the parents of in-migrants to the community and their occupations. Excluding from our study those marriages where the social status of either the man or the woman is not recorded leaves just under 1,500 marriages on which to base our analysis.

Most of the marriages excluded from the study are those of women marrying men from other parishes where the social status of the fathers is unavailable. The seemingly higher propensity for girls to marry someone from another parish is the result of two phenomena. One is the longstanding custom of marriages taking place at the church attended by the wife-to-be. Therefore, if the groom came from a parish outside Rendalen and the bride from Rendalen itself the marriage would still only appear in the marriage records in Rendalen – even if the couple were to settle in the groom's parish. Because of this, there is a corresponding "hidden" exclusion of men from Rendalen marrying girls from a neighbouring parish. Parish birth records document the birth of a legitimate child to a couple, from which the assumption may be made that a wedding has taken place somewhere else. If the cross-parish marriages were to be included, the number of marriage partners of unknown social status would be the same for sons and daughters of farmers. Still, the marriage of a Rendalen girl to a groom of unknown social

20. A comprehensive description of the database is currently obtainable only in Norwegian. See Martha Cecilie Gjelseth, "Relasjonsdatabaser som verktøy i en historisk-demografisk studie" (unpublished dissertation, University of Oslo, 2000).

21. The censuses of 1801, 1865, and 1875 were made available by the Digital Archives at www.digitalarkivet.no; the censuses of 1865 and 1875 are also available from the Norwegian Historical Data Centre at www.rhd.uit.no. The digitized census of 1875 covers only part of the country.

Table 2. *Geographic origin and knowledge of fathers' social status for couples marrying in Rendalen, 1750–1900*

	Family from Rendalen		Social status known	
	Number	Per cent	Number	Per cent
Both	1,322	65	1,488	73
Only wife	424	21	316	16
Only husband	200	10	173	8
Neither	92	5	61	3
Total	2,038	100	2,038	100

Source: Rendalen database.

status occurred to a much higher degree among the daughters of farm workers (26 per cent; see Table 1, p. 50). This is the result of another phenomenon: the migration of men seeking employment in the expanding forestry industry in the nineteenth century. These would normally marry girls from the lower social class. In this way the daughters of farm workers found a larger number of possible marriage candidates within Rendalen.

HOMOGAMY AMONG FARMERS AND FARM WORKERS

Table 1 shows a clearly higher degree of homogamy among farmers than among farm workers. The percentage given in italics in certain cells refers to the proportion of brides from the given social class where the social origin of the groom is known. The corresponding percentage for grooms appears at the bottom of the cells. It may be seen that of the sons of farm workers, 53 per cent married farmers' daughters, while only 22 per cent of farmers' daughters married sons of farm workers. Actually, both sons and daughters of farm workers married children of farmers more often than they married a member of their own social class (53 per cent for men and 48 per cent for women). Over time, homogamy among children of farmers declined. In the marriages that took place in the years between 1840 and 1900, 73 per cent of men and 64 per cent of women married homogamously, compared with 86 per cent and 80 per cent respectively in the period before.

Children of farm workers experienced the opposite development. Here, the degree of homogamy rose from 27 per cent to 48 per cent, and from 35 per cent to 50 per cent for men and women respectively. In the middle of the eighteenth century up to 90 per cent of all those marrying were children of farmers. This was due in part to a larger proportion of farmers, but also to the fact that farmers usually had more children than cottars and workers. With the extensive population increase, combined with the limited number of new farms, proletarianization led to a rise in the number of cottars and workers. This process was in large part due to the downward social mobility experienced by the children of farmers. At the end of the nineteenth century 40 per cent of those marrying were children of farm workers. This structural development in the relative numbers of possible marriage partners from the two social groups may explain changes in the degree of homogamy over time.

One way to control for these structural changes is to calculate the *odds ratio*. The odds ratio is defined as the odds of, for example, the son of a farmer marrying the daughter of a farmer, divided by the odds of a man of other social origin (all other social groups) marrying the daughter of a farmer. Odds ratios are therefore independent of the relative size of the social groups.[22] The odds ratios in Figure 3 show an unstable pattern of homogamy in the eighteenth century, a pattern which is mostly explained by the low numbers of farm workers marrying. However, more importantly, it indicates a fairly stable pattern during the nineteenth century among both social groups. Consequently, at the end of the nineteenth century there is little evidence for a more open society when it comes to social homogamy.

For the group of farmers as a whole, there was a consolidating trend at the end of the nineteenth century towards marrying within one's own class. This is consistent with the idea of Löfgren and Sundt that a larger working class and a clearer stratification between the classes strengthened social homogamy. In Rendalen, where the social landscape consisted primarily of only two classes, the closeness among the group of farmers also limited the number of marriage candidates for the lower class. This may be seen in the increase in homogamy among farm workers at the end of the period. The paucity of possible marriage partners and work opportunities not only led children of farm workers to seek marriage candidates from other parishes, but also to leave Rendalen before marriage more often than the offspring of farmers (33 per cent compared with 20 per cent). For the young people who chose to marry and stay in Rendalen, the social boundaries that separated farmers from farm workers were definitely still in place in 1900.

DECIDING WHOM TO MARRY

It has been shown that social homogamy prevailed in Rendalen during the nineteenth century, but does the study of homogamy say anything about the decision about whom to marry? More exactly, does it indicate anything

22. Kalmijn, "Intermarriage and Homogamy", p. 405.

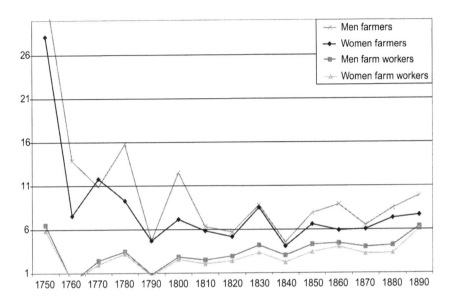

Figure 3. Odds ratio of marrying homogamously among children of farmers and farm workers, Rendalen, 10-year periods, 1750–1900.

about individual preferences versus parental control in spouse selection within these structural conditions?

An analysis of spouse selection between brothers within the sibling group gives some insight into the considerations governing the selection of marriage partner. Rendalen has been characterized as a stem family society. The freeholder inheritance law (*åsetesretten*) stipulated that the eldest son had the right to succeed his parents as head of the farm. In Rendalen the two generations would live together and share a common household after the marriage of the eldest son. Parents would therefore be more inclined to control the heir's choice of spouse than that of the younger sons.[23] If parental influence played an important role in the decision of the eldest son to marry homogamously, a difference might be seen between the eldest son and his younger brothers. The unique position of the farmer's eldest son is reflected in the way he married at a clearly lower age than his younger brothers.[24]

The fathers of almost half of the men marrying for the first time were no longer alive at the time of the wedding. The death of a father could affect the degree of homogamous marriage in two ways. The economic capital and social position of the family could be reduced if the father died early.

23. Telste, "Familien som kjenslefellesskap", p. 136.
24. Gjernes, "Relasjonsdatabaser som verktøy", p. 101.

Frans van Poppel *et al.* found that the death of a father, particularly before the sons had reached the age of fifteen, had a negative effect on their opportunities in the marriage market.[25] Another possibility is that the death of a father enabled the children to choose their partners more freely, enabling some of them to find partners outside their own social group. Our study tries to separate these two effects and determine whether the father's death had any impact on his sons' choice of marriage partner.

The results of logistic regressions of marrying homogamously for the children of farmers in Rendalen in the years 1750–1900 are presented in Tables 3 and 4. Only first marriages for the sex in question are included. The analysis is also limited to families from Rendalen in order to determine the position (youngest or eldest for example) within the group of siblings and the presence of parents. The same analysis was also performed for the children of farm workers, but, since this gave no significant results other than for the time periods, it is not included here. In the models we are controlling for time and the changing proportion of brides (Table 3), and grooms (Table 4) belonging to the group of farmers. Apart from these variables, which indicate changes in the relative size of the social groups over time, all the explanatory variables used are binary (dummy) variables. The averages of the explanatory variables are presented in the first column. The second column gives the coefficient estimate of the variables, where the reference variable is null and the values give a positive or negative effect compared with this variable. The third column gives the t-statistics, and the statistically significant values (two-tailed test) at the 10-per-cent level are marked in bold.

The models for sons of farmers are discussed first. Model 1 shows a clearly negative effect on marrying homogamously of fathers dying when the sons are still young. This indicates a negative economic development before the time of marriage which affected the young man's position in the marriage market. Statistical tests were also conducted to discover whether it was the widow's new husband which had the effect of reducing the opportunities for her sons from her first marriage. It appears that this had no effect, and hence the results are not shown here.

Surprisingly, there is no difference between the eldest son and his younger brothers in model 1. At first glance it seems that fathers did not influence the choice of marriage of their eldest sons in a way that made them marry more homogamously. But model 2 includes an interaction of the eldest son marrying after the father had died while the son was fairly old. This clearly lowered the propensity to marry homogamously, suggesting that the father did put pressure on the eldest son to marry homogamously (the main effect is strengthened). Since the death of the

---

25. Frans van Poppel *et al.*, "The Effects of Paternal Mortality on Sons' Social Mobility: A Nineteenth Century Example", *Historical Methods*, 31:3 (1998), pp. 101–112.

Table 3. *Logistic regression coefficients of marrying homogamously for sons of farmers: men marrying for the first time, 1750–1900*

	Mean	Model 1		Model 2	
		Value	t-value	Value	t-value
(Intercept)		1.44	5.99	−1.23	−0.92
Marrying a widow	(0.06)	0.72	1.55	0.71	1.52
Position in group of siblings (ref.	(0.26)				
second oldest)					
Eldest brother	(0.43)	0.12	0.56	0.33	1.31
Younger brothers	(0.29)	0.14	0.60	0.12	0.50
Parents unmarried	(0.02)	−0.07	−0.12	−0.02	−0.05
Age at marriage (ref. 25–34)	(0.58)				
Under 25	(0.18)	0.22	0.82	0.22	0.82
Over 34	(0.24)	**−0.50**	**−2.34**	**−0.52**	**−2.41**
Parents' position					
Father dead before age 15	(0.15)	**−0.62**	**−2.35**	**−0.58**	**−2.16**
Father dead after age 15	(0.30)	−0.27	−1.26	0.01	0.03
Mother dead	(0.29)	−0.20	−1.02	−0.19	0.00
Time period (ref. 1790–1830)	(0.25)				
1750–1790	(0.22)	**0.74**	**1.82**	**0.72**	**1.78**
1830–1870	(0.28)	0.40	1.27	0.44	1.37
1870–1900	(0.26)	0.47	1.14	0.50	1.22
Percentage daughters of farmers	(0.70)	**3.52**	**2.04**	**3.59**	**2.07**
marrying					
Eldest brother * Father dead after age	(0.10)			**−0.69**	**−1.75**
15					
−2LogL		2582.1		2592.6	
1−(Residual deviance/Null deviance)		0.060		0.063	
N		860		860	
Events		689		689	

Bold = significant p < 0.10.
Source: Rendalen database.

father late in life did not have a substantial effect on the younger sons marrying exogamously, it seems that they sought a farm girl more in response to their own preferences. While the eldest son already had a firm economic position as a farmer, a younger son was more inclined to choose a marriage partner with the economic resources to secure his position.

In theory, sons could not marry against their father's will as long as they were under the age of majority (twenty-five until 1869). Yet the results of our study do not show any higher degree of socially homogamous marriages before this age. One reason for this might be that the children were under their fathers' authority as long as they were living at home. In this way the death of the father could have more effect on sons' marriage choices. On the other hand, sons of farmers who had postponed marriage

Table 4. *Logistic regression coefficients of marrying homogamously for daughters of farmers: women marrying for the first time, 1750–1900*

	Mean	Value	t-value
(Intercept)		−1.18	−0.89
Marrying a widower	(0.07)	0.23	0.71
Position in group of siblings (ref. second oldest)	(0.29)		
Eldest sister	(0.37)	0.18	0.93
Younger sisters	(0.32)	0.03	0.13
Parents unmarried	(0.02)	−0.23	0.33
Age at marriage (ref. 23–32)			
Under 23	(0.26)	**0.41**	2.00
Over 32	(0.19)	**−0.81**	−3.98
Parents' position			
Father dead before age 15	(0.15)	−0.06	−0.24
Father dead after age 15	(0.21)	−0.16	−0.77
Mother dead	(0.26)	−0.26	−1.42
Time period (ref. 1790–1830)	(0.24)		
1750–1790	(0.21)	0.53	1.51
1830–1870	(0.28)	0.02	0.08
1870–1900	(0.27)	0.22	0.59
Percentage sons of farmers marrying	(0.68)	**3.41**	1.88
−2LogL		2953.6	
1−(Residual deviance/null deviance)		0.070	
N		966	
Events		729	

Bold = significant p < 0.10.
Source: Rendalen database.

until their mid-thirties were less attractive marriage candidates for the daughters of farmers.

It has been claimed that in a male-dominated society, men represent the demand and women represent the supply in the marriage market.[26] Men seek the partners with the most sought-after characteristics, and the most eligible marriage partners marry first, that is, at an early age. In a subsistence agricultural society, the attractive characteristic is thought to be wealth. Hence, the age effect for daughters in Table 4 can be interpreted as a selection effect whereby the wealthiest daughters marry first, most often the sons of farmers. The least eligible women on the other hand had to build their own economic basis, and because their impecuniousness made them less attractive to sons of farmers, they were more often obliged to settle with someone from a lower class.

However, the theory that attractiveness is predicated on wealth is disturbed by the lack of effect on the daughter's choice of marriage partner

26. Ståle Dyrvik, *Historisk demografi* (Bergen, 1982), p. 141.

Figure 4. A farmer's family in Rendalen, c.1870; four of the five daughters married sons of farmers.
Nordosterdalsmuseum, Tynset. Used with permission.

when the father died at an early age. For sons this was interpreted as a possible economic hardship in the time between the death of the father and the marriage. One possible explanation for the absence of this effect among daughters is that when the father had died, the daughters had more disposable wealth than they would otherwise have been entitled to through a dowry. This wealth would have been attractive to potential marriage partners. The probate registers from Rendalen show that the dowry could be quite small compared to the inheritance they later received.

HOMOGAMY AND SOCIAL MOBILITY

An analysis of the social mobility of men and women who married and settled in Rendalen sheds even more light on the importance of parents in making economically strategic partner choices. In Table 5 the results of a logistic regression of being a farmer as an adult are presented. Here, only those couples are included whose social status we know. Becoming a farmer is taken as the most attractive economic outcome in Rendalen, since other sources of income outside agriculture were limited during the whole period. A negative effect is taken as a sign of reaching a lower social position compared with being a farmer.

The social origin of both men and women is highly important when it comes to social mobility. When both the man and the woman were the children of farmers, the chance of their becoming farmers was greater. Of the 519 couples included in the study, 386 managed to maintain their social position as farmers. It was a different story for the children of farm workers marrying homogamously. Only 33 of 95 couples in this category rose in terms of social position (22 became farmers). Many of these were cottars who managed to buy their cottar farm and become freeholders. The results in Table 5 demonstrate how important it was for the children of farmers to group their economic resources. Marrying exogamously led to a higher propensity to downward mobility for the children of farmers. Here the eldest son of a farmer was in a unique position (as the interaction effect displays) since he was entitled to the family farm.

The results in Table 5 indicate that the death of the father before the marriage of his offspring affected the likelihood of that offspring's becoming a farmer as an adult. This was the case both for the bride and the groom. The effect of the father's death for men has already been picked up in the form of socially mixed marriages, but there was an additional effect on social mobility. Perhaps fathers had an important role in selecting economically viable partners for their children from within the group of farmers. This effect would have been lost when the father was no longer present. Without his influence, the choice of marriage partners that the children made on their own might not have been as economically successful.

CONCLUSIONS

The study of homogamy in Rendalen shows that, among farmers, social homogamy was declining in the nineteenth century. This was due to the rural proletarianization of the eighteenth and nineteenth centuries, which increased the size of the group of farm workers, thereby expanding the

Table 5. *Logistic regression coefficients of becoming a farmer after marriage: first marriages of men and women from Rendalen, 1750–1900*

		Mean	Value	t-value
(Intercept)			0.58	1.76
Position in group of siblings (ref. second oldest)				
Man	Eldest brother	(0.45)	−0.47	−1.54
	Younger brothers	(0.25)	−0.09	−0.43
	Parents unmarried	(0.05)	0.48	1.13
Woman	Eldest sister	(0.39)	−0.00	−0.02
	Younger sisters	(0.29)	−0.04	0.19
	Parents unmarried	(0.05)	−0.40	−0.93
Age at marriage (ref. man 25–34, woman 23–32)				
Man	Under 25	(0.14)	0.23	0.91
	Over 34	(0.27)	−0.16	−0.83
Woman	Under 23	(0.25)	−0.16	−0.83
	Over 32	(0.19)	−0.03	−0.15
Parents' position at time of marriage (ref. alive)				
Man	Father dead before age 15	(0.18)	**−0.44**	−1.86
	Father dead after age 15	(0.29)	**−0.33**	−1.86
	Mother dead	(0.29)	−0.03	−0.17
Woman	Father dead before age 15	(0.19)	−0.07	−0.30
	Father dead after age 15	(0.21)	**−0.54**	−2.58
	Mother dead	(0.26)	−0.09	−0.46
Social origin of fathers of the couple (ref. man farmer, woman farm worker)		(0.12)		
	Both farmers	(0.57)	**1.13**	4.76
	Man farm worker, woman farmer	(0.17)	−0.35	−1.09
	Both farm workers	(0.10)	**−0.93**	−2.59
	Farmer and other group	(0.02)	0.37	0.72
	Farm worker and other group	(0.02)	−0.53	−0.81
	Both other group	(0.00)	−4.49	−0.94
Time period (ref. 1830–1870)		(0.39)		
	1750–1790	(0.21)	**−1.00**	−4.42
	1790–1830	(0.25)	**−0.53**	−2.59
	1870–1900	(0.15)	**−0.42**	−1.74
Eldest son of a farmer		(0.31)	**1.10**	3.17
−2LogL			2842.8	
1−(Residual deviance/Null deviance)			0.181	
N			911	
Events			527	

Bold = significant p < 0.10.
Source: Rendalen database.

number of possible marriage candidates from this group. Controlling for this structural development, our study shows that the boundaries in the marriage market between children of farmers and farm workers prevailed at least until the end of the nineteenth century.

The inhabitants of Rendalen had fairly limited economic possibilities during the eighteenth and nineteenth centuries. It was not until the second half of the nineteenth century that emigration to America or migration to the expanding Norwegian cities became an attractive option for a larger segment of young rural men and women. For those that remained in the district, farming and forestry continued to be the dominant industries, and the boundaries between landowners and workers continued in the marriage market. There was little opportunity to break out of the two-class system by staying in Rendalen. Educational opportunities were limited and a solid economic basis was needed in order to advance socially. For those young people that chose to marry and settle in the home parish there are few traces of a more open society even by the late nineteenth century.

This contributes to and supports the findings of other Norwegian studies dealing with homogamy and social mobility, but it also expands our knowledge to include the second half of the nineteenth century. The limited number of new industries in rural areas made landholding the key determinant of social position, and fear of falling socially virtually compelled the children of farmers to marry among their own class. For farm workers, social boundaries compelled them to marry homogamously too. Sundt concluded that the peasants were more inclined to prioritize the material benefits of marriage than "the mutual tender love of a man or a woman".[27]

This article also tries to discern the parents' role in deciding whom to marry, and the subsequent effect on homogamy. A remnant from pre-industrial society was the feeling that parental consent and blessing were needed to ensure a happy marriage.[28] This study shows that parents exerted influence on the choice of their children's marriage partners. Through the institution of night-courting, young men and women could meet each other and form relationships based on personal affection. But if the father disapproved of the union, the parents could put pressure on their children to end this "courtship". Eldest sons in particular were pressured and encouraged to marry farmers' daughters, as one can see from the way the son's options widened after the death of the father. This is supported by Telste's findings that parents exercised substantial influence on marriage choices until the end of the nineteenth century.[29]

It seems as if, through their influence, fathers were successful in maintaining the social position of their children. The death of the father before the children married had a negative effect on their socio-economic future. Young men and women concerned about their own economic wellbeing therefore took pains to maintain a good relationship with their

27. Sundt, *On Marriage in Norway*, p. 153.
28. Ørnulf Hodne, *Kvinne og mann i norsk folkekultur* (Oslo, 2002), p. 99.
29. Telste, "Familien som kjenslefellesskap", p. 137.

parents. Making their own choice, based on personal attraction, might result in an economically less favourable marriage, and parental influence was therefore not necessarily regarded as running counter to their own interests.

IRSH 50 (2005), Supplement, pp. 65–91 DOI: 10.1017/S0020859005002075
© 2005 Internationaal Instituut voor Sociale Geschiedenis

"We Have No Proletariat": Social Stratification and Occupational Homogamy in Industrial Switzerland, Winterthur 1909/10–1928[*]

RETO SCHUMACHER AND LUIGI LORENZETTI

SUMMARY: The aim of this study is to examine, by analysing marital origin-related homogamy and mobility, the fluidity of a system of social stratification marked by a heterogeneous working class and likely to lead to increasing social-group solidarity during the phase of a more active labour movement in the early twentieth century. Data from Winterthur, a Swiss town characterized by the expansion of an important engineering industry, reveal that occupational homogamy was most pronounced at the top, among higher managers and professionals, and at the bottom of the social hierarchy, among unskilled factory workers. There is no empirical evidence of increased homogamous behaviour after the nationwide general strike of 1918, which is said to have had a long-term impact on workers' class-consciousness. Our analyses show, however, that the association between the social background of spouses depended on their geographical origin. This result may point to a regionally determined class-consciousness.

INTRODUCTION

Inspired by sociological research, during the last few decades social historians have widely explored processes of social stratification and class formation in the past. In this regard, analyses of the patterns and dynamics of partner choice have played a crucial role. Whereas high degrees of homogamy have been interpreted as an indicator of a social group's closeness, frequent heterogamy has often been seen as a sign of relative fluidity within the system of social stratification.

The question whether this mobility between social groups was affected by industrialization has proved to be of particular interest among historians and sociologists and provoked a longstanding debate. In the abundant literature, the opposition between pre-industrial society, characterized by its highly static and closed social hierarchy, and the industrializing world, marked by a rapidly changing occupational

* This paper is part of the "Histoire de la population en Suisse, 1815–1945" research project, funded by the Swiss National Science Foundation (no. 1114–058899/1).

structure and a regime of almost unlimited social mobility,[1] most often represented little more than a caricatured starting point that was either completely rejected by some or qualified by others. Among the former, sociologists have often had doubts about the reality of any gradual trend towards increasing mobility during industrialization,[2] while among the latter, historians have tried to distinguish different stages of industrialization. In a theoretical article on social mobility, Franklin Mendels concluded that "interactions between mobility and economic change vary according to the type or phase in which a given local, regional, or national economy finds itself",[3] and assumed that during the phase of proto-industrialization downward mobility must have been stronger than upward mobility.[4]

Hartmut Kaelble, in turn, has distinguished three eras of social mobility in the period of industrialization.[5] He determined that social mobility must have been increasing, especially during the second industrial revolution (which was characterized by the rise of large-scale enterprises), and he argued that the growth of white-collar work and improved access to higher education created numerous opportunities for upward social mobility among the working class.

The debate regarding the impact of industrialization on the degree of openness of systems of social stratification has, however, essentially focused on the temporal dimension of economic modernization. Where different phases of this process, such as the proto-industrial period and the first and second waves of industrialization, have been distinguished, industrialization has often been taken as a standardized independent variable of social fluidity. In other words, the variety of specific regional itineraries that this process could follow has regularly been neglected. Nonetheless, the course and the characteristics of this evolution were mainly country-specific and dependent on the availability of different factors of production, such as labour and physical and financial capital, as well as on existing pre-industrial economic organization.[6] The develop-

---

1. Ilja Mieck, "Wirtschaft und Gesellschaft Europas von 1650–1850", in Wolfram Fischer *et al.* (eds), *Handbuch der europäischen Wirtschafts- und Sozialgeschichte*, 6 vols (Stuttgart, 1987), vol. 5, pp. 1–234, 192.

2. Robert Erikson and John H. Goldthorpe, *The Constant Flux: A Study of Class Mobility in Industrial Societies* (Oxford, 1987); Ivan K. Fukumoto and David B. Grusky, "Social Mobility and Class Structure in Early Industrial France", in Andrew Miles and David Vincent (eds), *Building European Society: Occupational Change and Social Mobility in Europe 1840–1940* (Manchester, 1993), pp. 40–67.

3. Franklin Mendels, "Social Mobility and Phases of Industrialization", *Journal of Interdisciplinary History*, 7 (1976), pp. 193–216, 216.

4. *Ibid.*, p. 202.

5. Hartmut Kaelble, *Social Mobility in the Nineteenth and Twentieth Centuries: Europe and America in Comparative Perspective* (Leamington, 1985).

6. Patrick Verley, *L'échelle du monde* (Paris, 1997), pp. 69 ff.

ment of and changes in industrial occupational structures were therefore heavily dependent on the specific national model of industrialization. In that sense, the process of social-class formation was subject to national and even regional characteristics of economic modernization.[7] In particular, the composition and consciousness of the so-called working class, as well as its relationship to the non-industrial population, must have been dependent on the type of industrialization, its leading sectors, and their dominant organizational structures.

In a European comparative perspective, the Swiss case is particularly interesting because it represents a variation on the British model of industrialization. Switzerland's route to economic modernization followed the path predetermined by the proto-industrial development of the eighteenth and early nineteenth centuries and was characterized by the dominance of geographically delocalized manufacturing industries. As a consequence, the Swiss working class never formed a proletariat analogous to that of other countries and therefore also developed a different, less clear-cut form of class-consciousness.[8]

The main objective of this article is to analyse the internal coherence, evolution and regional specificity of the Swiss working class. Based on data from Winterthur, one of Switzerland's most industrialized towns at the beginning of the twentieth century, this article suggests an examination of the fluidity and rigidity of the system of social stratification in that peculiar context by analysing origin-related marital homogamy before and after World War I. In order to refine the main characteristics of Switzerland's occupational and social-class system in general and of the Swiss working class in particular, we will first outline this country's specific model of industrialization and the related process of social-class formation at the end of the nineteenth and the beginning of the twentieth centuries. After presenting Winterthur as representing a specific type of industrialization in Switzerland, we will analyse marital homogamy and mobility patterns using log-linear modelling.

INDUSTRIALIZATION AND SOCIAL-CLASS FORMATION IN SWITZERLAND

In Switzerland industrial development had always been subject to specific geographical and demographic constraints. On the one hand, geographical space is limited; Switzerland is characterized by an important alpine and pre-alpine area representing about 60 per cent of its territory. There is no direct access to the sea, which limited access to international markets. But most importantly, the country is lacking in raw materials.

7. Mieck, "Wirtschaft und Gesellschaft Europas von 1650–1850", p. 188.
8. Jean François Bergier, *Histoire économique de la Suisse* (Lausanne, 1984), p. 239.

The demographic situation, on the other hand, has been determined by substantial population growth during the entire nineteenth century. This growth provoked not only emigration, but also had a decisive impact on economic development. Specializing in cattle-breeding and hence available for additional activities, the mainly rural population constituted an abundant and inexpensive labour force that contributed to the development of an important proto-industry.[9] Spinning and weaving had been widespread activities on the plateau between the Alps and the Jura Mountains since the first half of the eighteenth century, whereas the watch-and-clock proto-industry was concentrated in Geneva and, since the 1830s, in the French-speaking Jura Mountains too. The highly specialized production was organized on the basis of the putting-out system,[10] and was essentially destined for the international markets.

Since the first decade of the nineteenth century, mechanized spinning companies were created mainly in the northeast of Switzerland. The development of the engineering industry since the middle of the nineteenth century was closely related to the rapidly expanding textile sector. Implemented mainly in the northeast of the country, this sector produced spinning frames for local industries but quickly diversified its fabrication: heating installations for the internal market, steam engines, steamships, and diesel engines destined for the export market. At the beginning of the twentieth century, Switzerland was one of the world's most industrialized countries.[11] During that period, the three main sectors were the textile manufacturing industry, the engineering industry, and the watch-and-clock industry. They employed approximately 70 per cent of the industrial labour force and 30 per cent of the economically active population.[12]

With respect to the development of the occupational structure and the process of social-class formation, the following specific characteristics of the Swiss model of industrialization[13] have to be emphasized. First of all,

---

9. The concept of proto-industry was developed by Franklin Mendels, who used it to describe the first stage of the industrialization process. Mendels and Deyon cited three main characteristics of this phase of economic development: (1) production output destined for national and international markets; (2) a mainly rural labour force which, in addition to its agricultural activities, worked temporarily for an urban merchant on the basis of the putting-out system; and (3) the regional development of a commercialized agriculture. See Franklin Mendels and Pierre Deyon, "La proto-industrialisation: Théorie et réalité", *Revue du Nord*, 53 (1981), pp. 11–16.

10. The putting-out system, or *Verlagsystem*, was a proto-industrial form of production in which an urban entrepreneur sent raw materials to rural home workers and brought the finished product back to town. This organizational form can be distinguished from the *Kaufsystem*, where home workers were independent and commercialized their products on their own, and from the factory system, which concentrated the workers in large units of production; Patrick Verley, *La Révolution industrielle* (Paris, 1997), pp. 82, 87 ff., 408.

11. *Ibid.*, p. 463.

12. Francesco Kneschaurek, "Wandlungen der schweizerischen Industriestruktur seit 1800", *Schweizerische Zeitschrift für Volkswirtschaft und Statistik*, 100 (1964), p. 155.

13. Bergier, *Histoire économique de la Suisse*, p. 182.

the lack of raw materials largely determined the organizational form of production. Since it was too expensive to import coal for the newly born textile manufactures, steam power was replaced by hydraulic power. The factories were therefore localized along rivers, most often in rural areas. As a consequence, industrial activity remained geographically de-localized. This distinctive characteristic of the Swiss model of industrialization prevented the development of larger industrial agglomerations as well as the formation of a proletariat comparable with that of other countries. Furthermore, the enterprises remained relatively small-scale. In 1911, 49 per cent of all factory workers were employed in enterprises with fewer than 100 employees and only 17 per cent worked in factories with more than 500 employees.[14]

Secondly, given the absence of raw materials, Swiss industries were inevitably processing industries, processing and finishing imported and often expensive materials. The only source of success on the international market was therefore the added value resulting from work, and this added value had to be higher than elsewhere. To achieve such added value, products had to be specialized and of good quality. However, only skilled workers could produce such sophisticated goods. Drawing on a long-standing proto-industrial tradition, this qualification was maintained by a high degree of education and literacy, notably in Protestant areas, where most industrial activity was concentrated. The phenomenon of "relegating" the industrial labour force to mainly unskilled work, as happened in countries with an important heavy industry, was unknown in Switzerland.

Finally, this country experienced what can be called *dualist* in-dustrialization.[15] Until the beginning of the twentieth century the factory system cohabited with the proto-industrial putting-out system. Especially in the watch-and-clock sector, the role of home workers remained important. Until 1910, a minority of the industrial population were factory workers: home workers, craftsmen, and construction workers still accounted for over 50 per cent.[16]

These specificities of the Swiss model of industrialization directly affected the process of social-class formation in general and the develop-ment of the industrial labour force in particular. The coexistence of the factory system, the putting-out system, and traditional crafts meant that the working class never formed a homogenous social group with a commonly shared class-consciousness and solidarity.[17] Factory workers,

---

14. Erich Gruner, *Arbeiterschaft und Wirtschaft in der Schweiz 1880–1914*, 3 vols (Zurich, 1987), vol. 1, p. 141.

15. Verley, *La Révolution industrielle*, p. 461.

16. Kneschaurek, "Wandlungen der schweizerischen Industriestruktur seit 1800", p. 139.

17. Hans Jörg Siegenthaler, "Die Schweiz 1850–1914", in Fischer *et al.*, *Handbuch der europäischen Wirtschafts- und Sozialgeschichte*, vol. 5, pp. 443–473, 455.

home workers, and artisans lived in different economic and social realities and must have developed different class identities.

The diversity of orientation among trade unions testifies to this heterogeneity. While home workers, who numbered about 100,000 in 1900,[18] were almost completely devoid of any organization, craftsmen defended their interests mainly through the Schweizerische Gewerbeverein, founded in 1879. This organization basically represented independent master craftsmen as well as employed masters in smaller industrial enterprises. Their standard of living probably did not differ considerably from that of ordinary factory workers, and in highly industrialized regions where they had a subcontracting relationship with larger enterprises their independence was more formal than real. Nevertheless, these craftsmen and masters generally felt closer to the *Bürgertum* than the working class.[19]

In 1880 the factory workers formed the Schweizerische Gewerkschaftsbund. Inspired by the international labour movement, towards the end of the nineteenth century this umbrella organization of industrial trade unions increasingly adopted the discourse of a class struggle. Even if in 1908 the "proletarian class struggle" became the declared objective, its main concern during the first decade of the twentieth century remained opposition to higher food prices. After 1905 strikes became more and more frequent and coordinated. The nationwide general strike (*Landesstreik*) of 1918 represented a culminating point for the labour movement in Switzerland. The mobilization of the army against protesting workers, a symbol of the "class struggle from above",[20] intensified class-consciousness among workers and the conflict between them and the liberal establishment. In that sense, those few days had a lasting impact on the sense of class affiliation among workers as well as on society's perception of this social group.

Throughout the first three decades of the twentieth century, farmers comprised Switzerland's second most important social group. Until 1930, their proportion of the active population never fell below 21 per cent, and it was only in the biggest towns that they had almost completely disappeared. The main characteristic of the Swiss farming community was the small size of the units of production. Thus, in 1905, 41 per cent of all farms worked less than three hectares.[21] In spite of the heavy mortgage debts owed by farmers, at the beginning of the twentieth century an agricultural origin no longer signified a socially and economically under-

18. Kneschaurek, "Wandlungen der schweizerischen Industriestruktur seit 1800", p. 139.
19. Gruner, *Arbeiterschaft und Wirtschaft in der Schweiz 1880–1914*, vol. 2, p. 1386.
20. Hans-Ulrich Jost, "Menace et repliement, 1914–1945", in *Nouvelle histoire de la Suisse et des Suisses*, 3 vols (Lausanne, 1983), vol. 3, pp. 91–178, 124–129.
21. Gruner, *Arbeiterschaft und Wirtschaft in der Schweiz 1880–1914*, vol. 2, p. 1399.

privileged situation.[22] The social status of farmers must actually have been similar to that of skilled workers and craftsmen. Yet the relationship between the farming and working classes changed decisively around the turn of the twentieth century.

During the 1890s these two social groups were relatively close, not only because most workers originated from peasant families but also because their political interests were similar. Anti-capitalistic tendencies within farmers' associations became manifest, and real "farmers' and workers' unions" were founded.[23] However, the debate on protective tariffs and inflation during the first decade of the twentieth century led to an estrangement between farmers and workers. While the first, represented by the Schweizerische Bauernverband, favoured a protectionist policy aimed at higher agricultural incomes, the latter deplored the rising prices of basic foodstuffs and held farmers responsible. The more frequent incidence of strikes especially provoked vehement reactions among the farming population, who bemoaned what they regarded as the breakdown in law and order and who increasingly considered themselves to be the only group still representing the interests of the state.[24]

As in many other industrializing countries, the number of white-collar workers or salaried employees[25] had been steadily increasing in Switzerland since the late nineteenth century: the ratio of non-manual to manual workers in the industrial and commercial sectors rose from 1:6.6 in 1900 to 1:3.8 in 1920.[26] This increase in the proportion of commercial employees, accountants, and office workers was related to the expansion of administrative units in large-scale enterprises as well as to the growth of the banking and insurance sector. In the engineering industry, in particular, this rise was also connected with the appearance of a new professional group, namely the "technicians". Though their education, received in technical schools, did not correspond to a university degree, it was graded higher than an apprenticeship. Their non-manual work, their educational background and, at least initially, the presence of

---

22. *Ibid.*, p. 454. The relatively high standard of living can also be explained by government subsidies for the farming population; Roland Ruffieux, "La Suisse des Radicaux. 1848–1914", in *Nouvelle histoire de la Suisse et des Suisses*, vol. 3, pp. 7–90, 71.

23. Gruner, *Arbeiterschaft und Wirtschaft in der Schweiz 1880–1914*, vol. 2, p. 1393. One example is the Bauern- und Arbeiterbund in the canton of Baselland.

24. *Ibid.*, p. 1409. In this regard, a comment by Ernst Laur, secretary of the Schweizerische Bauernverband, is instructive: "Ohne Bauernstand ist die Eidgenossenschaft dem Untergang geweiht".

25. In the German-speaking countries the most often used term was the *Angestelltenschaft*. See Jürgen Kocka, "Einleitende Bemerkungen", in *idem* (ed.), *Angestellte im europäischen Vergleich. Die Herausbildung angestellter Mittelschichten seit dem späten 19. Jahrhundert* (Göttingen, 1981).

26. Mario König, Hannes Siegrist, and Rudolf Vetterli, "Zur Sozialgeschichte der Angestellten in der Schweiz", in Kocka, *Angestellte im europäischen Vergleich*, pp. 169–195, 178.

management at their workplace gave white-collar workers a certain prestige and created a social distance between them and skilled workers and craftsmen.

With the radicalization of the labour movement during the first decade of the twentieth century, the distance between salaried employees and industrial workers became even more evident. The explicit approval of the capitalistic economic system by white-collar associations was just one sign of this increasing distance.[27] Even if, after World War I, the reduction in real wages and especially the expansion in scientific management in larger enterprises[28] modified the consciousness of white-collar workers, their interest groups continued to hold liberal positions.

Switzerland's social and economic elites were the main winners in the industrialization process. Since the period of proto-industrialization, the entrepreneurs of the leading exporting industries, who often combined commercial and financial activities as *marchands-banquiers*, had acquired most of the socio-economic and political power. In the second half of the nineteenth century, the industrialists constituted a loosely jointed ruling class, sharing pronounced meritocratic and liberal values and remaining open to entrepreneurial newcomers.[29] As many of them were members of the federal parliament, where they represented the dominant Radical Democratic Party, their claim to leadership was also democratically legitimized. Most of them were members of the Schweizerische Handels-und Industrieverein, an influential interest group that defended liberalism and the concerns of exporting industries.

At the beginning of the twentieth century, Swiss society was therefore characterized by an increasing contrast between its different components. The largely heterogeneous, mostly skilled working class began to radicalize in a context of increasing inflation and international unionism. Various authors have claimed that the labour movement in general, and the events of 1918 in particular, had an integrating effect on workers' class-consciousness.[30] Where diverse types of worker were still living in different realities, they might thereby have developed a shared sense of belonging. The farming community developed a marked self-confidence and feeling for political action, which was directed at the labour parties as well as the established Radical Democratic Party. At the same time, white-collar workers began to shape their own consciousness and defend their interests against the working and entrepreneurial classes. Given these

---

27. König, "Zur Sozialgeschichte der Angestellten in der Schweiz", p. 181.
28. Rudolf Jaun, *Management und Arbeiterschaft: Verwissenschaftlichung, Amerikanisierung und Rationalisierung der Arbeitsverhältnisse in der Schweiz, 1873–1959* (Zurich, 1986).
29. Siegenthaler, "Die Schweiz 1850–1914", p. 453.
30. Bernard Degen, "Arbeiter", in *Historisches Lexikon der Schweiz* [electronic publication HLS], version dated 28 September 2004; Philippe Kaenel, "L'histoire et les images. La figure de l'ouvrier en Suisse", *Revue Suisse d'Histoire*, 54 (2004), pp. 20–56, 28.

social transformations at the beginning of the twentieth century, we might suppose that marital homogamy increased after World War I.

WINTERTHUR: CENTRE OF THE SWISS ENGINEERING INDUSTRY

Winterthur was one of the leaders of industrialization in Switzerland. Throughout the second half of the nineteenth and the beginning of the twentieth century, it was also the town whose development was most closely connected with its industrial growth. For these reasons Winterthur is often taken as representative of industrial Switzerland.[31] During the first half of the nineteenth century, economic development was determined by the expansion of the textile manufacturing industry, while the second half was characterized much more by the implementation and growth of the engineering industry. The expansion of this latter sector also constituted the main impetus of demographic growth in the late nineteenth and early twentieth centuries. The population of the town and its agglomeration rose from 26,000 in 1880 to 46,000 in 1910 and 54,000 in 1930.

As Table 1 demonstrates, the engineering industry was the main economic sector of the town and therefore also its most important employer. The majority of workers were employed by one of the three leading firms. Founded during the first half of the nineteenth century, Gebrüder Sulzer AG was by far the biggest employer at the beginning of the twentieth century. The number of employees at Gebrüder Sulzer AG rose from 1,200 in 1880 to 3,200 in 1900 and 5,850 in 1920.[32] Production was mainly centred on diesel engines and ships, and on the engines used in the construction of railway tunnels. J.J. Rieter & Cie was the oldest of the three firms, and until the 1860s it was primarily a textile manufacturing company. By the turn of the century it had been converted into an engineering company; by then the construction of electric engines, bridge-building, and railway engineering constituted its main activities. Between 1880 and 1920 the number of workers stagnated at around 1,000. The Schweizerische Lokomotiv- und Maschinenfabrik was founded in the 1870s and focused on constructing steam engines and electric locomotives. The number of workers at this firm rose from 450 in 1880 to 1,300 in 1900 and 1,900 in 1920.

These three main engineering firms constituted the core of Winterthur's industry. They also shaped the town's appearance as a result of their industrial landscape and the housing estates built for their workers according to the principles of the French *cités ouvrières*. The most important estate was built by the Lokomotiv- und Maschinenfabrik, to the

---

31. François Walter, *La Suisse urbaine 1750–1950* (Carouge, 1994), p. 105.
32. Werner Ganz, *Geschichte der Stadt Winterthur* (Winterthur, 1979), p. 177.

Table 1. *Occupational structure of Winterthur (agglomeration), 1910–1930*

Sector (%)	1910	1920	1930
Agriculture	7.1	5.9	4.7
Food industry	4.8	4.7	3.9
Construction industry	10.9	8.5	11.6
Textile and clothing industry	18.6	15.7	11.3
Engineering industry	28.9	35.1	24.2
Other industries	4.0	4.3	3.0
Commerce, administration, services	20.4	20.4	35.3
Transport	5.3	5.5	5.9
Total	100	100	100

Sources: Bundesamt für Statistik, *Eidgenössische Volkszählungen* 1910, 1920, and 1930.

plans of its founder, Charles Brown. The terraced houses all had front and back gardens. As a consequence, at the beginning of the twentieth century Winterthur was one of Switzerland's rare garden cities.[33]

An investigation conducted in 1907[34] gives more detailed information on the workers employed in Winterthur's engineering industry. First of all, its findings show that at that time the engineering sector was a national employer of mostly skilled workers. Over 80 per cent of those working in Winterthur's engineering sector were skilled workers. Only 16 per cent of these workers came from Winterthur and its surroundings, whereas 31 per cent originated from the rest of the canton of Zurich, and 47 per cent from other Swiss cantons. Accounting for less than 6 per cent of the total, foreign workers were not numerous, though at more than 10 per cent they were over-represented among unskilled workers.

Broken down according to age and qualification, it appears that among skilled workers young people were much more numerous than among the unskilled workforce. One can thus assume that access to qualified work was guaranteed by a professional and vocational education rather than by accumulated experience. Gebrüder Sulzer ran its own educational establishment and employed about 340 apprentices in 1910.[35] Finally, the wage structure showed that skilled workers were better rewarded than unskilled employees. While only 37 per cent of skilled workers earned less than 1,500 francs per year, more than 87 per cent of unskilled employees did. A comparison with other industries and other Swiss regions at that time reveals that engineering workers had the highest real wages of all factory workers.

33. Walter, *La Suisse urbaine 1750–1950*, p. 412.
34. Heinrich Lothmar, "Die Lohn- und Arbeitsverhältnisse in der Maschinenindustrie zu Winterthur", *Zeitschrift für Schweizerische Statistik*, 43 (1907), p. 87.
35. Ganz, *Geschichte der Stadt Winterthur*, p. 174.

Figure 1. A foundry hall of Sulzer AG around 1900, Winterthur's most important employer at the beginning of the twentieth century.
Sulzer Archive

Figure 2. Workers operating the forge in a factory hall of Sulzer AG around 1900. In the early twentieth century, about 30 per cent of Winterthur's active population worked in the engineering industry.
Sulzer Archive

However, these relatively high wages and good housing conditions could not prevent class conflicts, even if at the beginning of Winterthur's period as the main centre of the Swiss engineering industry the relationship between workers and entrepreneurs was rather easygoing. The leaders of the three principal engineering firms in particular had moderate and almost paternalistic traits. Sulzer was one of the first to implement worker representation on its executive board, and it also introduced pension schemes and widows' and orphans' benefits. It is therefore not surprising that there were no strikes in this firm between 1869 and 1910.[36] It is also noteworthy that many industrialists, professors, and teachers joined the local section of the Schweizerische Gewerbeverein, the craftsmen's main interest group.[37] Furthermore, the local Labour Party had been represented in the municipal parliament since 1898. By creating an arbitration board for labour disputes, the town authorities also contributed to better mutual understanding between workers and entrepreneurs.

Yet the high inflation during the first decade of the twentieth century and the radicalization of the national and international labour movement also affected the local relationship between social classes. In 1909 Italian masons working at the Gebrüder Sulzer plant initiated a strike against Winterthur's industrialists. The movement spread to other professions when Sulzer accepted an order placed by an engineering firm in Geneva whose moulders had gone on strike. Sulzer's workers regarded the firm's decision as a provocation and interpreted it as part of a "conspiracy against the working class".[38] The strike was thus increasingly viewed within the international context of the class struggle. By October 1910 more than 2,000 workers at Sulzer and Rieter had come out on strike in sympathy with the masons. In 1918 Winterthur was one of the main centres of the *Landesstreik*, even though the agitations were less pronounced and violent than in Zurich.

In some respects Winterthur was representative of industrialized Switzerland at the beginning of the twentieth century. The mostly skilled and specialized workers clearly outnumbered the non-industrial labour force. As elsewhere in Switzerland, tensions between employers and the working class had been increasing since the first decade of the twentieth century, and at the end of World War I they had reached unparalleled levels. We can therefore expect occupational homogamy to have been higher in the 1920s than before the war. In some respects, however, Winterthur differed from other industrialized Swiss regions. Probably nowhere else in Switzerland was the spatial concentration of workers as

---

36. Peter Pfrunder and Giorgio von Arb, *Fabrikzeit. Spurensicherung auf dem Sulzer-Areal* (Winterthur, 1992), p. 53.
37. Ganz, *Geschichte der Stadt Winterthur*, p. 179.
38. The phrase appears in a letter written by a worker and quoted in Pfrunder and Von Arb, *Fabrikzeit. Spurensicherung auf dem Sulzer-Areal*, p. 45.

high as it was in Winterthur. Moreover, the relative proportion of factory workers within the industrial labour force was exceeded scarcely anywhere else in the country. Hence, one can expect homogamous behaviour to have been more pronounced among Winterthur's workers than among those elsewhere in Switzerland. For that reason, it will be necessary to analyse the impact of geographical origin on the marital behaviour of workers.

DATA

The data used in this paper are drawn from civil marriage certificates for the municipality of Winterthur. Marriage registers are an often-used historical source to study occupational homogamy and intergenerational marital mobility since they usually indicate the professions of the two spouses and their fathers. In Switzerland, however, such "complete" certificates were exceptional. Even if the federal law on civil registration led to a degree of uniformity as from 1876, its application still differed substantially between cantons, towns, and from one period to another. As a consequence, the professions of brides and fathers were often lacking. That may be one reason why historical studies of marital homogamy in Switzerland are still very rare.[39]

Unlike the marriage certificates for late nineteenth-century Winterthur, those for the early twentieth century are of exceptionally good quality because the professions of the fathers of the two spouses are most often mentioned, even if the fathers were deceased when their children married. Our dataset contains all marriage certificates for the years 1909, 1910, and 1928. A total of 845 out of 989 certificates for both periods include the professions of both fathers and can therefore be used for analyses of origin-related occupational homogamy. All professions were first coded according to the Historical International Standard Classification of Occupations (HISCO).[40] On the basis of these profession codes and any further information that the marriage certificates might contain, such as the individual's position in a firm (master, subordinate, apprentice, for example) or other details which might indicate social position (proprietor, doctor, for example), twelve occupational classes (HISCLASS) were

---

39. To our knowledge, the three studies on nineteenth-century Geneva are the only systematic investigations of partner-choice patterns in Switzerland: Eric Widmer, *De coeur et de raison. Le choix du conjoint à Genève au 19ᵉ siècle* (Geneva, 1993); Reto Schumacher, "De l'analyse classique à l'analyse différentielle. Nuptialité, fécondité et mortalité à Genève pendant la première moitié du 19ᵉ siècle" (MA thesis, University of Geneva, 2002); Grazyna Ryczkowska, "Accès au mariage et structures de l'alliance à Genève, 1800–1880" (MA thesis, University of Geneva, 2003).

40. Marco H.D. van Leeuwen, Ineke Maas, and Andrew Miles, *HISCO: Historical International Standard Classification of Occupations* (Leuven, 2002).

defined.[41] For the purpose of our study, the HISCLASS categories were then further amalgamated into seven occupational class groups, each containing one, two, or three categories.

Table 2 gives an overview of the distribution by class of grooms and their fathers for the years 1909/10 and 1928. The table shows, first of all, that for both periods and among the grooms, as well as their fathers, skilled workers constituted the most important class group. In all cases, lower-skilled and unskilled workers were clearly less numerous. This result confirms, for Switzerland in general and Winterthur in particular, the high degree to which the working class had a professional education. It also appears that lower managers and professionals, clerical, and sales were more frequently represented among grooms than among fathers, even if the relatively small numbers of observed cases do not permit us to be certain about this conclusion. This is true too for the farmers, much more numerous among fathers than among grooms. The farm workers, finally, were by far the smallest group, which can be explained by the particular structure of Swiss agriculture, characterized by small and often independent farms.

The differences in class distribution between grooms and fathers reflect not only intergenerational changes in the occupational structure but also the spouse's geographical origin. Only 27 per cent of grooms and 26 per cent of brides were actually born in Winterthur. As a consequence, most of their families lived elsewhere, often in the canton of Zurich and the German-speaking part of Switzerland. These differences can thus also be related to regional variations in the occupational structure. The distribution of spouses by place of birth also shows that Winterthur was part of a regional or even national marriage market, including cantons in northern and northeastern German-speaking Switzerland.

Both the distribution of and the composition within the seven class groups differed between grooms and fathers. Among higher managers and professionals, more than 35 per cent of grooms were graduate engineers, while only 8 per cent of fathers had the same profession. In the group of lower managers and professionals, clerical, and sales, merchants (*Kaufleute*) were the most important group mentioned in both cases. It is interesting, however, to note that among the grooms the second most important profession was that of technician, while among the fathers it was innkeeper. Similar differences existed among the group of skilled workers. Among grooms, professions related to the engineering industry clearly outnumbered classic mechanic activities, while among the fathers, professions such as carpenter and shoemaker were numerous. Finally, the likelihood ratio shows that, at least for the fathers, the class distribution

41. For this purpose we used an SPSS syntax file created by Ineke Maas and Marco van Leeuwen, Amsterdam, 25 May 2004.

Table 2. *Distribution of fathers and grooms by class in 1909/10 and 1928*

Occupational class groups (HISCLASS codes)	Fathers		Grooms	
	1909/10 %	1928 %	1909/10 %	1928 %
Higher managers and professionals (1+2)	4.9	2.9	5.7	5.7
Lower managers and professionals, clerical and sales (3,4,5)	18.3	15.7	29.1	22.5
Skilled workers (6+7)	36.4	36.1	30.3	33.5
Farmers and fishermen (8)	14.2	11.7	0.6	2.6
Lower-skilled workers (9)	14.7	17.6	19.9	21.1
Unskilled workers (11)	9.9	14.1	12.9	13.4
Farm workers (10+12)	1.5	2.0	1.4	1.2
Number of observations	1,800		981	
Likelihood ratio	18.465		11.835	
Degrees of freedom	6		6	
P-value	0.005		0.066	

Sources: Staatsarchiv Zürich, Zivilstandsregister, Eheregister Winterthur, A2 NN 492.43, A2 NN492.60.

differed significantly between the two periods. Given the standard errors, however, it is impossible to say whether the proportion of any given group had increased or declined between the two dates.

TOTAL HOMOGAMY AND MOBILITY RATES

In this first part of our analysis we will examine total homogamy and mobility rates. We will concentrate on origin-related homogamy and mobility by comparing the class affiliation of the groom's father with that of the groom's father-in-law. In doing so, we compare the profession of two individuals of about the same age. In this way, origin-related homogamy should not be sensitive to biases related to career mobility, as would be the case with intergenerational marital homogamy. Indeed, a comparison between the groom's social status and that of his father-in-law is problematic, because the individuals being compared are not at the same stage in their life course. The groom is at the beginning of his professional career and therefore likely to climb the social ladder, while his father-in-law is probably at the end of his career and will have attained his ultimate social status.

Total homogamy and mobility rates have often been considered crude and imprecise measures. It has been argued that, especially when rates for different sub-tables are compared, variations might be due to shifts in the occupational structure (differences in the marginal distributions of origin and destination).[42] While we share the view that the distinction between total, structural, and relative mobility is important, its importance should not be overestimated in the case of marital homogamy. Marginal distributions do not have the same meaning in every type of mobility table. Whereas in an intergenerational mobility table in which the son's class affiliation is cross-tabulated with that of his father the margins are fixed quantities, marital mobility tables do not have fixed marginal distributions. In other words, every son inevitably has a father, but nobody is forced to marry. The numbers of brides and grooms are therefore variable quantities reflecting the "interplay of preference for marriage partners of particular types, and opportunity to marry according to these pre-ferences".[43] In that sense, total homogamy rates are important measures that mirror the interplay of supply and demand in the marriage market.[44]

Table 3 shows more precisely the outcome of this interplay and permits one to compare the situations in 1909/10 and 1928. In 1909/10 the total origin-related homogamy rate was of 30.4 per cent. Accordingly, about 70 per cent of spouses were socially mobile, which means that the occupational classes of their fathers were different. The direction of the mobility differed, however, according to the sex of the spouse. About 39 per cent of brides experienced upward social mobility,[45] while only 31 per cent of grooms did so. In 1928, at 28.3 per cent, the total homogamy rate was only slightly lower than around 1910. Among socially mobile spouses, the differences between the two sexes with respect to the direction of class changes were less pronounced than in 1909/10. However, women were still more likely to experience upward mobility than men. With respect to the temporal evolution of homogamy, one can conclude that the total rates differed only slightly between the two dates. Nevertheless, it seems that the internal association between the social origin of the two spouses diminished between 1909/10 and 1928. As shown in Table 3, Somers' D and gamma, two measures of ordinal association in a two-way contingency table, are both substantially lower in 1928 than in 1909/10. Thus, at this stage of the analysis, the hypothesis that homogamy increased after World War I cannot be confirmed.

Total homogamy rates are interesting and important indicators of the mating process. However, they do not permit us to distinguish between

42. Robert McCaa, "Isolation or Assimilation? A Log-Linear Interpretation of Australian Marriages, 1947–60, 1975, and 1986", *Population Studies*, 43 (1989), pp. 155–162.
43. Alan Gray, "Measuring Preference for In-Marriage: A Response to McCaa", *Population Studies*, 43 (1989), pp. 163–166, 164.
44. *Idem*, "Intermarriage: Opportunity and Preference", *Population Studies*, 41 (1987), pp. 365–379, 366.
45. At this stage of our analysis we suppose a hierarchical order among the seven class groups, and regard the first group, the higher managers and professionals, as the highest social class, and the last one, the farm workers, as the lowest. In that sense, a person experienced upward social mobility when marrying someone belonging to a socially higher class.

Table 3. *Occupational class mobility table, Winterthur, 1909/10 and 1928*

1909/10	Class of bride's father							Total
	(I)	(II)	(III)	(IV)	(V)	(VI)	(VII)	
Class of groom's father								
Higher managers and professionals (I)	4	10	4	4	2	2	0	26
Lower managers, professionals, clerical and sales (II)	6	25	27	8	8	5	0	79
Skilled workers (III)	1	20	66	22	23	13	2	147
Farmers (IV)	2	7	16	12	16	5	1	59
Lower-skilled workers (V)	3	5	20	9	10	6	2	55
Unskilled workers (VI)	0	0	22	3	7	9	1	42
Farm workers (VII)	0	1	3	1	1	0	0	6
Total	16	68	158	59	67	40	6	414

Total homogamy rate	30.4%		Somers' D	0.214***
Upward mobility rate (men)	30.7%		Gamma	0.272***
Upward mobility rate (women)	38.9%			

1928	Class of bride's father							Total
	(I)	(II)	(III)	(IV)	(V)	(VI)	(VII)	
Class of groom's father								
Higher managers and professionals (I)	3	5	3	0	0	2	0	13
Lower managers, professionals, clerical and sales (II)	4	17	22	7	9	6	3	68
Skilled workers (III)	3	21	58	24	25	21	4	156
Farmers (IV)	2	4	14	11	8	5	1	45
Lower-skilled workers (V)	1	11	36	10	17	12	2	89
Unskilled workers (VI)	0	8	19	4	6	16	1	54
Farm workers (VII)	0	1	1	2	0	2	0	6
Total	13	67	153	58	65	64	11	431

Total homogamy rate	28.3%		Somers' D	0.124**
Upward mobility rate (men)	34.6%		Gamma	0.158**
Upward mobility rate (women)	37.1%			

Note: ***p < 0.001 **p < 0.01 *p < 0.05.

homogamous marriages due simply to the class distribution in the marriage market (structural homogamy), and those reflecting individual preference (often referred to as relative homogamy). As mentioned above, it is not possible completely to disentangle structural and relative homogamy in a marital mobility table. Still, this does not, we believe, mean that the distinction should be ignored.

Log-linear modelling is a method widely used to study relative homogamy. Such models predict the cell frequencies of a multidimensional contingency table as a function of the table's marginal distributions and a series of interaction terms. In the simplest case, the independence model, the observed cell frequencies can be predicted sufficiently closely by the margins of the table. In terms of marriage patterns, such a distribution would correspond to a situation where all homogamy is purely structural. In the most complicated case, the so-called saturated model, however, all possible interaction terms between the variables presented in the table are necessary to reproduce a cell distribution close enough to the observed frequencies. Such a model contains more parameters than there are cells in the table and is therefore not really helpful.

When applied to a marital mobility table, the objective of log-linear analysis is to replace the full interaction between the social origin of the two spouses by a series of homogamy parameters serving as cell co-variates in the model. In our case we substitute the forty-nine interaction parameters of the 7x7 marital mobility table by a reduced number of homogamy coefficients, measuring the association between the occupational class of the two spouses.

DISTANCES BETWEEN OCCUPATIONAL CLASSES

To refine the study of the association between origin (class affiliation of the groom's father) and destination (class affiliation of the bride's father) in the martial mobility table, we have specified a series of log-linear association models. These models assume that categories are ordinal, meaning that they are ranked on a scale.[46] The assignment of these scale values is an important topic in categorical data analysis.

The easiest way to impose an interval structure to categories is the integer-scoring method, which assigns consecutive integers to classes. However, when using this method one has to be sure that the classes are correctly ordered. Furthermore, it is assumed that distances between any two adjacent categories are uniform across all values. Another way to assign class scores is to estimate them from the data themselves, which means on the basis of the classes' crossings through marriage. Goodman's

---

46. Daniel A. Powers and Yu Xie, *Statistical Methods for Categorical Data Analysis* (San Diego, CA, 2000), p. 119.

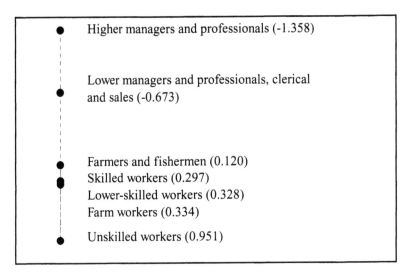

Figure 3. Estimated scores of class positions.

homogenous equal row and column effects model II[47] allows one to estimate these scale values without previous knowledge of the correct ordering of the categories.

Figure 3 shows the estimated relative positions of our seven occupational class groups for Winterthur in 1909/10 and 1928.[48] The model has a likelihood ratio of 35.0 with 30 degrees of freedom and is thus a well-fitting model. Primarily destined to be used for subsequent log-linear modelling, these estimated scale values are highly instructive in themselves since they give an idea of the class hierarchy and the distances between these groups.

The model actually points to a social structure consisting of four main classes, with higher managers and professionals constituting the upper class, and lower managers and professionals, clerical, and sales forming the upper-middle class. The lower-middle class included farmers, skilled, and lower-skilled workers, while the lower class comprised the unskilled workforce. These results confirm our assumption, outlined in the first part of this article, of a heterogeneous working class.

The social distance between skilled and unskilled workers was indeed important. This gap certainly reflects the opposition between the crafts-

47. Leo Goodman, "Simple Models for the Analysis of Association in Cross-Classifications Having Ordered Categories", *Journal of the American Statistical Association*, 74 (1979), pp. 537–552.
48. The model has been estimated using Jeroen K. Vermunt's LEM 0.11 program.

men, representing the overwhelming majority of skilled workers and an important part of the lower-skilled labour force, and the factory workers, most of whom were unskilled. But it may also be related to a concrete difference in the standard of living, as suggested by the data on wage distribution in the engineering industry in Winterthur. Yet, the social distance between farmers and workers, which the political events of the early twentieth century could have provoked, existed only partly in Winterthur. According to our model, farmers and skilled or lower-skilled workers did indeed belong to the lower-middle class, but the distance between farmers and unskilled workers was important. It also seems that the distance between the *Arbeiterschaft* and the *Angestelltenschaft* was real and significant.

LOG-LINEAR ASSOCIATION MODELS

The final step in our analysis of homogamy and marital mobility patterns in early twentieth-century Winterthur centres on the two hypotheses outlined in the first part of this study. First of all, we want to find out whether there was a rise in homogamy – as our historical arguments lead us to expect. Secondly, we want to examine whether the mobility between occupational classes was affected by the geographical origins of the spouses.

The first question implies analysing the association between origin, destination and time in a three-way contingency table. As we focus on the relation between origin (O) and destination (D), its full interaction term (OD) is replaced by a series of more parsimonious forms. Table 4 summarizes the different ways in which we have specified these interaction terms and their possible variation over time.[49]

The first model, the independence model, assumes that there was no interaction at all between the social origin of spouses, but asserts that the marginal distributions of the class affiliations of grooms and brides changed over time. This specification is not in itself particularly interesting, but it does serve as a baseline model for comparisons with more complex models. The quasi independence model includes six diagonal parameters (DIA_i) for the diagonal cells of the OD sub-table. Since the seventh cell on the diagonal (marriages between sons and daughters of farm workers) contains no observations, we have not specified a parameter for that cell. Specifying a different parameter for every diagonal cell actually means that homogamous behaviour varied according to occupational class.

---

49. Our model specifications were inspired by Marco van Leeuwen and Ineke Maas, "Log-linear Analysis of Changes in Mobility Patterns: Some Models with an Application to the Amsterdam Upper Classes in the Second Half of the Nineteenth Century", *Historical Methods*, 24 (1991), pp. 66–79.

Table 4. *Log-linear association models with respect to time, applied to occupational mobility in Winterthur, 1909/10–1928*

Model	df	LR	p > LR	BIC	AIC
–Independence model	72	140.06	0.000	−345.17	−3.94
$(O + D)^*T$					
–Quasi Independence model	66	88.98	0.031	−355.82	−43.02
$(O + D)^*T + DIA_I$					
–Quasi-uniform association model	65	60.13	0.648	−377.93	−69.87
$(O + D)^*T + DIA_i + U$					
–Semi dynamic QUA model	64	57.75	0.696	−373.57	−70.25
$(O + D)^*T + DIA_i + U^*T$					
–Full dynamic QUA model	58	54.83	0.594	−336.05	−61.17
$(O + D)^*T + DIA_i {}^*T + U^*T$					
–Full dynamic inheritance QUA model	63	57.47	0.673	−367.11	−68.53
$(O + D)^*T + DIA_i + INH^*T + U^*T$					

The third model, the quasi-uniform association model (QUA), contains one supplementary parameter U for the off-diagonal cells of the OD sub-table. This means that the diagonal cells are blocked out, that they are determined thus only by the log-linear homogamy parameters DIA_i. The frequencies of the cells above and below the diagonal are determined by a single parameter, measuring the association between the preliminary estimated class scores. The last three models contain three different specifications of the interaction between time and the association terms in the OD sub-table. The semi-dynamic quasi-uniform association model states that only the association parameter U differed across time, while the full dynamic QUA model also includes interactions between time and the diagonal homogamy parameters. The last model claims that these diagonal parameters differed over time, but uniformly across all occupational classes.

Table 4 indicates a series of goodness-of-fit statistics for these models. The likelihood ratio LR is a measure of the distance between the observed distribution of the contingency table and the one generated by the model. If the p-value for a given likelihood ratio and a number of degrees of freedom df exceeds 5 per cent, there is no significant difference between the observed and the predicted cell frequencies. In that case, the model fits the data. As we can see, all variations in the quasi-uniform association model are well-fitting models. When several models have an acceptable fit, it is usual to choose the most parsimonious – the one with the lowest Bayesian Information Criterion (BIC) or the lowest Akaike Information Criterion (AIC).[50] Considering the BIC and the AIC, we see that either the quasi-uniform association model without interaction with the time dimension or its semi-dynamic version should be retained.

Table 5 gives the parameter estimates for these two models as well as those for their full dynamic version. As to the diagonal parameters, it can be said that higher managers and professionals at the top of the occupational hierarchy and unskilled workers at the bottom of this class scheme had by far the most pronounced homogamous behaviour. To a much lesser extent, lower managers and professionals, clerical and sales, and farmers also showed homogamous tendencies. According to these log-linear models, however, skilled and lower-skilled workers did not behave homogamously at all, since their corresponding homogamy parameters are not significantly different from zero.

This pattern of marked homogamy at both the top and the bottom of the social ladder is certainly not specific to Winterthur. Such marital behaviour has already been observed in proto-industrial[51] as well as in industrial[52] settings. More surprising is the observed heterogamy among skilled and lower-skilled workers – a finding that must certainly be related to the characteristic heterogeneity of the Swiss working class. At the same time, we should also recall the social proximity between farmers, skilled, and lower-skilled workers, which also contributed to this result. The substantial homogamy found for unskilled workers nevertheless indicates a class-specific solidarity among underprivileged factory workers.

The uniform association parameter U for the off-diagonal cell frequencies is strong and highly significant. The interaction term β_{U*T} is negative and would thus point to a decline in the association between the class affiliation of the two spouses were it not for the fact that its standard error is slightly too high to eliminate doubt (p=0.13). The parameters reflecting the interaction between the time dimension and the class-specific intensity of homogamy, included in the full dynamic QUA model, are all statistically insignificant. It seems therefore that there was no clear shift in occupational homogamy patterns between 1909/10 and 1928.

Since many spouses originated from less or differently industrialized regions, their fathers' occupational class structure and composition would have been different from that of those born in Winterthur. Especially among workers therefore, class-consciousness and solidarity could have been different in these areas. It could be argued, therefore, that the mobility between class groups was different among immigrants than among natives. In order to test this second hypothesis, we have specified a

50. Adrian E. Raftery, "Bayesian Model Selection in Social Research", *Sociological Methodology*, 25 (1995), pp. 111–163. The $BIC=LR-dfln(N)$, and $AIC=LR-2df$. Both criteria combine model fit and parsimony.

51. For example in nineteenth-century Geneva: Widmer, *De coeur et de raison*, pp. 41 ff; Ryczkowska, "Accès au mariage et structures de l'alliance à Genève, 1800–1880", p. 83.

52. For example in nineteenth-century Liège: Anne Jacquemin, "Alliances et reproductions sociales à Liège, 1840–1890", in Guy Brunet, Antoinette Fauve-Chamoux, and Michel Oris (eds), *Le choix du conjoint* (Paris, 1998), pp. 107–132, 119.

Table 5. *Log-linear homogamy and association parameters for models with respect to time*

Parameter	QUA model	Semi dynamic QUA model	Full dynamic QUA model
DIA_1	1.863***	1.907***	1.628**
DIA_2	0.569**	0.596**	0.786**
DIA_3	0.145	0.135	0.286
DIA_4	0.595*	0.594*	0.404
DIA_5	0.242	0.235	0.081
DIA_6	1.164***	1.146***	1.182**
U	0.849***	1.062***	1.034***
β_{U*T}		−0.470	−0.405
β_{DIA1*T}			0.645
β_{DIA2*T}			−0.409
β_{DIA3*T}			−0.294
β_{DIA4*T}			0.401
β_{DIA5*T}			0.274
β_{DIA6*T}			−0.047

Note: ***$p < 0.001$ **$p < 0.01$ *$p < 0.05$.

second series of log-linear association models controlling this time for the groom's geographical origin. To facilitate the analysis we distinguish only between immigrants and natives. The models are basically the same as in the preceding section, except for the control variable T, which is replaced by I, indicating whether a groom was born in Winterthur ($I=0$) or not ($I=1$). Table 6 summarizes these models and indicates their statistical fit.

As is shown by Table 6 overleaf, it is difficult to obtain a satisfactory model when controlling for the groom's geographical origin. Neither the quasi-uniform association model nor its semi-differential version, including a parameter measuring the interaction between the off-diagonal association and the dichotomous I variable, fit the data. Even the last model, which states that not only the U parameter but also the diagonal homogamy parameters differ according to the groom's origin, is hardly significant, as its related p-value is only slightly higher than 5 per cent. All the same, this is an interesting result, since it highlights the fact that the association between the class affiliation of the two spouses must have been dependent on the groom's geographical origin.[53]

The parameter estimates presented in Table 7 overleaf corroborate this finding. The estimates of the first two models presented largely confirm the results of the previous analyses. Occupational homogamy was most

53. The preceding model has actually shown that the full interaction terms OD and ODT can be replaced by a series of homogamy parameters. It seems difficult, however, to substitute the full ODI interaction term. A hierarchical log-linear model selection procedure (Hiloglinear in SPSS)

Table 6. *Log-linear association models with respect to grooms' geographical origin, applied to occupational mobility in Winterthur, 1909/10–1928*

Model	df	LR	p > LR	BIC	AIC
–Independence model	72	168.05	0.000	–317.18	24.05
(O + D)*I					
–Quasi Independence model	66	116.56	0.000	–328.24	–15.44
(O + D)*I + DIA_i					
–Quasi-uniform association model	65	85.60	0.044	–352.46	–44.40
(O + D)*I + DIA_i + U					
–Semi differential QUA model	64	85.35	0.039	–345.97	–42.65
(O + D)*I + DIA_i + U*I					
–Full differential QUA model	58	74.47	0.071	–316.41	–41.53
(O + D)*I + DIA_i *I + U*I					

Table 7. *Log-linear homogamy and association parameters of models with respect to grooms' geographical origin*

Parameter	QUA model	Semi differential QUA model	Full differential QUA model
DIA_1	1.925***	1.926***	3.106**
DIA_2	0.538*	0.548*	0.266
DIA_3	0.146	0.144	−0.359
DIA_4	0.550*	0.550*	0.005
DIA_5	0.248	0.247	1.006*
DIA_6	1.206***	1.204***	1.289***
U	0.879***	0.759**	0.875**
β_{U*I}		0.166	0.023
β_{DIA1*I}			−1.502
β_{DIA2*I}			0.445
β_{DIA3*I}			0.727*
β_{DIA4*I}			0.562
β_{DIA5*I}			−1.066*
β_{DIA6*I}			−0.092

Note: *** $p < 0.001$ ** $p < 0.01$ * $p < 0.05$.

pronounced at the top and at the bottom of the social hierarchy, while it was least pronounced among skilled and lower-skilled workers. The association parameter U is high and statistically significant. However, in

applied to the four factors O, D, T, and I endorses this conclusion. The backward elimination procedure retains as the final model (O, D, T, I, TI, OI, DI, OD, ODI), with LR = 97.97, df = 96, p-value = 0.425. Unlike the ODT interaction, which can be removed from the model, the ODI term must be included in the model in order to fit data. The association between O and D seems dependent on I therefore.

the last model, which also includes interaction terms for the class-specific homogamy parameters, the estimates are considerably altered. The first homogamy parameter relative to higher managers and professionals is much higher than in the two preceding models. Its interaction with the control variable is strong and negative, even if it is not really significant (p=0.19). This may nevertheless indicate that in Winterthur the elites were much more insular towards other occupational classes than elsewhere.

Interestingly enough, the marital behaviour of skilled and lower-skilled workers depended on their geographical origin. Among skilled workers born in Winterthur there was no significant homogamous behaviour. In contrast, immigrants tended to marry within their social group, as is indicated by the significant and positive parameter β_{DIA3*I}. This result highlights a substantial degree of heterogeneity among the class of skilled workers and must be related to its origin-specific composition. Natives were mainly sons of highly specialized workers and foremen in Winterthur's engineering industry, while the fathers of immigrants were mostly artisans from traditional crafts.

A similar difference can be found for the marital behaviour of lower-skilled workers. The estimates reveal a marked tendency to homogamy among natives, while among immigrants this pattern is not confirmed, the interaction term being negative and of about the same importance. Once again, this distinctive behaviour may be related to the differential composition of this occupational group according to geographical origin. In Winterthur, the most important subgroup among the lower-skilled were the metalworkers, such as moulders and milling workers, while among the immigrants the professions mentioned covered a wide range of lower-skilled activities in the textile and the transport sectors. If, in this particular case, our finding points to a specific sociability among the lower-skilled workers of Winterthur's engineering industry, it shows in general that, especially among workers, class-consciousness and solidarity were regionally determined and dependent on local contexts.

CONCLUSION

"We have no proletariat" was an often-cited statement in late nineteenth-century Switzerland.[54] It shows that, in the nineteenth century, contemporaries were aware of Switzerland's very specific model of industrialization, which was characterized by geographically delocalized manufacturing industries (preventing the creation of large industrial agglomerations), and of the impact of this model on social-class

---

54. Kaenel, "L'histoire et les images", p. 20.

formation. The aim of this article has been to examine, by analysing marital homogamy and mobility patterns, the fluidity of a system of social stratification marked by a heterogeneous working class and likely to lead to increasing social-group solidarity during the phase of a more active labour movement in the early twentieth century. To do so, we have explored data from Winterthur, a town whose economic and social development was determined by the expansion of the engineering industry. The Swiss context in general and the local background in particular lead us to expect there to have been an increase in homogamous behaviour after World War I, especially among the working class. Given the town's specific industrial organization, we also assumed homogamy would be higher among spouses born in Winterthur than among immigrants.

Our analyses revealed that occupational homogamy was most pronounced at the top and bottom of the social hierarchy. The homogamy parameters were highest and statistically significant among higher managers and professionals on the one hand, and among unskilled workers – mostly factory workers – on the other. To a lesser extent, homogamous behaviour could also be found among the group of lower managers and professionals, clerical and sales. However, skilled and lower-skilled workers did not behave homogamously.

There is no empirical evidence of an increase in homogamy after World War I. Even if the statistical results remain ambiguous, the system of social stratification appears to have become more fluid between 1910 and 1928. The presumed intensification of class-consciousnesses and conflict cannot explain the evolution of partner-choice patterns during that period, therefore. However, we also found that the association between the social background of the spouses was dependent on their geographical origin. Especially among skilled and lower-skilled workers, the homogamy parameters were altered when this control variable was included in the analysis. If skilled workers born in Winterthur did not tend to marry within their group, immigrants belonging to the same social class, mostly sons of artisans from rural German-speaking Switzerland, showed significant homogamous behaviour. A similar difference could be observed among lower-skilled workers. Immigrants had no particular preference for homogamous marriage, while natives seemed to marry homogamously.

This study has shown that it is difficult to define and understand the working class in early twentieth-century Switzerland. Indeed, workers' identities must have been geographically and temporally unstable. On the one hand, class-consciousness and solidarity were regionally determined and dependent on local contexts. On the other hand, a sense of belonging might have been strong in phases of intense political struggle but have rapidly diminished in calmer times. Finally, the workers themselves might have considered their condition as temporary.[55] Especially in contexts of industrial immigration marked by a high turnover of professionals, there must have been a real possibility of social mobility – if not necessarily for first-generation immigrants, then at least for their daughters and sons.

---

55. Maurizio Gribaudi, *Itinéraires ouvriers. Espaces et groupes sociaux à Turin au début du XXe siècle* (Paris, 1987), p. 231.

IRSH 50 (2005), Supplement, pp. 93–122 DOI: 10.1017/S0020859005002087
© 2005 Internationaal Instituut voor Sociale Geschiedenis

Pyrenean Marriage Strategies in the Nineteenth Century: The French Basque Case

MARIE-PIERRE ARRIZABALAGA

SUMMARY: Marriage strategies in the rural Basque country of the nineteenth century differed according to social background and gender. Propertied families had more diversified strategies than landless families as a result of persistent single inheritance practices, population growth, urbanization, and industrialization which generated massive emigration. Propertied families helped some of their children to settle in local rural villages and others to emigrate to cities (women) or to America (men). Landless families, by contrast, continued to settle most of their children in local rural villages, others emigrating to America only later in the century, avoiding the cities at all cost. Men, no matter their social background, benefited the most from new economic opportunities because most of them married into families of equal or higher status. Women, by contrast, did not have equal opportunities because few married upward and outside their professional group. When women did not marry within their socio-professional group or remain single, they married into families of lower status (more often than men).

Through population statistics, historians and demographers have long observed and quantified the rural exodus and the massive emigration movements which the Pyrenees and France as a whole experienced in the nineteenth century. They used macro-structural arguments to justify the new demographic trends, blaming them on rural overpopulation, rural impoverishment, industrialization, and urbanization.[1] In this period, the Pyrenees did indeed experience massive emigration due to unprecedented demographic growth. Communities could not absorb the excess population as a result of their limited economic resources and their predominantly small-landowning agricultural activities. Further, land

---

1. On the demography of the Pyrenees, see G. Callon, "Le mouvement de la population dans le département des Basses-Pyrénées au cours de la période 1821–1920 et depuis la fin de cette période", *Bulletin de la société des sciences, lettres et arts de Pau*, 53 (1930), pp. 81–113; Michel Chevalier, *La Vie humaine dans les Pyrénées ariégeoises* (Paris, 1956); André Etchelecou, *Transition démographique et système coutumier dans les Pyrénées occidentales* (Paris, 1991); Théodore Lefebvre, *Les Modes de vie dans les Pyrénées-Atlantiques orientales* (Paris, 1933); Jacques Saint-Macary, *La Désertion de la terre en Béarn et dans le Pays Basque* (Pau, France, 1939).

partition imposed by the Civil Code risked impoverishing the entire population and ruining the region's economy. Ultimately, industrial activities in local towns and regional cities offered new resources and attractive opportunities for this excess population to find jobs to support themselves and their families.

Besides these macro-structural arguments, there were other issues at stake which explain the demographic evolution of the Pyrenees and massive emigration in the period. Historians and anthropologists have justified these patterns using micro-longitudinal methods to demonstrate how France's new egalitarian inheritance laws, those of the Civil Code of 1804, actually destabilized ancient customs and generated new behaviour. In order to perpetuate their ancient single inheritance practices and preserve their traditional "house system",[2] Pyrenean families elaborated new strategies which bypassed the new laws and excluded numerous cadets or "non-inheriting children" from land succession, forcing them to depart from the countryside to cities or overseas.[3] Rural depopulation and emigration were particularly observable in the traditional inegalitarian provinces south of the Loire River.[4] Conversely, provinces north of the Loire River, such as Brittany, were affected in later periods as a result of their traditional practices of egalitarian succession and land partition.[5]

Overpopulation, impoverishment, and the egalitarian laws of the Civil

2. The "house system" in the Pyrenees is a system which all propertied families respected and upon which they all depended. Families were recognized as household units comprising individuals with different roles and status, cohabiting in one house, all descending from the same family. The house was to be transmitted intact from one generation to the next and was the guarantor of family succession, lineage, and continuity. Family culture imposed these traditional values for the survival of the house so much so that the interests of the house prevailed over those of individuals. The Civil Code threatened these old traditional values, and therefore the integrity of the house, because it protected individual rights over property rights by imposing equal inheritance or the equal partition of land between siblings. As a result of partition, the house could no longer support a three-generational family living together (the stem family). The family business might then go bankrupt and successors be forced to sell the house. To avoid such tragedy, families had to circumvent the new law to maintain single inheritance and thus protect the house system.

3. Georges Ravis-Giordano and Martine Segalen (eds), *Les Cadets* (Paris, 1994), and Gérard Bouchard, John Dickinson, and Joseph Goy (eds), *Les Exclus de la terre en France et au Quebec (XVIIe–XXe siècles)* (Paris, 1998).

4. Rolande Bonnain, Gérard Bouchard, and Joseph Goy (eds), *Transmettre, hériter, succéder. La reproduction familiale en milieu rural, France–Quebec, XVIIIe–XXe siècles* (Paris, 1992), and D. Comas d'Argemir and J-F. Soulet (eds), *La familía als Pirineus* (Andorra, 1993). In addition, see works by: Isaac Chiva and Joseph Goy (eds), *Les Baronnies des Pyrénées. Maisons, mode de vie, société*, vol. 1 (Paris, 1981) and *Les Baronnies des Pyrénées. Maisons, espace, famille*, vol. 2 (Paris, 1986); Alain Collomp, *La Maison du père. Famille et village en Haute-Provence aux XVIIe et XVIIIe siècles* (Paris, 1983); Bernard Derouet, "Pratiques successorales et rapport à la terre: les sociétés paysannes d'Ancien Régime", *Annales ESC*, 1 (1989), pp. 173–206.

5. For publications on inheritance systems north of the Loire River, see Martine Segalen, *Quinze générations de Bas-Bretons. Parenté et Société dans le Pays Bigouden Sud, 1720–1980*

Code do help to explain why France, and the Pyrenees in particular, experienced rural depopulation and massive emigration in the nineteenth century, but only partially. The phenomenon, however, is more complex and we will here propose additional explanations. Using the Basque country as a case study and family reconstitution as a method, it appears that in this period rich and poor families from rural backgrounds all had difficulty in settling their children in the village. This was due to larger family sizes (of three or four children on average). It became an issue particularly for landed Pyrenean families who could settle only two (perhaps three) of their children comfortably in the village or nearby, marrying them into families of equal status. The other children, however, could not hope for homogamous marriages and a comfortable life because local options were limited. Settlement in their village environment, especially for women, often meant resorting to socially downward marriages or a life of subordination as unmarried "servants" in the family house.

From the mid-nineteenth century onwards, however, non-inheriting men and women from a rural agricultural background chose other destinies and destinations. Some (especially women) opted for urban migration (to the local towns, the regional cities of Bayonne and Pau, and also to Bordeaux and Paris) and others (especially men) for overseas emigration (to Argentina and Uruguay in South America, to Newfoundland and New Orleans, and later to Central America, the western states of the United States, and Canada around the turn of the century)[6] where, as a result of massive industrialism and greater employment opportunities, they had better chances of a decent life (see Table 1). Urban and overseas emigration thus became options which attracted many men and women from a rural background in the Pyrenees.[7] Departure was a strategy to avoid poor destinies, downward marriages, or life-long service labour as unmarried men and women.

(Paris, 1985); Gérard Béaur, "Land Transmission and Inheritance Practices in France During the *Ancien Régime*: Differences of Degree or Kind?", in David R. Green and Alistair Owens, *Family Welfare: Gender, Property, and Inheritance since the Seventeenth Century* (London, 2004), pp. 31–46.

6. On Basque emigration to America in the nineteenth and twentieth centuries, see William A. Douglass and Jon Bilbao, *Amerikanuak: Basques in the New World* (Reno, NE, 1975).

7. On Basque migration, see articles by Marie-Pierre Arrizabalaga: "Réseaux et choix migratoires au Pays Basque. L'exemple de Sare au XIXe siècle", *Annales de démographie historique*, (1996), pp. 423–446; "Comment le marché de l'emploi national et international a-t-il influencé les destins individuels au sein de familles basques et les modalités de transmission du patrimoine au XIX siècle?", in Christian Dessureault, John Dickinson, and Joseph Goy (eds), *Famille et marché (XVIe–XXe siècles)* (Sillery, Québec, 2003), pp. 183–198; "Migrations féminines – migrations masculines: des comportements différenciés au sein des familles basques au XIXe siècle", in Luigi Lorenzetti, Anne-Lise Head-König, and Joseph Goy (eds), *Marchés, migrations et logiques familiales dans les espaces français, canadien et suisse, XVIIIᵉ–XXᵉ siècles* (Berne, 2005), pp. 183–195.

Table 1. *Migration among the children and grandchildren of the 120 couples in the sample: second- and third-generation cohorts*

Residence	Children		Total		Grandchildren		Total	
	Men	Women	N	%	Men	Women	N	%
Rural	118	162	280	(61.5)	153	188	341	(42.4)
Urban	21	29	50	(11.0)	41	77	118	(14.7)
Abroad	36	20	56	(12.3)	96	43	139	(17.3)
Unknown	40	29	69	(15.2)	124	82	206	(25.6)
Total	215	240	455	(100)	414	390	804	(100)

Contrary to what the historiography has argued, emigration affected rich as well as poor families. More remarkably, the data on the Basque country show that, actually, men and women from richer families departed earlier and in greater number than those from poorer families. Poverty therefore is not a strong argument to explain rural depopulation and massive emigration in the Pyrenees in the nineteenth century.[8] Nor does it explain the destinies and destinations of emigrants.

Through an analysis of marriage strategies among rural Basque men and women of different socio-economic and professional backgrounds in the nineteenth century, we will attempt to explain these discernible behaviours, analysing the role which marriage opportunities played in explaining why some settled in their rural environment and others departed from it permanently. Did women from propertied or landless families have the same chance as men when it came to marrying into families of equal or higher social status, and if so why? Could women's marriage opportunities in the village explain their different socio-professional and migration destinies compared with men? Could the study of marriage patterns then give more complete and refined explanations for women's preference for urban migration and men's preference for overseas emigration?

METHODOLOGY

The Basque country in the western Pyrenees will here be used as a case study in the analysis of marriage strategies in an attempt to understand better the rural depopulation and the massive emigration phenomena which the Pyrenees experienced in the nineteenth century. In addition, family reconstitution will provide the data and illustrations to justify the greater

---

8. Historians specialized in inheritance and emigration in the Pyrenees in the nineteenth century have argued this, especially Antoinette Fauve-Chamoux and Rolande Bonnain. See also Gérard

diversity of marriage strategies and migration destinies among the richer families of the communities compared with the poorer ones. Finally, analysis of the data will help to explain the attraction of women to cities and that of men to America. For that purpose, we reconstituted 120 genealogies, 20 from each of the six villages selected as part of this sample study: 4 highland villages (Sare, Aldudes, Mendive, Alçay) and 2 lowland villages (Isturits and Amendeuix) scattered across the 3 French Basque provinces and remote from the regional, coastal city of Bayonne (Figure 1 overleaf).[9] Our genealogical research began with the selection of 120 couples who married during the first two decades of the nineteenth century, the reconstitution of their life experiences, as well as those of their children (second-generation cohort) who married between 1830 and 1860, and finally those of their grandchildren (third-generation cohort) who married after 1860: a three-generational family reconstitution which involved nearly 3,000 individuals from the early nineteenth century almost until today. To complete these genealogies, we consulted the civil registers (records of births, marriages, and deaths) of the 6 villages and of all neighbouring villages (within a 20-mile radius) over a period of 200 years.[10] The purpose of this regional research work was to reconstitute the destinies of the 120 original couples and all their descendants (children, grandchildren, and their respective spouses) who lived in their village of birth or elsewhere in the *département*, in neighbouring or distant villages, local towns, distant towns, or in the regional cities of Bayonne and Pau (see Table 1).

We also cross-analysed the genealogies with the land registers (*cadastre*), the succession registers (*enregistrement*) and the notarial records (*notaire*), which provided additional information on ownership, property size,

---

Bouchard, Joseph Goy, and Anne-Lise Head-König (eds), *Problèmes de la transmission des exploitations agricoles (XVIIIe–XXe siècles)* (Rome, 1998); Anne-Lise Head-König, Luigi Lorenzetti, and Béatrice Veyrassat (eds), *Famille, parenté et réseaux en Occident (XVIIe–XXe siècles)* (Geneva, 2001).

9. The French Basque country is located in the most western part of the Pyrenees between the Atlantic Ocean in the west and Béarn in the east in the French *département* of Pyrénées-Atlantiques, and between Spain in the south and the French *département* of Landes in the north. The country is divided into three provinces: Labourd, Basse-Navarre, and Soule (from west to east). The six villages are: Sare, a highland village in Labourd; Aldudes and Mendive, two highland villages in Basse-Navarre; Alçay, a highland village in Soule; and Isturits and Amendeuix, two lowland villages in Basse-Navarre. The regional capital city is Bayonne, a port city on the Atlantic Ocean. These isolated villages were deliberately selected away from Bayonne in order to make sure that the nearby regional city did not constitute a natural magnet to the excess rural population. As a result of the distances involved, people from isolated villages then had a wider variety of migration options.

10. Because some of the 120 couples' grandchildren, born in the late 1890s or early 1900s, lived long lives and died in the 1980s or 1990s, we systematically consulted the civil registers of the 6 villages and of all the 15–20 neighbouring villages from 1800 until the present.

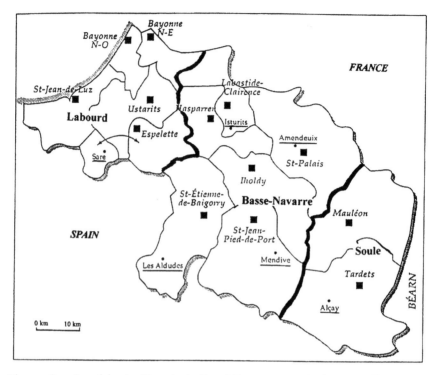

Figure 1. Location of the six villages in the French Basque country in the western Pyrenees.

dowries, and inheritance.[11] We proceeded to computerize the data, entering all available information by cohort: the 120 original couples (the first-generation cohort), their children (the second-generation cohort), and their grandchildren (the third-generation cohort). This multi-generational categorization subsequently provided material for an analysis of marriage strategies and their evolution.

The French Basque country being mainly a region of small farm ownership, we selected families who were representative of that population. As a result, 65 per cent of the 120 original couples in the early 1800s were propertied farmers or artisan farmers and 35 per cent landless farmers or artisan farmers. Family reconstitution showed that these 120 couples (first generation) had 567 children (4.7 children per couple), all born in the first half of the nineteenth century: 456 survived until adulthood (3.8 children per family).[12] The surviving second-generation cohort in turn had

11. This was the only way to study migration, because the nineteenth-century census data for all Basque villages were destroyed in two successive fires in the archives of Bayonne and Pau in the early twentieth century.

12. Children who died before the age of 21 were regarded as never having reached adulthood. A total of 111 of the 567 second-generation children (19.6 per cent of the cohort) and 230 of the 1,039 third-generation children (22.1 per cent of the cohort) died before reaching 21.

Table 2. *Marital status of the children and grandchildren of the 120 couples in the sample: second- and third-generation cohorts*

Marital status	Children		Total		Grandchildren		Total	
	Men	Women	N	%	Men	Women	N	%
Married	109	159	268	(58.8)	127	198	325	(40.2)
Unmarried	42	48	90	(19.7)	78	76	154	(19.0)
Unknown	64	34	98	(21.5)	213	117	330	(40.8)
Total	215	241	456	(100)	418	391	809	(100)

1,039 children (3.9 children per family), all born after 1840: 809 survived until adulthood (3 children per family). Of the 456 surviving second-generation children, 268 (58.8 per cent) married, and of the 809 surviving third-generation children 325 (40.2 per cent) married.[13] The focus of this study will be on these married individuals and their spouses (see Table 2).

It is important to note that, of the unknown cases, many were men and women who had emigrated to America or to cities, where a number remained single. We know more about women's marriage destinies than men's because women were less inclined than men to emigrate abroad, and therefore many women were located in villages, local towns, and regional cities.[14]

When computerizing the data, we created various socio-professional categories for all individuals and their parents. If they were married, we did the same for their spouses and their spouses' parents. These variables included information on their profession, property ownership, the size of their property, and their status. We also included a special category which combined all aspects, socio-economic and professional, along the lines of the HISCLASS classification.[15] Each individual, no matter what their

13. We were unable to locate the marriage certificates of all married descendants, especially those of emigrants who married in America or in large cities such as Bordeaux or Paris. As a consequence, our data suggest that only 40.2 per cent of the third-generation cohort married. It is likely that more of them actually married, but we were unable to reconstitute their lives, let alone their backgrounds. Nonetheless, many of this third-generation cohort probably remained single.
14. Women did not emigrate as much as men. Indeed, among the second- and third-generation cohorts, 67.5 per cent and 48.2 per cent of women respectively never left their rural environment, compared with 54.9 per cent and 37 per cent respectively for men (see Table 2). As a consequence, women's destinies were reconstituted in greater details than men's.
15. HISCLASS: a standard social-class scheme based on the Historical International Standard Classification of Occupations (HISCO). See the introduction to the present volume. The HISCLASS classification runs from 1 to 12: 1 and 2 referring to higher managers and higher professionals; 3, 4, and 5 to lower managers, lower professionals, clerical and sales personnel, and lower clerical and lower sales personnel; 6 and 7 to foremen and propertied medium-skilled workers; 8 to propertied farmers; 9 to landless lower-skilled workers; 10 and 12 to landless lower-skilled farm workers and unskilled farm workers; and 11 to unskilled workers. These have been restructured to form seven categories in the tables.

marital status, was assigned a "class" category, as were his or her parents. For comparative purposes, we assigned a "class" variable to all individuals' spouses and their parents. We were able to do so as a result of the cross-analysis of the various succession sources (land and succession registers). The purpose of creating such variables was to compare the socio-professional backgrounds of the parents and parents-in-law of married individuals within each cohort and between cohorts.[16] This analysis will then lead to an in-depth study of the evolution of the marriage patterns of men and women and of homogamy in the nineteenth century. Was there indeed a gender and socio-professional differentiation in marriage strategies which explains the different migration destinies of Basque men and women?

HOMOGAMY: THE DATA

The analysis of the three-generational computerized data on the married couples within each cohort clearly highlights the fact that, throughout the nineteenth century, the great majority of them married within their socio-professional group and subsequently enjoyed the same status as their parents. Indeed, of the men and women of the first-, second-, and third-generation cohorts who married – those who married in the early, mid-, and late nineteenth century respectively – the large majority had the same socio-professional background as their spouses, with their respective parents having the same profession and living within the same social environment (see Tables 3 and 4).[17] Indeed, the data indicate that throughout the nineteenth century 60 to 70 per cent of the married children in the sample married within their socio-professional group, choosing a spouse whose parents had the same socio-professional background as their own parents (see Tables 3 and 4).

When comparing men and women, however, it appears that men had greater chances of marrying a person within their socio-professional group than women: 65.7 to 74 per cent for men throughout the century compared with 60.8 to 68.9 per cent for women. Despite these gender differences, it is clear that, whenever possible, propertied or landless families ensured that

---

16. We were able to collect an extensive amount of information on the marriages of those who had settled in the local towns and the regional cities of Bayonne and Pau because we systematically consulted their registers from 1830 to 1950. We could not do the same for those who emigrated to America. Nevertheless, information on them was sometimes available in land and succession registers. Hence the number of unknown.

17. It is important to note that, for the purpose of our analysis, we disregarded all "unknown cases", individuals whose destinies were cases partially available or missing. Indeed, we sometimes know that specific individuals married, but we were either unable to collect information on the origins of their spouse or the data did not provide information on their in-laws.

Table 3. *Intergenerational mobility of married men: comparing the socio-professional status of their fathers and fathers-in-law, for first-, second- and third-generation cohorts (the original first-generation grooms, their sons, and their grandsons)*

Intergenerational mobility	First generation	Second generation	Third generation
Upward marriages	16.2%	14.3%	14.4%
Homogamy	65.7%	74.0%	69.9%
Downward marriages	18.1%	11.7%	15.7%

Note: We considered 105 of the 120 first-generation husbands; 77 of the 109 second-generation husbands (sons); and 83 of the 127 third-generation husbands (grandsons). We excluded all cases which provided no or partial information on in-laws.

Table 4. *Intergenerational mobility of married women: comparing the socio-professional status of their fathers and fathers-in-law, for first-, second- and third-generation cohorts (the original first-generation brides, their daughters and their granddaughters)*

Intergenerational mobility	First generation	Second generation	Third generation
Upward marriages	18.1%	20.6%	13.6%
Homogamy	65.7%	60.8%	68.9%
Downward marriages	16.2%	18.6%	17.5%

Note: We considered 105 of the 120 first-generation wives; 102 of the 159 second-generation wives (daughters); and 132 of the 198 third-generation wives (granddaughters). We excluded all cases which provided no or partial information on in-laws.

most of their children married into their own socio-professional group, in the rural environment with which they were familiar. What do family reconstitutions say additionally about these particular couples?

Family reconstitutions show that among propertied families (artisans, artisan farmers, and farmers) (categories 6, 7, and 8), the men and women who generally married within their own socio-professional group were mainly the heirs or heiresses to the family assets, one per family, who would take over the family farm or craft business of their parents, who lived and worked with them as stem families,[18] and who therefore enjoyed the same socio-professional status as their parents and in-laws (see Tables 5 to 9). The selected child, male or female, was in charge of perpetuating single-inheritance traditions to protect the ancient "house system", maintaining the family property undivided, and transmitting it intact to

18. Besides Frederick Le Play's works, see more recent contributions on the matter by Antoinette Fauve-Chamoux and Emiko Ochiai (eds), *Maison et famille souche: perspectives eurasiennes* (Kyoto, 1998).

Table 5. *Socio-professional status of husbands' fathers, compared with that of their in-laws: first-generation cohort (the couples in the sample, who married between 1800 and 1820)*

Status of husbands' fathers (down) and in-laws (across), by category	1+2	3,4,5	6+7	8	9	11	10+12
1+2 Higher managers and professionals	0			2			
3,4,5 Lower managers and professionals, clerical and sales		0		1			
6+7 Skilled workers			0	1	1		
8 Farmers and fishermen			4	57	1	12	
9 Lower-skilled workers				1	0	1	
11 Unskilled workers						0	
10+12 Farm workers		1		11			12

Table 6. *Socio-professional status of husbands' fathers, compared with that of their in-laws: second-generation cohort (the sons of the 120 couples in the sample, who married between 1830 and 1860)*

Status of husbands' fathers (down) and in-laws (across), by category	1+2	3,4,5	6+7	8	9	11	10+12
1+2 Higher managers and professionals	0						
3,4,5 Lower managers and professionals, clerical and sales		0					
6+7 Skilled workers			0	1		1	
8 Farmers and fishermen		2	3	46	2	1	
9 Lower-skilled workers			1		0	4	
11 Unskilled workers						0	
10+12 Farm workers				3	2		11

the next generation. The single heir was traditionally the first-born male or female child (*aînesse intégrale*), who would marry the non-inheriting son or daughter of a propertied family of similar background. The couple would then settle in the heir's family house as stem families.

In the nineteenth century, however, Basque families adapted their inheritance strategies to the new demographic and economic conditions, allowing their sons to emigrate in greater number than their daughters. As a result, they often opted for female inheritance, selecting their heirs from among their first-born or cadet daughters.[19] In addition, one or two of the siblings (male or female) of the heir or heiress experienced something

19. On the matter of Pyrenean single inheritance strategies (the Basque case included) in comparison with Asia, see Emiko Ochiai (ed.), *The Logic of Female Succession: Rethinking Patriarchy and Patrilineality in Global and Historical Perspective* (Kyoto, 2003). See too Rose

Table 7. *Socio-professional status of wives' fathers, compared with that of their in-laws: second-generation cohort (the daughters of the 120 couples in the sample, who married between 1830 and 1860)*

Status of wives' fathers (down) and in-laws (across), by category		1+2	3,4,5	6+7	8	9	11	10+12
1+2	Higher managers and professionals	0						
3,4,5	Lower managers and professionals, clerical and sales		0					
6+7	Skilled workers			1		2		2
8	Farmers and fishermen		3	7	50	3		12
9	Lower-skilled workers			1		1		
11	Unskilled workers						0	
10+12	Farm workers			1	7	2		10

Table 8. *Socio-professional status of husbands' fathers, compared with that of their in-laws: third-generation cohort (the grandsons of the 120 couples in the sample, who married after 1860)*

Status of husbands' fathers (down) and in-laws (across), by category		1+2	3,4,5	6+7	8	9	11	10+12
1+2	Higher managers and professionals	0						
3,4,5	Lower managers and professionals, clerical and sales		0					
6+7	Skilled workers			0	4		1	1
8	Farmers and fishermen				42		5	5
9	Lower-skilled workers				2	0	1	1
11	Unskilled workers					1	0	1
10+12	Farm workers				6	3	1	16

similar, marrying the heir or heiress to a farmhouse or other business of comparable size and status in the village or nearby. These were the men or women who received compensation for their legal shares of the inheritance (equal to the *préciput* share, or 25 per cent of the assets[20]), and used it as a dowry to marry into propertied families of the same status.[21] Thus, all

Duroux, "Emigration, Gender, and Inheritance. A Case Study of the High Auvergne, 1700–1900", in Green and Owens, *Family Welfare*, pp. 47–72.

20. To marry within their social group, men and women had to present a dowry equivalent to the *préciput* (equal to 25 per cent of the assets) or the extra share which the heir or heiress received upon marriage. If they were unable to save for such a dowry (as a result of the family being large), they could not marry within their social group.

21. The inheritance strategies to secure single inheritance were complex. They aimed at maintaining the house and property intact from one generation to the next while providing the non-inheriting siblings with compensation (generally less than their equal share) so that they

Table 9. *Socio-professional status of wives' fathers, compared with that of their in-laws: third-generation cohort (the granddaughters of the 120 couples in the sample, who married after 1860)*

Status of wives' fathers (down) and in-laws (across), by category	1+2	3,4,5	6+7	8	9	11	10+12
1+2 Higher managers and professionals	1	1		1			
3,4,5 Lower managers and professionals, clerical and sales		0	1	1	1		
6+7 Skilled workers		2	4	1			1
8 Farmers and fishermen	1	1		70	1		15
9 Lower-skilled workers			1	1	2		
11 Unskilled workers						0	
10+12 Farm workers				6	6		14

heirs and their spouses generally married men and women of similar socio-professional backgrounds. These homogamous marriage practices ensured continuity of property transmission (single inheritance) and family traditions, as well as stable social mobility for heirs, heiresses and their spouses in their rural environment.

Many children from landless families (categories 9 to 12) also married within their own socio-professional group. These men and women, whose parents were landless farmers, landless artisan farmers or landless artisans, married individuals whose parents had the same socio-professional backgrounds (see Tables 5 to 9).[22] They were engaged in the same profession as their parents and enjoyed the same status in their village of birth or nearby. Through these homogamous marriages they were assured of mutual help and family assistance in the environment they grew up in. We may thus conclude that marriage strategies among Basque rural families, whether propertied or landless, remained homogamous for the large majority of their descendants throughout the nineteenth century, and that couples experienced stable intragenerational and intergenerational social mobility.

could be comfortably settled and would not demand their equal share of the inheritance (this would have forced the estate to be partitioned). In this manner, the heir or heiress inherited the entire property, and one or two siblings generally received compensation for their share of the inheritance upon leaving the family house (generally in their youth, before their parents' death); this compensation they then used to marry into a propertied family or to emigrate to cities or overseas. The others remained single (at home or in the village, in towns or cities), never daring to force a partition of the estate to obtain their legal shares. All, however, enjoyed family solidarity. To survive, the system sometimes required family cohesion and individual self-denial.

22. Unlike propertied families, landless families rarely lived as stem families. Their rented farms were too small to house and occupy extended families. They often lived close to one another (as neighbours), but as nuclear families. Hence Peter Laslett's conclusions on the high frequency of simple households since the modern era.

When comparing the behaviour of men and women, however, we observe some gender differences. It appears that among the men and women of the second-generation cohort particularly, women had greater difficulty marrying within their socio-professional group (see Tables 3 and 4, p. 101). Though women from propertied families inherited the family's assets more often than men, or married heirs within their own socio-professional group, and women from landless families generally married landless men originating from landless families, homogamy was less prevalent among women than among men. Why? Why did more women marry men whose parents had different socio-professional backgrounds? Did women's parents have a higher or lower status than their in-laws? The analysis of marrying upward and downward will perhaps explain gender differences in migration destinies.

MARRYING INTO FAMILIES OF HIGHER STATUS (UPWARD MARRIAGES)

The data indicate that some men and women in the sample did indeed marry outside their socio-professional group, yet few among the first-, second-, and third-generation cohorts married men or women whose parents enjoyed a higher status than their own parents. Furthermore, in the course of the century it became difficult for women to marry into higher-status families. The data clearly show that, proportionally and over time, both men and women had less chance of marrying a person from a wealthier background: the figure for women was 18.1 per cent in the early nineteenth century (first-generation cohort), 20.6 per cent in the mid-nineteenth century (second-generation cohort), and 13.6 per cent in the late nineteenth century (third-generation cohort); for men it was 16.2 per cent, 14.3 per cent, and 14.4 per cent respectively (first-, second-, and third-generation cohorts) (see Tables 3 and 4). Why did women experience greater difficulty in marrying upward than men?

The men who were able to marry into a wealthier family were the sons of propertied farmers, artisan farmers or artisans (categories 7 and 8) who, through hard work and thrift, married the heiresses of these wealthier families (see Tables 5 to 9). Capable of amassing large savings, especially after a few years spent in America, they also amassed a sizeable dowry which allowed them to marry into a wealthier propertied family and move up the social ladder. Some men married the non-inheriting daughters of these wealthier families, before emigrating to America or purchasing a property locally. Though these cases were very few, it seemed easier for hard-working men to marry upward than for hard-working women, men being able to save a greater amount of money than women and being in a better position to bargain their way into a wealthier family.

By contrast, the daughters of propertied families (categories 7 and 8) experienced greater difficulty in marrying into wealthier families in the second half of the nineteenth century (third-generation cohort) because the job market and their lower level of education made it more difficult for them to find good jobs, to save a large amount of money, to amass a larger dowry than the *préciput* share, and to marry heirs of wealthier propertied families. As a result, some emigrated to cities, where they sometimes married into wealthier families – their husbands being merchants, professionals, or civil servants (higher or lower ones) (categories 1 to 5). These women were very few in number though, and became even fewer in the second half of the century (see Table 4, p. 101). Marriage opportunities were definitely not so favourable for women as for men.

Many men from less affluent backgrounds, whose parents were landless farmers, artisan farmers, artisans, or even unskilled workers (farmhands or artisan workers), (categories 9 to 12) could also improve their life and status through hard work and thrift, using their savings as dowries to marry into local propertied families (categories 7 and 8). They became farmers, artisan farmers, or artisans, all owning a house with a small or modest property in the course of their lives. By contrast, women from poorer backgrounds (daughters of landless families) could hardly ever marry upward into wealthier families in their rural environment because, as was the case for the daughters of propertied families, the job market and their lower level of education left them with no access to better-paid jobs. Consequently, they could not save enough to amass a dowry and marry a propertied man. The only instances when they could marry into a propertied family were if a widower remarried, when the heir's wife or the heiress of a farm or business died young. They then assumed the responsibilities of the late wife or heiress, taking care of the husband's young children (their stepchildren) until the next succession. In no other situation could the daughters of landless families marry upward.

The data conclusively indicate that the men in the sample were more conservative than the women, since the men remained more attached than the women to land, property ownership, and to rural life in the Basque country or in America. They saw marriage as a means of preserving or improving their lifestyles in their rural environment or abroad, and of ensuring the continuity of their traditional family practices.[23] The women, by contrast, seemed more emancipated, attached to status and property ownership, but far less to farm life and to their rural environment. When they could not marry into their socio-professional group, they sacrificed their lifestyles and environment to live more comfortable lives in cities,

23. Men valued their rural environment and their lifestyles as propertied farmers or medium-skilled workers. When they could not secure such a lifestyle in their rural environment, they emigrated to America, where they believed they had a greater chance of improving their lives than in cities, and where they could reproduce their family's lifestyle. For comparison, see Lorenzetti, Head-König, and Goy, *Marchés, migrations et logiques familiales*.

perhaps with men from higher social backgrounds, and in the process they were forced to break their ties with the family environment and with family traditions and practices.[24] As the following will show, explanations for the different marriage strategies of men and women will emerge more strikingly from the analysis of downward marriages. As a result of these observations, it will soon become clear that marriage opportunities had a great impact on the decisions of men and women in relation to rural, urban, or overseas migration.

MARRYING INTO FAMILIES OF LOWER STATUS (DOWNWARD MARRIAGES)

Through the century, many of the men and women of the second- and third-generation cohorts did marry into lower-status families (see Tables 3 and 4). These were particularly the granddaughters of the 120 couples; the parents of these granddaughters were higher or lower professionals, managers, or civil servants (categories 1 and 5) who had returned to agricultural labour or craft professions as property owners. They had married men and women from lower social backgrounds, especially the heirs or heiresses of propertied farmers, artisan farmers or artisans (categories 7 and 8), or landless artisans (category 9) (see Table 9, p. 104). However, these individuals were very few. They seemed to value rural life and their ancestral family environment more than status and social mobility.

Women who married men of lower status were sometimes heiresses whose parents valued the importance of the dowry rather than status. These families therefore preferred their heiresses to marry hardworking, thrifty men who, though from a lower social background, could amass a sizeable dowry and bring it into the marriage. As many non-inheriting sons often emigrated to America, the family seemed to resort to marrying off their heiresses to men from lower social backgrounds, men who brought a cash dowry into the house and showed submission.

The large majority of those who married down, however, were the non-inheriting children of propertied farmers, propertied artisan farmers or propertied artisans (categories 7 and 8), especially women who, among their numerous siblings, did not inherit a sufficient share of the inheritance (less than 25 per cent of the family's assets) and who therefore did not manage to marry into a propertied farming or artisan family of equal social status. They were individuals who were engaged in the professional activities of their parents as farmers, artisan farmers, or artisans, yet were

24. Recent comparative works on migration are numerous. See particularly Frans van Poppel, Michel Oris, and James Lee (eds), *The Road to Independence: Leaving Home in Western and Eastern Societies, 16th–20th centuries* (Berne, 2004).

unable to own the land they worked on or the business in which they worked. Most of them therefore became very small propertied or landless farmers, artisan farmers or artisans, and married landless sons and daughters of lower status. Thus, their marriages were downward not necessarily as a result of their different professional activities (parents and in-laws actually engaged in the same professions), but instead due to the lower social status of their in-laws as landless farmers, artisan farmers, or artisans in the community or nearby.

When comparing the marriage strategies of men and women, however, we observe that in the course of the century more women, especially heiresses and non-inheriting daughters from propertied families, married outside their social group and with men of lower status. They made up the large majority of those who accepted downward marriages, the men often preferring emigration to America instead. They were heiresses who married men of lower status – the sons of landless farmers, artisan farmers, and artisans who through hard work and thrift amassed sizable dowries. They were also non-inheriting daughters of propertied families who received small dowries (if at all), too small to marry heirs (even minor ones) and who refused to emigrate to America with their brothers. In that case, they opted for marriages with landless farmers or lower-skilled artisan workers, who might have been engaged in the same profession as their parents but who originated from families of lower social status, managing sometimes to acquire property in the course of their lives but not to the point of reaching their parents' status. All cases considered, it appears that on average 17.5 per cent of Basque women married downward in the nineteenth century (compared with 15 per cent of men).

The data thus indicate that in the course of the century there were indeed inequalities between the marital strategies of men and women, men generally marrying within their socio-professional group or upward while women more often married within their socio-professional group or downward (see Tables 3 and 4, p. 101). In an attempt to avoid downward marriages and downward social mobility, the sons of propertied families emigrated to America and daughters to cities. When emigrating to America, they generally maintained or improved their lives, some having more traditional behaviour as they lived in a familiar, rural environment which siblings and/or uncles had reconstituted, reproducing the family's lifestyle and practices. When settling in cities, women opted for emancipation, preferring to marry civil servants in cities, men of higher social status from elsewhere in France who offered them better lives, but away from their rural environment.[25] In the

---

25. Pierre Bourdieu also argued that women were more emancipated than men, adopting modern attitudes more rapidly than men in their quest for a better and easier life, especially in towns or cities; Pierre Bourdieu, *Le bal des célibataires. Crise de la société paysanne en Béarn* (Paris, 2002).

process, these women accepted having to break with their family, traditions, and practices.[26]

Most sons and daughters of landless families married men or women within their own socio-professional group and were engaged in the same professions as their parents and in-laws. They consequently maintained their status as farmers, artisan farmers, or artisan workers, renting a house and land. While the great majority of these men and women thus experienced stable social mobility, a few married upward, especially men who married heiresses, and others married downward, especially women who married sons of unskilled workers or farmhands. These men and women, however, were few. As the following will show, the sons and daughters of landless families had a greater chance of marrying homogamously or upwardly than the sons and daughters of propertied families. How did marriage patterns affect migration patterns within propertied and landless families?

HETEROGAMY AS AN EXPLANATION FOR EMIGRATION

The quantitative analysis of the data yielded rich findings and was helpful statistically to draw important conclusions on Basque marriage strategies in the nineteenth century. But a combined analysis of the computerized quantitative data with the qualitative observation of the genealogies will lead to an even more refined argumentation and further inferences. The conclusions will here draw our attention to the significance of marriage strategies in securing ancient single-inheritance practices. They will also give a more complete picture of the mechanisms which led men and women within the same family to have different marriage strategies. Finally, they will explain why men from all social backgrounds married upward more often than women, and what implications these situations had for migration, from a family perspective. The conclusions will differ depending on the socio-economic background of the families. We will consider propertied families first, and then non-propertied families.

The data and the genealogies clearly highlight the fact that as family size grew in the course of the nineteenth century it became more difficult for Basque *propertied families* (farmers, artisan farmers, artisans) to secure homogamous marriages and socio-economic stability for all of their children. They had no problem settling two or three of their children, marrying them off within their own social group – one as the heir or heiress of the family house or business, marrying the non-inheriting child of a propertied family, and one or two marrying heirs or heiresses. It was

26. For a comparative study on family in the age of urbanization, see Gérard Bouchard and Joseph Goy (eds), *Famille, économie et société rurale en contexte d'urbanisation (XVIIe–XXe siècles)* (Paris, 1990).

impossible, however, to settle all the children comfortably, especially when there were more than three; hence the high celibacy rate among the children of these families, men and women equally (19.7 per cent among the second-generation cohort and 19 per cent among the third-generation cohort).

To avoid treating sons and daughters unequally and discriminating against daughters with regard to marriage and inheritance, propertied families often selected their daughters as heiresses or married them into propertied families.[27] Women were considered suitable successors to and transmitters of traditions and property, even if they had brothers (whether older or younger). They were perhaps more submissive and more flexible, sometimes accepting undesirable conditions which their brothers refused; they might well, for instance, be prepared to marry the sons of landless farmers, artisan farmers, or artisans who had saved a lot of money.

Despite the favourable treatment of propertied families towards women, men had a greater chance of marrying within their socio-professional group or upward and of experiencing stable or upward social mobility. They sometimes preferred to receive a dowry which, added to their personal savings (from America sometimes), allowed them to marry upward into wealthier propertied families, and sometimes of becoming co-owners of a larger property. Indeed, whenever possible, men (even first-born sons) relinquished their inheritance rights as potential heirs, marrying the heiresses of richer families (farmers or artisan farmers), using their dowries to purchase the shares of the inheritance of the siblings of the heiress and thus gain power and respectability within the wealthier houses of their in-laws. When this option was not available, they instead emigrated to America, where they generally fared well as unmarried men. They thus enjoyed greater freedom of choice and movement than women, avoiding homogamous marriages at home under their parents' authority, as well as downward marriages into the lower-status families of landless farmers, artisan farmers, or artisans.

Non-inheriting children seemed to opt for celibacy rather than down-ward marriages, for three main reasons: because they could not engage in the same activity as their parents, in the same familiar environment; because they could not marry within their own socio-professional group; and because marriage did not guarantee them the same social status as that of their parents. At times, women from propertied families accepted marrying down and out of their parents' social group; but men did so more rarely. Indeed, the data indicate that among the second- and third-

---

27. This was also the case in other parts of the Pyrenees: in Béarn, as Jacques Poumarède and Christine Lacanette-Pommel have noted; in the Baronnies, as Rolande Bonnain has shown; and in Esparros, as Antoinette Fauve-Chamoux has explained. On the matter of inheritance strategies in a comparative perspective see Fauve-Chamoux and Ochiai, *Maison et famille souche.*

generation cohorts nineteen and seventeen daughters respectively from propertied families married downward, their in-laws enjoying a lower social status than their parents – being engaged in the same professions, but as landless farmers, artisan farmers or artisans (see Tables 7 and 9). By contrast, the same was true of only five propertied families' second-generation sons and six propertied families' third-generation sons (see Tables 6 and 8).

Men definitely refused downward marriages. Instead, they remained single in the village or emigrated to America where, as early as the mid-nineteenth century, they were engaged in either the same professions as their parents or better (as propertied cattle raisers, farmers, artisans, or professionals), often refusing marriage altogether in order to be able to return to their village of birth on retirement. Conversely, women did not emigrate in such frequent numbers, nor so early on in the century. If they could not inherit the family property or marry into a propertied family, they had two options it seems: downward marriage in their familiar rural environment, or celibacy in the village or nearby, in towns, or in cities. Only in the second half of the century did many of them envision exogamous marriages with men originating from wealthier families in cities, or homogamous marriages, perhaps before departing overseas.

Consequently, a great number of men were bound to marry into wealthier families than their sisters, and few married into lower-status families. Rather than accept downward marriages, they emigrated to America. Women for their part had fewer options available. If they could not inherit or marry into a propertied family of equal status (homogamous marriages with stable social mobility), which a great number of them did, their best chance to marry upward was by marrying the son of a higher or lower professional, of a manager or a civil servant in local towns or in cities. Emigration to America was a safe destination for the daughters of propertied families when they married men within their own social group before departure, each receiving a dowry to finance their fare to America and their settlement. They were, however, reluctant to settle in America permanently, perhaps because they considered life in La Pampa (Argentina) for example to be too hard and insecure. Clearly, marriage opportunities in the Basque country were not so favourable for women. This perhaps explains the higher celibacy rate of women throughout the century; celibacy was the only way to avoid downward marriage in the village or nearby, or homogamous marriages as housewives in America.

The sons and daughters of propertied families sometimes avoided marriage altogether in order to maintain their rights over the family assets, having the option of living and dying or returning to the family house on retirement. As they generally received no compensation for their shares of the inheritance before their departure from the family house, they remained co-owners of the family assets, maintaining in the process their status in the village as the sons and daughters of property owners. Before they died, they would donate their shares of the inheritance to the heir or heiress of the house.[28] Heirs or heiresses appreciated the sacrifice of their unmarried siblings because it meant that they need not provide additional dowries for them. In this manner, the family house and land remained intact through the century and was transmitted undivided to the next generation, despite the egalitarian laws of the Civil Code.

To illustrate the above arguments in relation to the marriage strategies of propertied families, we will use the example of the M. family from Sare (see family tree: case study 1). Martin M. and Magdeleine from Sare (first-generation cohort) married in 1802. Magdeleine inherited the 17-hectare property from her parents and Martin (the son of a propertied family who owned 12 hectares) brought a 1,000-franc dowry into the marriage. Their marriage was homogamous, both Martin and Magdeleine originating from the same village and marrying within their socio-professional group. Further, both were engaged in the same profession as their respective parents, and enjoyed the same status as those parents. As the family was relatively small, the couple managed to settle all three children equally comfortably, within their social group but sometimes outside their professional environment (second-generation cohort). However, all of them experienced stable social mobility during their lives.

Jean, the first-born son (second-generation cohort), inherited the family assets (the house and 12 hectares of land) when, in 1830, he married Marie D., born in Sare and the daughter of a propertied farmer who owned a house and 9 hectares of land. Marie brought a dowry of 1,000 francs to compensate at least one of Jean's siblings. Like their respective parents, Jean and Marie married within their socio-professional group, their marriage being as homogamous as their parents'. Jean-Etienne, the second-born son, was compensated for his share of the inheritance when, in 1854, he married Marianne B., born in Sare and the daughter of a local propertied farmer. After their marriage, they emigrated to America. Like their parents, they married within their socio-professional group (homo-gamy), but they had different destinies in America. Marie, the third-born daughter, was also compensated upon her marriage, in 1844, to Jean-Baptiste D., an urban propertied shoemaker, the son of a propertied shoemaker from the city of Bayonne. They too later emigrated to America.

---

28. This right was termed the "droit de chaise". It was derived from ancient family rights and, according to pre-revolutionary customs, entitled all unmarried siblings, men or women, who did not receive a dowry, to live and die in the family house. Though deprived of compensation which would otherwise have enabled them to marry decently into a propertied family, these men and women could enjoy a decent life with the heir or heiress until death. This was a way to avoid providing additional dowries which might burden the family financially, to limit land partition, and, consequently, to maintain the family assets (the house system, earlier explained) intact from one generation to the next, despite the egalitarian laws of the Civil Code.

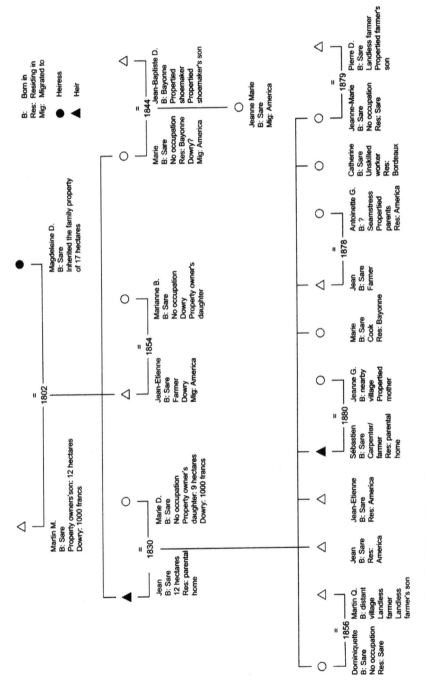

Figure 2. Case study 1: the M. Family from Sare.

Marie's marriage was not particularly homogamous, unlike her brother's. Though she married within the social environment of her parents, she did not marry within their professional environment.

One may conclude that as a result of this moderate family size the children were able to marry into propertied families (farmers, artisan farmers or artisans), each child receiving a decent dowry (worth 25 per cent of the family's assets), enough to marry a person of equal social status (homogamy). Though the three children had different destinies in the village (for Jean), in America (for Jean-Etienne), and in the city of Bayonne and later in America (for Marie), they all enjoyed the same social status as their parents.

In the next generation (third-generation cohort), marriage strategies evolved considerably as a result of Jean's larger family. Indeed, Jean (the first-born son above) had eight children. Given the large number of children to settle, it was difficult to marry off all eight of them comfortably. While in the previous generation, each child received a dowry worth 25 per cent of the assets (enough to marry within their socio-professional group), Jean's children were each legally entitled to just 9.4 per cent of the assets, which was not enough to marry within their social group.

Following our earlier arguments on large families, this third-generation case study will demonstrate that the men did indeed do better than the women, Jean's sons marrying into propertied families (Sébastien, his fourth-born son, and Jean, his sixth-born son) or emigrating to America (Jean, his second-born son, and Jean-Etienne, his third-born son), probably to avoid downward marriages, while his daughters sometimes married into lower-status families – Dominiquette (his first-born daughter) for instance married a landless farmer's son (Martin Q., from a distant village). The marriage of Jeanne-Marie (Jean's eighth-born daughter) was as homogamous, though, as her brothers' because she married the son (Pierre D. from Sare) of a propertied farmer. Nonetheless, she experienced downward social mobility since her husband became a landless farmer. The other daughters finally remained single in cities, probably to avoid downward marriages.

Thus, among Jean's four married children, three (one son and two daughters) married within the family's socio-professional group, and one (a daughter) married downward. Though homogamy remained prevalent, it did not secure stable social mobility – two of Jean's married daughters (Dominiquette and Jeanne-Marie) experiencing downward social mobility, their husbands being landless farmers. These marriage strategies, however, allowed them to settle in the village, in their familiar rural environment, avoiding celibacy and emigration. It was probably to avoid downward marriages and downward social mobility or because they were unable to make homogamous marriages with the sons of propertied families at home that Jean's two unmarried daughters (Marie and Catherine) probably migrated to the regional cities of Bayonne and Bordeaux respectively, where they died unmarried.

The only one to make a homogamous marriage and to enjoy stable social mobility was the heir, Sébastien, Jean's fourth-born son, who married the daughter of a propertied family and inherited the family property, enjoying the same status as his parents and in-laws. It was probably a privilege for him to inherit, yet he had to wait until 1880 before he could marry, by which time all his siblings had married and departed. His brothers, though, refused to marry either late or downward (probably for various reasons). They, therefore, accepted modest compensation in advance of their succession in order to emigrate to America as single men (as Jean, the second-born son, and Jean-Etienne, the third-born son, did) or as married men: Jean, the sixth-born son, married within his parents' socio-professional group (a homogamous marriage) before departing. In the case of large families, it was more difficult for parents to marry each child into a propertied family and to secure for them stable social mobility. Women seemed to pay the price for this, more of them either accepting downward marriages and experiencing downward social mobility or resorting to celibacy.

This case study clearly shows that, in the matter of marriage strategies and social mobility, women did not do so well as their brothers. Some opted for downward marriage strategies, marrying men of lower socio-professional backgrounds and enjoying a lower status in order to settle in their familiar rural environment. Others, though, opted for celibacy, refusing downward marriages and downward social mobility. Thanks to their sacrifice, single inheritance and the full transmission of the house and land to one child prevailed and family lineage and succession were thus secured.

Paradoxically, conditions with regard to marriage strategies were sometimes better for *sharecroppers' children*, especially men. The historiography argues that these families were so poor and the economic possibilities so limited that they could not survive in the village and therefore had to emigrate in order to secure themselves a decent life. This explains why, according to some historians, emigration affected the lower strata of rural society more than the higher strata. Yet the data on Basque families in the nineteenth century show a different picture. The great majority of the children of landless farmers, artisan farmers, and artisans managed to settle in their village of birth or nearby. They were very mobile, but only locally, moving perhaps within a few miles of their village of birth, where most of their relatives lived as well. It was a strategy to secure mutual assistance and family solidarity.

One may argue that they were too poor to afford emigration and that they lived within a familiar professional and geographical environment out of necessity and survival. They actually had new opportunities, especially the men. Their massive, permanent emigration took place only late in the century and they did not seem to be attracted to cities at all, but to America instead. We did locate some of them in local towns (towns near their village of birth), but hardly any in distant coastal towns and regional cities. Why did so many of them decide to settle in the rural environment, even after emigration agents had begun recruiting potential candidates for overseas settlement in 1860? And what were their marriage strategies and their destinies?

While some may argue that the majority of the sons and daughters of landless farmers, artisan farmers, and artisans had survival behaviours, all marrying within their familiar environment, their professional network, and their social group, the data sometimes provide material for a different interpretation. The large majority of them did indeed have homogamous behaviour as they married within their socio-professional group: men and women whose parents were engaged in the same professions and enjoyed the same status. Yet some had new possibilities for upward marriage and upward social mobility in their familiar rural environment. Most of them were men who filled the positions left behind by the sons of propertied families who did not inherit in order to marry an heiress, or emigrate to America, or remained single instead. Indeed, the sons of many propertied families relinquished their inheritance rights as heirs to marry out or upward, or else emigrate to America.

As a consequence, propertied families sometimes had difficulty finding sons-in-law within their social group in the village or nearby. As a replacement, they welcomed the sons of landless families into their house, men who were submissive, hardworking, and thrifty, capable of saving large sums of money and therefore of bringing a decent cash dowry into the marriage. The sons of these landless families (whether they were farmers, artisan farmers, or artisans) thus successfully married into propertied families. They avoided cities or emigration to America, not so much because they were too poor, but because they sometimes had an opportunity to improve their lives through upward marriages with heiresses in the village or nearby, or as propertied artisans. Only in the latter part of the century did they emigrate to America, emigration agents largely contributing to their massive departure by offering employment opportunities with a greater chance of upward social mobility than in the village. There were then fewer sons and daughters from landless families to marry in their villages or nearby.

Conversely, the daughters of landless families, who had difficulty amassing a dowry despite hard work and saving, hardly ever married upward in the village or nearby. They generally maintained their status by marrying the sons of landless farmers, artisan farmers, or artisans. These homogamous marriage strategies were vital, however, for their survival.

They rarely remained single, celibacy only securing them an even poorer and more insecure life as unskilled workers (servants) and therefore downward social mobility at mere subsistence levels. The conditions for women from landless families were therefore very hard, harder than for the men of their social group and also harder than for the women of higher social groups. For women from landless families, marriage was vital if they were to live a life above subsistence level.

A few women, however, improved their lot through upward marriage, occasionally marrying into propertied families, but only to widowers in order to take care of their husbands' underage children until the succession of the next generation. As time went by, though, the number of daughters of landless families available for marriage within their socio-professional group in their village of birth or nearby became fewer. Instead, they reverted to massive overseas emigration in the latter part of the century, especially as families, appealing to emigration agents to reunify them with their families and hopefully secure upward social mobility for them in America.

To illustrate the above arguments in relation to the marriage strategies of landless families, we shall look at the U. family from Aldudes (see family tree: case study 2, overleaf). Jean U and Marthe (first-generation cohort) married in Aldudes, their village of birth, in 1808. Both married within their social group (homogamy), their parents enjoying a higher status as propertied farmers. As the young couple had an illegitimate child, they were not entitled to inherit. As a consequence, they became landless farmers in Aldudes and experienced downward social mobility. Like their respective parents, they were farmers in the village, yet enjoyed a lower social status. Together, they had six surviving children, all born in Aldudes (second-generation cohort). As a result of their marriage strategies and the assistance of their families, none of them married downward and none of them experienced downward social mobility. They married within their own social group (homogamy) (marrying the sons or daughters of landless families) or upward (marrying the sons or daughters of propertied families). In the process, they either maintained their status as landless farmers, artisan farmers, or artisans in the village or nearby, or actually improved it as propertied farmers, artisan farmers, or artisans.

Guillaume, the first-born illegitimate son, experienced upward social mobility since he became a professional soldier in Bayonne, the regional capital. However, as a result of his illegitimacy perhaps, he remained single. Jean, the second-born son, married into two local landless families in the village since he married, successively, two sharecroppers' daughters, Catherine O. and Jeanne P., in 1852 and 1860 respectively. Finally, in 1859, Michel, Jean's sixth-born son, married Jeanne I., the daughter of a propertied farmer from Aldudes. His marriage was upward. He later experienced upward social mobility, settling as a property owner in the

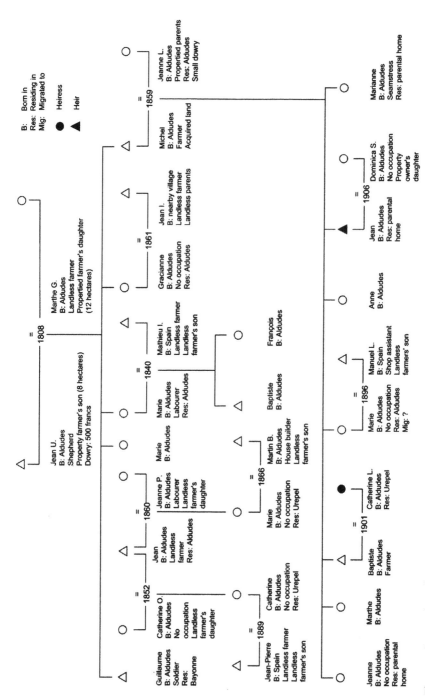

Figure 3. Case study 2: the U. Family from Aldudes.

village. Hence, the men of this family did relatively well, marrying within their social group or upward, and maintaining or improving their livelihood.

The women of the family, by contrast, did not do so well, all marrying sons of landless farmers. They thus maintained their status but did not improve it. No information was found on Marie, Jean's third-born daughter. However, Marie, his fourth-born daughter, married Mathieu I., the son of a landless farmer from Spain, in the village in 1840. Their marriage strategy was homogamous as both were born into landless families, were engaged in the same profession as their respective parents (as farmers), and enjoyed the same status (as a landless couple). Finally, the experience of Gracianne, the fifth-born daughter, was similar. In 1861 she married Jean I., the son of a landless farmer, born in a neighbouring village. Both married into families with the same socio-professional background, and both experienced stable social mobility. This landless family obviously had priorities: to settle their daughters within their socio-professional environment and help them to maintain their status and lifestyle as landless farmers in the village or nearby so that, through family solidarity, they did not experience downward social mobility and poverty.

In the next generation, Jean and Marthe's grandchildren (third-generation cohort) did exactly the same, especially the granddaughters. Indeed, Jean (Jean's second-born son above), a landless farmer, had two daughters. Catherine, his first-born daughter (from his first marriage), married the son of a landless farmer in 1889; Marie, his second-born daughter (from his second marriage), married a landless artisan worker (a house builder) in 1866; he himself was the son of a landless farmer. Both daughters married within their social group (homogamy). Yet Marie (the second-born daughter) had a different destiny, her husband being engaged in a different profession as a landless artisan. That was perhaps part of their strategy to maintain their lifestyle and their status in the village or nearby.

Michel (Jean's sixth-born son above), who had married into a wealthier family and acquired property using his savings and his wife's dowry, had seven surviving children. They had all been brought up as sons and daughters of property owners and probably wished to reproduce their father's marriage strategies, marrying into a propertied family and enjoying his status. Yet, as was typical of the marriage strategies of propertied families, men sometimes settled more comfortably than women. Indeed, while the men did as well as their parents, marrying into propertied families and enjoying the same status, women sometimes married downward, marrying men from landless families. Some therefore experienced downward social mobility. Michel's first-born and seventh-born daughters, Jeanne and Marianne, remained single in the family house, probably to avoid downward marriages or emigration. No information was found on Marthe and Anne, the second-born and fifth-born daughters respectively. However, the two sons did quite well, as Baptiste, the third-born son, married Catherine L., an heiress, in 1901, and Jean, the sixth-born son, inherited the family assets when he married Dominica S., the daughter of a propertied farmer, in 1906. The latter had to marry late though, after his siblings had married and departed from the house.

Clearly, it was difficult being one of the numerous daughters of a propertied family, as they had a much greater likelihood of marrying downward and of experiencing downward social mobility than the daughters of landless families and men in general. Hence their preference for remaining celibate in the village, in the town, or in cities, or for emigrating. They perhaps opted for celibacy as a strategy to avoid a hard life as the wives of landless farmers or landless artisans, with no authority, no decision-making power, and, more importantly, no ownership power. Celibacy did not secure better living conditions and social status, but it did enable the daughters to maintain their family ties and status as the daughters of propertied families, and to maintain their freedom of movement, with the possibility of retiring in the village and perhaps in their family home, and later to donate their shares of the inheritance to the house's single heir. By contrast, celibacy was an option which the daughters of landless families did not consider.

CONCLUSION

Marriage strategies generally aimed at ensuring that men and women married within the family's socio-professional group and enjoyed the same status as their parents, avoiding downward social mobility whenever possible. However, marriage was also used more generally as a strategy to perpetuate family traditions and maintain harmonious family relations. The priority of propertied families was to transmit their property to one child from one generation to the next. They therefore had to make great efforts to settle all their children comfortably, especially when they had a large family. They made sure that the unequal treatment of children did not lead to family strife and forced partition. One may therefore argue that marriage strategies within propertied families aimed at securing ancient practices of single inheritance and at keeping family property intact, so that the family's roots and lineage could survive over time. For landless families marriage was also vital for survival. The large majority married within their socio-professional group, settled within fifteen miles, and avoided celibacy and cities whenever possible. The data and family reconstitutions clearly indicate that landless families were more successful than propertied families in ensuring their children married either within their socio-professional group or upward.

While the great majority of the men and women in the three cohorts managed, no matter their social and professional background, to reproduce their parents' behaviour through the nineteenth century, marrying within their socio-professional group (homogamy), engaging in the same profession, and enjoying the same status as their parents, children from propertied families, especially daughters, were increasingly unable to reproduce these patterns, and were forced to marry into landless families, becoming landless farmers, artisan farmers, or artisans in the village or nearby. A few – mostly men – did marry into wealthier families with similar professional backgrounds in the village. As a result, it was the daughters of propertied families who, in the course of the century, married into lower-status families and experienced downward social mobility; the daughters of landless families did better than the daughters of propertied families as they generally contracted homogamous marriages. Men, however, no matter their social background (propertied or landless), were more likely to do better than their sisters, entering into homogamous or upward marriages or remaining celibate and/or emigrating.

The economic situation of the rural Basque country was certainly not so favourable for the non-inheriting sons and daughters of propertied families, who were able to maintain their status through homogamous marriages, as heirs or heiresses, marrying non-inheriting sons or daughters, or as the spouses of heirs or heiresses, engaged in the same profession as their parents and enjoying the same status. Few acquired new properties, as land was scarce. Over time, fewer remained single at home. However, in all other cases men and women (mostly women in the village or nearby) married into lower-status families and experienced downward social mobility. Thus, when homogamy was impossible, and to avoid downward marriages, the sons and daughters of propertied families emigrated to America (in the case of men) or to cities (in the case of women), where they settled, married within their own socio-professional group or higher, or remained single.

Landless families had different marriage strategies. Not only were there great differences in marriage strategies between men and women, their marriage strategies and their destinies also differed from those of proper-tied families. The sons and daughters of landless families were highly mobile, but only locally, within a small territory (within a fifteen-mile radius of their village of birth), and they reproduced the homogamous marriage strategies of their parents. As the sons of propertied families emigrated to America, or used their savings to marry into wealthier families, they created scope for others to assume the responsibilities of the family business or farm, most notably their sisters, who inherited the family business and sometimes married the hardworking and thrifty sons of landless families; these sons became spouses to these heiresses and improved their status through marriage. The daughters of landless families, like the daughters of propertied families, had difficulty securing a decent lifestyle and status for themselves through marriage. They avoided celibacy and cities though, making efforts to marry the sons of landless farmers. They occasionally moved to local towns in order to secure a decent marriage. They used similar marriage strategies there, marrying the sons of landless farmers, artisan farmers, or artisans.

In the first half of the century America was not so much an option for the sons and daughters of landless families because they could not afford the passage and probably feared failing (with no possibility of returning home). In the second half of the century, however, many envisioned that destination, as single men or as families, with the help of emigration agents who recruited massive numbers of Basque emigrants in the countryside and organized their passage safely across the Atlantic.

To conclude, our study of marriage strategies among Basque propertied and landless families in the nineteenth century has highlighted the concern of all these families to ensure their children married within their socio-professional group or better. Men, however, no matter their background, were more successful in this than women. Our study has also provided a better understanding of the migration destinies of men and women as a strategy to maintain family ties, secure mutual assistance, and perpetuate single inheritance.

IRSH 50 (2005), Supplement, pp. 123–148 DOI: 10.1017/S00208590051r50s139
© 2005 Internationaal Instituut voor Sociale Geschiedenis

Homogamy in a Society Orientated towards Stability: A Micro-study of a South Tyrolean Market Town, 1700–1900

Margareth Lanzinger

SUMMARY: In the German-speaking areas of Habsburg Tyrol, investigated here, the aim of regional politicians and communal representatives was to perpetuate the status quo of ownership and social structure. The most important instruments for realizing that aim were policies on marriage and settlement. In addition, inheritance was based on male primogeniture, which supported a tendency for the sizes of property to remain stable. Throughout the region there was an attitude generally hostile to industry, so when, in the nineteenth century, branches of the crafts producing wares for translocal markets became unprofitable, industrialization offered no alternative. In those circumstances, marriage can be regarded as practically a privilege. Does that relativize or augment the consideration of homogamy? It seems both cases are possible: slight tendencies to socially downward marriage support the first assumption; the second appears to be supported by the various shifts in marriage habits – reactions to changed social positions – among the most important groups over the course of the nineteenth century.

The choice of partner affected not only the bride and groom but should be seen as part of a complex network of relationships. Differing interests and expectations of the families of origin or close relatives, as much as of the wider society, always play a role, and can influence the decision as to who might be considered a suitable bride or groom. Social status is an important factor in forming the cultural patterns that define the criteria and parameters determining who was considered the "right" groom and the "right" bride.[1] Great significance is generally ascribed to economic considerations. These comprise not only property, inheritance, dowry, and so on, but also involve labour power, relevant professional training, and work experience or socialization. Finally, a marriage can provide a foundation for new local or translocal alliances and networks, or it can

---

1. See for example Pat Hudson and Steven King, "Marriage in Two English Textile Manufacturing Townships in the Eighteenth Century", in Christophe Duhamelle and Jürgen Schlumbohm (eds), *Eheschließungen im Europa des 18. und 19. Jahrhunderts. Muster und Strategien* (Göttingen, 2003), pp. 157–188.

further develop and stabilize existing ones. Increasingly in recent years, greater attention and significance have been given to emotional components: economic calculations do not exclude the existence of emotional ties, and ideally both coincide. In particular, familiarity, acquaintance with the same social milieu with common experiences in childhood and youth, "emotional security" based on kinship, and socio-economic or neighbourly relationships have proved in some studies to be important motives and a basis for subsequent marriage.[2]

The choice of partner was not independent of a broader social context: in the specific region investigated here, which can be roughly described geographically as German-speaking areas of the eastern part of the Habsburg Tyrol,[3] the legal framework, ideas of political authority and its influence, and transformations in those ideas all affected the frequency of marriage, and sometimes quite significantly. The objective of the communal representatives and a substantial proportion of regional politicians was to perpetuate the status quo of ownership and social structures. The most important instruments for realizing that were, on one hand, marriage restrictions – the possibility of marriage in the region tended to be linked to property – and on the other hand, restrictive settlement policies, which primarily regulated and controlled the influx of men from outside and thereby the possibility of anyone's marrying into the community. It can be presumed that these restrictions were more rigidly enforced in the economically more attractive markets and in cities more than in villages.

As well as the regulation of migration and settlement, conditions of acceptance into various crafts or trades and the concomitant fees could delay or even prevent marriage,[4] or suggest the expediency of wedding a local citizen's daughter or a master's daughter or perhaps his widow. Inheritance laws and practice created different starting conditions and so different opportunities for marriage.[5] Framework conditions were created

2. *Ibid.*; Heide Wunder *et al.*, "Ehepaare, Eheverläufe und Lebenslauf in Leipzig 1580–1730. Bericht über ein Forschungsprojekt", in Katharina Midell (ed.), *Ehe, Alltag, Politik. Studien zu Frauengeschichte und Geschlechterverhältnissen der frühen Neuzeit bis zur Gegenwart* (Leipzig, 1993), pp. 13–32, 20.

3. At that time Tyrol included – with certain territorial alterations – North and East Tyrol, which are part of present-day Austria, and South Tyrol and Trentino in Italy. The administrative unit also included Vorarlberg, located westward in the direction of Switzerland, and which today is part of Austria.

4. See Anne-Lise Head-König, "Les politiques étatiques coercitives et leur influence sur la formation du mariage en Suisse au XVIIIe siècle", in Duhamelle and Schlumbohm, *Eheschließungen im Europa*, pp. 189–214.

5. There were other restrictions that will not be discussed in further detail here. The marriage prohibitions vehemently propagated by the Catholic Church throughout the nineteenth century also hampered marriage between persons of different confessions or religions and between persons related by blood or marriage – far beyond the marriage restrictions provided for in the

which affected who was permitted to marry at all. Choice of partner too was strongly "economicized" in this way.

The range of general and regional factors delineated here, which flowed into the realization of marriage plans and could either foster, delay or prevent them, is to be examined in detail in the following section dealing with the specific location of this study, and this socio-political context provides a basis for the evaluations in the second part of the article. The focus here is first on the significance of social homogamy, and then on the extent to which the internationally standardized classification system HISCLASS, here tested, is congruent with or deviates from local criteria for outlining the social structure in that location.

Despite some specific exceptions, marriage can here be regarded practically as a privilege – does that relativize or augment the consideration of homogamy? In this context several other questions need to be raised: How can social equality between bride and groom be defined and how can it be operationalized? Do the criteria for assessing social status change when observed over 200 years, from 1700 to 1900? In what follows, I shall be able to address only a few points of these fundamental questions. I will concentrate on the socio-political, socio-economic, and socio-cultural circumstances of partner selection based on a micro-study focusing on marriage in local and family contexts. The setting is Innichen/San Candido, today a market town in South Tyrol/northern Italy; and the period under review is 1700 to 1900.[6] Innichen's character has been shaped by crafts, trade, and agriculture, and in a regional comparison it evinces an above-average commercial density: in 1790 every tenth resident in the town was a craftsman or tradesman.[7]

SOCIO-POLITICAL, SOCIO-ECONOMIC, AND SOCIO-CULTURAL CONTEXTS

Briefly, communal politics in those two centuries was characterized by the endeavour to maintain existing social structures,[8] a guiding principle

1811 Civil Code (Allgemeines Bürgerliches Gesetzbuch, ABGB). The bishops responsible for the diocese of Brixen, the region being studied here, were intent on maintaining the Catholic unity of the country and attempted to block interconfessional marriages. In relation to marriages between relatives and in-laws, canon law, which until 1917 allowed dispensation up to the fourth degree, continued to be followed, so the reduction in the statutory dispensation to just the second degree, as specified in the ABGB, was ignored.

6. See Margareth Lanzinger, *Das gesicherte Erbe. Heirat in lokalen und familialen Kontexten, Innichen 1700–1900* (Vienna [etc.], 2003).

7. See Rosa Lanzinger, "Gewerbetopographie des Landesgerichtes Sillian im Zeitraum von 1720 bis 1860" (Ph.D., Innsbruck, 1980), pp. 47 ff.

8. See Jon Mathieu's argument for paying greater consideration to the political aspects of the organization of society: Jon Mathieu, "From Ecotypes to Sociotypes: Peasant Household and

carried forward by a broad middle class of mainly craftsmen and large farmers, and by the local elite. Prevailing with rigidity and through mechanisms of exclusion, this principle was supported at the same time by measures of social integration.[9]

Until the mid-nineteenth century, communal representatives controlled and regulated influx and settlement through the granting of the right of communal citizenship or the temporary acceptance of residents as so-called *Inwohner* (roughly speaking, "dwellers"). The community decided in each individual case who was permitted to settle in the town as a citizen and who could then marry. A relatively high citizenship fee had to be paid upon acceptance. As case reconstructions have shown, the community made the settlement of men from other places dependent, with very few exceptions, on their economic potential, professional abilities, and prospects in the town. In many cases, acceptance as a citizen and marriage took place within a very short period of time, or acceptance was preceded by the purchase of a house, which indicates that a pre-condition for acceptance, frequently through marriage, was integration into local social fields.

The communal right of citizenship mainly regulated the settlement of men and to that extent the gender-specific differences in marriage patterns in terms of local endogamy and exogamy are certainly to be viewed in the same context. By contrast, women could marry into the town without having to surmount comparable hurdles, not least financial ones. What is conspicuous – and under the framework conditions described can perhaps be regarded as a kind of compensation – was the increasing proportion of couples in which the man was from Innichen and the woman from a different town. In the second half of the nineteenth century that was true in 57.4 per cent of the marriages in the sample described in the next section.[10] The *Inwohner* were at an intermediate stage. They were accepted for one year at a time and had to pay an annual fee to the community for residence.

Property was considered a prerequisite for marriage, a custom given a legal basis in 1820 with the introduction of the political marriage consensus. Every couple intending to marry had to bring the parish priest confirmation from the community that they were in possession of sufficient property to support a family – otherwise they could not be

State-Building in the Alps, Sixteenth–Nineteenth Centuries", *The History of the Family*, 5 (2000), pp. 55–74.

9. Jobs providing community services – such as the nightwatchman – were assigned to economically weaker people. The allocation of assistance from the communal funds for the poor or wood for the needy, which was linked to the status of communal citizenship, can also be interpreted in this sense.

10. The high proportion of women who married into the community resulted in gaps in the documented personal data, especially in the eighteenth century; this also extended to the occupations of the fathers.

married. The political marriage consensus was primarily conceived as a measure against pauperism in cities like Vienna and Prague, although it was hardly possible to administer it there, and it met with rejection in many parts of the Habsburg monarchy, being treated as a purely formal act. However, in broad sections of regional and communal politics in German-speaking Tyrol it was readily accepted and applied more rigidly than originally intended, as is evident from appeals. It was abolished throughout the monarchy in 1868 – except in Salzburg, where it remained in effect until 1883, and in Tyrol, where it remained in effect until 1921 (in South Tyrol until 1923).[11] In Innichen, the limitation in the marriage consensus to "servants, apprentices, and day-labourers", who received alms, pursued no employment and led an unsteady life, was ignored, and the decision-making competence remained with the community rather than being transferred to the district authorities, as is evident from the minutes of the meetings of the community council.

This "restrictive policy" is evident in a number of other areas, which in general resulted in an astonishing stability: there was barely any change at all in the number of residents between the mid-eighteenth century and the mid-nineteenth century – and that at a time when the population doubled or even tripled in other places. In 1751 there were 1,090 inhabitants in the town and on the mountain put together; in 1850 there were 1,120, of whom 927 lived in the town.[12] The number of houses also remained constant, although some were divided into two or three. In 1799 there was a report in conjunction with a new assessment of the well tax claiming that 40 years had passed since the last tariff regulation and that there was one house more since then.[13] The number of houses mentioned there remained constant at 128 for several more decades (see Figure 1). House-building activity is first documented again during the period of railway construction after 1870.

This supports the concomitant tendency for the size of property to remain stable due to the law of male primogeniture, with the undivided

11. See Elisabeth Mantl, "Legal Restrictions on Marriage: Marriage and Inequality in the Austrian Tyrol during the Nineteenth Century", *The History of the Family*, 4 (1999), pp. 185–207; Elisabeth Mantl, *Heirat als Privileg. Obrigkeitliche Heiratsbeschränkungen in Tirol und Vorarlberg 1820–1920* (Vienna [etc.], 1997).

12. For 1751 see Hans Kramer, "Beiträge zur Geschichte des Landgerichtes Sillian in Osttirol von ungefähr 1750 bis 1850", *Carinthia I*, 152 (1962), pp. 27–59, 30; for 1850 see Stiftsarchiv [hereafter, STA] Innichen, Familienbuch 1829 – Einwohner vom Markte Innichen und auf dem Innichberge [hereafter, Familienbuch 1829], Appendix.

13. See Tiroler Landesarchiv Innsbruck [hereafter, TLA], Verfachbuch Innichen [hereafter, VBI] 1799, fo. 1234r. There is documentation relating to a conflict involving the building of this house at the end of the eighteenth century between the community and the prospective builder, a new resident; TLA, VBI 1777, fo. 330r; VBI 1781, fos 880r–881r. See also Margareth Lanzinger, "The House as Demographic Factor? Elements of a Marriage Pattern under the Auspices of Hindrance Policies", *Historical Social Research*, 28 (2003), pp. 58–75, 71 ff.

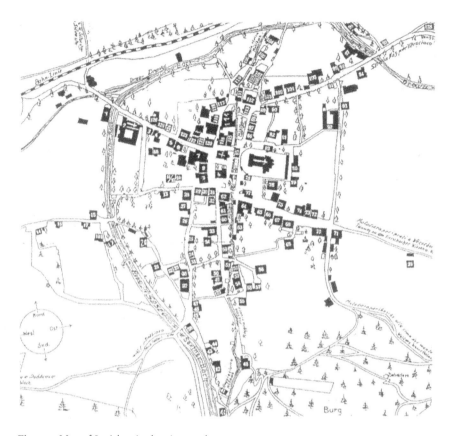

Figure 1. Map of Innichen in the nineteenth century.

transfer of property on succession.[14] Whereas in the eighteenth century a large degree of flexibility can be noted in the application of that model of property transfer, with younger brothers and even sisters frequently taking over property, a change was evident in the nineteenth century in the

14. The transition from the dominance of medium-sized and larger farms in the eastern Alpine region to the dominance of smaller farms in the western region runs right through what is today North Tyrol and South Tyrol. Whereas at the beginning of the nineteenth century the proportion of medium-sized and larger farms (10 hectares or more) ranged from over 40 per cent to 60 per cent in the eastern part of Tyrol (similar to the districts of Salzburg and Carinthia) – including the district of Lienz, with 58 per cent, to which Innichen belongs – the proportion of medium-sized and larger farms in the west – similar to Vorarlberg and Italian-speaking Trentino – was between just 1 per cent and 5 per cent. See *Ergebnisse der landwirtschaftlichen Betriebszählung vom 3. Juni 1902 in den im Reichsrate vertretenen Königreichen und Ländern, bearbeitet von dem Bureau der k.k. statistischen Zentralkommion* (Vienna, 1909), cited from Jon Mathieu, *Geschichte der Alpen 1500–1900. Umwelt, Entwicklung, Gesellschaft* (Vienna [etc.], 1998), Table A.5, pp. 214 ff.

direction of decreasing flexibility: in terms of property transfer within the family, in the nineteenth century the eldest son inherited significantly more often than in the eighteenth century.[15] Instead of a certain dynamic – the eldest son bought a different house, married an heiress, settled elsewhere – which allowed for more opportunities for younger siblings of either gender, there developed a relatively rigid and immobile system which more closely followed the normative model. At the same time, that model was more strongly orientated towards the male line. The thesis is that the property succession of the first-born male grew to be a kind of ideology in the course of the nineteenth century, becoming increasingly dominant and affecting actual inheritance practice.[16]

These manifestations of increasing rigidity can be explained by socio-economic changes, because overall changes in society in the nineteenth century did not stop at the threshold of the town. Due to changing markets and industrial competition, branches of crafts such as glove-making or linen weaving, producing particularly for translocal markets, became unprofitable; and new transport possibilities caused the carrying trade to dwindle. In the eighteenth century many people went to Vienna from Innichen as journeyman craftsmen – a distance of over 500 km – or settled somewhere in the Habsburg monarchy, in southern Germany or northern Italy. With industrialization and the end of journeyman wanderings, this reason for migration largely vanished. An attitude generally hostile to industry was predominant in the region of Innichen itself, so industrialization did not offer any alternatives.

The high proportion of unmarried people and the late age at first

---

15. Cf. the evaluation of a sample to compare the link between marriage and property in the sibling context for the years 1730–1750 and 1830–1850 in Lanzinger, *Das gesicherte Erbe*, pp. 242 ff.

16. Michaela Hohkamp and Jürgen Schlumbohm come to similar conclusions on this question. See Michaela Hohkamp, "Wer will erben? Überlegungen zur Erbpraxis in geschlechtsspezi-fischer Perspektive in der Herrschaft Triberg von 1654–1806", in Jan Peters (ed.), *Gutsherrschaft als soziales Modell. Vergleichende Betrachtungen zur Funktionsweise frühneuzeitlicher Agrar-gesellschaften* (Munich, 1995), pp. 327–341, 338; Jürgen Schlumbohm, *Lebensläufe, Familien, Höfe. Die Bauern und Heuerleute des Osnabrückischen Kirchspiels Belm in proto-industrieller Zeit, 1650–1860* (Göttingen, 1994), p. 391. For a different model see Marie-Pierre Arrizabalaga, "The Stem Family in the French Basque Country: Sare in the Nineteenth Century", *Journal of Family History*, 22 (1997), pp. 50–69, 54 ff., and also her article in this volume, pp. 93–122; Margareth Lanzinger, "Towards Predominating Primogeniture: Changes in the Inheritance Practices, Innichen/San Candido 1730–1930", in Hannes Grandits and Patrick Heady (eds), *Distinct Inheritances: Property, Family and Community in a Changing Europe* (Münster, 2003), pp. 125–144. A phenomenon in the convention of naming can also be seen parallel to this in the form of a stronger concentration on the father–son line: the most conspicuous change in the second half of the nineteenth century is the significant increase in naming children after paternal grandparents, and a decrease in naming them after godparents. A gender-specific analysis showed that this change was primarily related to the naming of boys. See Margareth Lanzinger, "Namenkultur – mikrohistorisch und auch quantitativ", *Historische Anthropologie*, 10 (2002), pp. 115–124, 121 ff.

marriage can be taken as indicators of the deterioration of the overall
situation in consequence of the circumstances briefly outlined here.
According to the census for 1880, in the district of Lienz, to which
Innichen belonged, almost half the men and women aged 41 to 50 (48.3 per
cent and 50.1 per cent respectively) and aged 51 to 60 (43.7 per cent and
49.8 per cent respectively) were unmarried.[17] The average age at first
marriage was comparatively high and rose in the course of the period
investigated: from 28.5 years for women and 30 years for men in the
second half of the eighteenth century to 31.5 years for women and 34.5
years for men respectively in the second half of the nineteenth century.

In the combination of these factors, marriage assumed a key role in
several respects: marriage constraints were intended to hinder as far as
possible the reproduction of those who were economically weaker and so
keep as low as possible the number receiving support from the local fund
for the poor. The number of marriages dropped in the period following the
introduction of the marriage consensus in the 1820s and again around the
mid-nineteenth century (Figure 2), which was a restorative phase on the
whole, both from a political perspective regionally and locally, when,
among other measures, the application of the marriage consensus was
intensified. The end of the communal right of citizenship following the
model of the *ancien régime* in the mid-nineteenth century did not result in
greater openness. The community laws newly passed and altered several
times until the end of the nineteenth century and intended to regulate the
pre-conditions for settlement meant that Innichen increasingly closed
itself off from the outside world. It became even more difficult and
increasingly rare for men from elsewhere to marry into the community.[18]

According to the picture so far sketched here, Innichen was a
comparatively restrictive and strongly self-regulated society that did not
seem to leave much scope for negotiation. However, a *liber status
animarum*, which documents the local populace for the 1830s and the
1840s, also lists "inmates", a term used to describe couples and families
without property according to the criteria of house ownership.[19] So, was
the marriage-consensus policy not so very rigorous after all? The
reconstruction of the lives of married couples who did not own a house
and lived as inmates in the 1830s and 1840 demonstrated a range of causes
showing that their situation was anything from a temporary solution while
awaiting inheritance to the result of loss of property, for instance due to
bankruptcy; and in a few cases, despite the marriage-consensus policy, a
marriage between persons without property. In 1849, for example, in a

17. See *Österreichische Statistik*, 2/1 (1882), pp. 154 ff.
18. See Lanzinger, *Das gesicherte Erbe*, pp. 102 ff.
19. STA Innichen, Familienbuch 1829. It contains household lists for the period 1829 to 1849,
with a gap from 1845 to 1848.

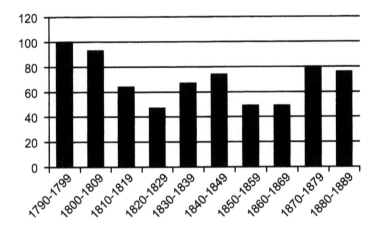

Figure 2. Number of marriages in the parish of Innichen, 1790–1889.

Source: STA Innichen, Liber Conjugatorum, Tomus II, 1761–1784; Tomus IIIa, 1784–1882; Trauungsbuch, Bd. 4, 1845–1927; Liber Baptizatorum, Copulatorum, Mortuorum vom Innichberg, 1786–1807. The figures for the individual decades are: 1790–1799: 99; 1800–1809: 93; 1810–1819: 64; 1820–1829: 47; 1830–1839: 67; 1840–1849: 74; 1850–1859: 49; 1860–1869: 49; 1870–1879: 80; 1880–1889: 76.

total of 154 households, there were 8 married couples, 8 parents with children, and 10 couples with children living in the town as inmates, of which 3 families and 3 couples did not fulfil the property criterion, neither at the time of marriage nor in realistic prospect.

Two patterns are evident in those cases, which are probably the reason why the couples in question nevertheless received permission to marry: the existence of illegitimate children, or that the women were past child-bearing age, so that, in other words, the motivation was towards moral virtue on the one hand, and on the other the calculation that the poor economic situation would not be continued into another generation, so preventing proletarianization.[20] The men are listed with the following occupations: butcher, weaver, fruit and crockery peddler, day-labourer, and a pair of former servants from East Tyrol, who were charged with the care of the hospice in return for their lodging.[21]

If we presume that social profiles are to be conceptualized in a very complex way, then I see the attempt undertaken here to pursue this

20. See Hans Henrik Bull in this volume, pp. 43–63. In Innichen one illegitimate child was obviously not "sufficient" to apply pressure for permission to marry; either there were already two, or the second was on the way. The illegitimacy rates are comparatively low here, between 0 per cent and 6 per cent per year in Innichen in the nineteenth century.
21. See Lanzinger, *Das gesicherte Erbe*, pp. 214 ff.

through an internationally standardized classification as a test case. Classification and the formation of categories are necessarily schematizing processes. The broader the area in which the classification is to be applied, the more removed is the classification from the actual social contexts of a certain time, a certain region, which means that according to its methodological conception it contradicts in fact a micro-historical procedure. However, it can be interesting to analyse the pivotal points where shifts and deviations can be noted between the results achieved with HISCLASS, as a "macro-model" coming in from outside, and a micro-historical approach which works with criteria derived from an actual local society. For this reason, this text is intended, to a certain extent, to be a contribution to an ongoing discussion that should, in my opinion, stimulate an important theoretical, methodological debate on the relationship between methods and results.

This must be qualified by noting that a number of aspects of real and symbolic capital, such as property and income, family prestige, and dignity of office or profession, cannot be taken into consideration in this evaluation because of the amount and complexity of data required; all the same, they contribute substantially to people's social positioning, which is composed of multiple factors.

THE DATASET

The evaluations are based primarily on information from the *Familien-buch* – "Book of Families beginning in 1700" – from the Innichen monastery archive.[22] This is a family reconstruction undertaken by a canon of the monastery in 1893–1894, and took nearly a year to complete.[23] The *Familienbuch* begins with the first marriage in 1700 and covers the period until the beginning of the twentieth century with subsequent additions. All married couples are listed alphabetically in chronological order according to the first letter of the husband's surname, with children's names added from baptismal registers.

In terms of exact data, the density of information is considerably greater for husbands than for wives. Missing data for local residents can be supplied in most cases from the relevant church registers; for the 1830s and 1840s gaps in information can be filled using data from the *liber status*

---

22. STA Innichen, Familienbuch angefangen vom Jahre 1700 [hereafter, Familienbuch 1700].
23. The origins of this *Familienbuch* thus belongs to an earlier period than the *Ortssippenbücher* ["Local Kinship Books"], a comparable type of source, which was drawn up in the 1930s in Germany and has a more reprehensible history. See John Knodel, *Demographic Behavior in the Past: A Study of Fourteen German Village Populations in the Eighteenth and Nineteenth Centuries* (Cambridge, 1988); John Knodel, "Ortssippenbücher als Quelle für die Historische Demographie", *Geschichte und Gesellschaft*, 1 (1975), pp. 288–324.

animarum mentioned above; information on craftsmen and tradesmen has been obtained from the thesis by Hermann Rogger.[24]

On the basis of this *Familienbuch* and the supplementary sources mentioned, I prepared a kleio database in the course of my thesis which largely follows the structure of the source.[25] For the market town, all families were included in the database, along with their branches, which had lived in Innichen over three generations in at least one line of descent. This enabled sources of error to be eliminated. For example, many women from Innichen married in the town but never lived there after their wedding, so that they and their husbands are registered as childless couples. The families from the Innichen mountain were all included, in order to provide a solid foundation for examining mountain-farming marriage circles and inheritance practice. In addition, property transactions and information on the whereabouts or activities of persons were included in the database from the *Verfachbuch* registers.[26]

The following evaluations include only first marriages. This is based on the assumption that first marriages are more important for social positioning than later marriages, which follow a different logic. Only those couples are taken into consideration for whom information is available about the occupation of the bride's father as well as the groom's. All occupations are classified using HISCO and then grouped using HISCLASS.[27]

HOMOGAMY IN RELATION TO THE FAMILIES OF ORIGIN

In the light of the regulated influx and marriage restrictions, and the inheritance practice of intact transfer, the market town is to be regarded in some areas as a quasi-"closed" and exclusive society with a dominant middle class of property owners. Marriage circles concentrated around these middle segments of craftsmen, tradesmen and farmers. The internal

24. Hermann Rogger, "Handwerker und Gewerbetreibende in Innichen seit dem 17. Jahrhundert. Ein Beitrag zur Familien- und allgemeinen Sozialgeschichte dieses Hochpustertaler Marktfleckens" (Ph.D, Innsbruck, 1986).

25. Margareth Lanzinger, "Heirat in lokalen und familialen Kontexten. Innichen 1700–1900" (Ph.D., Vienna, 1999). The structure of the database is similar to the model in Peter Becker and Thomas Werner, *Kleio. Ein Tutorial* (St Katharinen, 1991); see also Manfred Thaller, *Kleio: A Database System* (St Katharinen, 1993).

26. The *Verfachbücher*, which are unique to Tyrol, contain various types of contracts and agreements that were concluded in court as an instance of civil law, as well as purchase and transfer agreements. In the 1940s Josef Oberforcher prepared registers for, *inter alia*, the Verfachbuch Innichen (Bezirksheimatmuseum [hereafter, BHM] Lienz, Oberforcher Regesten [hereafter, OR]).

27. M.H.D. van Leeuwen and I. Maas, "HISCLASS", paper presented at the 5th European Social Science History Conference (Berlin, 24–27 March 2004); I. Maas and M.H.D. van Leeuwen, "SPSS recode job from HISCO into HISCLASS", May 2004.

distribution, however, may have shifted in some places over the course of time due to the socio-political changes outlined above. In order to be able to focus on these kinds of shift, the evaluation of the period from 1700 to 1900 is subdivided into fifty-year sections (Table 1).[28]

As is to be expected, marriage circles condense into three groups: skilled workers, farmers, and lower-skilled workers, who comprise between 85 per cent and just over 97 per cent in the individual time periods. From the perspective of the groom (row), the homogamy rate of sons of skilled workers dropped between 1700 and 1850 from 57.6 per cent to 25.5 per cent, and rose again in the second half of the nineteenth century to 41.7 per cent. With the exception of the first half of the nineteenth century, the separate occupational field of skilled workers is the most important one for the choice of partner. Among the sons of farmers one notes an increase from 68 per cent to 78.3 per cent in the eighteenth century and a decrease to 71.4 per cent between 1800 and 1849, followed by a renewed increase to 80.5 per cent, whereby marriages with daughters from the same occupational origins consistently reached the highest rates overall.

In comparison with skilled workers and farmers, the sons of lower-skilled workers consistently married less commonly within their own group – to a maximum of 27.3 per cent of cases (1700–1749) and a minimum of 13.6 per cent (1850–1899). Instead, they tended to marry – with an alternating preference or to the same extent in the first half of the nineteenth century – daughters of skilled workers (with 54.5 per cent most frequently in the first half of the eighteenth century) or farmers (with 44.4 per cent most frequently in the second half of the eighteenth century), evincing a clear tendency to marry upward. This can be interpreted as social mobility, but it could also indicate a need to "reconsider how we have categorized individual groups".

Whereas for the first half of the eighteenth century the findings in terms of marriage circles from the perspective of men and women are nearly identical (daughters of skilled workers married sons of skilled workers in 61.3 per cent of cases, daughters of farmers married sons of farmers in 68 per cent of cases, and daughters of lower-skilled workers married sons of skilled workers in 60 per cent of cases), differences emerged over the course of time, particularly in the relationship between farming origins and craft origins.

Homogamy is less characteristic of the farmer group: in the individual fifty-year segments between 1750 and 1899 farmers' daughters less often married farmers' sons than vice versa by respectively 23.8 per cent, 13 per cent, and 13.2 per cent. Consistently just over 20 per cent of farmers' daughters married sons of skilled workers. In comparison with craftsmen's

---

28. For the first half of the eighteenth century the information in the database is less dense, due to the mode of inclusion described above – some distortions are therefore possible.

Table 1. *Occupation of father of the groom (row) by that of father of the bride (column), first marriage of groom, according to HISCLASS*

Father of the bride

Count Row % Column % Total %	1+2*	3+4+5	6+7	8	9	11	Row Total
1700–1749 **Father of the groom**							
Lower managers and professionals, clerical and sales (3+4+5)		1 50.0 33.3 1.4	1 50.0 3.2 1.4				2 2.8
Skilled workers (6+7)	1 3.0 50.0 1.4	1 3.0 33.3 1.4	19 57.6 61.3 26.8	6 18.2 24.0 8.5	6 18.2 60.0 8.5		33 46.5
Farmers and fishermen (8)	1 4.0 50.0 1.4	1 4.0 33.3 1.4	5 20.0 16.1 7.0	17 68.0 68.0 23.9	1 4.0 10.0 1.4		25 35.2
Lower-skilled workers (9)			6 54.5 19.4 8.5	2 18.2 8.0 2.8	3 27.3 30.0 4.2		11 15.5
Column Total	2 2.8	3 4.2	31 43.7	25 35.2	10 14.1		71 100.0
1750–1799	1+2	3+4+5	6+7	8	9	11	Row Total
Higher managers and professionals (1+2)	1 25.0 20.0 0.7	1 25.0 10.0 0.7			2 50.0 10.0 1.4		4 2.9
Lower managers and professionals, clerical and sales (3+4+5)	2 15.4 40.0 1.4	3 23.1 30.0 2.1	4 30.8 10.8 2.9	1 7.7 1.5 0.7	3 23.1 15.0 2.1		13 9.3
Skilled workers (6+7)	2 4.1 40.0 1.4	3 6.1 30.0 2.1	20 40.8 54.1 14.3	16 32.7 24.2 11.4	8 16.3 40.0 5.7		49 35.0
Farmers and fishermen (8)		1 2.2 10.0 0.7	4 8.7 10.8 2.9	36 78.3 54.5 25.7	3 6.5 15.0 2.1	2 4.3 100.0 1.4	46 32.9

(*Continued overleaf*)

Table 1. *Continued*

1750–1799	1+2	3+4+5	6+7	8	9	11	Row Total
Lower-skilled workers		2	9	12	4		27
(9)		7.4	33.3	44.4	14.8		19.3
		20.0	24.3	18.2	20.0		
		1.4	6.4	8.6	2.9		
Unskilled workers (11)				1			1
				100.0			0.7
				1.5			
				0.7			
Column	5	10	37	66	20	2	140
Total	3.6	7.1	26.4	47.1	14.3	1.4	100.0

1800–1849	1+2	3+4+5	6+7	8	9	11	Row Total
Higher managers	1	2	1	2	2		8
and professionals (1+2)	12.5	25.0	12.5	25.0	25.0		5.2
	16.7	13.3	2.7	2.6	11.1		
	0.6	1.3	0.6	1.3	1.3		
Lower managers	1	4	4	2	1		12
and professionals,	8.3	33.3	33.3	16.7	8.3		7.8
clerical and sales	16.7	26.7	10.8	2.6	5.6		
(3+4+5)	0.6	2.6	2.6	1.3	0.6		
Skilled workers (6+7)	4	5	12	19	6	1	47
	8.5	10.6	25.5	40.4	12.8	2.1	30.5
	66.7	33.3	32.4	24.7	33.3	100.0	
	2.6	3.2	7.8	12.3	3.9	0.6	
Farmers and fishermen		2	11	45	5		63
(8)		3.2	17.5	71.4	7.9		40.9
		13.3	29.7	58.4	27.8		
		1.3	7.1	29.2	3.2		
Lower-skilled workers		1	9	9	4		23
(9)		4.3	39.1	39.1	17.4		14.9
		6.7	24.3	11.7	22.2		14.9
		0.6	5.8	5.8	2.6		
Unskilled workers (11)		1					1
		100.0					0.6
		6.7					
		0.6					
Column	6	15	37	77	18		154
Total	3.9	9.7	24.0	50.0	11.7		100.0

1850–1899	1+2	3+4+5	6+7	8	9	11	Row Total
Higher managers			1		1		2
and professionals			50.0		50.0		1.8
(1+2)			3.2		6.7		
			0.9		0.9		

(*Continued*)

Lower managers and professionals, clerical and sales (3+4+5)		2	4	2	2		10
		20.0	40.0	20.0	20.0		0.0
		18.2	12.9	4.1	13.3		
		1.8	3.6	1.8	1.8		
Skilled workers (6+7)	2	3	15	10	6		36
	5.6	8.3	41.7	27.8	16.7		32.4
	50.0	27.3	48.4	20.4	40.0		
	1.8	2.7	13.5	9.0	5.4		
Farmers and fishermen (8)	1	1	3	33	3		41
	2.4	2.4	7.3	80.5	7.3		36.9
	25.0	9.1	9.7	67.3	20.0		
	0.9	0.9	2.7	29.7	2.7		
Lower-skilled workers (9)	1	5	8	4	3	1	22
	4.5	22.7	36.4	18.2	13.6	4.5	19.8
	25.0	45.5	25.8	8.2	20.0	100.0	
	0.9	4.5	7.2	3.6	2.7	0.9	
Column Total	4	11	31	49	15	1	111
	3.6	9.9	27.9	44.1	13.5	0.9	100.0

* Value labels: 1+2 higher managers and professionals, 3+4+5 lower managers and professionals, clerical and sales, 6+7 skilled workers, 8 farmers and fishermen, 9 lower-skilled workers, 11 unskilled workers. Farm workers (10+12) existed only as servants, and they were not allowed to marry.

sons, daughters of skilled and lower-skilled workers more often married within the craft milieu than within the farming milieu: the proportion there is between 10 per cent and 20 per cent, with the exception of the first half of the nineteenth century, when 29.7 per cent of marriages were between daughters of skilled workers and farmers' sons and 27.8 per cent of marriages were between daughters of lower-skilled workers and farmers' sons.

Among the fourth largest group, the lower managers and professionals, clerical and sales, which includes publicans and tradesmen (substantial portions of the local elite), skilled workers comprised the most important marriage circle aside from their own group. In the second half of the nineteenth century, however, their daughters' husbands came from the ranks of lower-skilled workers in four out of ten cases – another indication of social mobility.

It is apparent that the first half of the nineteenth century was the phase with most noticeable shifts. Aside from the political, social, and economic upheavals and the introduction of the marriage consensus, another circumstance which must be mentioned concerns the consequences of the wars and upheavals of the Napoleonic era of the late eighteenth and early nineteenth centuries. The second half of the nineteenth century seemed to show a tendency to level out, so to speak, at the status of the second half of the eighteenth century. These findings to some extent contradict the presumption that those changes led to shifts in the social status of occupational groups, which were presumed as well to be reflected in marriage alliances. That will be examined in a more detailed analysis.

The question also should be raised of whether the occupation of the groom should be included in the discussion of homogamy. If it is not, one will fail to take into consideration the social mobility between a man's origins and his own subsequent occupation, achieved by the time of his marriage (and that not least because of his late age at marriage).[29] Was it a misalliance then when a day-labourer's son married the daughter of a publican? In the case of Josef Eisendle it was not, because although the son of a day-labourer, he had worked his way up to become a tradesman.[30]

It should be noted that not only was it possible to move up socially, there was also the risk of moving down, and for non-inheriting sons, for instance, that was a risk which increased especially in the nineteenth century. A drop in social status is not necessarily recognizable through occupational classification, however, because such men could certainly have learned a highly skilled trade. Detailed knowledge is needed of their actual working and property situations to be able to make a statement about their social status. If a man born to a lower-class family learned a skilled trade and married someone from a low-skilled or unskilled family, that would show up as homogamy rather than the downward marriage it arguably was in terms of current social status.

The particular question of social mobility illustrates that the links between individual occupational codes and generations and social status, being just collections of factors from more than one source and written registers, represent a leap to a different level qualitatively and so it is difficult to operationalize them.[31]

POINTS OF DISCUSSION AND DIFFERENT MEASURES FROM A LOCAL PERSPECTIVE

Starting from the results of the evaluation based on HISCLASS, we have alluded to several points of discussion from a local perspective. These will be addressed in more detail in the following. For some of the points it

29. See for example Maria Carla Lamberti, "Immigrate e immigrati in una città preindustriale: Torino all'inizio dell'Ottocento", in Angiolina Arru and Franco Ramella (eds), *L'Italia delle migrazioni interne. Donne, uomini, mobilità in età moderna e contemporanea* (Rome, 2003), pp. 161–205, 196.
30. Franz Eisendle moved to Innichen in the 1830s, and his father was listed as a day-labourer. Franz Eisendle worked in Innichen as a tradesman, had started with half a house rented with a colleague, married a publican's daughter, then owned first one half, later the other half also, of a house in the centre of town, subsequently held communal office, and eventually became mayor.
31. Yet the inclusion of the property dimension is still insufficient to determine questions of social stratification. In this context, Giovanni Levi refers, for instance, to the complex family strategies that also have an impact on the question of social positioning. See Giovanni Levi, *Das immaterielle Erbe. Eine bäuerliche Welt an der Schwelle zur Moderne* (Berlin, 1986), p. 48.

appears meaningful to focus additionally on several analyses modified specifically to take account of the local circumstances.

A first important point of discussion is the gender-specific difference in the extent of exchange between the crafts and the farming communities. That farmers' daughters frequently married into crafts households is probably due to the fact that virtually every trade and craft household had at least a small farm. It may be presumed that questions about the division of labour and the organization of work played a role in the choice of partner. In this form of mixed economy a relevant socialization of the wife in agriculture might have been more important than competence in the craft field, and in some sectors more than in others. The number of servants and the size of the agricultural property were factors to be taken into consideration, along with socio-cultural attitudes.

In fact, there were several sectors into which no farmers' daughters married, and some into which only a few married: among merchants, village barbers and surgeons, furriers, parchment makers, masons, and glazers there are no indications of connections in that direction. The proportion is just under or just over 10 per cent for first marriages among bakers, publicans, dyers, glove-makers, locksmiths, carpenters, and tailors, which suggests a stronger tendency among the middle sectors, primarily, to marry a woman from the farming milieu.

With respect to the marriage circles of farmers' sons, it should be noted that they did not necessarily become farmers themselves, for especially those who did not take over the farm often took different roads in life. In the evaluation it would be important therefore to start from the groom's occupation, not that of his father. That would allow a clearer insight into how important farming origins were for women who later became farmers.

In addition, in the Alpine context, it is worth making a distinction between farms in the valley and farms on mountain slopes. In Innichen, Innichberg ("Innich Hill"), located on the sunny side of the mountain, formed a separate municipality belonging to the same parish as the town but to a different court district. The Innichberg farms are found at an altitude of up to 1,500 metres, but the fields and meadows belonging to them reach even higher. In terms of labour techniques and conditions, farm work on the mountain slope placed different demands on people from farm work in the valley. Mountain farmers or their children could settle in the valley, but valley farmers on the mountain?

Using reconstructed ownership successions for the twenty-eight Innichberger farms for the period 1700 to 1900, we found only one farmer and town citizen who married up onto the mountain.[32] He married a

---

32. The person in question was Johann Schett, who married the widow from the Burgmann Farm in 1746; BHM Lienz, OR III 4, Verfachbuch Heinfels 1737 III 22, fo. 372 and STA Innichen, Familienbuch 1700, fo. 625.

widow whose husband had been a mountain farmer. Due to the system of separate marital property, the widow could not take over the farm as an owner, so her seven-year-old son became the owner and her second husband, the town citizen, took the farm on a fifteen-year lease: that is, until the son came of age and could assume control himself. Almost 90 per cent of the Innichberger farmers came from Innichberg itself, the remaining 10 per cent coming from outside to settle there. Did the choice of wives follow the logic of mountain-farmer origins just as strictly?

Several important parameters for classifying occupations according to the HISCLASS model could be added for the segment of crafts and trades to capture more accurately the complexity of Innichen's class structure, which was closely connected to the socio-political, socio-economic, and socio-cultural contexts outlined earlier. Certain categories of occupation were more highly regarded than others in Innichen, but that assessment did not necessarily run parallel to the distinction between the character of an occupation as skilled or lower-skilled. The social prestige of a craft apparently depended largely on the cost of the means of production required to carry out the profession, which ultimately meant property.

A tailor, for example, must have mastered the skills of his craft and was therefore a skilled worker according to HISCLASS, yet in terms of the preconditions for business he could just as well live and work somewhere as a lodger. Tanners require, in comparison, extensive equipment but they are ranked among the lower-skilled workers. Whereas tanning was often regarded as a less honourable craft in urban societies and banished to the outskirts of town or to remote streets because of the stench, it was one of the most prestigious guilds in Innichen. Marriage to a tanner or a tanner's son therefore tended to be linked with more social prestige in Innichen than marriage to a tailor or tailor's son. In the categorization of skilled and lower-skilled, however, that relation is exactly the reverse.

In addition, the status of being the only person in the town practising a craft which was important to local industry could also invest one with a special position. In Innichen this was true of the dyer's craft, for instance, which was passed on over generations in one highly respected family and was also one of the crafts requiring the most intensive means of production. HISCLASS, however, classifies dyers as lower-skilled workers.

Finally, the question should also be raised of the extent to which the importance and thus also attractiveness in the marriage market of certain occupations depended on their economic situation. A good test case from a local perspective would be that of the glove-maker. The manufacture of leather gloves flourished especially in the second half of the eighteenth century, and the number of glove-makers increased accordingly.[33]

33. The following data are available for the period at the end of the eighteenth century from an application to the regional parliament for a reduction in customs: eighteen master glove-makers,

Several of the discussion points mentioned here will be examined in more detail on the basis of individual occupational sectors or in groups somewhat different from those of HISCLASS, in an attempt to approximate the specific *local* scale of values in the town. In this scale of values, property is central, occupational skills are obviously subordinate to it.

HOMOGAMY IN RELATION TO HUSBAND'S OCCUPATION

The choice of partners from the perspective of the husbands' occupation compared with the perspective of the men's families of origin shows a tendency towards broader distribution at the level of individual occupations in the wife's family of origin, with the exception of glove-makers, cobblers, carpenters, and merchants. Differences are evident among mountain farmers, glove-makers, weavers, and publicans.

In comparison with the sons of mountain farmers in general, working mountain farmers largely married the daughters of other mountain farmers. It is highly probable that specific labour or technical requirements were a crucial factor in the choice of a wife. In dispensation applications for marriage among relatives, for example, there are references to the specific demands of the work of mountain farming, which were regarded as a factor making it more difficult to find a suitable spouse.[34] Yet thirteen daughters of market citizens married someone from Innichberg, of whom eight married into farms at a slightly lower level, while three married widowers, whose farms were among the more prosperous ones with several servants. The women mostly came from long-established farming families in the town.[35] It is evident especially in the nineteenth century that between 50 and 70 per cent of women who married in Innichberg were themselves from mountain-farming families.[36]

Glove-makers generally married farmers' daughters less often than did their sons. In this activity, which in Innichen emerged and flourished over

fourteen journeymen and apprentices, thirty-nine male and female helpers. See Bibliothek des Stiftes Innichen, Urkundenbuch, MS VIII, b 6, fo. 37 ff., cit. from Rogger, "Handwerker und Gewerbetreibende", p. 20.

34. An applicant for a marriage dispensation explained, for example, that "not everyone can be got up on the mountain, and not everyone can be used either"; Diözesanarchiv Brixen, Konsistorialakten 1874, Fasz. 22A, Römische Ehedispensen, no. 15; see also the article by Hilde Bras and Jan Kok in this volume, pp. 247–274.

35. Multiple ties of marriage between the town and the mountain could be reconstructed for a family of market farmers, the Kohlschneider Farm, which ran in both directions with a certain regularity. See STA Innichen, Familienbuch 1700, fos 14, 279, 283, 499, 760.

36. There is also a problem here with the high proportion of women marrying in from outside, because without specific knowledge of the area it is not possible to determine whether they came from the valley or the mountain. For this reason, these data represent minimum percentages; the actual percentages are probably higher.

the course of the eighteenth century, the social status of glove-makers and their children appears to have diverged, which could indicate a somewhat ambivalent in-between position. For the spectrum of families of origin whose daughters married a glove-maker is very broad, and ranges into the higher crafts and trades,[37] but, conversely, not a single glove-maker's daughter appears as a wife among the more prestigious sectors in the sample. The marriage relationships thus remained one-sided here.

Compared with their sons, weavers were more likely to have married the daughters of other weavers or – in the nineteenth century – the daughters of valley farmers, and since weaving was often practised as a secondary occupation to farming there was more scope for the marriage circles to overlap in these cases.[38] Weavers also married the daughters of bakers, millers, and tanners, but, most frequently, among the craft and trade branches, and unlike smiths or shoemakers for example, they married women from the same branch.

Among publicans, it is particularly noticeable that in the second half of the nineteenth century there was a broader distribution in the selection of partners among publicans' sons than among publicans. Among craftsmen and tradesmen, publicans show the highest proportion of occupational endogamy:[39] heirs and purchasers of public houses tended to marry publicans' daughters. In Innichen, publicans were simultaneously the owners of the largest farms, evident, for instance, in the number of maids and male servants working there – and so publicans were among the local elite. Here, it is relatively clear that occupational endogamy can be regarded as social homogamy too.

Relevant socialization among women and their familiarity with its demands was obviously an advantage, especially in the sectors where they contributed their labour, which was specifically sought, as was the case with wives of mountain farmers and publicans alike. Occupational endogamy and social homogamy coincided most clearly in those sectors.

DIFFERENTLY GROUPED

The social stratification of a *local* society depends to a certain degree on a specific system of values changing over time. From a micro-historical perspective, the central aim is to ascertain the elements of the prevailing system of values and to reconstruct their implications for the social profile

---

37. The situation was different among shoemakers and cobblers for example – other crafts that were widespread locally – the more prestigious spheres are hardly present; one baker's daughter and one smith's daughter are the exception.

38. A problem that cannot be addressed in greater depth here is that multiple professions and occupations can change the social profile of individual professions.

39. The marriage circle for commercial and merchant professions was similarly specific: here the marriage circle included daughters of tradespeople augmented by apothecaries and civil servants.

of a community. If this interconnection is a crucial point of the investigation, then the social classification too should be orientated by its values and implications.

To clarify the particular situation in Innichen in the second half of the nineteenth century, occupations are here grouped together in a social matrix constructed by the author to reflect detailed knowledge of social relationships among certain occupational groups from which the examples in the section above were taken, and to reflect the means of production required by craftsmen. We have in group 1: bakers, publicans, merchants forming the local elite;[40] group 2: high-level crafts requiring a sizeable means of production;[41] group 3: farmers; group 4: mid-level crafts – between groups 2 and 5 in terms of means of production; group 5: mass crafts requiring comparatively little in the way of means of production and carried out by comparatively many people in the town; group 6: various functions and offices (such as barber-surgeons, imperial and royal hunters, local court clerks, district court "commissars", and sextons); group 7: other.

Calculated in 50-year increments (Table 2 overleaf), sons of bakers, publicans, and merchants in group 1 married within their own group less and less often (from 66.7 per cent to 28.6 per cent). In the nineteenth century there was initially a shift towards the farmers, followed by a shift back towards the high-level crafts in the second half of the nineteenth century. This reversion could indicate that those sectors, which were among the most property-intensive, had meanwhile consolidated or reorientated in a better way; agriculture especially gained in importance in this context.[42] It is interesting here that the category "other", which ranked third in this period, is an expression of the tendency to change – revealing a habit of marrying downward if one examines actual cases. Of course, this conclusion is based on a very small group, but every single case counts in the sense of the scope of options for action.

Among daughters from this first group (Table 3 overleaf) the preferred sectors of origin remained more consistent. For the second half of the nineteenth century this evaluation confirms the HISCLASS conclusion of downward marriage, with daughters from group 1 marrying sons from

40. Bakers also had a licence to run a public house. The local publicans had the largest farms and the highest number of servants. From inventories and various contracts one finds a high level of property and/or means among this group of bakers, publicans, and merchants. They are addressed as "*Herr*" in contracts, registers and so on. They were very often engaged in communal functions, as mayors, as communal representatives, as administrators of communal funds (for the poor and orphans, for example) and they were also frequently engaged as guardians for minors after a father's death.

41. The results of the reconstruction of property transfers also indicate that special sectors are involved here: in these sectors there was a greater continuity of property and profession between fathers and sons or sons-in-law. See Lanzinger, *Das gesicherte Erbe*, pp. 234 ff.

42. For example, a master tanner opened a tavern in this period.

Table 2. *Occupation of father of the groom (row) by that of father of the bride (column), first marriage of groom in %*

	1	2	3	4	5	6	8	Total
1700–1749								
1 Bakers, publicans, merchants	66.7	11.1	11.1	11.1				9
2 High-level crafts*	23.1	30.8	15.4	15.4	15.4			13
3 Farmers	4.0	12.0	68.0	12.0			4.0	25
4 Mid-level crafts**	10.0	20.0		20.0	40.0	10.0		10
5 Mass crafts***		15.4	30.8	7.7	38.5		7.7	13
6 Various functions and offices		100.0						1
7 Other								
Total								71
1750–1799								
1 Bakers, publicans, merchants	57.1	28.6			14.3			7
2 High-level crafts*	10.5	26.3	42.1	15.8	5.3			19
3 Farmers		7.1	83.3	2.4	2.4	2.4	2.4	42
4 Mid-level crafts**	5.6	22.2	27.8	11.1	16.7	11.1	5.6	18
5 Mass crafts***	2.7	8.1	35.1	16.2	29.7	8.1		37
6 Various functions and offices	7.1			14.3	35.7	28.6	14.3	14
7 Other			66.7	33.3				3
Total								140
1800–1849								
1 Bakers, publicans, merchants	46.2	7.7	23.1		7.7	7.7	7.7	13
2 High-level crafts*	10.5	21.1	42.1		21.1	5.3		19
3 Farmers	1.6	3.2	71.4	7.9	12.7	1.6	1.6	63
4 Mid-level crafts**	3.6	14.3	39.3	25.0	7.1	7.1	3.6	28
5 Mass crafts***	4.5	4.5	36.4	9.1	31.8	4.5	9.1	22
6 Various functions and offices	16.7			50.0	16.7	16.7		6
7 Other	33.3				33.3		33.3	3
Total								154
1850–1899								
1 Bakers, publicans, merchants	28.6	35.7	7.1				28.6	14
2 High-level crafts*	22.2	11.1	33.3	5.6	11.1		16.7	18
3 Farmers	2.4	2.4	80.5	4.9	4.9	2.4	2.4	41
4 Mid-level crafts**		12.5	25.0	12.5	37.5	6.3	6.3	16
5 Mass crafts***	10.5		15.8	31.6	26.3	5.3	10.5	19
6 Various functions and offices		100.0						1
7 Other				50.0	50.0			2
Total								111

* Butchers, millers, tanners, dyers, smiths, glazers, and hat makers.
** All other crafts.
*** Tailors, cobblers, glove-makers, and weavers.

Table 3. *Occupation of father of the bride (row) by that of father of the groom (column), first marriage of groom in %*

	1	2	3	4	5	6	8	Total
1700–1749								
1 Bakers, publicans, merchants	54.5	27.3	9.1	9.1				11
2 High-level crafts*	7.7	30.8	23.1	15.4	15.4	7.7		13
3 Farmers	4.2	8.3	70.8		16.7			24
4 Mid-level crafts**	11.1	22.2	33.3	22.2	11.1			9
5 Mass crafts***		18.2		36.4	45.5			11
6 Various functions and offices				100.0				1
7 Other			50.0		50.0			2
Total								71
1750–1799								
1 Bakers, publicans, merchants	44.4	22.2		11.1	11.1	11.1		9
2 High-level crafts*	11.8	29.4	17.6	23.5	17.6			17
3 Farmers		12.7	55.6	7.9	20.6		3.2	63
4 Mid-level crafts**		20.0	6.7	13.3	40.0	13.3	6.7	15
5 Mass crafts***	4.5	4.5	4.5	13.6	50.0	22.7		22
6 Various functions and offices			10.0	20.0	30.0	40.0		10
7 Other			25.0	25.0		50.0		4
Total								140
1800–1849								
1 Bakers, publicans, merchants	46.2	15.4	7.7	7.7	7.7	7.7	7.7	13
2 High-level crafts*	8.3	33.3	16.7	33.3	8.3			12
3 Farmers	4.0	10.7	60.0	14.7	10.7			75
4 Mid-level crafts**			29.4	41.2	11.8	17.6		17
5 Mass crafts***	4.2	16.7	33.3	8.3	29.2	4.2	4.2	24
6 Various functions and offices	14.3	14.3	14.3	28.6	14.3	14.3		7
7 Other	16.7		16.7	16.7	33.3		16.7	6
Total								154
1850–1899								
1 Bakers, publicans, merchants	36.4	36.4	9.1		18.2			11
2 High-level crafts*	45.5	18.2	9.1	18.2		9.1		11
3 Farmers	2.1	12.8	70.2	8.5	6.4			47
4 Mid-level crafts**		8.3	16.7	16.7	50.0		8.3	12
5 Mass crafts***		12.5	12.5	37.5	31.3		6.3	16
6 Various functions and offices			33.3	33.3	33.3			3
7 Other	36.4	27.3	9.1	9.1	18.2			11
Total								111

* Butchers, millers, tanners, dyers, smiths, glazers, and hat makers.
** All other crafts.
*** Tailors, cobblers, glove-makers, and weavers.

group 5 (mass crafts).[43] In group 2 (tanners, dyers, smiths, glazers, etc.) the emphasis shifted from the same group, which was dominant in the first half of the eighteenth century, to farmers between 1750 and 1850. In the second half of the nineteenth century the spectrum of marriage circles became considerably more dispersed.

It is an indication of the strong position of the farming community in the second half of the nineteenth century that the rate remained high at 80.5 per cent for marriages between sons from farming families and daughters likewise from farming families (Table 2). Similarly, in the second half of the nineteenth century (1850–1899) and also in the first half of the eighteenth century (1700–1749) just over 70 per cent of farmers' daughters married within their own group (Table 3).

Access to marriage circles among farmers became less assured for the broad range of craftsmen in group 4: in the nineteenth century they initially married most frequently within their own group, and from the group of mass crafts in the second half of the nineteenth century. The situation for group 5 was similar: in the second half of the nineteenth century there were few marriages between men in group 5 and daughters of farmers; sons of tailors, cobblers, glove-makers, and weavers mostly married daughters from the mid-level crafts group. The order of the origins of marriage partners for daughters from group 5 was similar during that period.

CONCLUSION

The analyses based on occupational groups classified according to the international, HISCLASS scheme and based on the author's own scheme of occupational groups orientated towards local criteria correspond in terms of gender-specific differences in marriage preferences particularly between craftsmen and farmers: craftsmen's daughters married much less often into the farming community than farmers' daughters into the crafts community. That could support the theory that choice of partner involved not only status, but matters of socialization and labour requirements. Wives or daughters could play a role in the formation of alliances following a logic different from that governing the marriages of sons, conspicuously so for instance in the group of high-level crafts in the second half of the nineteenth century, where the marriage circles of daughters differed considerably from those of sons.

The impact of changes to the local system of values caused by socio-

43. In the light of the comparatively limited marriage opportunities, the question also arises as to whether in some cases prestige was not also expressed by more than one child being able to marry in the town. Perhaps this sometimes relativized the idea of homogamy and made it seem less important.

economic factors, which meant especially the unprofitability of numerous crafts that produced for a translocal market in the nineteenth century due to industrial competition, is clearly evident in the shifts in marriage circles between occupational groups.[44] This affords an even greater significance to property in comparison with crafts skills for instance. It was a development leading to a better position for farmers and helped the craftsmen possessing more property to achieve a certain consolidation or greater opportunities for reorientation. A degree of re-agrarianization can be noted in the second half of the nineteenth century. However, the property criterion seems to have outweighed everything else.

That might also be why this specific situation emerges less markedly using the HISCLASS scheme than it does using a local social matrix: whereas in the second half of the nineteenth century patterns are seen to deviate from earlier periods in several respects if we use a categorization relating to the local context, with the HISCLASS scheme the manifestations of change are shifted more towards the first half of the nineteenth century. From a micro-historical perspective focusing on Innichen, there is thus a need to introduce additional parameters coupled with spatial-temporal specifics into the link between occupational endogamy and social homogamy.[45] Arguably then, one should allow the open and variable formation of groups for these kinds of evaluation, since this would allow for the necessary differentiations and shifts in emphasis, albeit perhaps at the expense of comparability.

The central question is whether the socio-political context outlined in the beginning affected partner selection in the direction of a preference for homogamy. In the light of the actively and purposely pursued policy of social stability at the communal level, did a marriage "among equals" represent a further stabilizing factor? To a certain degree, a tendency of the kind can be presumed. In particular, shifts in the marriage circles in both the first and the second halves of the nineteenth century can be regarded as a consequence of new endeavours to compensate for changes in status due to economic and social upheavals. When social parameters were shifted, the choice of partner followed suit, although it took some time for it to become clear which course the new positionings would take.

44. Samples of community and court representatives (up to 1806) show a change between the late seventeenth and late eighteenth centuries from a composition comprising publicans especially to one reflecting a much broader base of craftsmen. Craftsmen were clearly less represented in the 1860s, when merchants and publicans too made up half of the community council. Although farmers were not more numerously represented here than before, in the late nineteenth century they increasingly took over communal offices held previously by all heads of households for one or two years at a time under a rotation system. See Lanzinger, *Das gesicherte Erbe*, pp. 105 ff.
45. See for example Detlev Mares, "Abschied vom Klassenbegriff? Viktorianische Arbeiterbewegung, politische Sozialgeschichte und linguistic turn in England", *Neue Politische Literatur*, 42 (1997), pp. 378–394.

It has also become clear that property defined social status.[46] The choice of partner also proved to have a stabilizing effect to the extent that its circles could only be expanded within a limited range – as is evident, for example, in the one-sided bands of marriage under flourishing conditions between women of a higher social position and glove-makers: there was no corresponding upward reciprocity in the next generation.

Strategies, but opportunities too, were different for the separate sectors, forming a bottleneck from top to bottom. That is especially evident in the case of farmers' daughters, who were increasingly acceptable to higher branches in the course of a re-evaluation of agriculture, but who were less often present in the less attractive segments of mid-level and mass crafts. Despite a strong orientation towards property, there were cases of downward marriages again and again – as shown particularly among the elite group of bakers, publicans and merchants. This relativization of homogamy should also quite probably be seen against the background of restrictive marriage policies.

46. See also the article by Martin Dribe and Christer Lundh in this volume, pp. 149–177.

IRSH 50 (2005), Supplement, pp. 149–177 DOI: 10.1017/S0020859005002105
© 2005 Internationaal Instituut voor Sociale Geschiedenis

Finding the Right Partner: Rural Homogamy in Nineteenth-Century Sweden[*]

MARTIN DRIBE AND CHRISTER LUNDH

SUMMARY: In pre-industrial society, choosing a marriage partner was a crucial process, and especially so for landowners. This study focuses on social aspects of mate selection in five rural parishes in southern Sweden between 1829 and 1894, using an individual-level database containing information on a large number of marriages and the social origins of the marrying couple regardless of whether they were born in the relevant parish or not. The information makes it possible to study homogamy without introducing the possible selection biases implicit in looking only at non-migrating population, a consideration which is of great importance in a society characterized by very high levels of geographical mobility. The results show a community marked by quite strong homogamy but with pronounced differences among social groups. Landholding peasants were the most homogamous. The pattern of homogamy also remained fairly constant despite fundamental economic and social change.

INTRODUCTION

In pre-industrial western Europe there was great importance attached to the economic aspects of marriage. In areas dominated by the western European marriage pattern, marriage was closely connected to family and household formation:[1] in order to marry, a young couple needed a secure income and accommodation to be able to set up an independent household. To peasants, access to land was vital, and marriage was often inextricably linked to intergenerational land transmission, which made the

* An earlier version of this article was presented at the 5th European Social Science History Conference (Berlin, 24–27 March 2004). We are grateful to Antoinette Fauve-Chamoux, Bart Van de Putte, Patrick Svensson, and the editors of this issue for comments and suggestions. Martin Dribe gratefully acknowledges financial support from the Swedish Council for Working Life and Social Research (FAS). Christer Lundh's research was undertaken as part of the projects "Age at Marriage in Sweden 1750–1900: Trends and Regional Variations", funded by the Swedish Council for Research in the Humanities and Social Science (HSFR), and "Early-Life Conditions, Social Mobility, and Longevity: Social Differences and Trends in Mortality in Sweden, 1650–1900", funded by the Swedish Council for Working Life and Social Research (FAS).
1. John Hajnal, "European Marriage Patterns in Perspective", in D.V. Glass and D.E.C. Eversley (eds), *Population in History. Essays in Historical Demography* (London, 1965), pp. 101–143; *idem*, "Two Kinds of Pre-industrial Household Formation System", in Richard Wall, Jean Robin, and Peter Laslett (eds), *Family Forms in Historic Europe* (Cambridge, 1983), pp. 65–104.

choice of marriage partner a crucial issue and one in which a lot more than love and affection was involved.[2] In addition to this important financial aspect, marriage constituted a method of linking lineages. Kinship alliance in itself could be an important motive for marriage, or it could be used as an instrument to find a socially and financially suitable partner in the marriage market,[3] so marriage strategies were closely tied to more general family strategies regarding social reproduction, where marriage was intimately connected to concerns about inheritance, land transmission, migration decisions, and so on.[4]

The aim of this article is to analyse social homogamy in a rural area of southern Sweden from 1829–1894. Our starting point is the claim of ethnologists and local historians that pre-industrial rural society was indeed characterized by a rather strong tendency to homogamy. Although such claims make sense in the light of what we have just seen, they are based mostly on qualitative sources or individual examples which show the *occurrence* of positive assortative mating (people with similar character-istics marrying each other), but not its *frequency*. The approach in this study will be to confront the picture given by ethnologists and local historians with demographic data, and so to undertake a quantitative analysis of the frequency of homogamy. More specifically, we shall ask if there was a general tendency to homogamy in rural areas of southern Sweden in the nineteenth century, and if it was similarly the case across social groups and over time.

In order to answer such questions we make use of a high-quality dataset based on family reconstitutions of five rural parishes in the province of Scania in southern Sweden. By tracing back to their place of birth all individuals living in a marital union in one of these parishes during the period 1829–1894, we create the opportunity to study social homogamy without introducing possible selection biases stemming from migration, which are otherwise common in family reconstitution studies.

BACKGROUND

If marriage were just an act of love and mate selection not restricted by institutions along social, religious, or ethnic lines or by geographic

2. See Lawrence Stone, *The Family, Sex and Marriage in England 1500–1800* (London, 1979), especially ch. 7; Michael Mitterauer and Reinhard Sieder, *The European Family* (Chicago, IL, 1982), ch. 6.

3. Joseph Ehmer, "Marriage", in David I. Kertzer and Marzio Barbagli (eds), *Family Life In the Long Nineteenth Century 1789–1913* (New Haven, CT [etc.], 2002), pp. 282–321; David W. Sabean, *Kinship in Neckarhausen, 1700–1870* (Cambridge, 1998).

4. See Pierre Bourdieu, "Marriage Strategies as Strategies of Social Reproduction", in Robert Forster and Orest Ranum (eds), *Family and Society: Selections from the Annales, Économies, Sociétés, Civilisations* (Baltimore, MD, 1976), pp. 117–144.

distance, the mix of mates into couples would be rather haphazard. For many reasons we know that this is not how marriage worked in olden times, nor does it today. Therefore, theories have been developed in order to explain individuals' assortative behaviour in the marriage market.

One line of argument is that mate selection aims at pooling wealth and status from two households into a third, new union.[5] Certain marriage strategies are developed in order to maximize the outcome of such unions depending on the social, religious, or ethnic origin of the spouses. For financial reasons, and for fear of punishment from family and social, or religious and ethnic groups, young people will prefer a spouse with similar economic characteristics – in accordance with the saying "birds of a feather flock together".

In economic theories of marriage it is considered that the assortative mating process is largely determined by the gender division of labour, the productivity (wage) of men and women in different tasks, and the effects of different time allocations on aggregate output in household production, i.e. whether spouses have similar characteristics (positive assortative mating) or different ones (negative assortative mating).[6] However, in a pre-industrial rural context mating has less to do with divisions of labour than with assets, and mainly with access to land and housing. Regardless of whether spouses were similar in terms of assets, they were always specialists in different jobs of work in accordance with the gender-based division of labour.[7] That implies that gains in specialization were not the point in different matches. Instead, strategies aimed at maintaining family estates and securing a viable landholding and social reproduction lay at the centre of the marriage decision, at least for landed groups.

In nineteenth-century southern Sweden people were homogeneous as far as religion and ethnicity were concerned but they were divided socially. There were many institutions in rural society, some connected to marriage, which make it reasonable to believe that certain marriage strategies were practised, especially among landholding peasants. For example, we know

5. See Matthijs Kalmijn, "Intermarriage and Homogamy: Causes, Patterns and Trends", *Annual Review of Sociology*, 24 (1998), pp. 395–421.On the other hand, people of lower status could make a social career through marriage, thereby increasing their wealth and status. By marrying a peasant head of household, a maid would immediately improve her position to that of mistress and supervisor of the female servants. A corresponding union between a farmhand and a farmer's daughter would mean a social career to the former, who would become the head of household, the guardian of his wife, and the manager of the farm. Though such cases were few (see Christer Lundh, "Remarriages in Sweden in the Eighteenth and Nineteenth Centuries", *History of the Family*, 7 (2002), pp. 423–450), they would counteract the tendency to homogamy.

6. Gary S. Becker, *A Treatise on the Family* (enlarged edn, Cambridge, MA, 1991), ch. 4.

7. See Orvar Löfgren, "Family and Household among Scandinavian Peasants: An Exploratory Essay", *Ethnologia Scandinavica*, 4 (1974), pp. 17–52; idem, *Arbetsfördelning och könsroller i bondesamhället – kontinuitet och förändring* (Lund, 1977); Louise A. Tilly and Joan W. Scott, "Women's Work and the Family in Nineteenth Century Europe", *Comparative Studies in Society and History*, 17 (1975), pp. 36–64.

that peasant couples developed various techniques to modify the principle of inheritance legislation, which prescribed equal inheritance among all children.[8] In Scania, the most common way seems to have been to transfer the family farm to a chosen child, often the eldest son, while at least one parent was still alive, in exchange for board and lodging for life. This was known as "peasant retirement".[9] However, it was not always the eldest son who became the new manager of the family farm, for quite often a younger son took on the job; or a daughter, which meant in fact a son-in-law.[10] To choose the right person must have been a crucial decision for the ageing couple: children who were not favoured in this respect were compensated in other ways, by parcels of land or movable property.[11]

It is easy to imagine that the marriage of children played an important role for the peasant couple in their plans for their own old age and succession between generations. The splitting of land through inheritance could be compensated for by the right marriage arrangement. A successful union between one of the children and a similarly wealthy party was a guarantee that the farm could maintain two households when the old couple retired. Beside the fact that they owned, and managed, the family farm, the institution of marriage gave the ageing couple an important role in the mating process.

According to the Marriage Act of 1734, no-one could be forced into marriage, and that applied both to men and women. On the other hand, the same act included provisions giving parents the power to influence their

8. Under Swedish inheritance legislation all children inherited from their parents. Up to 1845, sons inherited twice the amount that daughters did, but from 1845 all children inherited equally. Despite this general rule, the parents could to some extent favour one chosen child by separately bequeathing movable property or plots of newly acquired land. Even though all children had the right to their lawful portion, they could not always count on inheriting *land*. In cases where the farm was too small to divide, an heir with a larger share could buy out the others. This rule was valid up to 1845; after that a brother could buy out a sister. For a general description of the Swedish inheritance system, see Christer Winberg, "Familj och jord i tre västgötasocknar. Generationsskiften bland självägande bönder ca 1810–1870", *Historisk tidskrift*, 101 (1981), pp. 278–310, and Martin Dribe and Christer Lundh, "Gender Aspects of Inheritance Strategies and Land Transmission in Rural Scania, Sweden, 1720–1840", in Emiko Ochiai (ed.), *The Logic of Female Succession: Rethinking Patriarchy and Patrilinearity in Global Perspective* (Kyoto, 2003), pp. 53–73.

9. See Martin Dribe and Christer Lundh, "Retirement as a Strategy for Land Transmission: A Micro Study of Nineteenth Century Rural Sweden", *Continuity and Change*, 20 (2005), forthcoming; Christer Lundh and Mats Olsson, "The Institution of Retirement on Scanian Estates in the Nineteenth Century", *Continuity and Change*, 17 (2002), pp. 373–403; David Gaunt, "The Property and Kin Relationships of Retired Farmers in Northern and Central Europe", in Richard Wall, Jean Robin, and Peter Laslett (eds), *Family Forms in Historic Europe* (Cambridge, 1983), pp. 249–279; Löfgren, "Family and Household among Scandinavian Peasants".

10. Dribe and Lundh, "Gender Aspects of Inheritance Strategies".

11. Winberg, "Familj och jord i tre västgötasocknar"; Dribe and Lundh, "Retirement as a Strategy".

children's choice of partner. Unmarried women had no authority and were placed in the care of guardians, normally their fathers, who acted on their behalf in marriage negotiations. The institution of guardian is a reflection of the fact that marriage was a matter not only for the young couple, but for their elders too, in particular as far as women were concerned. The law also provided the right to disinherit daughters if they should marry against their parents' wishes. Even sons or widowed daughters could be disinherited if they remarried against the wishes of their parents, because they were part of their parents' household and a refusal to obey could be interpreted as disdain or contempt for their parents.[12]

Legislation therefore made it possible for marriages to be based on love, but at the same time, by virtue of their involvement in marriage negotiations and their right to disinherit children who did not obey them, made it possible for parents to influence the choice of a marriage partner. Ethnological researchers have made attempts to create a picture of how this worked in practice, by studying contemporary accounts of the subject.

In older ethnological literature, which dealt mainly with the customs of landed peasants, much emphasis was laid on parental influence on children's marriages and mention was even made of a "parental-power marriage system".[13] People were reluctant to see the homestead passed on to someone outside the family and wanted instead, as a result of marriage, to increase their own homestead's size by fusion with another one. An advanced expression of that sort of economic planning in connection with marriage was, among other things, the so-called "sibling-exchange" system, in which two siblings from one family married two from another.[14]

Contemporary sources often provide vivid accounts of parental power over children's choice of marriage partner. As mentioned above, it was mostly a matter of marriage strategies among wealthy farmers in southern and central Sweden. Contemporary narrators point out that these farmers endeavoured to marry off their children to their equals, which is to say within the same social group. Wealth and social status, not passion or love, were decisive qualities in the choice of marriage partner.[15] In 1847, Nicolovius, a pseudonym for the parson Nils Lovén, published a description of peasant customs he saw during his childhood at the turn of the century in the district of Skytt in southern Scania in which he stated:

---

12. *Sveriges rikes lag*, Giftobalken (Marriage Act), ch. 1: §2, §5; ch. 6: §§1–2.
13. Rob. K Wikman, quoted in John Granlund, "Bröllopsfunktionärer", *Fataburen* (1969), pp. 133–148, quotation p. 134.
14. Marianne Andersson, "Böndernas bönemän", *Fataburen* (1969), pp. 53–60, 53; Assar Jansson, "Giftermål med syskonbyte under 1700-talet", *Rig*, 38 (1955), pp. 82–88.
15. Eva Wigström, *Allmogeseder i Rönnebergs härad på 1840-talet* (Malmö, 1985, first pub. 1891), pp. 27–28; Nils G. Bruzelius, *Allmogelivet i Ingelstads härad i Skåne* (Lund, 1976, first pub. 1876), p. 34.

Similarity of wealth, but not the way of thinking or opinion, was the basis for marriage unions among farmers' families at the time. Beauty and grace were the least important in making their choice. These concepts did not even have corresponding words in the language of the farmers, and even now, when the word "charming" is used, I hear of a charming horse and even a charming pig, but, so far, never a charming girl.[16]

Marriage is often presented by contemporary narrators as a financial affair, even though that was not openly admitted; and a proposal was a negotiation in accordance with laid-down rules.[17] In 1976, Nils Bruzelius, a headmaster in the Ingelstad district of southern Scania, published an account of local customs. On marriage he wrote: "In the marriage settlement the most important question was always, 'What will you give the girl?' More than one proposal came to an abrupt end at the mere question, because the father-in-law refused to hand over the oxen demanded by the son-in-law."[18]

Contemporary narrators compare the peasants' conduct when choosing a marriage partner for their children with the efforts of higher social classes to retain or extend their family property. Whenever those efforts came into conflict with a youngster's love for someone other than the intended partner, or with a lack of affection for a chosen one, parents tried to impose their will and often succeeded.[19] If opposition from one of the marriage partners to the wishes of parents was too great, it was possible, within the framework of the marriage agreement between two families, to effect a change so that a brother or sister would be offered instead. However, fathers often forced daughters to marry against their will.[20] Eva Wigström, a teacher and writer describing peasant customs in the district of Rönneberg in western Scania in the 1840s, reported: "Just as Denmark has its legends about locked-up maidens, the Scanian rural people had theirs about girls who by force had to marry the men chosen for them by their parents and relatives."[21] Parents did not have the same jurisdiction to force sons into marriage, and traditional material shows that there were

---

16. Nicolovius, *Folklifwet i Skytts härad i Skåne vid början af detta århundrade* (Malmö, 1990, first pub. 1847), pp. 121–122.

17. Wigström, *Allmogeseder i Rönnebergs härad*, p. 29.

18. Bruzelius, *Allmogelivet i Ingelstads härad*, p. 34.

19. Wigström, *Allmogeseder i Rönnebergs härad*, p. 28; Bruzelius, *Allmogelivet i Ingelstads härad*, p. 34.

20. Nils-Arvid Bringéus, *Unnarydsborna. Lasses i Lassaberg anteckningar om folklivet i Södra Unnaryd vid 1800-talets början* (Stockholm, 1967), p. 105. On the initiative of the ethnologist Nils Gabriel Djurklou, Lars Andersson (called Lasse in Lassaberg), who was an active farmer, recorded his notes on peasant life in Unnaryd in Småland, the province north of Scania, during the period 1870 to 1872. The original manuscript by Lasse in Lassaberg was published in 1967 by Nils-Arvid Bringéus, Professor of Ethnology.

21. Wigström, *Allmogeseder i Rönnebergs härad*, p. 27.

instances when boys refused to follow their parents' directions and the parents had to yield.[22]

In addition to these parentally controlled marriages of convenience, there was always room for marriages based on love and affection above all, and in fact the use of parental power to influence children's choice of marriage partners was most evident among the nobility, bourgeoisie, and farmers, where children's marriages had an effect both on the transfer of resources between generations and on the organization of security in old age for parents.[23] Since parents controlled property, the threat of disinheritance had real significance. For the landless in rural areas, parental influence on children's choice of marriage partner was smaller.[24]

Contemporary accounts show that parental influence on children's marriages was greater in southern Sweden than it was in northern parts of the country, and that might have been due to differences in social structure. In the south, as we have seen, social differences were large and farmers with considerable landholdings gave their daughters large dowries, which is why they had good reason to try to get their children to avoid marrying the "wrong" partner. In the north, the social structure was more egalitarian, which reduced the need for strong parental influence on the choice of marriage partner.[25]

So, ethnological studies based on traditional material emphasize that farmers tried to prevent their children from marrying someone from a landless background.[26] Even contemporary descriptions call attention to the fact that children of landed peasants usually married their equals.[27] During the latter half of the eighteenth century there was extensive growth of landless groups. It has been shown that this growth was not due to fertility rates being higher among the landless than among the landed, but to increased downward social mobility. It is probable that, in the process, there was an increase in the proportion of marriages between peasants and the landless. It can also be expected that marriages across social boundaries were more common in areas, for example western Scania, with early proletarianization. Considering that "marrying down" socially was strongly resisted by peasant children, the increased proletarianization of rural areas should have resulted in an alternative strategy of remaining in

---

22. See Bringéus, *Unnarydsborna*, p. 105.

23. Orvar Löfgren, "Från nattfrieri till tonårskultur", *Fataburen* (1969), pp. 25–52, 35–36; Gunilla Kjellman, *Bröllopsgåvan* (Lund, 1979); see also Stone, *The Family, Sex and Marriage*, p. 182.

24. Andersson, "Böndernas bönemän", p. 53.

25. Löfgren "Från nattfrieri till tonårskultur", pp. 35–36. For a discussion of the link between dowries and homogamy, see Sabean, *Kinship in Neckarhausen*, pp. 466–469.

26. Löfgren "Från nattfrieri till tonårskultur", pp. 35–36.

27. Wigström, *Allmogeseder i Rönnebergs härad*, pp. 27–29; Nicolovius, *Folklifwet i Skytts härad*, p. 121; Bruzelius, *Allmogelivet i Ingelstads härad*, p. 34.

the parental home and postponing marriage, or even abstaining from it completely.[28]

Within sociological theories of modernization it is often believed that the nineteenth and early twentieth centuries brought fundamental changes to mating patterns. Industrialization brought not only economic changes that through new employment opportunities for young people reduced parental control over marriage, but also changes of mentality, implying an increased importance of "romantic love" in choosing a marriage partner.[29] As a result, it is argued that economic factors and family strategies became less important throughout the nineteenth century and that this development ultimately led to increased heterogamy. Empirical studies, however, sometimes find it difficult to substantiate these hypotheses of modernization.[30] Instead, mating patterns, as well as the family system more generally, seem to have been quite robust in resisting the economic and social changes that followed industrialization.[31]

AREA AND DATA

The data used are based on family reconstitutions carried out within the Scanian Demographic Database[32] for five rural parishes in western Scania in southern Sweden: Hög, Kävlinge, Halmstad, Sireköpinge, and Kågeröd. They are all about ten kilometres from the coast in the western part of Scania, which is the southernmost province of Sweden (see Figure 1). The social structure of these parishes varied somewhat. Hög and Kävlinge were

28. Christer Winberg, *Folkökning och proletarisering. Kring den sociala strukturomvandlingen på Sveriges landsbygd under den agrara revolutionen* (2nd edn, Lund, 1977), pp. 261–262; Christer Lundh, "Marriage and Economic Change in Sweden during the 18th and 19th Century", in Isabelle Devos and Liam Kennedy (eds), *Marriage and Rural Economy: Western Europe since 1400* (Turnhout, 1999), pp. 217–241.

29. See in particular William J. Goode, *The Family* (Englewood Cliffs, NJ, 1964), pp. 108–109; Edward Shorter, *The Making of the Modern Family* (Glasgow, 1977), pp. 152–163, 250–262. See also Marco van Leeuwen and Ineke Maas, "Partner Choice and Homogamy in the Nineteenth Century: Was There a Sexual Revolution in Europe?", *Journal of Social History*, 36 (2002), pp. 101–123.

30. See Van Leeuwen and Maas, "Partner Choice and Homogamy".

31. See Michael Anderson, *Family Structure in Nineteenth Century Lancashire* (Cambridge, 1971); Tamara K. Hareven, *Family Time and Industrial Time* (Cambridge, 1982); Angélique Janssens, *Family and Social Change: The Household as a Process in an Industrializing Community* (Cambridge, 1993).

32. The Scanian Demographic Database is a collaborative project between the Regional Archives in Lund and the Research Group in Population Economics at the Department of Economic History, Lund University. The source material is described in Elisabeth Reuterswärd and Franceska Olsson, "Skånes demografiska databas 1646–1894. En källbeskrivning", *Lund Papers in Economic History*, 33 (1993), pp. 1–62, and the quality of data is analysed in Tommy Bengtsson and Christer Lundh, "Evaluation of a Swedish Computer Program for Automatic Family Reconstitution", *Lund Papers in Economic History*, 8 (1991), pp. 1–43.

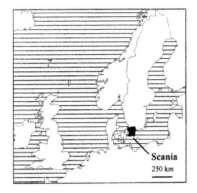

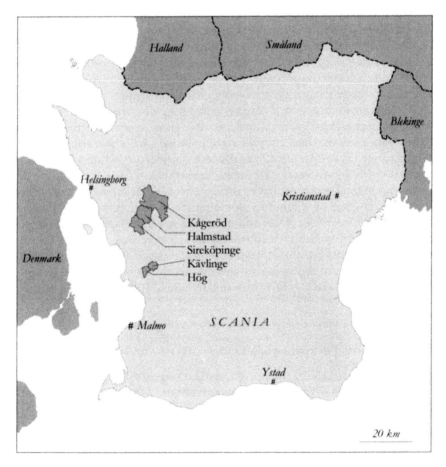

Figure 1. Location of the sample of parishes.

dominated by farmers on freehold and crown land with rather similar social characteristics, while the other three parishes were totally dominated by tenant farmers on manorial land.[33] Besides the peasant group, the parishes also contained various landless and semi-landless groups, who made their living working for other people. In 1830, the five parishes had 3,978 inhabitants. By 1895 that figure had increased to 5,539: an average annual increase of 0.5 per cent during this 65-year period, a somewhat slower rate of growth than for rural Sweden as a whole during the same period, which was 0.6 per cent per year.[34]

The family reconstitutions were carried out using data for births, marriages and deaths for the period from the late seventeenth century until 1894. The material is of high quality. The reconstitutions were carried out automatically using a computer programme.[35] They have also been checked manually and linked to other sources, chiefly poll-tax registers (*mantalslängder*) and the catechetical examination registers (*husförhörslängder*). The database contains all individuals born in the different parishes, or migrating into them. Instead of sampling any particular group (a birth cohort for example) each individual is followed from birth, or time of arrival in the parish, to death, or migration out again.

Since this study deals with mating behaviour, we need information on the social background of both spouses in a given couple. In the period 1829–1894, 4,040 married couples were counted in the 5 parishes under investigation. From them we sampled the couples for whom the social origin of both husband and wife could be established.

One potential problem with family reconstitution studies is that migration can lead to a family's demographic events being spread over several different parishes. Depending on how we deal with this problem, results derived from family reconstitution data may be biased in various ways.[36] In this study we are dependent on information about conditions in the parental home of individuals living in marital unions in the parishes. Using traditional family reconstitution data would have forced us to limit

33. See Martin Dribe, *Leaving Home in a Peasant Society: Economic Fluctuations, Household Dynamics and Youth Migration in Southern Sweden, 1829–1866* (Lund/Södertälje, 2000).

34. Statistics Sweden, *Befolkningsutvecklingen under 250 år. Historisk statistik för Sverige* (Stockholm, 1999), p. 42.

35. See Bengtsson and Lundh, "Evaluation of a Swedish Computer Program".

36. See Steven Ruggles, "Migration, Marriage and Mortality: Correcting Sources of Bias in English Family Reconstitution 1580–1837", *Population Studies*, 46 (1992), pp. 507–522; *idem*, "The Limitations of English Family Reconstitution: English Population History from Family Reconstitution 1580–1837", *Continuity and Change*, 14 (1996), pp. 105–130; E.A. Wrigley, "The Effect of Migration on the Estimation of Marriage Age in Family Reconstitution Studies", *Population Studies*, 48 (1994), pp. 81–97; Sune Åkerman, "An Evaluation of the Family Reconstitution Technique", *Scandinavian Economic History Review*, 25 (1977), pp. 160–170; Poul Thestrup, "Methodological Problems of a Family Reconstitution Study in a Danish Parish Before 1800", *Scandinavian Economic History Review*, 20 (1972), pp. 1–26.

the sample to couples where both husband and wife were born in the same parish they resided in after marriage. Due to very high rates of migration in this area,[37] such an approach would be likely to suffer from selection bias because the sample couples would have been taken from among non-migrants, who, most probably, would therefore have been selected by reference to landholding, physical ability, and so forth.[38]

To avoid that problem, we have traced all married individuals back to their parish of birth, regardless of whether their marriages took place in the parish of residence or not, and added information about their fathers' social status at birth. Information about the occupations of fathers was taken from the birth records or, if available, the catechetical examination registers, and data on access to land or croft were taken from poll-tax registers.[39] In that way we obtained information about the social origin of both husband and wife in married couples without introducing too much selection bias stemming from migration. However, due to missing or incorrect information about date and place of birth in the registers, we were not able to link data on the parental home to all individuals in the sample. For about 30 per cent of the couples we lack information about the social origin of either husband or wife, sometimes both, which leaves us with 2,724 couples for whom we have data on the social background of both husband and wife.

Table 1 overleaf shows couples distributed by spouses' social origin according to the HISCLASS classification.[40] Since the area of investigation in this study is entirely rural, for practical reasons, some minor regrouping within the HISCLASS framework has to be undertaken. Classes 1–5 ("managers and professionals") must be excluded from the analysis, since these groups are too small to be analysed by themselves, as is evident from Table 1, and too different to be conflated with any of the other groups.

In the present context "skilled workers" (classes 6–7) consists only of

37. See Dribe, *Leaving Home*; *idem*, "Migration of Rural Families in 19th Century Southern Sweden: A Longitudinal Analysis of Local Migration Patterns", *History of the Family*, 8 (2003), pp. 247–265; Martin Dribe and Christer Lundh, "People on the Move: Determinants of Servant Migration in Nineteenth Century Sweden", *Continuity and Change*, 20 (2005), pp. 53–91.
38. See Dribe, *Leaving Home*, ch. 2 for a discussion.
39. Information on individual birthplaces was gathered from the catechetical examination registers. The data were linked as part of the research project "Early-Life Conditions, Social Mobility, and Longevity", headed by Tommy Bengtsson and financed by the US National Institutes of Health/National Institute of Ageing (1P01AG18314-02), the Swedish Council for Social Research, and the Bank of Sweden Tercentenary Foundation. For details on the source material see Dribe, *Leaving Home*, ch. 2.
40. M.H.D. van Leeuwen and I. Maas, "HISCLASS", paper presented at the 5th European Social Science History Conference (Berlin, 24–27 March 2004). This classification is based on the more detailed occupational classification in HISCO; see Marco H.D. van Leeuwen, Ineke Maas, and Andrew Miles, *HISCO: Historical International Standard Classification of Occupations* (Leuven, 2002).

Table 1. *Cross-classification of spouses' social origin in five Scanian parishes, 1829–1894, using HISCLASS, all marriages*

Husband	Wife									N
	1+2	3+4+5	6+7	8a	8b	9	10a+12a	11	10b+12b	
1829–1864										
Higher managers and professionals (1+2)	0	0	0	2	0	0	2	0	1	5
Lower managers and professionals, clerical and sales (3+4+5)	0	0	0	0	0	0	0	0	1	1
Skilled workers (6+7)	0	0	3	0	9	0	14	1	15	42
Farmers on freehold and crown land (8a)	2	0	12	81	46	7	48	0	49	245
Tenant farmers on manorial land (8b)	0	1	11	31	205	2	92	0	103	445
Lower-skilled workers (9)	0	0	3	2	7	5	7	0	13	37
Semi-landless farm workers (10a+12a)	1	1	13	43	143	14	128	0	106	449
Unskilled workers (11)	1	0	0	0	0	0	0	0	0	1
Landless farm workers (10b+12b)	0	2	17	27	84	13	74	0	94	311
N	4	4	59	186	494	41	365	1	382	1,536
1865–1894										
Higher managers and professionals (1+2)	1	0	0	1	1	0	1	0	1	5
Lower managers and professionals, clerical and sales (3+4+5)	0	0	1	1	1	0	0	0	1	4

	(1+2)	(3+4+5)	(6+7)	(8a)	(8b)	(9)	(10a+12a)	(11)	(10b+12b)	N
Skilled workers (6+7)	0	0	5	6	3	5	11	1	41	72
Farmers on freehold and crown land (8a)	1	2	5	35	10	1	24	0	38	116
Tenant farmers on manorial land (8b)	0	0	9	17	27	1	40	0	58	152
Lower-skilled workers (9)	0	1	2	2	6	3	15	0	22	50
Semi-landless farm workers (10a+12a)	1	1	21	27	31	21	102	0	152	356
Unskilled workers (11)	0	0	0	0	0	0	0	0	0	0
Landless farm workers (10b+12b)	2	1	19	19	28	26	111	0	227	433
N	5	4	62	108	107	57	304	1	540	1,188

1829–1894

	(1+2)	(3+4+5)	(6+7)	(8a)	(8b)	(9)	(10a+12a)	(11)	(10b+12b)	N
Higher managers and professionals (1+2)	1	0	0	3	1	0	3	0	2	10
Lower managers and professionals, clerical and sales (3+4+5)	0	0	1	1	1	0	0	0	2	5
Skilled workers (6+7)	0	2	8	6	12	5	25	2	56	114
Farmers on freehold and crown land (8a)	3	1	17	116	56	8	72	0	87	361
Tenant farmers on manorial land (8b)	0	2	20	48	232	3	132	0	161	597
Lower-skilled workers (9)	0	0	5	4	13	8	22	0	35	87
Semi-landless farm workers (10a+12a)	2	2	34	70	174	35	230	0	258	805
Unskilled workers (11)	1	0	0	0	0	0	0	0	0	1
Landless farm workers (10b+12b)	2	3	36	46	112	39	185	0	321	744
N	9	8	121	294	601	98	669	2	922	2,724

Sources: Family reconstitutions, poll-tax registers, and catechetical examination registers for Halmstad, Hög, Kågeröd, Kävlinge, and Sireköping parishes, the Scanian Demographic Database, Department of Economic History, Lund University.

artisans, such as shoemakers, tailors, or carpenters; in a rural environment such as the parishes under study, artisans were not specialized skilled workers as were urban artisans, for whom both education and establishment were controlled by the guilds.[41] Rural artisans often worked for different peasants in the parish, rather than in their own workshops like urban artisans; sometimes they even lived in a peasant household while doing the work. Usually they were unable to live by their trade alone but had to work as farm labourers to supplement their income, and in the historical sources the same person might easily be recorded as a shoemaker one year and a landless worker another. Hence, rural artisans are grouped together with landless farm workers in this analysis.

The class of farmers (8) is divided into two subgroups by reference to their type of property rights and land tenure. Class 8a consists of farmers on freehold and crown land who had at least enough land at their disposal to provide for their families and to pay land rents or taxes.[42] Freeholders owned their land and paid land taxes, while crown tenants farmed land belonging to the Crown and paid land rent for it. Although there were important differences between those groups, for example when it came to inheritance and subdivision of land,[43] their situations were in many respects closely similar, especially if we compare them with other social groups. Consequently, in this analysis they will be analysed together and hereafter be jointly referred to as farmers.[44]

Class 8b consists of tenant farmers on manorial land with holdings above subsistence level. They were part of a manorial system and their conditions differed both socially and legally in important respects from

41. For a detailed analysis of rural artisans, see Carl-Johan Gadd, *Självhushåll eller arbetsdelning? Svenskt lant- och stadshantverk ca 1400–1860* (Gothenburg, 1991).

42. We have used 1/16 *mantal* as the limit of subsistence. *Mantal* is an old tax unit, originally meaning "the number of men". During the sixteenth century, every landholding was supposed to constitute one *mantal*, i.e. be large enough to support one peasant and his family as well as produce a surplus to be paid as tax to the crown. With few exceptions, this was indeed the case during the sixteenth century. Thus, at this time a *mantal* simply meant that the peasant had land and was supposed to pay tax to the crown. However, due to repeated subdivisions of landholdings, farmsteads typically got smaller and smaller fractions of a *mantal* assigned to them. Furthermore, reclamation of new land, as well as changed methods of cultivation, led to increased land productivity, which makes a comparison over time of the size of different farms almost impossible. Nevertheless, the *mantal* can be used at least as a rough measure of the size of a farm relative to other farms in the village in the same period. Thus, by comparing the different *mantal* peasants had, the relative productive potential of the landholdings can be determined. See Dribe, *Leaving Home*, pp. 26–27. It has been calculated that in the Harjager district, where Hög and Kävlinge are situated, one *mantal* was equivalent to about 200 acres in 1820. See Emil Sommarin, *Det skånska jordbrukets ekonomiska utveckling 1801–1914*, vols 2–3 (Lund, 1939), p. 25.

43. See Dribe and Lundh, "Gender Aspects of Inheritance Strategies"; Carl-Johan Gadd, *Den agrara revolutionen 1700–1870. Det svenska jordbrukets historia, band 3* (Stockholm, 2000).

44. See also Dribe, *Leaving Home*, ch. 2.

those of farmers on freehold and crown land. At least up to the 1860s they paid most of their rent as labour rent, working on the demesne. Often the exact amount of labour to be paid was not specified in contracts.[45] After the 1860s, the manorial system changed towards more specific contracts and less labour rent, which made conditions between the different farming groups more similar. From contemporary descriptions we also know that freeholders in the area generally looked down on tenants, despite the fact that they often farmed land of equal size.[46]

Class 9, "lower-skilled workers", consists of soldiers. The organization of the Swedish military system meant that the local community put at the disposal of a soldier a cottage or croft, with a small garden plot, in exchange for military service. He was given some payment too, usually in a combination of cash and benefits in kind, but the wage was not sufficient to live off, so the soldier had to work as a labourer to earn some more. In any case, being a soldier was by no means a full-time job, for usually a man spent only a couple of weeks with the army, during the off season for agriculture. The remainder of the year he spent at home, and worked on the land.[47] Accordingly, in this analysis, soldiers are merged into the group of landless farm workers.

The class of farm workers (10 and 12) is also divided into two subgroups. The "landless" includes farm workers without access to land, i.e. contract workers (*statare*), day labourers, servants, and lodgers (10b and 12b): the "semi-landless" (10a and 12a) consists of occupational groups who often had access to some land. Here we find peasants with land below subsistence level as well as of cottagers (*gatehusmän*) and crofters (*torpare*), who sometimes had landholdings equal to that of smallholding peasants, but frequently had only small garden plots. Unfortunately, it is impossible to distinguish in the sources between cottagers and crofters with and without arable land, which makes the semi-landless group somewhat heterogeneous, containing peasants and cottagers/crofters with land below subsistence level, as well as some cottagers and crofters lacking arable land altogether. Finally, the group of unskilled (non-farm) workers (11) is very small, which is only to be expected since the area under study was completely rural until the last decades of the nineteenth century.

Because of the small number of observations in some of these categories and the difficulty in distinguishing different occupations in this rural context, either from the sources or from the actual work individuals performed, an example being that artisans and soldiers were farm labourers most of the time, we chose a less detailed social categorization in order to

45. See Mats Olsson, *Storgodsdrift. Godsekonomi och arbetsorganisation i Skåne från dansk tid till mitten av 1800-talet* (Lund/Stockholm, 2002).
46. See Wigström, *Allmogeseder i Rönnebergs härad.*
47. See Lars Ericson, *Svenska knektar. Indelta soldater, ryttare och båtsmän i krig och fred* (Lund, 2002).

arrive at meaningful interpretations of the patterns of homogamy. Four different groups will be analysed: farmers on freehold and crown land (hereafter called "farmers"), tenants on manorial land (hereafter called "tenants"), "semi-landless", and "landless". The first two groups are identical to class 8a and 8b respectively, while the semi-landless group is the same as class 10a+12a. In the landless group classes 6, 7, 9, 10b, 11, and 12b are merged together.

In the Malthusian situation of eighteenth- and early nineteenth-century rural Sweden resources were scarce and so access to marriage varied between social groups. Since the social norm was that a marriage should result in the building of a separate household, a pre-condition for marriage was that along with a secure income access be available to a dwelling suitable for a family. Compared with youths of landless and semi-landless origin, the children of farmers and tenants were favoured in this respect and they were generally younger when they married, men being about thirty and women twenty-seven.[48] Young people of non-peasant origin often had to work as servants for a longer time and on average married a year or two older.

In the second half of the nineteenth century a substantial decrease occurred in mean age at first marriage for non-peasants, for women a drop of two or three years and for men two years. The average marriage age of peasants did not change much though, and in the late nineteenth century the difference was small between social groups. One interpretation of the decrease in the mean age at first marriage of the non-peasant group is that it reflected the social transformation in the countryside. Population pressure and the commercialization of agriculture perhaps gave rise to new employment and housing circumstances for married people such as crofters, cottagers and contract workers (*statare*), so access to marriage for landless people probably became easier and they could marry younger.[49]

Total marital fertility for women over twenty was around 7.[50] In the mid-nineteenth century about two-thirds of all newborn children survived to their thirtieth birthday, which implies that usually more than one potential heir was available when farms were transferred and that the choice of successor was consequently not a trivial decision.[51]

48. Christer Lundh, "Swedish Marriages: Custom, Legislation and Demography in the Eighteenth and Nineteenth Centuries", *Lund Papers in Economic History*, 88 (2003), p. 50. Recalculation of means for 1740–1849 and 1850–1894 from the data in figures 7 and 8 respectively.

49. *Ibid.*, pp. 49–51.

50. The figure refers to the period 1766–1865 in the same area; see Tommy Bengtsson and Martin Dribe, "Agency, Social Class, and Fertility in Southern Sweden 1766–1865", in George Alter, Noriko O. Tsuya, and Wang Feng (eds), *Prudence and Pressure* (forthcoming), ch. 4.

51. Calculated from period life tables for Sweden 1846–1850, Statistics Sweden, *Befolknings-utvecklingen under 250 år. Historisk statistik för Sverige* (Stockholm, 1999), pp. 119–120. See

A special problem with family reconstitution data is that for inward-migrating couples we do not know whether one or both spouses was remarried, or married for the first time. This distinction can be made only for couples married in any of the five parishes under examination here. In cases of remarriage, it was noted in the marriage record if either spouse had been married before. In our sample both first marriages and remarriages are included (a total of 2,693 couples). In order to make clear whether or not the pattern of mate selection is different for spouses marrying for the first time, a smaller sample of first marriages is studied (1,374 couples), the latter sample considered because it could highlight possible differences in homogamy which might depend on the marital status of spouses when the marriage itself was entered into. On the other hand, we are well aware that results may be biased, since this population is selected on the basis of the couple marrying and settling down in the area of investigation.

MEASURING AND MODELLING HOMOGAMY

Tables 2 and 3 present the number of couples distributed by reference to the social origin of the spouses. In Table 2 all marriages are included, while Table 3 includes only first marriages. In these cross-classification tables, homogamous unions are counted in the diagonal cells. As can be seen in these tables, the number in the diagonal cell is larger than the rest of the numbers in the respective rows or columns for farmers, tenants, and landless, which is an indication of positive assortative mating.

Given the four-group occupational classification used here, total homogamy over the entire period 1829–1894 was about 40 per cent in the two populations studied (see Table 4). Comparing the two periods it seems that homogamy became if anything stronger over time, but the differences between the periods are rather small (38 and 39 per cent in the first period and 44 and 42 per cent in the second). Table 5 indicates that for the whole period 1829–1894, the percentage of males who were married to a social equal was higher for landless and tenants and lower for semi-landless and farmers. For landless and tenants, homogamy was also stronger among males than among females, while the opposite was true for farmers and semi-landless. While homogamy was more pronounced in the first period for individuals of tenant origin, the opposite was true for individuals of landless background. These tendencies counterbalanced each other, which may help to explain why no changes could be observed in total homogamy over time.

Tables 4 and 5 indicate the occurrence of homogamy in the rural population we are studying. However, to compare the preference for

also Dribe and Lundh, "Retirement as a Strategy for Land Transmission"; *idem*, "Gender Aspects of Inheritance Strategies".

Table 2. *Cross-classification of spouses' social origin in five Scanian parishes,*
1829–1894, all marriages

Husband	Wife				
	Farmers	Tenants	Semi-landless	Landless	N
1829–1864					
Farmers	81	46	48	68	243
Tenants	31	205	92	116	444
Semi-landless	43	143	128	133	447
Landless	29	100	95	164	388
N	184	494	363	481	1,522
1865–1894					
Farmers	35	10	24	44	113
Tenants	17	27	40	68	152
Semi-landless	27	31	102	194	354
Landless	27	37	137	351	552
N	106	105	303	657	1,171
1829–1894					
Farmers	116	56	72	112	356
Tenants	48	232	132	184	596
Semi-landless	70	174	230	327	801
Landless	56	137	232	515	940
N	290	599	666	1138	2,693

Source: See Table 1.

homogamous marriage among the separate occupational groups, or over
time, we must take into consideration their social structure. Not only must
we analyse absolute homogamy, but relative homogamy too, and one
possible way to approach the latter is log-linear analysis.

Log-linear analysis has been widely used to model cross-classification
count data of the kind available to us here.[52] Log-linear models have often
been used, for instance, in analysing social mobility,[53] but also in analyses of

52. See Leo A. Goodman, "On the Measurement of Social Mobility: An Index of Status
Persistence", *American Sociological Review*, 34 (1969), pp. 831–850; Leo A. Goodman,
"Multiplicative Models for the Analysis of Occupational Mobility Tables and Other Kinds of
Cross-Classification Tables", *American Journal of Sociology*, 84 (1979), pp. 804–819.
53. For examples in historical research see Jan van Bavel, Hilde Peeters, and Koen Matthijs,
"Connections between Intergenerational and Marital Mobility: A Case Study, Leuven, 1830–
1910", *Historical Methods*, 31 (1998), pp. 122–134; Marco van Leeuwen and Ineke Maas, "Log-
linear Analysis of Changes in Mobility Patterns: Some Models with an Application to the
Amsterdam Upper Classes in the Second Half of the Nineteenth Century", *Historical Methods*,
24 (1991), pp. 66–79; Frans van Poppel, Jurjen de Jong, and Aart C. Liefbroer, "The Effects of
Paternal Mortality on Son's Social Mobility: A Nineteenth-Century Example", *Historical
Methods*, 31 (1998), pp. 101–112.

Table 3. *Cross-classification of spouses' social origin in five Scanian parishes, 1829–1894, first marriages*

Husband	Wife				
	Farmers	Tenants	Semi-landless	Landless	N
1829–1864					
Farmers	36	13	20	21	90
Tenants	13	131	51	58	253
Semi-landless	22	86	70	71	249
Landless	17	60	51	69	197
N	88	290	192	219	789
1865–1894					
Farmers	14	4	14	18	50
Tenants	5	19	19	52	95
Semi-landless	14	21	41	94	170
Landless	10	15	75	170	270
N	43	59	149	334	585
1829–1894					
Farmers	50	17	34	39	140
Tenants	18	150	70	110	348
Semi-landless	36	107	111	165	419
Landless	27	75	126	239	467
N	131	349	341	553	1,374

Source: See Table 1.

Table 4. *Total homogamy*

	All marriages		First marriages	
	Couples (per cent)	N	Couples (per cent)	N
Total homogamy	41	2,693	40	1,374
1829–1864	38	1,522	39	789
1865–1894	44	1,171	42	585

Source: See Table 1.
Note: Total homogamy = total number of couples where both spouses had the same social origin expressed as a percentage of the total number of couples.

mating patterns both in historical and contemporary populations.[54] In log-linear analysis the count in the cells of a cross-classification table is modelled multiplicatively. In the simplest case – what is usually referred to as the "independence model" – the count in a cell is assumed to depend only on the marginal distributions in the table:

54. See Matthijs Kalmijn, "Status Homogamy in the United States", *American Journal of Sociology*, 97 (1991), pp. 496–523; *idem*, "Assortative Mating by Cultural and Economic

Table 5. *Homogamous males and females*

	All marriages				First marriages			
	Males		Females		Males		Females	
	%	N	%	N	%	N	%	N
1829–1864								
Farmers	33	243	44	184	40	90	41	88
Tenants	46	444	41	494	52	253	45	290
Semi-landless	29	447	35	363	28	249	36	192
Landless	42	388	34	481	35	197	32	219
1865–1894								
Farmers	31	113	33	106	28	50	33	43
Tenants	18	152	26	105	20	95	32	59
Semi-landless	29	354	34	303	24	170	28	149
Landless	64	552	53	657	63	270	51	334
1829–1894								
Farmers	33	356	40	290	36	140	38	131
Tenants	39	596	39	599	43	348	43	349
Semi-landless	29	801	35	666	26	419	33	341
Landless	55	940	45	1138	51	467	43	553

Source: See Table 1.

$$ln(f_{ij}) = u + h_i + w_j$$

where u is the grand mean, h_i is the row effects (social structure of husbands), w_j is the columns effects (social structure of wives). If this model fits the observed data there is nothing structuring the mating process except the availability of spouses of different social origins, so the mating process itself is completely random. This model will be included only for comparisons. The modelling strategy will be to identify a number of theoretically relevant models which can be tested and compared. Since we are interested in studying homogamy over time we have divided the sample into two different time periods (see Table 2 above). The first model to test is the independence model taking into account changes in social structure over time, which is done both by including a parameter for time period, and interaction terms between time period and row and column effects. This model can then be compared with different homogamy models.

Occupational Status", *American Journal of Sociology*, 100 (1994), pp. 422–452; Robert D. Mare, "Five Decades of Educational Assortative Mating", *American Sociological Review*, 56 (1991), pp. 15–32; Robert McCaa, "Isolation or Assimilation? A Log Linear Interpretation of Australian Marriages, 1947–60, 1975, and 1986", *Population Studies*, 43 (1989), pp. 155–162; Bart Van de Putte, "Homogamy by Geographical Origin: Segregation in Nineteenth-Century Flemish Cities (Gent, Leuven, and Aalst)", *Journal of Family History*, 28 (2003), pp. 364–390; Van Leeuwen and Maas, "Partner Choice and Homogamy".

Table 6 presents an overview of the different models. As already mentioned, the independence model assumes that there are no systematic differences between the different cells in the table, which will be used for comparison. The equal homogamy model assumes that people have a tendency to marry homogamously, i.e. to marry someone from the same social group, and that this tendency does not differ between social groups. In other words, all social groups are equally likely to marry someone from the same social group.

In the case of pre-industrial rural society we expect the mating process to be different in different social groups. Landholding peasants, and especially farmers on freehold and crown land, can be expected to have wanted to marry homogamously in response to the importance to them of access to land in securing social status. The landless, on the other hand, cannot be expected to have preferred to marry, for financial reasons at least, other landless people. On the contrary, marrying a landholding peasant would imply upward social mobility. Of course, some may have been forced to marry a landless spouse from lack of alternatives, but we may still expect to find differences between social groups in the strength of their tendency to homogamy. The differential homogamy model allows for different homogamy effects in different social groups.

Sometimes it is argued that the main social difference in pre-industrial rural society was between the landed and the non-landed, while differences were much smaller within those groups.[55] In order to test this hypothesis we use a land homogamy model, which has one parameter for peasants marrying peasants, and one for non-peasants marrying non-peasants.

Since partner choice was intimately connected with social mobility, marrying upward (hypergamy) was most probably a goal desired by many of the landless and semi-landless. It could be argued that it should have been easier for women to marry upward, since they were not the managers of farms, while a farmer son in the process of taking over the family farm might have been more inclined to marry a spouse of landless origin, since there could be no transfer to her of responsibility over the farm. It is also possible that parents might look more favourably upon such a match for their son than if their daughter were to marry a landless man, who would then, in effect, become manager of the farm. In order to test that hypothesis we use three different hypergamy models: one model with a separate parameter each for males and females marrying upward, one model for women marrying upward and one for men marrying upward.

55. See Ingrid Eriksson and John Rogers, *Rural Labor and Population Change: Social and Demographic Developments in East-Central Sweden during the Nineteenth Century* (Uppsala, 1978), pp. 57–64. For demographic evidence see Bengtsson and Dribe, "Agency, Social Class, and Fertility"; Dribe, *Leaving Home*; Martin Dribe and Christer Lundh, "Husmäns och torpares demografi 1815–1865", in Kerstin Sundberg and Christer Lundh (eds), *Gatehus och gatehusfolk i skånska godsmiljöer* (Lund, 2002), pp. 143–156.

Table 6. *Models of homogamy*

Independence

Husband	Wife			
	FA	TE	SL	LL
FA	0	0	0	0
TE	0	0	0	0
SL	0	0	0	0
LL	0	0	0	0

Equal homogamy (d)

Husband	Wife			
	FA	TE	SL	LL
FA	d	0	0	0
TE	0	d	0	0
SL	0	0	d	0
LL	0	0	0	d

Differential homogamy (d_k)

Husband	Wife			
	FA	TE	SL	LL
FA	d_1	0	0	0
TE	0	d_2	0	0
SL	0	0	d_3	0
LL	0	0	0	d_4

Land homogamy (c_m)

Husband	Wife			
	FA	TE	SL	LL
FA	c_1	c_1	0	0
TE	c_1	c_1	0	0
SL	0	0	c_2	c_2
LL	0	0	c_2	c_2

Hypergamy* (h_n)

Husband	Wife			
	FA	TE	SL	LL
FH	0	h_1	h_1	h_1
NT	h_2	0	h_1	h_1
SL	h_2	h_2	0	h_1
LL	h_2	h_2	h_2	0

Female hypergamy* (h^f)				
Husband	*Wife*			
	FA	TE	SL	LL
FA	0	h^f	h^f	h^f
TE	0	0	h^f	h^f
SL	0	0	0	h^f
LL	0	0	0	0

Male hypergamy* (h^m)				
Husband	*Wife*			
	FA	TE	SL	LL
FA	0	0	0	0
TE	h^m	0	0	0
SL	h^m	h^m	0	0
LL	h^m	h^m	h^m	0

FA = Farmers
TE = Tenants
SL = Semi-landless
LL = Landless
* Marrying upward

The next step is to compare the different models. Different tests are available to check the fit of each model.[56] The most commonly used is the likelihood ratio test of the null hypothesis that the model fits the data: high values of the test statistic (the deviance statistic, G^2) indicate a poor fit and significance levels below 0.05 testify that the model does not fit the data, which in itself can give useful information about mating strategy. For example, a rejection of the independence model implies that the mating process is not random, but that there are some underlying structures determining who marries whom.

Nested models can be compared using a similar test where the difference in the deviance statistics between the two models is χ^2-distributed under the null hypothesis of no difference between a larger and a smaller model, with the degrees of freedom equal to the difference in the number of parameters estimated.[57] There is also an alternative way of comparing models that does not require models to be nested, namely the Bayesian Information Criterion (BIC):

56. For a description of log-linear models see Alan Agresti, *An Introduction to Categorical Analysis* (New York, 1996); Daniel Zelterman, *Advanced Log-Linear Models Using SAS* (Cary, NC, 2002).
57. Nested models are built hierarchically so that a larger model contains the same variables as the smaller model with some additional variables. In most cases statistical tests devised for model comparisons, such as the likelihood ratio test, require models to be nested in this way.

$$BIC = G^2 - df \, log(N)$$

where G^2 is the deviance statistic (the likelihood ratio test statistic), df the degree of freedom, and N the number of observations. A model with a lower BIC is preferred, and models with a negative BIC can be considered to have a reasonable fit.[58] Table 7 displays the fifteen different models estimated and the statistics used for model check.[59]

As expected, the independence model is clearly rejected (the critical value for G^2 at the 0.01 level with 25 degrees of freedom is 54.9), which shows that the mating process is not random. Taking into account the changed social structure (model 3) significantly improves the model fit, but the model is still rejected. In fact only the differential homogamy model has a reasonable fit, as shown both by the BIC and the likelihood ratio test (p-value>0.1). The differential homogamy model which controls for changes over time is not preferred to the one which does not control for period differences, which suggests that the pattern of homogamy did not change significantly between the two time periods. There seems to be no difference in which of the two models is preferred between the sample of all married couples and the sample of first marriages. These comparisons show that the data are best described by a model controlling for changes over time in the social structure and allowing homogamy to differ between all social groups.

Apparently the marriage pattern was characterized by a high degree of homogamy, but the strength of it differed among social groups, and an analysis of the estimated parameters (d_k) can inform us more exactly how homogamy differed among different groups. Table 8 shows the parameter estimates for the period as a whole and for each of the separate sub-periods. In the latter case, the coefficients shown in the table are the net effects calculated from the estimated interaction model (model 7), and the $p_{interac.}$ is the p-values for the interaction effects. The coefficients show the effects of the diagonal parameter on $ln(f_{ij})$ in each period while the exponentiated coefficients show the effect on the expected count (f_{ij}): a value of 2 implies that the estimated count in the cell is twice as high as could be expected taking into consideration only the marginal distributions (social structure).

In panel A of Table 8, farmers show the strongest homogamy with an effect of about 5, which indicates that cases of farmer marrying farmer are more than five times as frequent as could be expected from a random match, controlling for changed social status over time. Tenants show a weaker tendency, but still quite powerful, and the landless have a statistically significant homogamy effect, albeit lower than for tenants.

58. See Adrian E. Raftery, "Choosing Models for Cross-Classifications", *American Sociological Review*, 51(1986), pp. 145–146.

59. Model estimations were made using the GENMOD procedure in SAS. For log-linear models in SAS, see Zelterman, *Advanced Log-Linear Models*.

Table 7. *Model comparisons*

Model	All marriages			First marriages[+]		
	G^2	df	BIC	G^2	df	BIC
1 Independence (h_i, w_j)	756.5	25	669.8	435.9	25	349.2
2 Time difference (h_i, w_j, t)	710.6	24	627.4	405.5	24	322.3
3 Changed social structure $(h_i, w_j, t, h_i{}^*t, w_j{}^*t)$	236.5	18	174.1	141.8	18	79.4
4 Equal homogamy $(h_i, w_j, t, h_i{}^*t, w_j{}^*t, d)$	100.9	17	42.0	86.3	17	27.4
5 Equal homogamy, time difference $(h_i, w_j, t, h_i{}^*t, w_j{}^*t, d, d^*t)$	98.4	16	42.9	83.1	16	27.6
6 Differential homogamy $(h_i, w_j, t, h_i{}^*t, w_j{}^*t, d_k)$	11.9*	14	−36.6	15.2*	14	−33.4
7 Differential homogamy, time diff. $(h_i, w_j, t, h_i{}^*t, w_j{}^*t, d_k{}^*t)$	10.9*	10	−23.8	13.1*	10	−21.6
8 Land homogamy $(h_i, w_j, t, h_i{}^*t, w_j{}^*t, c_m)$	159.6	17	100.7	110.1	17	51.2
9 Land homogamy, time diff. $(h_i, w_j, t, h_i{}^*t, w_j{}^*t, c_m, c_m{}^*t)$	151.2	16	95.7	108.4	16	53.0
10 Hypergamy $(h_i, w_j, t, h_i{}^*t, w_j{}^*t, h_n)$	99.0	16	43.5	84.6	16	29.1
11 Hypergamy, time diff. $(h_i, w_j, t, h_i{}^*t, w_j{}^*t, h_n, h_n{}^*t)$	95.5	14	47.0	81.0	14	32.4
12 Female hypergamy $(h_i, w_j, t, h_i{}^*t, w_j{}^*t, h^f)$	127.2	17	68.2	93.7	17	34.8
13 Female hypergamy, time diff. $(h_i, w_j, t, h_i{}^*t, w_j{}^*t, h^f{}^*t)$	124.6	16	69.1	92.4	16	37.0
14 Male hypergamy $(h_i, w_j, t, h_i{}^*t, w_j{}^*t, h^m)$	158.2	17	99.3	112.0	17	53.1
15 Male hypergamy, time diff. $(h_i, w_j, t, h_i{}^*t, w_j{}^*t, h^m, h^m{}^*t)$	158.1	16	102.6	109.4	16	53.9

Source: See Table 1.
[+] Only marriages recorded in the parishes.
* p>0.1, which implies that the model cannot be rejected at the 10 per cent level. All other models can be rejected below the 5 per cent level of significance.
h_i husband's social origin (row effects).
w_j wife's social origin (column effects).
t time period (1829–1864, 1865–1894).
For explanations of other parameters see Table 6.

Only in the case of the semi-landless can we find no indication of homogamy. Most probably that is explained by the fact that this group is quite heterogeneous, including both smallholders and virtually landless cottagers – groups that can be expected to have married in opposite

Table 8. *Parameter estimates, differential homogamy*

A. All married couples observed

	1829–1894			1829–1864			1865–1894		
	β	e^β	p	β	e^β	$p_{interac.}$	β	e^β	$p_{ref.cat.}$
FA	1.63	5.09	0.000	1.59	4.92	0.762	1.68	5.38	0.000
TE	0.70	2.02	0.000	0.68	1.97	0.694	0.79	2.19	0.001
SL	−0.02	0.98	0.882	0.06	1.06	0.386	−0.12	0.88	0.445
LL	0.43	1.53	0.000	0.40	1.49	0.661	0.48	1.62	0.000

B. First marriages (only marriages recorded in the parishes)

	1829–1894			1829–1864			1865–1894		
	β	e^β	p	β	e^β	$p_{interac.}$	β	e^β	$p_{ref.cat.}$
FA	1.93	6.88	0.000	1.98	7.22	0.568	1.81	6.11	0.000
TE	0.86	2.35	0.000	0.82	2.27	0.482	0.92	2.50	0.003
SL	−0.18	0.84	0.224	0.04	1.04	0.288	−0.42	0.66	0.077
LL	0.29	1.33	0.028	0.20	1.22	0.756	0.44	1.55	0.024

Source: See Table 1.

Note: Estimates for the sub-periods are net effects (main effect plus period interaction effect) in the interaction model (model 7). 1865–1894 is the reference category and p-values for 1829–1864 ($p_{interac.}$) refer to significance tests of interaction effects between period and the diagonal parameters (d_k).

FA = Farmers
TE = Tenants
SL = Semi-landless
LL = Landless

directions. Apart from the semi-landless there seems to be a clear hierarchy in homogamy, with farmers being clearly the most homogamous, tenants taking the middling position, and the landless being least homogamous. Looking at panel B, it is clear that the same hierarchy applies to couples in their first marriages: the only noteworthy difference between the whole sample and the sample of first marriages is that homogamy among farmers is even stronger when only first marriages are considered.

These results are quite as expected. Landholding farmers had most to risk in the mating game and most to gain by marrying a like individual. Consequently they showed the strongest homogamy. It also seems reasonable that homogamy in this group was stronger in first marriages, partly because parental control over first marriages was greater, partly because of higher availability of potential spouses of similar social status among never married individuals than would be found among widows or widowers. Migration-related selectivity could be at work here, too. We know that farmers showed lower mobility than the landless or semi-landless[60] and it may be that those children of farmers chosen to take over the family holding were even less likely to move, which would contribute to the stronger likelihood of homogamy we have observed in first marriages among farmers.

Turning to changes over time, none of the interaction terms is statistically significant, which implies that we cannot show any clear changes in the pattern of homogamy over time; that was also the conclusion drawn from the model comparisons in Table 7. If we consider the estimated effects there seems to be a strengthening of homogamy among farmers when looking at all marriages, but a weakening when we look only at first marriages. For the semi-landless there is a tendency to heterogamy over time, as indicated by the negative coefficient relating to the second period. For the other social groups the differences between the periods are small. Taken together, the data suggest that homogamy remained strong during the entire period, which does not support hypotheses of fundamental change in mating patterns over the nineteenth century such as are envisaged by modernization theories: at least, not in rural areas.

CONCLUSION

Finding the right partner was a crucial thing for many people in pre-industrial society. Marriage was not only an act of love but a financial transaction as well. That is especially true for landowning peasants (farmers and tenants), since they had most to risk from a bad match.

60. Dribe, *Leaving Home*; *idem*, "Migration of Rural Families".

Parental control over marriage was strong, but peasant children themselves anyway preferred a partner from a similar background. Most probably, the economic concern was only one reason for preferring homogamy. More intangible aspects related to differences in social status, while self-identification with one's own group also contributed. Ethnological evidence and contemporary accounts give many examples of the importance of such perceived differences between social groups in pre-industrial rural Sweden.

In this article we have studied quantitatively the pattern of homogamy in a rural community in southern Sweden during the nineteenth century – a period with quite dramatic economic and social changes following agricultural transformation. The results show a society characterized by a relatively strong tendency towards homogamy. Given the occupational classification in this study, about 40 per cent of couples were homogamous unions. However, homogamy was not uniform across social groups. Farmers were considerably more homogamous than landless labourers, with tenants taking a middle position. Only the semi-landless did not show any homogamy at all, in that they were no more likely than could be expected from the observed social structure to marry someone from the same social origin, which can probably be explained by the fact that this was a heterogeneous group positioned between the landed groups and landless labourers.

Homogamy was also stronger for first marriages, especially among farmers, probably as a result of more parental control and a larger supply of potential marriage partners than in cases of remarriage. Interestingly, mating patterns remained fairly constant over time. Despite this being a period of quite rapid changes in Swedish society, homogamy did not weaken. Apparently, the choice of marriage partner remained an important financial and social concern, which does not support ideas in the literature that changes following modernization in the mentality or structure of opportunity for young people implied a transition to a more heterogamous society in which love replaced economics as the driving force in the choice of partner.

The rather strong homogamy characterizing landowning peasants in particular makes perfectly good sense in the light of the economic realities of peasants in a rural society. The landless, on the other hand, did not have much reason to marry within their group, since marrying a farmer or a tenant would be a major step up the social ladder. Instead, the homogamy we observe in this group is to a large extent a function of the preference for homogamy in the landed group; in most cases there were simply no alternatives for the landless except to marry other landless people.[61] The

61. See Kalmijn, "Intermarriage and Homogamy", p. 397.

profound economic changes during the nineteenth century following agricultural transformation and early industrialization did not change that situation. If anything, homogamy among farmers became stronger, testifying that mating habits were part of a very slowly changing structure which was deeply rooted in rural society.

IRSH 50 (2005), Supplement, pp. 179–218 DOI: 10.1017/S0020859005002117
© 2005 Internationaal Instituut voor Sociale Geschiedenis

Migration, Occupational Identity, and Societal Openness in Nineteenth-Century Belgium*

Bart Van de Putte,** Michel Oris, Muriel Neven,
and Koen Matthijs

Summary: This article examines social heterogamy as an indicator of "societal openness", by which is meant the extent to which social origin, as defined by the social position of one's parents, is used as the main criterion for selection of a marriage partner. We focus on two topics. The role first of migration and then of occupational identity in this selection of a partner according to social origin. And in order to evaluate the true social and economic context in which spouses lived, we do not use a nationwide sample but rather choose to examine marriage certificates from eleven cities and villages in Belgium, both Flemish and Walloon, during the nineteenth century. By observing different patterns of homogamy according to social origin we show in this article that partner selection was affected by the relationship between migration, occupational identity and class structure. It seems difficult to interpret all these divergent patterns in terms of modernization. In our opinion the historical context creates a complicated set of conditions reflected in differences in the type and strength of migration and in the sectoral composition and evolution of the local economy. The whole exerts an influence over partner selection.

This article examines social heterogamy as an indicator of "societal openness". We refer to the extent to which social origin, considered as the social position of one's parents, is used as the main criterion to select other people for social interaction, in our case most particularly for the selection of a marriage partner. An important claim of modernization theory is that in response to a range of changes, such as the growth of meritocracy or the decline of parental control, societies tend to become more open so that social origin is less rigidly adhered to as a determinant in partner choice.[1] A

---

* The authors would like to thank Etienne van der Straten for his help in the database management, and Anne Jacquemin who made the Liège marriage certificates available.
** Bart Van de Putte is Postdoctoral Fellow of the Fund for Scientific Research – Flanders (Belgium).
1. Marco H.D. van Leeuwen and Ineke Maas, "Social Mobility in a Dutch Province, Utrecht 1850–1940", *Journal of Social History*, 30 (1997), pp. 619–644.

variant claim is that societal openness at the end of the nineteenth century meant "demographic class formation",[2] a concept applied, in general, to the declining importance of both objective and subjective differences among the lower classes, for instance in the selection of a partner. According to the class-formation perspective, this modern openness was limited to the lower classes while boundaries between them and the middle class remained strong.[3]

In this article we consider the importance of occupational identities to the evolution of societal openness according to social origin, and try to shed light on the role of migration. The specifically sectoral composition of the economy and the level and type of migration are key elements in the economic and social context of any society. Both factors are perhaps important reasons for the greater complexity of the trend towards "modern" societal openness and why that trend is less linear than is sometimes assumed. In other words, they help to explain why the level of societal openness is dependent on historical context. We include the main criticisms of modernization theory and do not expect to find simple continuous processes, nor any progressive uniformity,[4] but we wish to understand why real patterns of partner selection diverge from the theoretical trend.

The data consist of marriage certificates from several Flemish and Walloon cities and villages. The advantage of the database is that it allows us to evaluate the social and economic context in which these spouses lived in more detail than we can by using a nationwide sample of "individuals". We present the data and give some background information. We then go on to discuss theoretical issues and empirically explore questions of migration, occupational identity, and social origin. We also discuss the methodology used to examine partner selection according to social origin. This methodology is applied later in our study.

DATA AND CONTEXT

We have used marriage certificates from civil registration registers which are available for the entire nineteenth century. The certificates contain information about the actual marriage, some demographic history of the spouses and their parents, their occupations, their places of residence, and

---

2. Andrew Miles, *Social Mobility in Nineteenth- and Early Twentieth-Century England* (Basingstoke [etc.], 1999).
3. Jürgen Kocka, "Family and Class Formation: Intergenerational Mobility and Marriage Patterns in Nineteenth-Century Westphalian Towns", *Journal of Social History*, 17 (1984), pp. 411–433, 423.
4. Simon Szreter, *Fertility, Class and Gender in Britain 1860–1940* (Cambridge, 1996), pp. 23–29; Steve Hochstadt, *Mobility and Modernity. Migration in Germany, 1820–1989* (Ann Arbor, MI, 1999).

Figure 1. Wedding photograph, Liège, c.1880.
E. Van Driessche (ed.), Des accordailles aux épousailles, Galerie CGER, Bruxelles, 19 février–1 mai 1988 *(Brussels, 1988), p.32. Used with permission.*

so on. Table 1 gives an overview of the places used for this study. Different sampling strategies were used: for Ghent, one in twelve marriage certificates was included, for Liège one in ten; for Verviers an alphabetical sample was extracted based on the letter B, while for Leuven and Aalst we abstracted one in three marriage certificates. For the other places we included all marriages. Altogether, we have available 38,502 marriage certificates, and in 9,152 cases we know the social position of the fathers of both bride and groom.

In the nineteenth century Belgium pioneered industrial revolution on the European continent, but in a highly polarized way. For the cotton and woollen textile industry, Ghent and Verviers were most advanced from the end of the eighteenth century and into the very early nineteenth. Ghent was a large and historic city, its economy based mainly on cotton, though other branches of the textile sector and engineering were important too. In the first half of the nineteenth century its population doubled and migration increased, and with that came a lower standard of living.[5] In the second half of the nineteenth century population growth slowed.[6] Unlike Ghent, Verviers was a small centre which underwent a phase of urban crisis similar to Ghent's in the first half of the nineteenth century.[7] An agglomeration progressively grew along the river Vesdre, and Limbourg was among the last villages to be integrated after 1846.

Aalst, like Limbourg, participated in a second wave of industrialization. In the first half of the nineteenth century it was a quiet, almost medieval city, where before 1880–1890 factories were still small, with fewer than 100 workers. But from about that time industry expanded, factories became larger, and in both Aalst and Limbourg newly established manufacturers appeared who had to compete with already well-established firms in the big cities, so they exploited their labour forces intensively, imposing working conditions even worse than elsewhere.[8]

Between the almost precocious development of Ghent and Verviers on

---

5. Chris Vandenbroeke, "Voedingstoestanden te Gent tijdens de eerste helft van de 19de eeuw", *Belgisch Tijdschrift voor Nieuwste Geschiedenis*, 4 (1973), pp.109–169; Peter Scholliers, *Wages, Manufactures and Workers in the Nineteenth-Century Factory: The Voortman Cotton Mills in Ghent* (Oxford [etc.], 1995).

6. Joël Mokyr, *Industrialization in the Low Countries, 1795–1850* (New Haven, CT [etc.], 1976), p. 27.

7. Claude Desama and Catherine Bauwens, "Une petite ville au coeur de la révolution industrielle: Verviers et le travail de la laine", in Bart Van der Herten, Michel Oris, and Jan Rogiers (eds), *La Belgique industrielle en 1850: deux cents images d' un monde nouveau* (Brussels, 1995), pp. 87–128.

8. Catherine Capron, "Une analyse statistique des migrations à partir d'un registre de population. Application au cas de Limbourg (est de la Belgique), 1847–1866", in Dominique Barjot and Olivier Faron (eds), *Migrations, cycle de vie familial et marché du travail* (Paris, 2002), pp. 65–94, 69.

Table 1. *Data and settings*

Location	Region	Period	Number of certificates	Population in 1806	Population in 1900	Economy
Ghent	Flanders	1800–1913	8,575	58,199	160,133	Industrial: textile
Aalst	Flanders	1800–1913	5,496	12,151	29,203	Industrial: textile
Leuven	Flanders	1800–1913	9,330	23,910	42,070	Artisanal-commercial
Verviers	Wallonia	1846–1890	2,176	9,821	*48,907	Industrial: textile
Limbourg	Wallonia	1807–1884	1,183	1,945	**4,118	Industrial: textile
Tilleur	Wallonia	1831–1881	1,055	496	**4,311	Industrial: coal, iron, suburb
Liège	Wallonia	1840–1890	4,461	46,983	*147,660	Industrial: coal and iron
Appelterre	Flanders	1800–1913	1,185	1,256	1,475	Agricultural
Bierbeek	Flanders	1800–1913	2,130	1,936	3,317	Agricultural
Ardennes	Wallonia	1811–1890	1,690	2,837	*3,495	Agricultural
Pays de Herve	Wallonia	1847–1890	1,221	5,991	*4,679	Agricultural

* population in 1890; ** population in 1880.

the one hand and Aalst and Limbourg on the other during the 1820s, mechanization in the textile industry prompted the modernization of the iron industry, with its coke-fired blast-furnaces, and of coal mining in the area around Liège. Liège itself was a large city, like Ghent, with many professional men and shopkeepers working alongside both old-time artisans, such as weapon-makers, and newer types of worker such as coal miners.[9] As Bairoch pointed out, Liège was a "historical opportunity" since an old town was located right in the centre of a coal basin and attracted a more or less coherent industrial agglomeration around itself.[10] Tilleur, a small village in which the Society of Sclessin invested in 1828, and whose population exploded from 617 to 6,642 inhabitants between 1831 and 1900, is a typical component of the area.[11]

Like Aalst and Limbourg, Leuven was originally a mid-sized town with no very strong industrialization in the nineteenth century, but Leuven lost the traditional craft and agricultural roots of its economy.[12] The transition was very gradual and did not lead to many large-scale business enterprises or factories, but Leuven played an important part in administration and education.

Local economic histories find an echo in the socioprofessional profiles of the fathers of grooms, although this echo is altered by geographical and intergenerational social mobility (Table 2).[13] Liège has a more diverse social structure and, globally, appeared to be a wealthy city with a large elite (10.6 per cent of fathers) and few unskilled workers (12.2 per cent). Lower managers and professionals were also some 12.5 per cent, and almost half (47.5 per cent) of the fathers in our sample were skilled or semiskilled workers. Leuven presents a similar profile but is obviously a smaller centre. Ghent was more comparable with Liège as an urban centre but had fewer elite citizens and more unskilled workers. In Ghent, in Limbourg, and even more so in Verviers, skilled and semiskilled workers were a large majority. While in Liège this group were mostly craftsmen, in the latter three cities their importance was mainly owing to the textile industry, a sector where production was highly segmented and a corresponding professional vocabulary very well established. Different

9. Anne Jacquemin, "Alliances et reproductions sociales à Liège entre 1840 et 1890", in Guy Brunet, Antoinette Fauve-Chamoux, and Michel Oris (eds), *Le choix du conjoint* (Paris, 1998), pp. 107–130, 108–109.

10. Paul Bairoch, *De Jéricho à Mexico. Villes et économie dans l'histoire* (Paris, 1985), p. 344.

11. Muriel Neven, "Mortality Differential and the Peculiarities of Mortality in an Urban-Industrial Population: A Case Study of Tilleur, Belgium", *Continuity and Change*, 15 (2000), pp. 297–329.

12. Koen Matthijs, Jan Van Bavel, and Ilse Van de Velde, *Leuven in de 19de eeuw. De bevolking: een spiegel van het dagelijkse leven* (Leuven, 1997).

13. We chose to use the social position of the fathers as it is the position of the fathers that is used in the analysis of partner selection.

Table 2. *Social position of the father of the groom, percentages (HISCLASS)*[14]

HISCLASS	Ghent	Aalst	Leuven	Limbourg	Verviers	Liège	Tilleur	Bierbeek	Appelterre	Pays de Herve	Ardennes
Higher managers and professionals (1+2)	5.5	3.2	7.0	8.8	5.0	10.6	2.2	1.2	0.4	2.7	1.5
Lower managers and professionals, clerical and sales (3+4+5)	17.1	11.5	15.1	9.2	11.0	12.5	6.1	3.2	5.1	4.3	3.8
Farmers and fishermen (8)	10.1	20.0	16.4	19.4	8.9	9.9	15.5	73.5	68.8	47.6	69.1
Skilled workers (6+7)	24.1	18.5	34.3	18.7	20.0	22.2	15.5	7.0	6.5	12.4	8.5
Lower-skilled workers (9)	21.5	15.6	14.1	26.2	45.9	25.3	21.9	2.2	3.6	16.5	5.0
Farm workers (10+12)	2.0	2.7	2.8	8.7	4.7	7.3	19.2	10.7	13.7	15.0	9.7
Unskilled workers (11)	19.8	28.5	10.3	9.2	4.7	12.2	19.8	2.4	1.9	1.5	2.3
N	3,730	2,470	4,047	565	967	1,298	510	1,063	474	582	975

14. For HISCO, see Marco H.D. van Leeuwen, Ineke Maas, and Andrew Miles, *HISCO: Historical International Standard Classification of Occupations* (Leuven, 2002). For HISCLASS, see M.H.D. van Leeuwen and I. Maas, "HISCLASS", paper presented at the 5th European Social Science History Conference (Berlin, 24–27 March 2004); I. Maas and M.H.D. van Leeuwen, "SPSS recode job from HISCO into HISCLASS", May 2004.

evidence collected in previous studies[15] contrasts the paternalistic family enterprises of Verviers with the more aggressive and anonymous firms of Ghent and the more recently established manufacturers in Limbourg and Aalst. Indeed, there were few unskilled workers in Verviers, rather more in Limbourg and Ghent, and a lot in Aalst (28.5 per cent). A high level was also observed in Tilleur, where the industrial revolution clearly led to a sort of "dequalification" and an increase in the number of unskilled there.[16]

Our databases cover the Belgian countryside too. Appelterre belongs to a region in which farming was often combined with a domestic textile industry. The cultivation of tobacco was a profitable extra source of income for many inhabitants. Bierbeek is located in a fertile region where farming took place on a fairly large scale. Before the French Revolution abbeys owned large farms, but later those properties came into private hands and were gradually divided up. The Pays de Herve was particularly famous for a very elaborate combination of cattle-breeding and textile proto-industrial production for the merchant-clothiers of Verviers. This area experienced a major collapse of this proto-industry between 1810 and 1830, and as a result the region "ruralized", with small peasant properties being replaced by large-scale concerns managed by local farmers for urban owners.[17] In the Ardennes, Sart, and Polleur municipalities was a group of small hamlets on the fringes of Fagnes, some of the poorest ground to be found in Belgium. A majority of semi-landless peasants used the large tracts of common land and forests to eke out an existence, which was anyway quite miserable. In the villages farmers were of course the huge majority (69 to 73.5 per cent), except in the Pays de Herve where some 29 per cent of fathers of grooms were classed as skilled or semiskilled workers – a reminder of the area's proto-industrial past. To this must be added that there was no general decrease in the number of farmers.

Nationally, if we compare our samples and Belgium as a whole, we miss several rural areas, the industrial basins of Hainaut, and the capital, Brussels, a major place of interaction between social groups, migrants, and others.[18] We cannot claim our results are valid for the whole country, but

15. Capron, "Une analyse statistique"; Desama and Bauwens, "Une petite ville"; Peter Scholliers, *De Gentse metaalbewerkers in de 19de eeuw: de enquête van L. Varlez* (Brussels, 1985).

16. Muriel Neven, "Espaces ruraux et urbains au XIXe siècle: trois régimes démographiques belges au coeur de la révolution industrielle", *Popolazione e storia*, 2 (2002), pp. 35–62, 50.

17. *Idem, Individus et familles: les dynamiques d'une société rurale. Le Pays de Herve dans la seconde moitié du XIXe siècle* (Liège, 2003).

18. Machteld De Metsenaere, "Le choix du conjoint, indicateurs des changements linguistiques à Bruxelles au XIXe siècle", in Brunet, Fauve-Chamoux, and Oris, *Le choix du conjoint*, pp. 77–92.

our data do cover a wide range of contexts and histories while we aim precisely at showing the effects of context on the paths taken by societies, as far as openness in choice of partner is concerned.

THEORY

Partner selection

To explain the influence on partner selection of modernization, migration, and occupational identities, we present a simple framework to examine partner selection. We distinguish three general determinants:[19] structural causes, preferences, and social control.

Partner selection is influenced by the supply of potential partners (*structural causes*). There are two important elements to this. First, *social structure* determines group sizes in the marriage market; that is, the number of potential partners who belong to a specific social category (for example, the number of farmers or skilled workers). Second, the supply of potential partners is in practice influenced by *meeting opportunities* between different "types" of partner. Potential partners belonging to a specific category (farmers, for instance) can sometimes more easily meet similar individuals (other farmers) instead of members of other groups (workers, for example), for instance, because of spatial segregation according to social position.[20]

Individual evaluation criteria (*preferences*) are applied to partner selection. There are three main principles of evaluation that inform the "development" of preference patterns in partner selection:

Rational-instrumental selection ("he or she is the most suitable choice"). This principle was highly valued in the contemporary literature.[21] It may be applied to the social position of the father (social origin) or to the social position of the spouses, reflecting their personal "merit", in which case the level of intergenerational social mobility is an important cause of heterogamy according to social origin.

19. Marco van Leeuwen and Ineke Maas, "Huwelijksmobiliteit in Friesland tussen 1850 en 1929", *It Beaken*, 63 (2001), pp. 64–178; Frans van Poppel, Aart Liefbroer, Jeroen Vermunt, and Wilma Smeenk, "Love, Necessity and Opportunity: Changing Patterns of Marital Age Homogamy in the Netherlands, 1850–1993", *Population Studies*, 55 (2001), pp. 1–13; Bart Van de Putte, "Het belang van de toegeschreven positie in een moderniserend wereld. Partnerkeuze in 19de-eeuwse Vlaamse steden (Leuven, Aalst en Gent)" (Ph.D., Catholic University of Leuven, 2003).

20. On the role of spatial proximity, see Jacquemin, "Alliances et reproductions socials", pp. 121–122.

21. Denis Bertholet, *Le bourgeois dans tous ses états: le roman familial de la Belle Epoque* (Paris, 1987); George Alter, *Family and the Female Life Course: The Women of Verviers, Belgium, 1849–1880* (Madison, WI, 1988), pp. 145–147.

Romantic-expressive selection ("he or she is the only 'true' partner"). If this principle is applied, heterogamy according to social origin may be expected to increase,[22] although the consequences of romantic love for heterogamy are sometimes questioned.[23]

Selection based on *"group belonging"* ("he or she is an insider"). If this principle is applied, cultural values and prejudice against outsiders are important causes of homogamy (for example the identification of sons with the occupational group of their father, aversion to migrants). If, for example, social groups are defined by the occupation of one's father, one can expect the selection of a marriage partner to be restricted to this "in-group".[24]

Partner selection is often controlled or at least influenced by the preferences of third parties (*social control*), whether parents, peers, priests, or perhaps colleagues: some argue, for example, that spouses, especially the young and the upper classes, married the "right" partner often because of social control.[25]

Underlying the idea of modernization and the increase in societal openness are the claims that, (1) rational-instrumental selection was applied increasingly to the social position of the spouses instead of to the social position of the father, which suggests a meritocratic element; or (2) that romantic-expressive selection increasingly replaced rational-instrumental selection; or, (3) that there was a de-identification with the occupation of the father; or, (4) that there was a weakening of traditional forms of social control. Of course, these causes are not mutually exclusive. The idea of demographic class-formation adds to this the notion that definitions of the identifiable social group did not simply disappear but

22. Marco van Leeuwen and Ineke Maas, "Partner Choice and Homogamy in Sweden in the Nineteenth Century: Was there a Sexual Revolution in Europe?", *Journal of Social History*, 36 (2002), pp. 101–123; Edward Shorter, *The Making of the Modern Family* (New York, 1975), pp. 157–159; Bart Van de Putte and Koen Matthijs, "Romantic Love and Marriage: A Study of Age Homogamy in Nineteenth-Century Leuven", *Belgisch Tijdschrift voor Nieuwste Geschiedenis*, 21 (2001), pp. 579–619; Frans van Poppel, Aart Liefbroer, and Wendy Post, "Vers une plus grande homogamie d'âge entre conjoints: différences entre les classes sociales et différences régionales aux Pays-Bas, 1812–1912", *Annales de Démographie Historique*, (1998), pp. 73–110, 75–76.
23. Peter Borscheid, "Romantic Love or Material Interest: Choosing Partners in Nineteenth-Century Germany", *Journal of Family History*, 11 (1986), pp. 157–168; François Héran, "Finding a Spouse: A Survey of How French Couples Meet", *Population: An English Selection*, 1 (1989), pp. 91–121.
24. William Sewell, "Social Mobility in a Nineteenth-Century European City: Some Findings and Implications", *Journal of Interdisciplinary History*, 7 (1976), pp. 225–230.
25. Steve Hochstadt, "Demography and Feminism", in P. Robertson (ed.), *An Experience of Women: Pattern and Change in Nineteenth-Century Europe* (Philadelphia, PA, 1982), pp. 541–560, 544.

Figure 2. Parents exercised social control by accepting or refusing marriage candidates. "*L'album moral*" *d'aprés Jules David, 19ᵉ siècle, from: E. Van Driessche* (ed.), Des accordailles aux épousailles, Galerie CGER, Bruxelles, 19 février–1 mai 1988 *(Brussels, 1988), p.31. Used with permission.*

became broader and included the whole lower class instead of just the one specific occupational group.

In the next sections we shall show how migration and occupational identity fit into this scheme and describe how those variables differ in the selected locations.

The role of migration

There are four reasons to associate migration with social heterogamy. First, migration can lead to a decline in social control. If parents are not present, that is to say if children and parents do not migrate together, marriage candidates may behave more freely.[26] Not only might traditional preferences be less strongly "controlled" by the parents of those who, as a

---

26. Michel Oris and Emiko Ochiai, "Family Crisis in the Context of Different Family Systems: Frameworks and Evidence on When Dad Died", in Renzo Derosas and Michel Oris (eds), *When Dad Died: Individuals and Families Coping with Distress in Past Societies* (Berne [etc.], 2002), pp. 17–79, 45–47.

result of this mobility[27] before marriage, became, as it were, emancipated; we also see obvious cases in nineteenth-century Belgium where young men and women quite literally "escaped" from the parental control exercised in their strictly Malthusian villages.[28]

Second, migration can limit the use of the social network of parents. Even if parents are present, their ability to support their children in their selection of a partner might be limited because of their migration, in much the same way as the deaths of parents could have the same effect.[29] Consequently, social origin is, in a sense, less useful when considered for migrants than for natives. If partner selection is based on rational-instrumental selection by reference to the social position of parents, then following this logic we should expect migrants to be more likely to marry a partner of lower social origin.

Third, migration is frequently, although not systematically, linked with social mobility. The decision to migrate is often related to an individual's perception of the future within the community of origin. Since the Belgian countryside reached its demographic climax only in the late nineteenth century, without any real easing before 1890 of the Malthusian brake of late marriage and high rates of celibacy,[30] we can say that those who could, stayed.[31] Sons and daughters of farmers usually migrated to the city if the possibility of earning a living in their home village was limited. If the lower social position of a child who had migrated were to be taken into account, it would become difficult to marry a partner of the same social origin. But of course, migrants could avoid that pitfall by marrying other migrants.

Fourth, the presence of migrants and the desire to marry homogamously according to geographical origin can have consequences for partner selection according to social origin. If geographical origin is the main principle used in partner selection, and if there is a large migrant group available for marriage, it becomes more difficult to marry a partner of the same social origin. Indeed, if the number of potential partners is reduced to those of the same geographical origin, the chances of marrying somebody

27. Didier Blanchet and Denis Kessler, "La mobilité géographique, de la naissance au mariage", in Jacques Dupâquier and Denis Kessler (eds), *La société française au XIXe siècle. Tradition, transition, transformations* (Paris, 1992), pp. 343–377, 346.
28. Michel Oris, Catherine Capron, and Muriel Neven, "Le poids des réseaux familiaux dans les migrations en Belgique orientale au 19e siècle. Peut-on quantifier?", in Eugenio Sonnino (ed.), *Living in the City* (Rome, 2002), pp. 151–178.
29. Grazyna Ryczkowska, "Accès au mariage et structures de l'alliance à Genève, 1800–1880", (M.A. thesis, University of Geneva, 2003), esp. pp. 106–110, 121–123.
30. Bierbeek is an exception since the mean age at marriage declined earlier. See Koen Matthijs, *De mateloze negentiende eeuw. Bevolking, huwelijk, gezin en sociale verandering* (Leuven, 2001).
31. Muriel Neven, *Individus et familles*, ch. 9; Michel Oris, "The Age at Marriage of Migrants During the Industrial Revolution in the Region of Liège", *The History of the Family: An International Quarterly*, 5 (2000), pp. 391–413, 408–409.

of the same social origin are automatically smaller.[32] While the first three reasons imply that migrants are more heterogamous, this fourth reason implies a higher level of heterogamy more generally.

Table 3 overleaf shows the proportion of migrants among spouses in the Belgian cities and villages. The difference between grooms and brides is largely an artefact and can be explained by the custom of celebrating the marriage in the bride's locality. The table shows that in most locations the population of spouses had a large component of migrants. Given the relatively high levels for the villages, especially Pays de Herve and Appelterre, spatial mobility was not a characteristic unique to urban populations. As such, the large presence of migrants justifies this more thorough discussion of the role of migration in the process of partner selection. Furthermore, in Flanders natives tended to stay dominant, but in Wallonia they were a minority, except in the Ardennes. Clearly, in small industrial suburbs like Tilleur and Limbourg migration created new populations.

The migrant group was diverse. They were both rural and non-rural, foreigners and Belgians, Flemish and French-speaking. Particularly important, because of the spectacular growth there, was the presence in both Liège and Tilleur of the Flemish: in Liège from 1874–1890 26 per cent of grooms were either Flemish or foreign, while before 1850 only 12 per cent had been so; in Tilleur the figures were 43.1 per cent and 23.9 per cent respectively (this was less the case for native brides, with fewer Flemish brides compared with Flemish grooms).

Consequently, the native Liège and Tilleur brides were increasingly operating in a marriage market on which there were many potential marriage candidates speaking a different language. Obvious discrimination against the Flemish[33] and endogamy among them have been observed in Liège and Tilleur.[34] Furthermore, as, in Tilleur at least, these spouses did not come from the same or even adjacent villages, this endogamy of the

32. Van de Putte, "Het belang van de toegeschreven positie". The role of migration is probably somewhat different in the countryside. Most migrants are born rather close to the village of marriage and are not necessarily "special"; they did not come from far away nor did they "leave" their old social environment.

33. Yves Quairiaux and Jean Pirotte, "L'image du Flamand dans la tradition populaire wallonne depuis un siècle", *Res publica. Revue de l'Institut belge de science politique*, 20 (1978), pp. 391–406; Jacquemin, "Alliances et reproductions socials". For other studies of segregation according to geographical origin on the marriage market, see Van de Putte, "Het belang van de toegeschreven positie", on Flanders; Jacquemin, "Alliances et reproductions socials", on the Flemish in Liège; Leslie Page Moch, *Moving Europeans: Migration in Western Europe since 1650* (Bloomington, IN [etc.], 1992), pp. 143–147; Patricia van den Eeckhout and Peter Scholliers, "Social History in Belgium: Old Habits and New Perspectives", *Tijdschrift voor Sociale Geschiedenis*, 23 (1997), pp. 147–181,160.

34. Anne Jacquemin, "Un éclairage de la sociabilité en milieu urbain à partir des actes de mariages liégeois (1840–1890)", *Congrès de Liège des 20–23 octobre 1992* (Liège, 1994), pp. 346–360; Oris, "The Age at Marriage".

Table 3. *Percentage of spouses not born in the place of marriage*

Location	Grooms		Brides	
	%	N	%	N
Aalst	31.0	5,194	24.8	5,171
Leuven	40.7	8,437	36.7	8,623
Ardennes	41.7	1,690	24.2	1,690
Bierbeek	42.2	2,118	18.6	2,112
Ghent	43.2	8,565	40.0	8,555
Liège	54.8	4,461	51.4	4,461
Appelterre	57.4	1,173	27.5	1,164
Verviers	58.6	2,176	50.0	2,176
Pays de Herve	66.3	1,221	40.8	1,221
Limbourg	75.3	1,183	61.3	1,183
Tilleur	92.2	1,055	77.3	1,055

Flemish was not the result of the marriages of "almost married couples" marrying in the city of destination, but rather from rejection and marginality. It differs from endogamy among, for example, native weapon-makers in Liège – which was done from choice. A calculation of the association between the two variables "geographical origin of groom" and "geographical origin of bride" (using a variable with three categories: natives, foreigners, and Flemish, other migrants) shows that homogamy was strong (Cramers V is 0.43 for Liège and 0.64 for Tilleur, while much lower for the other cities, in which the value is maximally about 0.2).

Occupational identity

By "occupational identity" we mean the tendency of individuals to define their social identity in terms of their own occupation or that of their family. We refer specifically to a son's identification with the occupation of his father. Occupational identity was traditionally important as an organizing principle of social life, as a shaper of social contacts between persons and families with the same occupation.[35] First, as observed by Sewell for nineteenth-century Marseilles,[36] occupational identity stimulates intergenerational immobility, which will probably lead to more

---

35. See for example Scarlett Beauvalet-Boutouyrie, *La démographie de l'époque moderne* (Paris, 1999), p. 125; Miles, *Social Mobility*, p. 145; Kathlijn Pittomvils, "De Gentse maatschappijen van onderlinge bijstand in de eerste helft van de negentiende eeuw. Solidariteit, staking en/of segmentering?", *Belgisch Tijdschrift voor Nieuwste Geschiedenis*, 25 (1994–1995), pp. 433–479.
36. Sewell, "Social Mobility in a Nineteenth-Century European City"; see also Miles, *Social Mobility*, ch. 4.

homogamy according to social origin. Second, occupational identity might have tended to stimulate homogamy because it contributed importantly to a sense of belonging to an occupational group.[37]

Industrialization, urbanization, and the rise of modern cities, with their greater opportunities for anonymous meeting and the availability of new occupations, challenged "traditional" occupational identities and occupational immobility down the generations, which can always result in a more open pattern of partner selection. Yet this "modernization" view needs to be qualified, because industrialization does not necessarily lead to the gradual decline of occupational identities. First, especially during the first stages of industrialization, large industrial sectors were created, the textile and mining industries being examples. Some of these modernized occupational groups, especially the miners, are well known to have developed a strong sense of identity and formed cohesive groups.[38] So, industrialization might in some cases even reinforce the role of occupational identities and help them stimulate homogamy.

Second, although there are signs of decreased differences among the lower classes, due for example to proletarianization and de-skilling,[39] the transformation of modern industrial and other workers into one large group of "the lower class" was by no means a smooth process. Even if a modern labour movement wanted to alter group boundaries, in some situations sector-based social life and identity remained strong for a long time; indeed, the organizational outlook of the labour movement was originally based on those segmentations.[40] In other words, in modern times too, not only class but occupation as well shaped social life and bolstered social dignity.

Third, some "traditional" occupational groups kept intact their tight social network and probably their homogamous marriage pattern for a very long time. Most survived the first industrial revolution, which was limited to a few leading sectors, but progressively they were weakened by the diffusion of mechanization and industrial organization into craft sectors of production.[41] The Liège weapon-makers are a good example of

37. Grazyna Ryczkowska and Gilbert Ritschard, "Mobilités sociales et spatiales. Parcours intergénérationnels d'après les mariages genevois, 1830–1880", paper presented at the 5th European Social Science History Conference (Berlin, 24–27 March 2004).

38. Diana Cooper-Richet, *Le peuple de la nuit: mines et mineurs en France (XIX–XXe siècle)* (Paris, 2002); Claude Gaier, *Huit siècles de houillerie liégeoise: histoire des hommes et du charbon à Liège* (Liège, 1988).

39. Neven, "Mortality Differential and the Peculiarities of Mortality in an Urban-Industrial Population", pp. 297–329; Scholliers, *De Gentse metaalbewerkers*, p. 36.

40. In Verviers, as late as 1906 the Textile Workers Federation included The Federation of Combed Woolworkers, The Federation of Carded Woolworkers, The General Association of Weavers, The Wool Washers, and five others groups.

41. Michel Oris, "Le contexte économique et social", in *Histoire des Sciences en Belgique* (Brussels, 2001), pp. 37–70, 41.

that.[42] Also farmers usually have a strong occupational identity, which is reinforced by the importance of the rational-instrumental criterion in partner selection.[43] For children of farmers who are themselves farmers, it is often important to marry a partner from a farming background, perhaps to pool property or just because farming skills are an attractive quality in a spouse. The higher level of social control in the countryside strengthens this narrow group life.[44] Consequently, the differences in absolute homogamy between locations and their evolution over time are possibly strongly influenced by the size of the group of farmers. This is not as trivial as it might seem, since it was precisely those levels of absolute homogamy that were rather important to the daily experience of societal openness.[45]

To assess the strength of occupational identities in the cities and villages we calculated the percentage of grooms working in the same sector (HISCO, first two digits) as their fathers. We found, first, that there was no general and strong decline in occupational immobility, although in Aalst in the period after 1890 and in Liège and Tilleur after 1850 there was a modest decrease of about 10 per cent. Second, the level of intergenerational occupational immobility was surprisingly high for some occupations, not only in traditional but also in some new sectors. In Tilleur and Liège the percentage of sons who followed their fathers into mining was high, respectively 74.6 per cent and 62.1 per cent, while among the fathers miners accounted for respectively 70 per cent and 20 per cent of lower-skilled workers. Among the textile workers of Verviers and Limbourg intergenerational occupational immobility was the most frequent option too, especially in Limbourg (76.4 per cent compared with 54.5 per cent in Verviers, while among the fathers textile workers accounted for respectively 60 per cent and 72 per cent of the lower-skilled workers). In Flanders there were no occupations that showed such high levels of "immobility" and only textile workers showed a distinct pattern. In Ghent, where about 29 per cent of the lower-skilled were textile workers, the general level of intergenerational occupational immobility was about 30 per cent, while for textile workers it was one of the highest (at 40 per cent), which shows indeed that industrialization did not necessarily lead directly to strong occupational mobility, implying the absence of a potentially strong stimulus to heterogamy.

A particular case revealing the importance of occupational identity can

42. Claude Gaier, *Quatre siècles d'armurerie liégeoise* (Liège, 1976); René Leboutte, *Reconversions de la main-d'oeuvre et transition démographique. Les bassins industriels en aval de Liège. XVIIe–XXe siècles* (Paris, 1988).

43. Martine Ségalen, *Mari et femme dans la société paysanne* (Paris, 1980).

44. Muriel Neven and Michel Oris, "Contrôle religieux, contrôle social: la fécondité dans l'est de la Belgique dans la seconde moitié du XIXe siècle", *Annales de Démographie historique*, 2 (2003), pp. 5–32.

45. Van de Putte, "Het belang van de toegeschreven positie".

be observed in Verviers. After 1873, Verviers' industry declined more steeply than elsewhere and was in fact the Walloon "pioneer" of industrial decline. Simultaneously there was an early process of class formation there. That resulted in many trade unions, federations, cooperatives, an affiliation to the Belgian Workers' Party in 1885 and, although only later, in the 1890s, widespread strikes. Verviers was thus a pioneer city in the labour movement, a city where a new sense of belonging emerged quite early and quickly, at least more so than in Liège or Tilleur. The combination of economic stagnation and early labour movement activity perhaps initially (say before 1890) stimulated occupational- and sector-based social life, just as traditional occupational organizations did. It is plausible to suggest that this strengthening of group bonds itself led to homogamy. This period of stagnation must be distinguished from the phase of urban crisis in the first half of the nineteenth century, conditions in which heterogamy was favoured.[46] We assume that the restoration of occupational identity by early class formation is strongest for the rooted population. In many eighteenth- and nineteenth-century cities, such as Grenoble or Geneva,[47] a distinction is made between the rooted population, seen as the "core" of the city, who own and proudly transmit its local civic culture, and the mobile population, who are just "passing through".

Ghent's history shows similarities: economic expansion was less strong after 1850, and, although the number of textile enterprises and workers increased, their proportion within the whole economy declined.[48] The labour movement in Ghent too became important, especially after 1890, but before then there were important associations, of spinners and weavers for example, which were organized on the basis of their occupation.

Finally, in the villages, high levels of occupational immobility were habitual among farmers. The highest level is observed in Appelterre (72.5 per cent), the lowest in Bierbeek (58.3 per cent), and there was great immobility (68 per cent) in the Ardennes and the Pays de Herve.

Occupational identity, class, and migration

Occupational identity, class, and migration were clearly related. Some occupational sectors, for example the textile industry in early nineteenth-century Ghent or weapon-making in Liège, were preferred mainly by native city dwellers. Also, some "classes" were populated by specific groups.

46. *Ibid.*
47. For Grenoble, see Emmanuel Le Roy Ladurie, "La démographie des Lumières", in *Histoire de la France urbaine, t. 3. La ville des temps modernes de la Renaissance aux Révolutions* (Paris, 1998), pp. 293–347, 301. For Geneva, see Ryczkowska and Ritschard, "Mobilités sociales et spatiales".
48. André Capiteyn, Johan Decavele, Christine Van Coile, and Herman Vanderlinden, *Gentse torens achter rook van schoorstenen. Gent in de periode 1860–1895* (Ghent, 1983).

The association between occupational structure, social structure, and migration adds complexity to the possible influence of those factors on partner selection. First, opportunities for meeting between partners of different social origin may be restricted if migrants have a specific social origin or if migrants are over-represented in specific groups or, for that matter, under-represented in others. For example, if migrants usually meet other migrants, and if most migrants are sons and daughters of farmers while the natives are not, that will stimulate homogamy among farmers, irrespective of the preferences those migrants and natives might have for any specific social origin. This principle is the so-called by-product effect,[49] and occurs if two conditions are fulfilled: that there is a difference in the socio-economic profile of migrants in relation to natives, and that there is homogamy according to geographical origin.

Second, the mechanisms behind the isolation of migrants and natives and behind the isolation of specific occupational sectors (strong and narrow in-group definitions) may reinforce each other, which makes them potentially strong obstructors of societal openness, since they help produce strong senses of identity.[50] A language boundary, for example, might reinforce the formation of separate social networks.

Third, the association between social and geographical origin can alter social structure and so change group sizes. In our view, that is more important for the villages where, perhaps due to changing economic activities such as those brought about by the rise of rural industry, immigration of non-farmers could open the closed social systems of farming communities.

We briefly discuss here the socio-economic profile of migrants and natives in the Belgian cities and villages. In general, associations between geographical origin (natives/migrants) and social (HISCLASS) were not very strong. In most cities and villages Cramers V was about 0.2. Yet in Leuven, Cramers V was about 0.43, in Ghent and Liège about 0.34, and in Verviers 0.32. The strength of the association fluctuated somewhat over time, but without a consistent trend. There is a lot to be said about specific associations, but to be concise we highlight only three. First in Flanders, French-speaking migrants with an urban background were disproportionately recruited to state institutions there, which led to overrepresentation of those migrants in the category of higher and lower managers and professionals. Second, in the Walloon textile cities, particularly in the recently developed town of Limbourg, natives and those born in the

---

49. Wilfred Uunk, *Who Marries Whom? The Role of Social Origin, Education and High Culture in Mate Selection of Industrial Societies During the Twentieth Century* (Nijmegen, 1996).
50. Jan Dhondt, "La région gantoise. L'industrie cotonnière", in Pierre Lebrun, Marinette Bruwier, Jan Dhondt, and George Hansotte (eds), *Essai sur la révolution industrielle en Belgique, 1770–1847* (Brussels, 1979), pp. 75–160; Claude Gaier, *Huit siècles de houillerie liégeoise* (Liège, 1988).

neighbouring countryside dominated among lower-skilled workers, while urban migrants and foreigners were concentrated in skilled and leading positions. Third, in Tilleur 69 per cent of foreign grooms were lower-skilled workers, most of them coal miners, while 64 per cent of Flemish grooms were unskilled. But all this is just because foreigners arrived first, at the very beginning of the industrial revolution, before the rapid rise of the unskilled Flemish day labourer.[51]

In the villages the socio-economic profile of migrants was to some extent different from that of the natives. In Bierbeek (80 per cent as against 66 per cent) and the Ardennes (80 per cent as against 52 per cent) there were more sons of farmers among the natives than among migrants. It is clear that, particularly in the Ardennes, migration altered social structure and therefore had consequences for marriage patterns. The pattern was different in the Pays de Herve migration, as farmers were more numerous among migrants there (55 per cent as against 40 per cent among natives). Among the natives there were more sons of skilled workers and farm workers. In Appelterre there was not much difference between the natives and migrants.

In the Ardennes this difference might have led to a by-product effect, since in the Ardennes there was a degree of homogamy according to geographical origin. Consequently, those who were homogamous according to geographical origin had a greater chance of marrying homogamously according to social origin. In a comparison between migrants and farmers, the difference in the percentage of farmers decreased from 33 per cent before 1850 to 17.5 per cent from 1874–1890. We can see that the by-product effect would therefore decline over time.

Conclusion

In an attempt to introduce the influence of historical context formally into the debate about the increase of societal openness during the nineteenth century, we have identified possible patterns in which migration and occupational identities may be linked to partner selection by social origin. Table 4 gives an overview. In a short description of the historical context of these Belgian cities and villages we evaluated the importance of these factors. Apart from the general importance of migration, occupational identity, and, to some extent, the association between geographical origin and class, we saw that in some locations those factors created a specific societal context. We refer to the peculiar position of Flemish and

51. Michel Oris, "Une démographie des familles dans le tourbillon de la révolution industrielle", in Anne-Lise Head-Hönig, Luigi Lorenzetti, and Béatrice Veyrassat (eds), *Famille, parenté et réseaux en Occident (XVIIe–XXe siècles). Mélanges offerts à Alfred Perrenoud* (Geneva, 2001), pp. 37–52.

Table 4. *Overview of determinants of heterogamy*

Determinant	Specific reason	Partner selection by social origin
Migration	Social control	Heterogamy
	Lack of network, support	Heterogamy
	Social mobility	Heterogamy
	Wish to avoid migrants	Heterogamy
Occupational identity	Industrial occupational identities	Homogamy
	Early labour movement	Homogamy
	Persistency of traditional identities	Homogamy
Occupational identification, class and migration	Social structure	?
	Meeting opportunities	Homogamy
	Reinforced closed social groups	Homogamy

foreigners in Liège and Tilleur after 1850, the economic stagnation and early class-formation seen in Verviers, and the variety of rural economic and social contexts. Next, we shall try to establish whether migration and occupational identity were related to partner selection and if they determined a trend in this selection.

METHODOLOGY

In this section we give an overview of the models and variables used in our empirical analysis of partner selection by social origin. We use a series of models to analyse partner selection stepwise. In a first step we measure the basic trend in absolute heterogamy in each location. This first step aims to outline the general pattern of partner selection. In a second step we use logistic regression analyses[52] to compare the levels of heterogamy between locations and over time. The outcome variable is "marrying hetero-gamously" versus "marrying homogamously". For categorical variables, the coefficients of the logistic regression analysis show the factor by which the odds of marrying heterogamously are higher (if the parameter is higher than 1) or lower (if the parameter is lower than 1) depending upon whether one belongs to a specific category of variable compared with the reference category of that variable. For non-categorical variables, the coefficients

---

52. We chose to use logistic regression analysis rather than log-linear analysis because the latter is difficult to use if there are many cells with zero or low frequencies in the mobility (or partner selection) table. This problem is particularly acute when adding many variables (with many categories) to the analysis. The advantage of log-linear analysis is the neat control of the effect of group sizes. We cope with this problem by introducing a group size variable in the logistic regression analysis; Van de Putte, "Het belang van de toegeschreven positie".

refer to the difference in odds when there is a one point change in the independent variable.[53] The models will help us to see if group sizes, occupational identity, and migration are connected to partner selection patterns, and whether the pattern of homogamy is explained by this connection.

In model 1A we use period, location, and group size as the independent variables. Periods have been defined to reflect broadly the main structural socio-economic transformations: the first industrial revolution before 1850, an ascending phase from 1851 to 1873, the long depression in both industry and agriculture from 1874 to 1890, and a new ascending Kondratieff from 1891 to 1913. The group size variable controls for the influence of changing social structure on the chance of marrying heterogamously. We look at things from the perspective of the groom. For each category of social origin, we calculate the percentage of brides' fathers belonging to that same category. The percentage shows the chance of marrying homogamously.[54]

We also add an interaction variable between period and location. In a model containing interaction effects, the main effects of the variables included in the interaction effect (here: period and location) show the effects within the reference group of the other variable in the interaction effect. For example, the parameters for location show the difference in the chance of marrying heterogamously between the locations in the reference period. The period effect shows the coefficients for the reference location. The interaction effects of location and period show how that period effect differs in the other locations: the parameter of the interaction effect for a specific location by a specific period shows the factor by which the main effect of this period must be multiplied to become the period effect for the specific location.

In model 2A we add variables for migration, occupational identity, geographical homogamy, and presence of parents. The migration status of groom and bride is measured by the type of area where they were born. We distinguish among natives, Flemish (or "Walloon" in Walloon locations) rural migrants, Flemish (Walloon) non-rural migrants, foreigners, unknown, and Walloon (Flemish) migrants. Occupational immobility is measured as $1 =$ groom has the same occupation as father (reference), while $2 =$ groom does not have the same occupation as father. We assume

---

53. In technical terms, the parameters are odds ratios (of the odds of marrying heterogamously for a category of the independent variable divided by the odds of marrying heterogamously for the reference category).

54. The introduction of this group size variable controls for the distribution of the social origin of both brides and grooms. If the distribution of the social origin of the grooms changes, that leads to changing numbers of grooms assigned to specific group size values. If we take the perspective of the bride, the same results appear. We take the perspective of the groom simply to demonstrate the logic of controlling for group sizes, as a didactic trick.

that occupational identity is strongest in the reference category. Geographical homogamy is simply measured as: 1 = marriage is homogamous according to geographical origin (reference); 2 = marriage is heterogamous according to geographical origin. We use the migration status of groom and bride to measure this dimension of homogamy. If there is an association between social origin and geographical origin (by-product), then geographically homogamous marriages will tend to be more homogamous according to social origin. Parental presence is measured as: 1 = father lives in the city of marriage; 2 = father does not live in the city of marriage; and 3 = no information. This variable is only available for the Flemish locations.

In model 3A we add the social origin of the groom. This model tests whether the evolution of homogamy is caused by change of social structure. If groups who are traditionally more homogamous (farmers, the elite, for example) decrease in number, that will affect the level of homogamy. Social origin is measured using HISCLASS.

We perform separate analyses for cities and villages, because, as will be shown in Table 5, p. 202, the pattern of partner selection is so different in them that direct comparison would lead us to focus on merely trivial differences, and would anyway require the introduction of an incomprehensible number of interaction effects. Furthermore, analysing the role of farmers requires a somewhat different approach. So to analyse the second step in the villages we used slightly different models. First, we dropped the interaction variables between period and location so as to avoid numerous interaction effects (1B, 2B, and 3B). While for cities there are specific contextual characteristics in each period which can be interpreted, and which allow useful comparisons over time between cities, that is not true, or is less so, for villages. Second, to assess the effect of the evolution of the farmers' group size, models 1B and 2B are compared with models 1C and 2C, which exclude the group size variable, the reason for which is that the partner selection pattern is strongly related to the number of farmers. Finally, to avoid categories with very few observations we replaced "social origin" ("farmers" and "non-farmers") and "geographical origin" ("natives" as opposed to "migrants") by a dichotomous variable.

The models of step 2 naively assume that these factors produce the same results in every location and at all times. More detailed examination is needed to evaluate whether there are interaction effects of these variables with period and location. In step 3 we therefore examine the results obtained in steps 1 and 2 by connecting them with their historical contexts, for example with the position of the Flemish in Liège and Tilleur and with the process of early class formation in Verviers. For the cities we make some additional comparisons (heterogamy by migration status and by geographical homogamy). For the villages we applied the models 1B, 1C, 2B, and 3B to each location separately.

A MULTIVARIATE ANALYSIS OF HETEROGAMY

Partner selection in the cities

We start with the analysis of the general trend in absolute heterogamy in the cities (step 1, Table 5). The main and, seen from a modernization perspective, rather puzzling finding is the difference in the evolution of heterogamy before 1890. In the first half of the nineteenth century, the highest levels of heterogamy found are for Ghent, Liège and Verviers, the lowest for Aalst. In the period 1874–1890 the situation changed. The level of heterogamy in Verviers became lower than for other industrial cities. The reason for that is the moderate increase in heterogamy in particular for Liège[55] and the decrease in heterogamy in Verviers.[56] If we consider the situation in the period 1891–1913 we observe that, due to a strong rise in heterogamy after 1890, the level of heterogamy in Aalst was by then comparable to the level in Ghent and Leuven, cities in which heterogamy did not increase.

To understand how those patterns emerged we examine these observations in more detail. First, we discuss the pattern before 1890, focusing on the different situations in Liège and Verviers. Second, we address the increase in heterogamy in Aalst after 1890.

Heterogamy before 1890: First we test whether the differences in heterogamy are related to the direct influence of changing group sizes, occupational immobility, and migration (step 2). Table 6 shows the evolution of heterogamy using the logistic regression models 1A, 2A, and 3A.

The results of model 1A confirm the diverging patterns in the level of homogamy in those cities. In the reference period 1874–1890 heterogamy is highest for Liège, as all coefficients of the other cities are lower than 1. In Leuven, Aalst, and Verviers the level of heterogamy is significantly lower. The period effects show that in Liège heterogamy was lower before the period 1874–1890.[57] For Verviers, these period effects are very different. There was no similar increase. If we were to recode "location" with Verviers as the reference category, the parameters for period (referring now to Verviers) would show a higher, and significant, level of heterogamy during the periods 1800–1850 and 1851–1873 than during 1874–1890. The

---

55. The increase in heterogamy in Tilleur and Limbourg is not significant. The social structure changed over time. The number of lower-skilled workers among Limbourg fathers (of both brides and grooms) declined after 1873, as did the number of farmers (but only of grooms); the number of unskilled workers rose, although only among fathers of brides. Such changes in Limbourg's social structures are not easy to interpret. They are essentially artificial and due to territorial changes in the early 1880s.

56. Note that though these changes might not be very large, the contrasting trends between Liège and Verviers are striking.

57. The borderline significance is partly related to the rather low number of observations for the first periods. If we use Liège as the reference category, and Tilleur (which is in fact part of Liège and shares similar characteristics, such as the large number of Flemish and foreign migrants), then the period effects are significant (0.637 for period 1 and 0.658 for period 2).

Table 5. *Percentage of absolute heterogamy according to social origin*

Period	Ghent	Aalst	Leuven	Limbourg	Verviers	Liège	Tilleur	Bierbeek	Appelterre	Pays de Herve	Ardennes
1800–1850	71.2°	58.2	65.4°	64.5	67.5	67.7	62.8	37.3°	30.1°	50.0	31.4°
1851–1873	65.3*	60.3	61.5	68.6	63.6	69.2	65.8	23.5*	46.9*	46.3	41.1*
1874–1890	68.9#	56.2	62.7	71.9#	55.9	75.8*#	69.2#	33.0#	47.7	45.5	51.2*
1891–1913	68.2	70.1*	66.2					22.2*	39.8		
N	1,934	1,351	2,093	350	521	612	324	660	264	328	715

* = difference with period 1800–1850 is significant at the 0.05 level.
° = difference with Aalst in period 1800–1850 is significant at the 0.05 level.
= difference with Verviers in period 1874–1890 is significant at the 0.05 level.

Table 6. *Logistic regression analysis of the chance of marrying hetero-gamously according to social origin (Flemish and Walloon cities, 1800–1890)*

Variables	Model 1A		Model 2A		Model 3A	
	Sig.	Exp(B)	Sig.	Exp(B)	Sig.	Exp(B)
Period						
1800–1850	0.104	0.651	0.060	0.604	0.071	0.615
1851–1873	0.057	0.682	0.030	0.642	0.031	0.642
1874–1890 (ref.)						
Location						
Leuven	0.002	0.568	0.000	0.502	0.000	0.505
Ghent	0.132	0.748	0.048	0.678	0.060	0.689
Aalst	0.001	0.531	0.000	0.465	0.019	0.612
Limbourg	0.229	0.713	0.120	0.636	0.126	0.638
Verviers	0.015	0.585	0.003	0.514	0.006	0.539
Tilleur	0.363	0.751	0.633	0.869	0.726	0.889
Liège (ref.)						
Group size	0.000	0.964	0.000	0.965	0.000	0.949
Location * Period						
Leuven by 1800–1850	0.058	1.763	0.028	1.943	0.021	2.020
Leuven by 1851–1873	0.161	1.427	0.095	1.536	0.087	1.554
Ghent by 1800–1850	0.088	1.691	0.046	1.866	0.060	1.805
Ghent by 1851–1873	0.443	1.220	0.276	1.331	0.274	1.335
Aalst by 1800–1850	0.393	1.317	0.185	1.541	0.451	1.285
Aalst by 1851–1873	0.130	1.510	0.065	1.668	0.181	1.463
Limbourg by 1800–1850	0.465	1.343	0.350	1.468	0.263	1.591
Limbourg by 1851–1873	0.277	1.481	0.298	1.463	0.266	1.510
Verviers by 1800–1850	0.007	3.588	0.008	3.563	0.004	4.158
Verviers by 1851–1873	0.007	2.157	0.004	2.282	0.002	2.418
Tilleur by 1800–1850	0.721	1.168	0.784	1.128	0.962	1.022
Tilleur by 1851–1873	0.582	1.236	0.541	1.272	0.666	1.192
Occupational mobility			0.000	1.502	0.000	1.544
Occupational immobility (ref.)						
Migrant status groom						
Native (ref.)						
Rural migrant			0.017	0.791	0.234	0.884
Non-rural migrant			0.002	0.724	0.014	0.774
Foreigner			0.000	0.528	0.003	0.586
Unknown			0.332	0.830	0.443	0.861
Walloon migrant			0.000	0.565	0.002	0.636
Migrant status bride						
Native (ref.)						
Rural migrant			0.221	1.124	0.161	1.147
Non-rural migrant			0.512	0.933	0.596	0.945
Foreigner			0.039	1.525	0.066	1.462
Unknown			0.876	1.030	0.997	1.001
Walloon migrant			0.197	0.807	0.269	0.831
Geographically heterogamous			0.000	1.383	0.000	1.376

(Continued overleaf)

Table 6. *Continued*

Variables	Model 1A		Model 2A		Model 3A	
	Sig.	Exp(B)	Sig.	Exp(B)	Sig.	Exp(B)
Geographically homogamous (ref.)						
Social origin						
Higher managers and professionals (1+2)					0.000	0.484
Lower managers and professionals, clerical and sales (3+4+5)					0.964	1.006
Skilled workers (6+7)					0.000	1.715
Farmers (8)					0.005	0.708
Lower-skilled workers (9)					0.001	1.461
Farm workers (10+12)					0.145	1.355
Unskilled (11) (ref.)						
Constant	0.000	6.052	0.000	4.949	0.000	5.536

Model information.
Model 1A: N = 4983; model fit: chi² = 212.4; p = 0.000; Nagelkerke R^2 = 0.058.
Model 2A: N = 4983; model fit: chi² = 294.3; p = 0.000; Nagelkerke R^2 = 0.080.
Model 3A: N = 4983; model fit: chi² = 400.9; p = 0.000; Nagelkerke R^2 = 0.107.

interaction effects of Verviers by "period" do indeed make clear that there was an evolution there of opposite character to that in Liège. The period effects for Tilleur and Limbourg differ less and not significantly. Finally, the parameter for group size indicates that the larger the number of equals among fathers of brides, the less the chance of a heterogamous marriage, which is of course not surprising.

The results of model 2A show that occupational mobility and geographical heterogamy increase the chances of marrying heterogamously according to social origin. The latter shows that there is possibly a by-product effect, although the effect might also mean that preferences for homogamy according to social and geographical origin simply happen to coincide. The findings on geographical heterogamy and occupational mobility confirm the role of those factors in partner selection. These relationships are consistent, that is, present in each location (data not shown), which shows that in analysing partner selection according to social origin these variables should be taken into account. The role of migration is less clear. Migrant grooms have less chance of marrying heterogamously, but that is not so for migrant brides. On the contrary, even foreign brides have more chance of marrying heterogamously. That might signify that the role of migration is more complex than was envisaged in the theoretical section. For example, there might be interaction of migration by location, period, class, etc., or, perhaps, migrants might have had less chance than natives of experiencing upward mobility.

However, adding these variables does not mean that the differences between Liège (and Tilleur) and the other cities are explained by them. On the contrary, the main effects of location in model 2A show that the general level of heterogamy was still highest in Liège. The effect is significant for Verviers, Ghent, Leuven, and Aalst. In Tilleur the level of heterogamy is not significantly different. This means that, according to model 2A, in the period 1874–1890 the level of heterogamy in Liège (and Tilleur) was higher than in the other cities but was not caused by, for example, a different level of occupational immobility.

In model 3A social origin of the groom is added. Farmers and higher managers or professionals are shown to have been less heterogamous than unskilled workers. Skilled and lower-skilled workers were more heterogamous, and farm workers, who are rather unskilled, and lower managers and professionals do not differ in terms of heterogamy. Adding this variable to the model does not change the above observation.

In step 3 we connect these observations with the location-specific findings discussed earlier. First we return to the presence of the Flemish in Liège and Tilleur. We recall that in their situation priority was perhaps given to homogamy by geographical origin, which avoids having a partner who speaks a different language, and that in some cases it may be supposed that the principle of marrying a partner of the same social origin cannot be applied. The presence of Flemish and foreign migrants made it increasingly difficult to marry homogamously according to social origin if one wished to marry homogamously according to geographical origin.

This explanation is confirmed in Tables 7 and 8 for Liège, where we observe that native brides married more heterogamously according to social origin, since brides faced great difficulty in finding native partners, and that couples homogamous according to geographical origin were increasingly less homogamous by social origin, as a result of the increasing difficulty of combining both those criteria. In fact, the increase in heterogamy was limited to those groups. The increase in heterogamy for couples who were homogamous according to geographical origin is observed likewise for Tilleur.[58] The same pattern did not appear for Verviers, Ghent, and Limbourg. The very fact that the increase in heterogamy so closely tallied with the composition of couples according to their geographical origin shows that more was taking place than simple modernization. In our opinion, the arrival of foreigners and Flemish people made it difficult especially for native brides to find native partners of the same social origin. This form of heterogamy was an indirect product of industrialization – since the rise of migration was itself the product of

---

58. For Tilleur the conclusions are more difficult, because of the low number of observations and the more complicated situation due to the extremely large number of migrants. We assume that the main schism lay between Walloon natives and migrants on the one hand and foreigners and Flemish migrants on the other.

Table 7. *Percentage of heterogamy according to social origin, by migration status of bride, Walloon cities and Ghent*

Period	Ghent	Limbourg	Verviers	Liège	Tilleur
Natives					
1800–1850	70.7	58.5	66.7	63.6	64.3
1851–1873	65.1	68.5	59.1	66.7	62.1
1874–1890	67.0	74.1	48.5*	79.4*	67.9
Total	68.1	65.7	56.1	71.1	64.6
N	827	134	243	325	99
Migrants					
1800–1850	73.2	69.1	69.2	72.7	62.0
1851–1873	66.0	68.6	68.2	72.1	66.7
1874–1890	72.6	71.0	64.6	71.9	70.3
Total	70.7	69.4	67.1	72.1	65.8
N	314	216	278	287	225

* = difference between period 1800–1850 and period 1874–1890 significant at the 0.05 level.

Table 8. *Percentage of heterogamy according to social origin, by homogamy according to geographical homogamy, Walloon cities and Ghent*

Period	Ghent	Limbourg	Verviers	Liège	Tilleur
Homogamous					
1800–1850	68.8	64.3	56.3	61.8	48.8
1851–1873	63.8	62.2	52.6	66.7	60.7
1874–1890	67.5	65.4	49.3	78.6*	65.0*
Total	67.3	63.9	51.8	70.4	57.1
N	1,131	119	197	304	119
Heterogamous					
1800–1850	75.5	64.9	75.0	75.0	71.4
1851–1873	67.3	70.9	70.2	71.6	68.9
1874–1890	70.8	74.6	59.8*	73.2	71.1
Total	70.2	70.1	67.0	72.7	70.2
N	803	239	324	308	205

* = difference between period 1800–1850 and period 1874–1890 significant at the 0.05 level.

industrialization – but we are rather a long way from claiming that it was meritocracy that caused societal openness.

Second we turn to Verviers. In the theoretical section we argued that in some cases industrialization might have reinforced the role of occupational identity and so stimulated homogamy because, for instance, during industrialization large, modern industrial sectors were created with strong group bonds and because the organizational outlook of the labour movement was based upon occupational segmentations. The timing of the effect (contrast between urban crisis and a period of stagnation) and the location (not evident in either Limbourg nor Aalst; a similar but perhaps less marked pattern in Ghent[59]) suggest that this was indeed the case in Verviers.

Another indication may be found in the behaviour of the rooted population. In Table 8 we see that in Verviers couples who were homogamous according to geographical origin showed some lessening of heterogamy according to social origin. Distinguishing between native and migrant homogamous couples, we see that there was no decrease in heterogamy according to social origin for migrant homogamous couples, the least rooted couples (from 70 per cent before 1874, to 69.1 per cent thereafter). All other combinations do show a decrease, of at least 7 per cent, but the largest decrease (16 per cent) is for couples of whom the bride was native but the groom migrant. At first sight, this seems strange, as we can assume that natives who married endogamously were more rooted and so can be expected to show the greatest decrease in heterogamy. Yet the mixed nature of these marriages is itself perhaps proof of the integration of the migrants involved. Alter has shown that, among migrants, marrying a native bride was seen as a good strategy for stabilization and integration in the city. Much more so than elsewhere, a male migrant marrying a native bride in Verviers was a man who wanted to move from the mobile to the rooted group and his very marriage was inherently a success as well as a promise of further integration into the group of real Verviétois.[60]

Heterogamy after 1890: The next issue concerns the increasing level of heterogamy in Aalst after 1890. The timing of the effect is not surprising since Aalst experienced industrialization only late in the nineteenth century. At the same time it is important to note that although economic changes in Aalst were dramatic, they did not produce the same kind of changes of migration status in the composition of the population as occurred in the Walloon cities, and that after 1890 the majority of spouses were born in Aalst (75.2 per cent of brides and 69 per cent of grooms), percentages which are perhaps even slightly higher in comparison to earlier periods. A distinctive factor, however, is that Aalst industrialized in a period during which the labour movement attained its full strength, so the circumstances in which partners were selected were different from those in cities which industrialized earlier.

Table 9 shows the results of model 1A.[61] The parameters for location

59. Van de Putte, "Het belang van de toegeschreven positie". This observation for Ghent was made using a different class scheme (SOCPO scheme). In the period 1800–1850 the level of heterogamy was 6 per cent higher than in the period 1851–1890, but 10 per cent higher if the observation is limited to the lower classes, for whom the strongest effects are expected. Using HISCLASS, which differs in some ways from SOCPO, this decrease is less sharp.

60. Alter, *Family and the Female Life Course*.

61. We limit the analysis to the Flemish cities, as it is only for these cities that we have observations for the period 1891–1913.

show the difference in the chance of marrying heterogamously between locations in the reference period 1891–1913. The level of heterogamy in Ghent and Leuven did not differ significantly in 1891–1913 from the level of heterogamy in Aalst. The parameters for period show the period effects for the reference location, Aalst. It is clear that in Aalst heterogamy was highest in the period 1891–1913. The interaction effects for period and location signify that in the periods 1800–1850 and 1874–1890 heterogamy was significantly higher in Leuven and Ghent than it was in Aalst.

In model 2A migration status of groom and bride, homogamy by geographical origin, occupational identity, and parental presence are added. Geographical heterogamy and occupational mobility have a positive effect on heterogamy. Grooms whose father was present in the city of marriage had a greater chance of marrying heterogamously.[62] It is also clear that migration in general did not have major effects on heterogamy. In this analysis the period effects for Aalst are still present after controlling for those factors, which shows that while occupational mobility and geographical heterogamy are important, they do not in themselves constitute the explanation for the increase in heterogamy in Aalst.

In model 3A we add "social origin groom" to the previous model. The difference between 1891–1913 and the other periods disappears after controlling for this variable, apart from the difference in the period 1800–1850. This is probably related to the increased number of lower-skilled textile workers as a result of industrialization in Aalst and, from 1891–1913, the decreasing number of unskilled workers and farmers, two groups which differ in their "traditional" level of heterogamy. Before 1890 the lower skilled too were a heterogamous group while the unskilled and farmers were more homogamous.

To sum up, the increase in heterogamy in Aalst was not caused by changes in migration nor occupational identity. That does not necessarily mean that meritocracy alone was on the rise. Van de Putte found that heterogamy after 1890 in Aalst, as in Ghent,[63] was for the most part

---

62. It is difficult to explain this, but we must add here that heterogamy might also mean upward mobility, and one cannot exclude the notion of the father as a tool for upward mobility rather than as a "keeper of homogamy".

63. It took some time for the labour movement to become a nationwide mass movement. In our opinion, it was only after 1890 that the broader process of demographic class formation started, understood as the process by which boundaries among the lower classes disappeared while the boundary between the middle class and the lower classes remained. This period is not under observation for Verviers, so we cannot consider whether heterogamy among the lower classes increased after that date. Van de Putte ("Het belang van de toegeschreven positie") observed this pattern of demographic class-formation for the industrial cities of Aalst and Ghent after 1890. Using a different class scheme (SOCPO scheme) an increase was observed in heterogamy for both Ghent and Aalst. The different results for Ghent are mainly the result of the use of some sector-based social classes by HISCLASS (SOCPO does not use sector as a criterion). The effect

heterogamy within the lower classes, so it indicated a process of demographic class formation. In other words, apart from possible changes in the meritocratic outlook of society, changes in group belonging were probably important: one saw, in effect, the rise of a broad lower-class group. Moreover, nor can one rule out the possibility that in the case of Aalst there was more than simply modernization or demographic class formation, for while the Belgian socialist labour movement became a mass movement during 1890–1913 the Catholic labour movement also emerged and became a formidable opponent. In that period, workers were divided ("pillarization") by these competing ideologies. In Aalst the Catholic labour movement was especially strong ("Daensisme") and it is probable that group belonging was to some extent based on the "pillar" one belonged to, Catholic or socialist. Partner selection might have been limited to those groups and so led to heterogamy by social origin, since social origin became relatively less important, or rather more difficult to combine with partner selection based on one's "pillar", just as group belonging based on geographical origin to some degree dominated partner selection in Tilleur and Liège. In short, the impression of openness observed in Aalst may be undermined by other societal rifts which are not revealed by the data presented here.

The villages

Before we discuss the differences among the villages and their evolution over time, we must briefly point to the difference between the cities and the villages. In Table 5 we saw that there was a big difference in absolute homogamy between the cities and the villages: in the villages the majority of marriages were homogamous, while in the cities that was not so, which is not surprising given the presence of large groups of farmers in the villages.

The differences between the villages are analysed in a logistic regression analysis presented in Table 10. Compared with the Ardennes (model 1C), there was a higher level of homogamy in Bierbeek, while in Pays de Herve and Appelterre heterogamy was more common (although not significantly so). The pattern is dominated by the group sizes, in particular of farmers, absolute heterogamy being highest in the Pays de Herve, where the number of farmers was lowest. But there is more: the difference in heterogamy was not especially large (compared with Appelterre, 6 per cent, and with the Ardennes, 9 per cent), while the difference in the percentage of farmers was 20 per cent or more. In Bierbeek the level of heterogamy was lowest, although the number of farmers was the same as in Appelterre or the Ardennes.

of the different classification is strongest in the period 1851–1890 in Ghent, so there is no recognition of an increase in heterogamy for the period 1891–1913 compared with 1851–1890.

Table 9. *Logistic regression analysis of the chance of marrying hetero-gamously according to social origin (Flemish cities, 1800–1913)*

	Model 1A		Model 2A		Model 3A	
	Sig.	Exp(B)	Sig.	Exp(B)	Sig.	Exp(B)
Period						
1800–1850	0.001	0.578	0.006	0.636	0.021	0.673
1851–1873	0.015	0.670	0.031	0.699	0.153	0.782
1874–1890	0.002	0.629	0.006	0.657	0.381	0.867
1891–1913 (ref.)						
Location						
Leuven	0.369	0.900	0.571	0.935	0.407	0.903
Ghent	0.363	0.899	0.582	0.936	0.313	0.884
Aalst (ref.)						
Group size	0.000	0.973	0.000	0.971	0.000	0.949
Location * Period						
Leuven by 1800–1850	0.029	1.549	0.050	1.492	0.064	1.471
Leuven by 1851–1873	0.554	1.133	0.533	1.143	0.963	1.010
Leuven by 1874–1890	0.289	1.238	0.369	1.200	0.600	0.895
Ghent by 1800–1850	0.001	1.980	0.005	1.828	0.012	1.735
Ghent by 1851–1873	0.225	1.295	0.298	1.251	0.538	1.146
Ghent by 1874–1890	0.015	1.653	0.024	1.599	0.348	1.227
Occupational mobility			0.000	1.443	0.000	1.464
Occupational immobility (ref.)						
Migrant status groom						
Native (ref.)						
Rural migrant			0.324	0.886	0.658	0.946
Non-rural migrant			0.398	1.107	0.286	1.138
Foreigner			0.757	1.075	0.510	1.169
Unknown			0.690	1.155	0.496	1.285
Walloon migrant			0.057	0.735	0.147	0.789
Migrant status bride						
Native (ref.)						
Rural migrant			0.886	0.983	0.919	0.988
Non-rural migrant			0.319	0.891	0.339	0.894
Foreigner			0.508	0.844	0.539	0.853
Unknown			0.736	0.883	0.800	0.909
Walloon migrant			0.217	0.798	0.255	0.811
Geographically heterogamous			0.000	1.360	0.000	1.341
Geographically homogamous (ref.)						
Parents groom present						
Parents not present (ref.)						
Parents present			0.000	1.616	0.000	1.463
No information			0.618	1.181	0.844	1.069
Parents bride present						
Parents not present (ref.)						
Parents present			0.501	0.928	0.489	0.926
No information			0.877	1.053	0.947	1.022
Social origin groom						
Higher managers and professionals (1+2)					0.000	0.420

(*Continued*)

Table 9. *Continued*

	Model 1A		Model 2A		Model 3A	
	Sig.	Exp(B)	Sig.	Exp(B)	Sig.	Exp(B)
Lower managers and professionals, clerical and sales (3+4+5)					0.388	1.108
Skilled workers (6+7)					0.000	1.856
Farmers (8)					0.022	0.753
Lower-skilled workers (9)					0.000	1.677
Farm workers (10+12)					0.562	1.169
Unskilled (11) (ref.)						
Constant	0.000	4.053	0.000	2.169	0.000	3.047

Model information:
Model 1A: N = 5379; model fit: chi² = 115.5; p = 0.000; Nagelkerke R² = 0.029.
Model 2A: N = 5379; model fit: chi² = 204.6; p = 0.000; Nagelkerke R² = 0.052.
Model 3A: N = 5379; model fit: chi² = 330.9; p = 0.000; Nagelkerke R² = 0.083.

After controlling for group sizes (model 1B), we can see that the level of heterogamy was much lower in Pays de Herve than in the Ardennes. The higher level of absolute heterogamy measured in Pays de Herve was the result only of the relatively small number of farmers, meaning that at the level of daily experience as reflected in the level of absolute heterogamy we see societal openness caused by the presence of a large number of skilled and lower-skilled workers, such as those in the textile industry. Nonetheless, preference is strong for a partner from the same social origin, as is shown by controlling for the effect of group sizes.

In model 2C we add variables. Migrant grooms were more likely to marry heterogamously. After controlling for group sizes, the effect disappears (model 2B). The reason for that is the relationship between the number of migrants and the number of farmers (see above). Migration altered social structure, which resulted in more heterogamy. There is no similar effect to be seen in the migration status of brides. In the villages occupational immobility was related to homogamy, but that does not explain the lower level of heterogamy in Bierbeek and Pays de Herve (model 2B).

As far as the evolution of heterogamy is concerned, in general there was a higher level of heterogamy from 1874–1890 than in the first half of the nineteenth century (Table 10, model 1C), but after controlling for group sizes we do not find any period effect (model 1B). Furthermore, Table 5 showed that the evolution of heterogamy was quite different in the villages. Only in the Ardennes was there a consistent increase in absolute heterogamy.

To examine the evolution of heterogamy in more detail, we applied a logistic regression analysis separately to each village (Table 11). In Bierbeek there was no rise in absolute heterogamy but the chance of

Table 10. *Logistic regression analysis of the chance of marrying heterogamously, villages*

Variables	Model 1C		Model 1B		Model 2C		Model 2B		Model 3B	
	Sig.	Exp(B)	Sig.	Exp(B)	Sig.	Exp(B)	Sig.	Exp(B)	Sig.	Exp(B)
Period										
1800–1850 (ref.)										
1851–1873	0.177	1.187	0.747	0.951	0.568	1.078	0.451	0.888	0.502	0.898
1874–1890	0.003	1.498	0.146	1.266	0.018	1.406	0.248	1.214	0.222	1.238
1891–1913	0.331	0.852	0.362	1.205	0.154	0.782	0.439	1.177	0.451	1.172
Location										
Bierbeek	0.006	0.702	0.130	0.790	0.003	0.668	0.072	0.752	0.065	0.744
Appelterre	0.322	1.168	0.921	0.981	0.748	1.057	0.732	0.930	0.767	0.939
Pays de Herve	0.080	1.290	0.002	0.599	0.367	1.146	0.003	0.597	0.004	0.603
Ardennes (ref.)										
Group size			0.000	0.957			0.000	0.958	0.000	0.960
Migrant groom					0.017	1.374	0.792	1.042	0.761	1.049
Native groom (ref.)										
Migrant bride					0.353	1.120	0.684	0.943	0.703	0.946
Native bride (ref.)										
Occupational mobility					0.000	2.213	0.000	1.945	0.000	1.943
Occupational immobility (ref.)										
Geographically heterogamous					0.148	1.216	0.370	1.154	0.379	1.152
Geographically homogamous (ref.)										
Non-farmers									0.687	1.170
Farmers (ref.)										
Constant	0.000	0.530	0.000	5.242	0.000	0.315	0.000	3.659	0.037	3.041

Model information

Model 1C: N = 1967; model fit: chi² = 48.8; p = 0.000; Nagelkerke R² = 0.034. Model 1B: N = 1961; model fit: chi² = 660.3; p = 0.000; Nagelkerke R² = 0.391. Model 2C: N = 1923; model fit: chi² = 145.9; p = 0.000; Nagelkerke R² = 0.100. Model 2B: N = 1918; model fit: chi² = 683.7; p = 0.000; Nagelkerke R² = 0.411. Model 3B: N = 1918; model fit: chi² = 683.5; p = 0.000; Nagelkerke R² = 0.411.

Table 11. *Logistic regression analysis of the chance of marrying heterogamously, villages (separate analysis)*

	Bierbeek								Appelterre							
	Model 1C		Model 1B		Model 2B		Model 3B		Model 1C		Model 1B		Model 2B		Model 3B	
	Sig.	Exp(B)	Sig.	Exp(B)	Sig.	Exp(B)	Sig.	Exp(B)	Sig.	Exp(B)	Sig.	Exp(B)	Sig.	Exp(B)	Sig.	Exp(B)
Period																
1800–1850 (ref.)																
1851–1873	0.010	0.518	0.108	0.591	0.134	0.607	0.141	0.612	0.054	2.052	0.212	1.701	0.393	1.482	0.607	1.286
1874–1890	0.476	0.829	0.478	1.282	0.475	1.289	0.455	1.307	0.051	2.118	0.605	1.249	0.445	1.503	0.926	1.060
1891–1913	0.001	0.481	0.049	1.810	0.046	1.839	0.045	1.916	0.187	1.532	0.586	0.812	0.756	0.879	0.478	0.721
Group size	0.000	0.952	0.000	0.952	0.000	0.952	0.000	0.949	0.000	0.965			0.000	0.968	0.009	0.949
Occupational mobility					0.155	1.392	0.148	1.402					0.050	1.908	0.051	1.904
Occupational immobility (ref.)																
Migrant groom					0.593	0.831	0.591	0.831					0.217	1.643	0.224	1.634
Native groom (ref.)																
Migrant bride					0.125	1.653	0.118	1.670					0.938	1.030	0.962	1.018
Native bride (ref.)																
Geographically heterogamous					0.918	1.037	0.941	1.026					0.327	0.674	0.369	0.696
Geographically homogamous (ref.)																
Non-farmers							0.703	0.749							0.298	0.298
Farmers (ref.)																
Constant	0.001	0.594	0.000	5.209	0.000	4.297	0.042	5.864	0.000	0.431	0.003	3.495	0.159	2.147	0.143	9.639

(Continued overleaf)

Table 11. Continued

	Ardennes								Pays de Herve							
	Model 1C		Model 1B		Model 2B		Model 3B		Model 1C		Model 1B		Model 2B		Model 3B	
	Sig.	Exp(B)	Sig.	Exp(B)	Sig.	Exp(B)	Sig.	Exp(B)	Sig.	Exp(B)	Sig.	Exp(B)	Sig.	Exp(B)	Sig.	Exp(B)
Period																
1800–1850 (ref.) (Ardennes)																
1800–1873 (ref.) (PDH)																
1851–1873	0.021	1.526	0.435	1.190	0.747	1.077	0.471	0.816								
1874–1890	0.000	2.297	0.085	1.521	0.225	1.351	0.724	0.884	0.819	0.948	0.305	1.326	0.255	1.378	0.343	1.311
Group size			0.000	0.959	0.000	0.961	0.000	0.928			0.000	0.944	0.000	0.946	0.528	1.024
Occupational mobility					0.000	2.151	0.000	2.097					0.001	2.516	0.000	2.735
Occupational immobility (ref.)																
Migrant groom					0.627	1.136	0.697	1.107					0.642	1.166	0.531	1.234
Native groom																
Migrant bride					0.311	0.782	0.273	0.767					0.295	0.744	0.290	0.739
Native bride																
Geographically heterogamous					0.138	1.485	0.116	1.519					0.869	0.946	0.868	0.945
Geographically homogamous (ref.)																
Non-farmers							0.091	0.106								
Farmers															0.035	22.902
Constant	0.000	0.457	0.000	4.335	0.000	2.563	0.024	36.145	0.343	0.879	0.000	4.491	0.002	2.888	0.123	0.048

Model information
Bierbeek

Model 1C: N = 660; model fit: chi^2 = 13.8; p = 0.003; Nagelkerke R^2 = 0.030.
Model 1B: N = 658; model fit: chi^2 = 253.4; p = 0.000; Nagelkerke R^2 = 0.459.
Model 2B: N = 654; model fit: chi^2 = 255.2; p = 0.000; Nagelkerke R^2 = 0.464.
Model 3B: N = 654; model fit: chi^2 = 255.3; p = 0.000; Nagelkerke R^2 = 0.465.

Appelterre:
Model 1C: N = 264; model fit: chi^2 = 5.5; p = 0.138; Nagelkerke R^2 = 0.028.
Model 1B: N = 260; model fit: chi^2 = 56.1; p = 0.000; Nagelkerke R^2 = 0.259.
Model 2B: N = 221; model fit: chi^2 = 51.3; p = 0.000; Nagelkerke R^2 = 0.279.
Model 3B: N = 221; model fit: chi^2 = 52.4; p = 0.000; Nagelkerke R^2 = 0.284.

Ardennes:
Model 1C: N = 715; model fit: chi^2 = 17.4; p = 0.000; Nagelkerke R^2 = 0.033.
Model 1B: N = 715; model fit: chi^2 = 250.4; p = 0.000; Nagelkerke R^2 = 0.403.
Model 2B: N = 715; model fit: chi^2 = 273.3; p = 0.000; Nagelkerke R^2 = 0.433.
Model 3B: N = 715; model fit: chi^2 = 276.2; p = 0.000; Nagelkerke R^2 = 0.437.

Pays de Herve:
Model 1C: N = 328; model fit: chi^2 = 0.1; p = 0.819; Nagelkerke R^2 = 0.000.
Model 1B: N = 328; model fit: chi^2 = 87.2; p = 0.000; Nagelkerke R^2 = 0.312.
Model 2B: N = 328; model fit: chi^2 = 100.6; p = 0.000; Nagelkerke R^2 = 0.353.
Model 3B: N = 328; model fit: chi^2 = 104.8; p = 0.000; Nagelkerke R^2 = 0.365.

marrying heterogamously, when the figures are controlled for group sizes, did increase during 1891–1913 compared with the first half of the nineteenth century (model 1B). Although occupational immobility for example decreased, this rise in heterogamy is not related to the variables introduced in model 2B. In the Ardennes, the increasing level of absolute heterogamy (model 1C) is connected to the decline in the number of farmers (model 1B). The high level of absolute heterogamy from 1874–1890 is no longer significant at the 0.05 level if the model controls for group sizes, but the parameter remains high and significant at the 0.10 level. Adding occupational immobility, migration and geographical homogamy reduces the parameter even further (no longer significant, model 2B). That is not unexpected given that occupational immobility and the by-product effect decreased after 1873 (see above). In Appelterre and the Pays de Herve there was no rise in heterogamy, even after adding the extra variables. Occupational mobility too in those villages was an important determinant of heterogamy.

The main conclusion is that there was no general rise in heterogamy in the villages, and the two villages which did show an increase took a different "path". In the Ardennes, heterogamy increased mainly because of the declining number of farmers, the decline of occupational immobility and the decline of the by-product effect; while in Bierbeek after controlling for group sizes we see that heterogamy increased but was linked neither to occupation nor migration-related factors.

GENERAL CONCLUSION

In this analysis we examined the effect of migration and occupational identity on partner selection according to social origin. A clear, general, consistent effect of migration was not found. The role of migration is probably more complicated than we have presented it to be in this research, but all the same a specific effect was found. Avoidance of the marginal group of Flemish migrants led to increased societal openness with regard to social origin. In Liège and Tilleur in the second half of the nineteenth century the number of strangers increased, both Flemish and foreigners. The native Walloon population, not very keen on intermingling with them, were exposed to an increasing difficulty finding partners of the same social origin in the "native marriage market".

We also found support for the idea that occupational identity is an important factor in partner selection. Sons having the same occupation as their father had a greater chance of marrying homogamously. But to this must be added that in industrial sectors high levels of intergenerational occupational immobility were observed as well and the lack of any decrease in intergenerational immobility is perhaps a reason why there was no general increase in societal openness during the course of industrialization. An interesting finding is the decrease in heterogamy in Verviers during 1874–1890. Early lower-class formation succeeded the urban crisis in the first half of the nineteenth century and that transition was accompanied by a decrease in societal openness. In our interpretation, that reflects the increasing use of modern occupational identities as a means to impart structure to social life and social bonds and to claim social dignity.

In addition, the relationship between migration, occupational identity and class structure did have effects on partner selection. Migration sometimes changed social structure and consequently affected partner selection, which is clearly seen in some of the villages. There was possibly a by-product effect as well. The association between geographical and social origin and the sometimes only moderate tendency to marry homogamously according to geographical origin also caused homogamy by social origin, but that did not significantly affect the main trend in homogamy. Whether the combination of specific geographical and social positions led to increased feelings of group belonging was difficult to demonstrate because there were no large social groups with a distinctive migrant status. Consequently, we believe that factor was probably not responsible for dramatic changes in the pattern of partner selection.

As a result of the interplay of these factors, we observed in this analysis of partner selection in Belgian cities and villages different patterns of homogamy according to social origin. We do not claim that our interpretation of these patterns cannot be refined. More detailed research will add more information about these complex issues, but at least one general conclusion emerges: it is difficult to interpret all these diverse patterns in terms of modernization. In our opinion, the historical context creates a complicated set of conditions, reflected in differences in the type and strength of migration and in the sectoral composition and evolution of the local economy, and context influences partner selection. Of course, that does not exclude the possibility that in a later phase a coherent pattern did emerge. In Aalst for example, there was an increase in heterogamy but only after 1890, in a period when industrialization was expanding and a modern mass labour movement was born – a situation very different from that in Verviers before 1890.

Finally, we discuss some specific implications of this study. First, it is difficult and maybe in some cases misleading to look at a country as a whole. That is true even for the countryside alone. Villages vary greatly in terms of migration, the number of farmers or the different profile of migrants and natives. Those factors influence partner selection, so it might be advisable to use the variables formally in analysis. Second, partner selection is not determined only by an individual's or his family's social power, status, achievements, and so forth. As shown by the role of early class formation in Verviers and the position of the Flemish in Liège and

Tilleur, group belonging too is important as it shapes social life and contacts and thereby affects partner selection. Not only are groups related by occupation important, but so too are groups based on geographical origin; and possibly religion. The formal introduction of these considerations can definitely help to explain partner selection according to social origin.

IRSH 50 (2005), Supplement, pp. 219–246 DOI: 10.1017/S0020859005002129
© 2005 Internationaal Instituut voor Sociale Geschiedenis

Migration and Endogamy According to Social Class: France, 1803–1986*

JEAN-PIERRE PÉLISSIER, DANIÈLE RÉBAUDO, MARCO
H.D. VAN LEEUWEN, AND INEKE MAAS

SUMMARY: Does intra-national migration matter for partner choice? A number of conflicting hypotheses on the effects of migration on the likelihood of endogamy according to social class of origin are formulated and tested on the French historical record over the past two centuries. We conclude that migrants were less likely to marry endogamously, especially if they migrated from rural villages to cities; this is explained mainly by the fact that they thereby escaped the social pressure of their parents and peers and met more people from different social backgrounds. Contrary to what we expected, the relationships between migration characteristics and endogamy changed hardly at all over the two centuries. We also investigated whether temporal differences in endogamy could be explained partly by changes in migration patterns. We found that they could. The increase in the number of men and women living in or moving to cities was one particularly important cause of the decreasing likelihood of endogamy. Finally, we were interested in the possible bias in regional studies on endogamy. Our results show that this bias is especially large if these regions include only rural areas or cities. This is because the likelihood of endogamy differs between rural areas and cities, and is also especially low for people who move between these two types of region.

INTRODUCTION

During young adulthood, finding an attractive partner is one of the main aims of life. People go to great lengths to fulfil this aim. Some "try out" several partnerships before they settle, others search for a long time until they find their true love. Some marry their neighbour's son or daughter, with whom they played as a child; others migrate and meet someone in their new place of residence who finally becomes their partner. It is this

* We would like to thank Marie-Pierre Arrizabalaga, Margarida Duraes, Antoinette Fauve-Chamoux, Leslie Page Moch, Elyce Rotella, Frank van Tubergen, and Richard Zijdeman for their valuable comments on an earlier draft of this article, as well as the participants of two seminars where this paper was discussed: a seminar on "Familles, mariages et domesticités: modèles historiques comparés (XVIe–XXe siècle)" at the École des Hautes Études en Sciences Sociales in Paris, and the Utrecht Mobility and Stratification Seminar.

difference that is the topic of this article. Does intra-national migration matter for partner choice? And, more specifically, does it matter for the likelihood that the marriage will be endogamous, i.e. that both partners originate from the same social class?

Many studies have shown that people tend to marry over a short geographical distance.[1] At first sight it seems likely that their marriage will be endogamous because neighbours tend to be from the same social class. However, one could also argue that long-distance marriages are more likely to be endogamous because a partner found at a great geographical distance might indicate a large investment in searching for a partner, and therefore an especially close fit between the partners. Alternatively, the long-distance migration might have been triggered by something totally unrelated to searching for a spouse, such as further education or finding a job. A number of conflicting hypotheses on the effects of migration on the likelihood of endogamy will be examined in this article.

In the following we will study the consequences of migration for endogamy by class of origin in France between 1803 and 1986. The choice of spouse has been the topic of a great many quantitative historical studies, in France as well as elsewhere, but they have tended to focus on geographical endogamy or on age differences between spouses.[2] The same applies to qualitative historical studies on marriage patterns, such as those by Flandrin and Segalen.[3] More attention has been paid to the study of class mobility in sociological studies of post-World-War-II France.[4] A few

1. See, for example, Alice Bee Kasakoff and John W. Adams, "Spatial Location and Social Organisation: An Analysis of Tikopian Patterns", *Man*, New Series, 12 (1977), pp. 48–64; Barrie S. Morgan, "A Contribution to the Debate on Homogamy, Propinquity, and Segregation", *Journal of Marriage and the Family*, 43 (1981), pp. 909–921; Thomas W. Pullum and Andres Peri, "A Multivariate Analysis of Homogamy in Montevideo, Uruquay", *Population Studies*, 53 (1999), pp. 361–377; Gillian Stevens, "Propinquity and Educational Homogamy", *Sociological Forum*, 6 (1991), pp. 715–726.
2. See *inter alia* Guy Brunet, Antoinette Fauve-Chamoux, and Michel Oris (eds), *Le choix du conjoint* (Paris, 1996).
3. J.L. Flandrin, *Les amours paysannes XVIe–XIXe siècles* (Paris, 1975), and Martine Segalen, *Love and Power in the Peasant Family: Rural France in the Nineteenth Century* (Oxford, 1983).
4. See for instance Michel Bozon and François Héran, "La découverte du conjoint. I. Évolution et morphologie des scènes de rencontre", *Population*, 6 (1987), pp. 943–986; *idem*, "La découverte du conjoint. II. Évolution et morphologie des scènes de rencontre", *Population*, 1 (1988), pp. 121–150; *idem*, "L'aire de recrutement du conjoint", *Données sociales* (1987), pp. 338–347. See too Michel Forsé and Louis Chauvel, "L'évolution de l'homogamie en France", *Revue française de sociologie*, 36 (1995), pp. 123–142; Alain Girard, *Le choix du conjoint. Une enquête psycho-sociologique en France* (Paris, 1981); Louis-André Vallet, "Forty Years of Social Mobility in France: Change in Social Fluidity in the Light of Recent Models", *Revue Française de Sociologie: An Annual English Selection*, 42, Supplement (2001), pp. 5–64; and various studies by Singly, including his recent study of France, and other European studies. François de Singly and Vincenzo Cicchelli, "Contemporary Families: Social Reproduction and Personal Fulfilment', in D.I. Kertzer and M. Barbagli (eds), *Family Life in the Twentieth Century: The History of the European Family* (New Haven, CT, 2003), pp. 311–349.

articles deal with the integration of migrants in parts of France, based on either the conscription registers[5] or marriage records.[6]

We used the large TRA dataset for the purpose of our present investigation.[7] This dataset is especially suitable for our study. First, because France is a relatively large country we will be able to study the consequences of both short-distance and long-distance migration. Secondly, the long period allows us to study whether the consequences of migration have changed with the almost universal availability of modern means of transport, and also whether temporal differences in endogamy can be explained, in part at least, by variations in the occurrence of migration. Thirdly, because the data cover both urban and rural regions we can investigate whether the direction in which one migrates matters.

Methodologically, this study might be useful because many historical studies on endogamy are restricted to stable populations in a specific area. By investigating the effects of migration on endogamy it will become possible to evaluate to what extent the results of regionally restricted studies are biased. From a societal point of view it is interesting to see to what extent migrants integrate into their new region of residence. If the marriages of migrants are less likely to be socially endogamous than those of non-migrants, and especially if they are more likely to marry downward, this can be seen as a sign of imperfect integration.

ENDOGAMY AND MIGRATION: RECENT THEORIES

Whether migrants win or lose on the social ladder has been the subject of a

5. Jean-Claude Farcy and Alain Faure, *La mobilité d'une génération de français. Recherches sur les migrations et les déménagements vers et dans Paris à la fin du XIXe siècle* (Paris, 2003).
6. Antoine Prost, "Structures sociales du XVIIIe arrondissement en 1936", in J. Girault (ed.), *Ouvriers en banlieue, XIXe–XXe siècles* (Paris, 1998), pp. 50–64. Philippe Rygiel, "Dissolution d'un groupe ethnique. Origines des témoins et des conjoints des enfants des familles polonaises implantées dans le Cher", *Mouvement Sociale*, 191 (2000), pp. 69–89.
7. On TRA, see Jacques Dupâquier and Jean-Pierre Pélissier, "Mutations d'une société: la mobilité professionelle", in J. Dupâquier and D. Kessler (eds), *La société française au XIXe siècle* (Paris, 1992), pp. 121–236; C. Motte and J.-P. Pélissier, "La binette, l'aiguille et le plumeau", in *ibid.*, pp. 237–342; J.-P. Pélissier and D. Rébaudo, "Une approche de l'illettrisme en France", *Histoire et Mesure*, 19 (2004), pp. 161–202. On studies of migration and marriage using the TRA data, see Didier Blanchet and Dennis Kessler, "La mobilité géographique de la naissance au mariage", in Dupâquier and Kessler, *La société française au XIXe siècle*, pp. 343–378; Paul-André Rosental, *Les sentiers invisibles. Espace, familles et migrations dans la France du 19e siècle* (Paris, 1999); *idem*, "La migration des femmes (et des hommes) en France au XIXᵉ siècle", *Annales de Démographie Historique*, 1 (2004), pp. 107–136. See also Noël Bonneuil and Paul-André Rosental, "Changing Social Mobility in Nineteenth-Century France", *Historical Methods*, 32 (1999), pp. 53–73, and Jérôme Bourdieu, Gilles Postel-Vinay, and Akiko Suwa-Eisenmann, "Défense et illustration de l'enquête des 3000 familles. L'exemple de son volet patrimonial", *Annales de Démographie Historique*, 1 (2004), pp. 19–52.

number of sociological[8] studies, and several historical studies, mostly by American historians working with census data. Thernstrom assumed the existence of a "permanent floating proletariat" in America in the nineteenth century, an "underclass" of men, permanently on the move to nowhere.[9] This image has been strong and persistent, despite statistical reanalyses of Thernstrom's work which reached quite different conclusions.[10] Upton, Kousser, and others stress that the likelihood of social advancement after migration depends on rational factors, notably age: the younger one is at migration, the longer one has to reap what has been sown, that is to recapture the "costs" of migration. Other, more recent studies on careers in the past have also stressed factors such as age and schooling.[11] This reappraisal of migrants can, in fact, be seen as part of a broader movement in the historiography of the Western world. Where migrants were once seen as a marginal minority of losers, it is now common to claim that migration was not marginal at all but touched the lives of a great many Europeans, possibly the majority, and that as a consequence there was no such thing as a selection effect of an underclass of less talented men and women who would always be less fortunate than the rest.[12]

What migration meant for the family domain, however, is still largely unknown. Broadening the study of the consequences of migration from the economic to the family domain is interesting not only for methodological and societal reasons, as discussed above, but also for theoretical reasons. Theoretical progress can be made by systematically comparing

8. See for example John L. Rodgers and Joan R. Rodgers, "The Economic Impact of Rural-to-Urban Migration in the United States: Evidence for Male Labor-Force Participants", *Social Science Quarterly* (1997), pp. 937–954, and Michael Wagner, "Zur Bedeutung räumlicher Mobilität für den Erwerbsverlauf bei Männern und Frauen", in Akademie für Raumforschung und Landesplanung (ed.), *Regionale und biographische Mobilität im Lebensverlauf* (Hanover, 1992), pp. 149–167.

9. S. Thernstrom, *The Other Bostonians: Poverty and Progress in the American Metropolis 1880–1970* (Cambridge, MA, 1973), pp. 40–42, 231–232.

10. J. Morgan Kousser, "Log-linear Analysis of Contingency Tables: An Introduction for Historians with an Application to Thernstrom on the 'Floating Proletariat'", *Historical Methods*, 15 (1982), pp. 152–169. Graham J.G. Upton, "A Note on 'Log-linear Analysis of Contingency Tables'", *Historical Methods*, 18 (1985), pp. 147–154.

11. For a survey see John C. Brown, Marco H.D. van Leeuwen, and David Mitch, "The History of the Modern Career: An Introduction", in David Mitch, John C. Brown, and Marco H.D. van Leeuwen (eds), *Origins of the Modern Career* (Ashgate, 2004), pp. 3–41.

12. See for example, Leslie Page Moch, *Moving Europeans: Migration in Western Europe since 1650* (Bloomington, IN, 1992); Colin Pooley and Jean Turnbull, *Migration and Mobility in Britain since the 18th Century* (London, 1998), and the discussion of their book in the *Annales de Démographie Historique* in 2002 by Lucassen, Kasakoff, Kok, and Schwartz: Leo Lucassen, "Introduction", *Annales de Démographie Historique* (2002), pp. 101–105; Jan Kok, "Comment on Pooley and Turnbull", *ibid.*, pp. 113–118; Robert M. Schwartz, "Steady State Mobility", *ibid.*, pp. 119–123. See also Anne Winter, "'Vagrancy' as an Adaptive Strategy: The Duchy of Brabant", *International Review of Social History*, 49 (2004), pp. 249–278.

competing hypotheses from several theories, and, as we will see below, several partly conflicting hypotheses on the consequences of migration for endogamy can be derived. Furthermore, differences with respect to endogamy between migrants and non-migrants might add to the explanation of regional and temporal differences in the likelihood of endogamy if these regions or periods vary in terms of the extent of migration. These regional and temporal differences have been the focus of much research on endogamy.[13]

Why would we expect migrants to show more or less endogamy than non-migrants? In general, social endogamy is thought to be the consequence of, first, people's preferences for a partner from the same social class; second, the pressure of significant others (parents, peers, the priest for example) on one to marry within one's own social class; and, third, social segregation, making it more likely that one meets and consequently marries someone from one's own class.[14] If migrants differ from non-migrants with respect to one or more of these determinants of endogamy, we may expect the two groups to differ too with respect to the likelihood of endogamy. Research on the effects of international migration on integration, however, has shown that it makes sense not only to distinguish between migrants and non-migrants but also to look at the characteristics of the place of destination and the place of origin of migrants and the specific combination of the two (the distance between place of origin and destination for example).[15]

In the literature on migration and endogamy we found one hypothesis that predicts a direct effect of migration on partner preferences. According to Sherkat, endogamy might be more attractive for people who have been uprooted.[16] They feel strangers in their place of destination and try to compensate for this by seeking friends and a partner who will make them feel at home. This is likely to be someone with the same social origins as themselves. We extend this hypothesis because we expect individuals who move over a larger distance to feel more uprooted and therefore even more likely to seek a partner from their own social class (H1a). Additionally, the effect of migration might be greater if the place of origin and destination

13. See for example, Robert D. Mare, "Five Decades of Educational Assortative Mating", *American Sociological Review*, 56 (1991), pp. 15–32; Wilfred Uunk, "Who Marries Whom? The Role of Social Origin, Education and High Culture in Mate Selection of Industrial Societies during the Twentieth Century" (Ph.D., University of Nijmegen, 1996).

14. M. Kalmijn, "Intermarriage and Homogamy: Causes, Patterns, Trends", *Annual Review of Sociology*, 24 (1998), pp. 395–421.

15. Frank van Tubergen, "The Social-cultural and Socio-economic Integration of Immigrants in Cross-National Perspective: Origin, Destination, and Community Effects" (Ph.D., University of Utrecht, 2005).

16. Darren E. Sherkat, "Religious Intermarriage in the United States: Trends, Patterns, and Predictors", *Social Science Research*, 33 (2004), pp. 606–625.

are less alike (H1b). Someone who moves from a small village to another small village probably feels less alone than someone who moves from a small village to a city, or vice versa. Sherkat's hypothesis would also be supported if people who were uprooted for reasons other than migration were also more likely to marry endogamously. We will therefore investigate whether men and women were more likely to marry endogamously in the years immediately after the end of a war than in times of peace (H1c).

While being uprooted as a consequence of migration is thought to increase endogamy, there are also scholars who claim that, for an altogether different reason, migration will decrease endogamy according to social origin. It is sometimes assumed that individuals who are ambitious and highly motivated in their occupational career will also be more eager to escape their social class of origin by marrying upward (i.e. not endogamously). The research on the economic consequences of migration shows that it is unclear whether migrants are in general positively selected with respect to characteristics such as ambition, capacities, and intelligence.[17] However, certain circumstances might favour the positive selection of migrants.

Such a positive selection tends to be stronger if people migrate for economic reasons rather than family or political reasons. Even if we do not know why people migrate, we may assume that migration from rural to urban regions is more likely to be economically motivated than migration in the opposite direction or migration between rural areas or between urban regions. Positive selection is also more likely if people migrate over a longer distance. Such migration requires a relatively large investment. Highly motivated individuals who expect to be able to compensate for this investment in the future will be more inclined to take this risk than those who do not. We therefore expect less endogamy among long-distance migrants (H2a) and among migrants moving from rural to urban regions (H2b).

These effects would disappear if we could take these selections into account. We cannot do this with the data at hand, except in the following, admittedly restricted, way by distinguishing the intergenerationally upward mobile from those in the same class or an even lower class than their father. We assume that the intergenerationally upward mobile are more ambitious and therefore more likely to marry exogamously than the latter (H2c).

Social pressure, the second determinant of endogamous marriages, might be directly affected by migration. The larger the distance migrated, the more difficult it is for parents or peers to effectively influence the

17. Barry R. Chiswick, "Are Immigrants Favorably Self-Selected?", *American Economic Review*, 89 (1999), pp. 181–185.

behaviour of the migrant (H3a).[18] Again, however, it is useful to look at the characteristics of the place of origin and place of destination of the migrant.

Social control of the choice of marriage partner in the French country-side has often been described. Unmarried youngsters would have met long before the age of courtship, either on the farm, during work evenings in the village, as members of local fraternities, in the fields during sowing and reaping, at feasts and fairs, in church during Mass, or at school. Work evenings – in French *veillées* – were common throughout the country-side.[19] In the long winter evenings, the unmarried girls of the village, their mothers, and potential suitors would join one another in a communal barn to work, mostly to spin, sing and talk, perhaps dance, and to eat and drink. What the ballroom was for the urban *jeunesse dorée*, the *veillée* was for rural populations, except that the former had leisure, while the latter also had to work. It is often said that marriages were made in the *veillée*: "the spinning-room gave the lads an opportunity to observe the girls' abilities at what would be one of their most important tasks in the household. In a traditional rural society, such criteria were extremely important for the choice of a partner."[20]

Not only was social control in evidence during the *veillées*, it pervaded village life and it favoured endogamy, as has often been noted with regard to geographical endogamy and sometimes social endogamy. Many proverbs expressed a desire for endogamy in the countryside, and none disapproved of it:[21] "Qui se marie loin trompe ou est trompé (Provence); Épouse ton voisin, tu connaîtras son chien (Gascogne, Languedoc)".[22] As elsewhere in Europe, village youngsters accepted this collective oral wisdom and protected the stock of unmarried men and women by beating up "outsiders" (unless they had, literally, been bought off). "Fools" who were courting outside their age group, their village, or social group were paraded through the village sitting back to front on a donkey; another technique was to deposit a trail of rotting vegetables or manure between the houses of the two lovers. Intense staring and vile gossiping by the women at the communal washing place or a rough *charivari* in front of the houses of the culprits were also used to express disapproval.[23] In the very

18. Sherkat, "Religious Intermarriage in the United States".

19. M. Mitterauer, *A History of Youth* (Oxford, 1990), pp. 178–184. Edward Shorter, *The Making of the Modern Family* (New York, 1975), pp. 125–127.

20. Mitterauer, *A History of Youth*, p. 181. See too, Segalen, *Love and Power in the Peasant Family*, p. 16.

21. Flandrin, *Les amours paysannes*, p. 139.

22. Martine Segalen, *De l'amour et du mariage autrefois* (Paris, 1981), p. 34.

23. Flandrin, *Les amours paysannes*, pp. 140–145; Segalen, *Love and Power in the Peasant Family*; Eugene Weber, *Peasants into Frenchmen: The Modernization of Rural France 1870–1914* (Stanford, CA, 1976), pp. 399–413. See too the articles in Jacques Le Goff and Jean-Claude Schmitt (eds), *Le charivari* (Paris, 1981).

many small villages in France in the nineteenth century, the village might to a large extent consist of family and so, it has been claimed, it was the families who did the marrying rather than the couples themselves.[24]

In cities, social pressure and control is presumably less effective than in rural areas.[25] Migrants who moved from a village to the city were therefore, by and large, less subject to social control, although we know that migrants from the same region often flocked together and so did not entirely escape this control.[26] Indeed, the presence of kin might have been an impetus to migrate to a particular town,[27] and one might also have migrated as a young child with one's parents to a town. Nonetheless, one might expect migration from rural to urban areas to weaken social control and thus endogamy (H3b).

Migrants moving in the other direction might, however, leave behind a relatively tolerant climate and move to a situation where neighbours watch one another closely. In this case, social pressure to marry an appropriate partner (i.e. from the same social class) might decrease to a much lesser extent, or even increase.[28] We expect that a similar mechanism might make first marriages more likely to be endogamous than later marriages (H3c). Social pressure from family and peers is probably much more effective and stronger for first marriages than for second marriages, because in the latter case the bride and groom no longer live with their parents; they are older, and more independent. Social pressure might also be especially high in regions with traditional family values (H3d).

Alternatively, individuals who experienced little social control might also be more likely to migrate than those experiencing a great degree of social control. Where families exercised little control, their children might be more likely to marry outside their own social class and to leave their place of origin. The less social control, the further children would migrate both with respect to distance (H4a) and with respect to urbanization (H4b); and the more likely it is that they would marry exogamously. We expect these effects to disappear if the strength of social control within the family and at the place of origin is taken into account.

Examples of families with little control over their children might include incomplete families (H4c) and families without much capital (H4d). The first have more difficulty in influencing the behaviour of their children because two parents can do that more effectively than one parent. The second type of family has less influence because they cannot threaten to disinherit their children if they refuse to conform. It has been argued that

24. Weber, *Peasants into Frenchmen*, pp. 167–168.
25. Louise Tilly and Joan Scott, *Women, Work and Family* (New York, 1978), pp. 121–122.
26. See for example Weber, *Peasants into Frenchmen*, pp. 281–282.
27. Leslie Page Moch, *Paths to the City* (Thousand Oaks, CA, 1983), pp. 199–200.
28. Sherkat, "Religious Intermarriage in the United States".

the extent to which social control was exerted was closely linked to the transmission of property down the generations. This was one reason for the high degree of social control among farmers: they had to ensure that the farm remained intact over centuries. Segalen writes:

> In traditional society, problems that would today be considered personal, whether to do with the intimacies of the heart or of the body, were the responsibility of the community. The formation of the couple, as well as concerning the young people themselves, involved the two families and the entire social group.[29] [...] Family considerations weigh heavily on the individuals who, tend to disappear in the face of the wider aims of economic and social improvement of the family line. In these terms the couple is merely a link in the chain leading to the growth of patrimony or resisting the fragmentation of landholdings through inheritance. The individuality of the couple, or rather, its tendency towards individuality, is crushed by the family institution, and also by the social pressure exercised by the village community as a whole.[30]

This is also said to be the case for the propertied classes in the city: "Curieusement le modèle bourgeois se rapproche du modèle paysan, dans la mesure où l'institution matrimoniale coïncide avec un 'établissement'. Au mariage, les parents transmettent une partie de leurs biens à leurs enfants; ils doivent donc en contrôler soigneusement la formation."[31]

If regions are relatively homogeneous with respect to social class, social endogamy within a certain region will result even if people do not prefer to have spouses with characteristics similar to their own.[32] Migration to another region, especially at a large distance, would then foster intermarriage by providing the opportunity to meet people from different backgrounds (H5a). However, in some cases (the elite of small villages for example) it might be necessary to migrate to find a partner of approximately the same age and from the same social class, and indeed the geographical marriage horizon of the elites is, generally speaking, large, although the same applies to servants.[33] But we will assume that this latter case is an exception.

Again, the characteristics of the place of origin and destination might play a decisive role. First, if one migrates but ends up in a place similar in terms of composition to one's place of origin (from rural village to rural

29. Segalen, *Love and Power in the Peasant Family*, p. 38.
30. *Ibid.*, p. 41.
31. Segalen, *De l'amour et du mariage autrefois*, pp. 68, 85. See too George Alter, *Family and the Female Life Course: The Women of Verviers, Belgium, 1849–1880* (Madison, WI, 1988), pp. 148–150, on the town of Verviers.
32. P.M. Blau and J.E. Schwartz, *Crosscutting Social Circles* (New York, 1984). William R. Catton, Jr and R.J. Smirich, "A Comparison of Mathematical Models for the Effect of Residential Propinquity on Mate Selection", *American Sociological Review*, 29 (1964), pp. 522–529. Stevens, "Propinquity and Educational Homogamy".
33. Pooley and Turnbull, *Migration and Mobility in Britain since the 18th Century*, p. 158.

village for example), then migration might have little effect on endogamy (H5b).[34] Secondly, if one migrates from a village to a city, the marriage market increases enormously; migrating in the opposite direction, there is little to be gained in terms of the number of potential marriage partners (H5c). These marriage-market hypotheses are also supported if members of large classes of origin marry endogamously more often than members of small classes of origin (H5d). We will investigate whether this is the case.

Conversely, migration might also restrict the opportunities of migrants, if, for example, migrants and the original population do not interact. In that case migrants are forced to marry among themselves. This might restrict their choices, especially if they are a small group. Also, in this case migration will result in a higher degree of geographical endogamy but also a lower degree of social endogamy. Segregation of migrants and the original population is more likely to happen if both groups have a different lifestyle or if the original population feels threatened (economically or culturally) by the migrants. We may assume that lifestyle differences increase with the distance migrated (H6a) and with the relative degree of urbanization between the place of origin and destination of the migrants (H6b).[35] Fear of migrants might be positively related to the size of the migrant group.[36] However, because it is easier for larger migrant groups to find an appropriate partner within their own group, the result of this is unclear.

Some characteristics of society changed so much during the nineteenth and twentieth centuries that hypotheses formulated for the nineteenth century might no longer be true in the twentieth century, and vice versa. First, distance measured in kilometres (rather than time) meant something very different in the early nineteenth century from what it did in the late twentieth century.[37] Whereas it once took weeks to travel from northern to southern France, this distance can now be covered in a day by car and even faster by aeroplane. We therefore expect distance to play a much smaller role in explaining endogamy today than it did two centuries ago (H7).

Secondly, as a consequence of improved transportation, but also of the mass media, differences in norms and lifestyles between rural and urban areas have become narrower. Even the occupational distribution in villages and cities sometimes hardly differs any more. All hypotheses predicting an effect resulting from moving between rural and urban areas should

34. Morgan, "A Contribution to the Debate on Homogamy, Propinquity, and Segregation".
35. See for example, Bart Van de Putte, "Het belang van de toegeschreven positie in een moderniserende wereld. Partnerkeuze in 19de-eeuwse Vlaamse steden (Leuven, Aalst en Gent)", (Ph.D., Catholic University of Leuven, 2003).
36. Hubert M. Blalock, *Toward a Theory of Minority Group Relations* (New York, 1967).
37. See for example Pooley and Turnbull, *Migration and Mobility in Britain since the 18th Century*, p. 303.

therefore be less valid now than they would have been in the early nineteenth century. More specifically, we expect decreasing effects of the difference in urbanization between the places of origin and destination (H8) and the degree of urbanization of the place of destination (H9).

Hypotheses 7, 8, and 9 also follow from the claim that social control has decreased in Europe in general and France in particular since the end of the eighteenth century.[38] Flandrin stated that:

> [...] la multiplication des conceptions prenuptials vient de ce que les jeunes gens ... ont alors été moins soumis a leurs parents que dans le passé; ils ont fréquenté plus librement les filles; ils ont davantage choisi leur future épouse par attrait sexuel et ont imposé plus souvent ce choix à leurs parents.[39]

Shorter claimed that "the most important change in nineteenth- and twentieth-century courtship has been the surge of sentiment [...]. People started to place affection and personal compatibility at the top of the list of criteria in choosing marriage partners. These new standards became articulated as romantic love."[40] And he added: "Once the heart began to speak, it would give instructions often entirely incompatible with the rational principles of family interest and material survival on which the small community was ordered. Marry the woman you love, the heart might say, even though your parents disapprove."[41]

Others have argued that social control was less in evidence in cities – although by no means absent there, especially among the bourgeoisie – than it was in the countryside[42] and thus the continuous growth in the percentage of the population living in cities would mean that, over all, social control decreased in France over the past two centuries. We also know that *veillées*, bundling, and *charivari* are now virtually absent in France, while they were common at the beginning of the nineteenth century, and thus in the countryside too the degree of social control over the choice of marriage partner must have diminished. The *charivari* declined in number and force during the nineteenth century, so much so that by the end of the century it could be found only in small remote places.[43] Although they remained a feature in many places until the 1880s, by the turn of the century the *veillées* too were wasting away.[44] And with them went the collective oral wisdom,[45] codified in proverbs, which had

---

38. Flandrin, *Les amours paysannes*; J.M. Phayer, *Sexual Liberation and Religion in Nineteenth Century Europe* (London, 1977); Shorter, *The Making of the Modern Family*, pp. 125–127; James F. Traer, *Marriage and the Family in Eighteenth-Century France* (Ithaca, NY, 1980).
39. Flandrin, *Les amours paysannes*, p. 243.
40. Shorter, *The Making of the Modern Family*, p. 148.
41. *Ibid.*, pp. 19–20.
42. Tilly and Scott, *Women, Work and Family*, p. 1211.
43. Weber, *Peasants into Frenchmen*, p. 406.
44. *Ibid.*, p. 416.
45. *Ibid.*, pp. 419–428.

long expressed and enforced the desire for endogamy. Still, in remote areas of France, a strong sense of "us" versus "strangers" continued to exist until the 1950s.[46] All told, however, we predict that the effect of social control and thus the difference in endogamy between migrants and non-migrants diminished over time.

These hypotheses are summarized in Table 1.

DATA, MEASUREMENT, AND MODELS

Data

The data we use are drawn from the "3,000 families survey", better known as the TRA dataset. The name originates from the sample procedure used in the survey. The survey aims to collect birth, marriage, divorce, and death certificates for all French persons whose surnames begin with the three letters TRA (e.g. Tranchant, Travers). This results in patronymic genealogies of about 3,000 couples who married between 1803 and 1832 and a sample rate of about one per 10,000 inhabitants in 1806. TRA was chosen because surnames starting with these three letters occur in all languages spoken in France (including Alsatian, Breton, Catalan, and French itself). For this research we use marriage register information. All marriages for the nineteenth century have been computerized. The dataset for the twentieth century is not yet complete.[47] The dataset includes 74,562 marriage certificates. However, because information on crucial characteristics, especially the father's occupation, is missing from many certificates, models will be estimated using data from 23,641 marriage certificates for men and 23,313 marriage certificates for women.

Measurement

Endogamy is measured by comparing the social class of the father of the bride with the social class of the father of the groom at the time of the marriage. To arrive at the class variable, all occupational titles were first coded using HISCO.[48] These codes were then automatically recoded using

---

46. Claude Karnoouh, "L'étranger ou le faux inconnu. Essai sur la définition spatiale d'autrui dans un village lorrain", *Ethnologie française*, 2 (1972), pp. 107–122.

47. Analyses (not shown in this article) show that weighting the data to take the lower representation of rural areas in the twentieth century into account has no effect on the results. We therefore refrain from presenting results of analyses based on weighted data.

48. Marco H.D. van Leeuwen, Ineke Maas, and Andrew Miles, *HISCO: Historical International Standard Classification of Occupations* (Leuven, 2002). J.-P. Pélissier, D. Rébaudo, and D. Nicolas, "La mobilité professionnelle en France aux XIX et XXe siècles d'après les actes de mariage" [HISMA. Occasional Papers and Documents] (IISG, Amsterdam, 2004).

Table 1. *Summary of hypotheses on the effect of migration on social endogamy*

	Effect on endogamy			
	Migration distance	Difference in urbanization	Urbanization of destination	Individual characteristics
Preferences				
1. Endogamy as a response to migrants being "uprooted"	+ (H1a)	+ (H1b)		+ turmoil * indicated by postwar years (H1c)
2. Composition: those who prefer exogamy migrate	– (H2a)		– (H2b)	– ambition * measured by upward mobility (H2c)
Social pressure				
3. Endogamy due to less social control over marital behaviour	– (H3a)		– (H3b)	– less social control * indicated by second marriage (H3c); * and less traditional family values (H3d)
4. Composition: those generally subject to little social pressure migrate	– (H4a)	– (H4b)		– less social pressure * indicated by the death of a parent (H4c); * and absence of property (H4d)
Marriage market				
5. Broadening the geographical marriage horizon	– (H5a)	– (H5b)	– (H5c)	+ size of class of origin (H5d)
6. Endogamy due to spatial segregation	– (H6a)	– (H6b)		
Time				
7. Better means of transport and less social control	decreasing over time (H7)			
8. Decrease in cultural differences and less social control		decreasing over time (H8)	decreasing over time (H9)	

Figure 1. Portrait of a marriage in Oeuilly (Marne), 1905. Bride, groom, their parents, and relatives all lived in three villages situated five kilometres from one another. They were farmers or farm workers.
Source: Private collection D. Rébaudo. Used by permission.

HISCLASS.[49] This taxonomy comprises twelve classes ranging from higher managers to unskilled farm workers. For reasons of comparability these twelve classes were combined into seven classes: (1+2) higher managers and professionals, (3, 4, 5) lower managers, professionals, clerical and sales, (6, 7) skilled workers, (8) farmers and fishermen, (9) lower-skilled workers, (11) unskilled workers, and (10, 12) farm workers.

In this type of source, information on the occupation of the father is usually missing in about 50 per cent of all cases. Since this is true for both the father and the father-in-law, valid cases for about 25 per cent of all marriages could be expected. Actually, endogamy was apparent in 26,480 cases, which is clearly above what we expected. Although the likelihood of having complete information on the classes of the father and the father-in-law is greater for the stable rural population, the dataset contains enough

49. M.H.D. van Leeuwen and I. Maas, "HISCLASS", Paper presented at the 5th European Social Science History Conference (Berlin, 24–27 March 2004); I. Maas and M.H.D. van Leeuwen, "SPSS Recode Job from HISCO into HISCLASS", May 2004.

cases of complete information on urban migrants to allow us to estimate our models.

Migration distance is operationalized as the distance in kilometres between the place of birth and place of residence at the time of marriage. Although the way this crucial concept of geographical "distance" is measured is both clear as well as generally valid, there might be a few less fortunate aspects to it. To begin with, differences in topography and accessibility between places are not taken into account, even though a mountain range or a major watershed can make places that are close to one another on a map very distant in terms of access.[50] Furthermore, if the two places are identical, the migration distance will be zero, even in the case of a large city like Paris, where there might have been a sizeable distance between the actual address at birth and the address at marriage. This presumably presents only a small problem, but another characteristic of these migration-distance data is potentially more disturbing: about half the individuals were immobile; in half the cases the value for migration is zero. We therefore add a dummy variable distinguishing migrants from non-migrants. The effect of migration distance then only applies to those who actually migrated.

Urbanization is measured using a five-category scale in increasing order of urbanization: rural towns and villages, capital of a canton, capital of an arrondissement, capital of a *département*, or department, and the national capital, Paris. The level of urbanization of the place of birth is unknown for those born abroad and for a small percentage of the rest of the population. They are excluded from our analyses. We measure the *difference in urbanization between place of birth and residence* by subtracting the category scores. The maximum difference is 4 (between Paris and rural towns and villages), the minimum is 0.

During the nineteenth and twentieth centuries France was involved in several wars (1812–1815: the Napoleonic Wars; 1870–1871, the Franco-Prussian War; 1914–1918: World War I; 1939–1945: World War II). We believe that marriages in the years immediately after these wars would have been especially affected. *Postwar years* are distinguished from other years by a dummy variable.

Upward mobility is measured by comparing the class of the father of the groom/bride with the class of the bride/groom when the latter married. In both cases the seven-class version of HISCLASS is used, in which mobility from classes at the bottom of this taxonomy to classes higher up is regarded as upward mobility. Because a large proportion of women and a smaller proportion of men had no occupation at marriage, we add an extra dummy

50. R.J. Johnston and P.J. Perry, "Déviation directionelle dans les aires de contact: deux exemples de relations matrimoniales dans la France rurale du XIXe siècle", *Études Rurales*, 46 (1972), pp. 23–33.

variable to distinguish these groups from men and women who did have an occupation at marriage.

French marriage registers give information on the survival status of the parents. We measure separately whether the *father is deceased* and whether the *mother is deceased*. Two classes are deemed to have had property: the *higher managers and professionals* (class 1+2) and the *farmers and fishermen* (class 8). As this is a proxy variable, not all members of these classes will in effect have had property. There must have been a certain proportion without property, especially among the very large class of farmers. The occupational titles seldom make this clear however (if they did, there would be no problem; not only does the HISCLASS taxonomy place cotters among the group of rural labourers and large landowners among the elite, HISCO itself has a subsidiary variable noting property). Although there is thus a certain amount of "noise" in the data, it is reassuring that other French data make it clear that a large proportion of farmers and the elite did, generally speaking, leave something to inherit at their death.[51] *First marriages* of brides and grooms are distinguished from second and later marriages.

Having *traditional family values* has not been measured at the individual level. Instead, we used information from Todd on departmental differences in family values.[52] France consists of almost 100 departments. They have all been scored on the relationship between parents and children (more or less authoritarian) and the relationship between siblings (more or less egalitarian). Both characteristics have been combined into three categories: (0) egalitarian and not very authoritarian; (1) either authoritarian or inegalitarian; and (2) authoritarian and inegalitarian. These departmental characteristics have been linked to the individuals by using the department in which they were born.

Class size is measured by the percentage of brides' fathers that belong to

51. Luc Arrondel and Cyril Grange, "Successions et héritiers dans la société rurale du XIXe siècle: l'exemple des familles 'TRA' de Loire-Inférieure", *Annales de Démographie Historique* (2004), pp. 53–77.

52. Emmanuel Todd, *La nouvelle France* (Paris, 1988), p. 88. Todd claims his data are valid for at least the past two centuries. It should be noted though that he does not break them down by sub-period. Although we are fortunate in having a measure of traditional family values at all, we would have preferred to have had more than one measurement point (and to have had individual-level rather than departmental-level data). As we cannot distinguish between sub-periods, it is unclear if there were changes in the position of departments relative to one another with regard to family values. Preliminary results from a national survey in 1980 among French notaries concerning the transmission of property in villages and small cities seem to suggest stability. This, at least, is Goy's conclusion ("la permanence, près de deux siècles après la promulgation du Code civil des comportements régionaux pré-1789 malgré les transformations juridiques, économiques et sociologiques"). See Joseph Goy, "Pour une cartographie des modes de transmission successorale deux siècles après le Code civil", *Mélanges de l'École française de Rome*, 100 (1988), pp. 431–444; the quotation is on p. 441.

a specific class. Class size is estimated separately for every five years. Since class and the sex of the children are not correlated, this percentage is a good indicator of the availability of partners for both men and women.

Finally, we take the *year of marriage* into account because it is generally assumed that endogamy of class of origin decreased over time. To test hypotheses on the changing importance of migration over time, interaction effects of year of marriage and migration distance, urbanization of the place of residence, and difference between urbanization of place of birth and place of residence respectively are created. Before these variables were multiplied, they were centred around their mean. As a consequence, the main effect of – say – migration distance in models including the interaction effect of migration distance and year of marriage can be interpreted as the effect of migration distance in the mean year of marriage (around 1900).

Models

Because the dependent variable has only two categories, we use logistic regression analyses. In the first model only migration characteristics (distance, urbanization of place of residence, and difference in urbanization between places of birth and residence) are included. In a second model, individual characteristics are added. In a third model, interaction effects between the migration characteristics and time are included. A separate set of logistic regression models is used to investigate to what extent changes in the migration characteristics explain trends in the likelihood of endogamy. We present exponentiated effect parameters, so-called odds ratios. Odds ratios above 1 indicate positive effects; odds ratios between 0 and 1 indicate negative effects.

RESULTS

Description

Before we disentangle the effects of several migration characteristics and other variables, we investigate whether migration and endogamy are related. A comparison between migrants and non-migrants with respect to the percentage of marriages that were endogamous offers preliminary support for a strong relationship. Whereas only 40 per cent of male and female migrants married within their own class of origin, 53 per cent of male non-migrants and 52 per cent of female non-migrants did so (Table 2). The longer the distance migrated, the greater the likelihood of an exogamous marriage. Male migrants who married exogamously migrated over an average distance of 96 kilometres, while for those who married endogamously the average distance migrated was only 69 kilometres. For

Table 2. *Migration and social endogamy in France, 1803–1986*

	Men	Women
Endogamous marriages (%)		
migrants	40.1	40.1
non-migrants	53.4	51.8
Migration distance (mean km, migrants only)		
endogamous	69.4	59.6
exogamous	96.1	79.1
Endogamous marriages (%)		
urban–rural migrant	33.2	31.2
urban–urban migrant	32.4	29.6
rural–urban migrant	29.9	29.1
rural–rural migrant	53.3	48.7

Source: TRA survey, INRA/CNRS.

female migrants the difference was somewhat less (79 kilometres compared with 60 kilometres), but still substantial.

An initial investigation of the direction of migration reveals two different types of migrant. Those who migrated from one rural place to another differed from non-migrants hardly at all with respect to the likelihood of endogamy. All migrants who moved either to or from a city were much less likely to marry endogamously. The patterns for men and women are strikingly similar.

Finally, we investigate whether the relationship between migration and endogamy changed over time (Figure 2). Figure 2 shows two interesting patterns. First, the likelihood of marrying endogamously changed little during the nineteenth century, but decreased thereafter. Secondly, around 1930 the marriage patterns of migrants and non-migrants converged slightly. Before 1930 the "spread" between endogamous marriages among migrants and non-migrants tended to be about 10 per cent. After 1930, this slowly decreased to about 5 per cent in 1986.

Models

Tables 3 and 4 present the logistic regression models for men and women respectively. We will describe the results in the order of the hypotheses listed in Table 1. According to the first hypothesis, endogamy should increase with the distance migrated because migrants feel more uprooted than non-migrants, especially when they migrate over a long distance (H1a). We find no support for this hypothesis. In all models for men and women there is a clear negative relationship between being a migrant and endogamy: migrants were less likely than non-migrants to marry endogamously. However, distance did not seem to matter: none of the

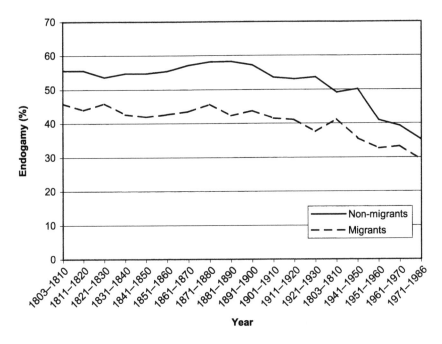

Figure 2. Social endogamy of migrants and non-migrants in France, 1803–1986.
TRA survey, INRA/CNRS

effects of migration distance is significant. This means that although we found a bivariate negative association between distance migrated and endogamy, this association is caused by the fact that men and women who migrated over a large distance were also more likely to migrate to a city and to migrate between places that differed greatly with respect to urbanization (the two other variables in model 1).

According to the first preference hypothesis, migrants who migrated between places that differed greatly with respect to urbanization should also feel more uprooted and be more likely to marry endogamously (H1b). Again, we find the opposite for both men and women. The greater the difference in urbanization, the less likely the marriage would be endogamous. A 1-point difference on the urbanization scale leads to an odds ratio of 0.955 for men and 0.909 for women. The odds of men who migrated between rural villages and Paris marrying endogamously were 0.832 (0.955^4) times the odds of men who migrated between places with the same level of urbanization. The corresponding odds for women were 0.683 (0.909^4).

Finally, the first preference hypothesis predicted that men and women would be more likely to marry endogamously in postwar years than in

Table 3. *Logistic regression analyses of social endogamy in France, 1803–1986 (men)*

	Model 1		Model 2		Model 3	
	odds ratio	sig.	odds ratio	sig.	odds ratio	sig.
Migrant	0.727	***	0.851	***	0.857	***
Distance place of birth and residence (/10)	0.998		0.997		0.995	
Urbanization place of residence	0.745	***	0.927	***	0.935	***
Difference in urbanization	0.955	*	0.901	***	0.898	***
Postwar years			1.149	*	1.150	*
Upward mobility			0.467	***	0.468	***
Not in the labour force			0.782	***	0.778	***
First marriage			1.083		1.083	
Father deceased			0.934		0.936	
Mother deceased			0.986		0.991	
Origin class with property:						
Higher managers and professionals			3.223	***	3.221	***
Farmers and fishermen			3.042	***	3.038	***
Marriage values:						
authoritarian or inegalitarian			1.180	***	1.179	***
authoritarian and inegalitarian			1.294	***	1.294	***
Size class of origin			1.022	***	1.022	***
Year since 1800 (/100)			0.932	*	0.893	*
Migrant * year centred around 1900 (/100)					1.117	
Distance * year centred around 1900 (/100)					1.008	*
Urb. * year centred around 1900 (/100)					0.960	
Diff. urb. * year centred around 1900 (/100)					0.989	
Constant	1.811	***	0.381	***	0.387	***
N	23,641		23,641		23,641	
Chi²	1121.6		5227.1		5238.8	
Degrees of freedom	4		16		20	

Source: TRA survey, INRA/CNRS.
* p < 0.05; ** p < 0.01, *** p < 0.001.

other years (H1c). We find some support for this hypothesis in the case of men. In the years immediately following a war, the odds of men marrying endogamously were 15 per cent higher than the corresponding odds in other years. Women seemed less affected by war and its aftermath.[53]

53. Interestingly, for Britain, Pooley and Turnbull found that wars had little permanent effect on migration patterns; while wars did result in population movements, after the war most people returned home; Pooley and Turnbull, *Migration and Mobility in Britain since the 18th Century*, pp. 261, 273.

Table 4. *Logistic regression analyses of social endogamy in France, 1803–1986 (women)*

	Model 1		Model 2		Model 3	
	odds ratio	sig.	odds ratio	sig.	odds ratio	sig.
Migrant	0.793	***	0.916	**	0.918	*
Distance place of birth and residence (/10)	1.002		1.002		1.000	
Urbanization place of residence	0.745	***	0.932	***	0.937	***
Difference in urbanization	0.909	***	0.863	***	0.860	***
Postwar years			1.077		1.078	
Upward mobility			0.604	***	0.604	***
Not in the labour force			0.757	***	0.755	***
First marriage			1.188	*	1.188	*
Father deceased			0.982		0.982	
Mother deceased			0.979		0.981	
Origin class with property:						
Higher managers and professionals			2.537	***	2.539	***
Farmers and fishermen			2.832	***	2.829	***
Marriage values:						
authoritarian or inegalitarian			1.266	***	1.265	***
authoritarian and inegalitarian			1.369	***	1.369	***
Size class of origin			1.027	***	1.027	***
Year since 1800 (/100)			0.899	**	0.886	*
Migrant * year centred around 1900 (/100)					1.047	
Distance * year centred around 1900 (/100)					1.005	
Urb. * year centred around 1900 (/100)					0.971	
Diff. urb. * year centred around 1900 (/100)					1.007	
Constant	1.706	***	0.328	***	0.328	***
N	23,313		23,313		23,313	
Chi^2	1018.7		5011.9		5014.9	
Degrees of freedom	4		15		20	

Source: TRA survey, INRA/CNRS.
* $p < 0.05$; ** $p < 0.01$; ** $p < 0.001$.

According to the second preference hypothesis, the distance migrated should be negatively related to endogamy, because those who were keenest to escape their local fate migrated over a large distance and were also less likely to marry endogamously (H2a). As discussed above, there is indeed a negative relationship between being a migrant and endogamy, but not between distance migrated and endogamy. More consistent with this hypothesis is the negative relationship between urbanization of place of

residence and endogamy for both men and women (H2b). This relationship is rather strong in model 1. For both men and women a 1-point
difference on the scale of urbanization of their place of residence is
associated with 25 per cent lower odds of marrying endogamously. Those
living in Paris were 68 per cent less likely to marry endogamously than
those living in rural villages.

The second preference hypothesis also predicts that the differences in
marital patterns between cities and villages would disappear if we took the
ambitions of men and women into account (H2c). This is very hard to do
with the data at hand, but we may assume at least that men and women
who are upwardly mobile compared with their father are more ambitious.
This variable is included in the second model. Upwardly mobile men and
women were indeed much less likely to marry endogamously than men
and women who were not mobile, not even downwardly.

The association between endogamy and urbanization of the place of
residence is much smaller in the second model than in the first. However,
models in which the variables of model 2 are excluded one by one (results
not shown in the tables) show that upward mobility explains only a very
small part of this change.[54] Together, these results may be summarized as
follows. The negative relationships between endogamy on the one hand
and being a migrant and urbanization of place of residence on the other
seem to support the second preference hypothesis, namely that those who
preferred to marry exogamously migrated. However, the finding that these
relationships are "explained" hardly at all by the ambitions of men
indicates that it might be fruitful to search for other explanations for these
negative relationships – explanations perhaps formulated in some of the
other hypotheses.

According to hypothesis 3, the social pressure of family and peers
weakened due to migration (H3a), and this was especially the case for
those who migrate toward a city (H3b). This hypothesis is thus also
consistent with the negative relationships between being a migrant and
endogamy, and between urbanization of place of residence and endogamy.
We expected social pressure to weaken between first and second marriages.
This was the case for women. The odds of a woman's first marriage being
endogamous were 19 per cent higher than the odds of a second or later
marriage being endogamous. This is additional support for the hypothesis
that under certain circumstances family and peers were less able to affect
marriage behaviour. Finally, social pressure of family and peers on
marriage behaviour is expected to be stronger for persons originating
from a department with more traditional family values (H3d). Our
findings support this hypothesis. Men and women born in departments

---

54. If upward mobility is omitted, the effect of urbanization of place of residence of men in
model 2 becomes 0.916, which is much closer to 0.927 than to 0.745.

where family values are more traditional were more likely to marry someone from the same class of origin.[55]

According to the rival hypothesis on social pressure, those who migrate are a select group of people who experienced little social pressure before migration. Based on this hypothesis, both migration distance (H4a) and the difference in the level of urbanization (H4b) are expected to be negatively related to endogamy. As discussed above, the difference in the level of urbanization was indeed negatively related to endogamy and migrants in general were more likely to marry outside their class of origin.

This second social-pressure hypothesis also predicts, though, that these relationships should disappear if we take initial differences in social pressure into account. We do so by adding to the model a variable indicating whether the parents were alive at marriage (H4c), and whether the parents belonged to the propertied classes (H4d). The survival status of the parents does not show the predicted effect, but in the models family property has the predicted relationship with endogamy. Women, and especially men, from the propertied classes were much more likely to marry endogamously than women and men from other classes. However, these characteristics do not completely explain the effects of being a migrant and the difference in urbanization between place of birth and residence. The effect of the latter variable in particular hardly differs between models 1 and 2. People who experienced little social pressure were more likely to marry outside their own social class, but they were not more likely to migrate between places that differed much with respect to urbanization.[56]

Both of the two marriage-market hypotheses predict negative relationships between distance migrated and difference in urbanization (between place of birth and residence) on the one hand and endogamy on the other. According to the first marriage-market hypothesis, a negative relationship may be expected because those who married over a large distance, or moved to a larger city, or moved between places that differed strongly, were more likely to meet people from a different social background (H5a, b, c). According to the second marriage-market hypothesis, those who migrated over a large distance and between very different places would be more segregated from the population in the place of destination and would therefore be forced to marry among the migrant group. Given those restrictive circumstances it was probably more difficult to marry someone

---

55. The fact that family values were not measured at the individual level but at the level of department means that our non-multi-level analyses might overestimate the significance of their effect.

56. Note, however, that the effect of urbanization of place of residence is explained to a large extent by the smaller percentage of the population originating from a propertied, i.e. farming, class in the cities.

from the same social background (H6a, b). With the exception of the effect of migration distance, these predicted relationships are borne out by the data.

According to the mechanism behind the first marriage-market hypothesis, men and women from larger social classes would be more likely to marry endogamously, because the likelihood of them meeting others from their own social background was relatively high (H5d). The positive effects of size of the class of origin on endogamy for both men and women support this hypothesis. If one class of origin is 10 per cent larger than another class, the odds of marrying endogamously in the first class will be 24 per cent higher for men and 31 per cent higher for women than the corresponding odds in that other class.

Even after taking characteristics of migration and many individual characteristics into account, there is still an effect of year of marriage. In the early nineteenth century people were more likely to marry within their own class of origin than they were in the late twentieth century. We will return to this in the next section.

The last three hypotheses in Table 1 predict that the effects of migration will have decreased over time. In general, this is not what we find. Only the effect of long-distance migration decreased for men. We did not find an overall effect of migration distance on the likelihood of men marrying endogamously, evidently because this effect disappeared over time.[57] Cultural differences, as indicated by differences in urbanization, are just as important predictors of endogamy in the nineteenth century as they are in the twentieth century.

Explaining changes in endogamy over time

In the introduction we assumed that changes in the likelihood, distance, and direction of migration might explain changes in rates of endogamy over time. For example, we found a rather strong negative effect on endogamy of the difference in urbanization between place of birth and place of residence. If this type of migration has become more frequent over time, this might explain the decrease in the likelihood of endogamy. To further investigate this, we estimate three more models (Tables 5 and 6). The first model shows the bivariate relationship between endogamy and the year of marriage. The second model includes the three migration variables, and the third model the other individual characteristics. A full model including all variables has already been shown in Tables 3 and 4 (model 2); this model shows a small unexplained trend toward less endogamy.

---

57. The positive interaction effect indicates that the odds ratio for migration distance moved closer to 1.

Table 5. *Explaining changes in social endogamy in France, 1803–1986 (men)*

	Model 1 odds ratio	sig.	Model 2 odds ratio	sig.	Model 3 odds ratio	sig.
Year since 1800 (/100)	0.633	***	0.742	***	0.843	***
Migrant			0.741	***		
Distance place of birth and residence (/10)			0.999			
Urbanization place of residence			0.751	***		
Difference in urbanization			0.969			
Postwar years					1.152	*
Upward mobility					0.444	***
Not in the labour force					0.719	***
First marriage					1.134	*
Father deceased					0.910	*
Mother deceased					0.974	
Origin class with property:						
Higher managers and professionals					3.256	***
Farmers and fishermen					3.484	***
Marriage values:						
authoritarian or inegalitarian					1.160	***
authoritarian and inegalitarian					1.303	***
Size class of origin					1.020	***
Constant	1.358	***	2.280	***	0.311	***
N	23,641		23,641		23,641	
Chi²	280.8		1231.4		5007.9	
Degrees of freedom	1		5		12	

Source: TRA survey, INRA/CNRS.
* $p < 0.05$; ** $p < 0.01$; *** $p < 0.001$.

The bivariate relationship between endogamy and year of marriage is strongly negative (see too Figure 2). The likelihood of an endogamous marriage decreased by about 37 per cent (1 to 0.63) over 100 years and by about 60 per cent during the whole period. The three migration variables explain a substantial part of this trend. For men, the effect of year of marriage weakened from 0.64 to 0.74 after taking migration into account; for women the effect changed from 0.63 to 0.73. For both men and women this was due mainly to increasing numbers of men and women living in large cities (analyses not shown). The migration characteristics and the other variables offer separate (hardly overlapping) explanations of the trend toward less endogamy. This can be seen from the fact that the difference in the effect of year of marriage between models 1 and 2 (both in Tables 5 and 6) is of approximately the same size as the difference in the effect of year of marriage between model 3 in these tables and the full model (model 2) in Tables 3 and 4.

Table 6. *Explaining changes in social endogamy in France, 1803–1986 (women)*

	Model 1		Model 2		Model 3	
	odds ratio	sig.	odds ratio	sig.	odds ratio	sig.
Year since 1800 (/100)	0.631	***	0.728	***	0.822	***
Migrant			0.817	***		
Distance place of birth and residence (/10)			1.004			
Urbanization place of residence			0.750	***		
Difference in urbanization			0.923	***		
Postwar years					1.079	
Upward mobility					0.591	***
Not in the labour force					0.770	***
First marriage					1.259	**
Father deceased					0.952	
Mother deceased					0.957	
Origin class with property:						
Higher managers and professionals					2.597	***
Farmers and fishermen					3.242	***
Marriage values:						
authoritarian or inegalitarian					1.257	***
authoritarian and inegalitarian					1.372	***
Size class of origin					1.025	***
Constant	1.358	***	2.192	***	0.268	***
N	23,313		23,313		23,313	
Chi^2	279.8		1140.1		4835.7	
Degrees of freedom	1		5		12	

Source: TRA survey, INRA/CNRS.
* $p < 0.05$; ** $p < 0.01$; *** $p < 0.001$.

Together, the other variables (model 3) explain a somewhat larger part of the trend than the migration characteristics. By far the most important are changes in class sizes (analyses not shown). At the beginning of the nineteenth century a very large proportion of the French population were farmers. As a consequence, the likelihood of a farmer's son meeting and eventually marrying a farmer's daughter was very high. At the end of the twentieth century the class structure was more heterogeneous, resulting in more contacts between members of different classes, and more exogamy.

CONCLUSION

The main aim of this article was to test hypotheses on the effects of migration on endogamy by social origin. We formulated six hypotheses. One of them predicted that endogamy would increase with the distance migrated, and with the difference in urbanization between place of birth and place of residence at marriage; five hypotheses predicted the opposite. The one exceptional hypothesis was not supported by our findings. Although people might have felt uprooted after migration, this was not followed by an increased likelihood of endogamy. Nevertheless, some support for the effect of feeling uprooted was found: men were more likely to marry endogamously in the years immediately following a war than in other years.

Of the remaining five hypotheses, two predicted that migration and endogamy would be negatively related because the group of migrants is composed differently from the group of non-migrants: with respect to preferences (ambitious people were more likely to migrate) and with respect to social pressure (individuals under less social pressure were more likely to migrate). These hypotheses are supported by several findings. First, we found that men and women who migrated were less likely to marry within their own class of origin. Secondly, for men, in the nineteenth century this was less likely in the case of long-distance migration. Thirdly, men and women were less likely to marry endogamously when they lived in cities and when they migrated between places that differed greatly with respect to urbanization (between rural villages and Paris for example). Furthermore, several indicators of ambition and social pressure show the predicted relationship with endogamy. Nevertheless, these two composition hypotheses are not fully supported because ambition and social pressure do little to explain the effects of migration characteristics.

There is support for the hypothesis that social pressure declines when men and women "move away" from their parents. Moving away can take the form of either migration, especially to a city, or a second marriage. Women (but not men) who remarried were more likely to marry someone from a different social background than women who married for the first time.

Finally, two hypotheses stated that migration should be negatively related to endogamy because migration affects the marriage market. Although the mechanisms behind these two hypotheses are very different (greater opportunity to meet others compared with forced marriage within the group of migrants), both predict the same relationship between migration and endogamy; and both are supported. The mechanism of greater opportunity to meet is also supported by the finding that endogamy was strongly related to size of class.

We conclude that migrants were less likely to marry endogamously, especially if they migrated from rural villages to cities; this is explained mainly by the fact that they thereby escaped the social pressure of their parents and peers and met more people from different social backgrounds.

Contrary to what we expected, the relationships between migration characteristics and endogamy changed hardly at all over the two centuries to which our data relate. One would expect it nowadays to be much easier for parents to visit their children even if they live elsewhere. It is also easier for men and women to meet people from different social backgrounds without having to migrate. Nevertheless, migration was almost as strongly related to endogamy at the end of the twentieth century as it was almost two centuries earlier.

Our second aim was to investigate whether temporal differences in endogamy could be explained partly by changes in migration patterns. We found that they could. The increase in the number of men and women living in or moving to cities was one particularly important cause of the decreasing likelihood of endogamy. Another was the more equal division of men and women across social classes.

Thirdly, we were interested in the possible bias in regional studies on endogamy. Our results show that this bias is especially large if these regions include only rural areas or cities. This is because the likelihood of endogamy differs between rural areas and cities, and is also especially low for people who move between these two types of region.

Finally, we were interested in the fate of migrants. Our finding that migrants were less likely to marry endogamously suggests that they were not fully integrated in their place of destination. Further analyses should reveal whether exogamy for migrants meant marrying upward or downward.

IRSH 50 (2005), Supplement, pp. 247–274 DOI: 10.1017/S0020859005002130
© 2005 Internationaal Instituut voor Sociale Geschiedenis

"They Live in Indifference Together": Marriage Mobility in Zeeland, The Netherlands, 1796–1922

Hilde Bras* and Jan Kok**

SUMMARY: This article investigates developments in and antecedents of socially mixed marriage in the rural Dutch province of Zeeland during the long nineteenth century, taking individual and family histories, community contexts, and temporal influences into account. A government report of the 1850s said of Zeeland that farmers and workers lived "in indifference together". However, our analysis of about 163,000 marriage certificates reveals that 30 to 40 per cent of these rural inhabitants continued to marry outside their original social class. Multivariate logistic regressions show that heterogamous marriages can be explained first and foremost by the life-course experiences of grooms and brides prior to marriage. Previous transitions in their occupational careers (especially to non-rural occupations for grooms, and to service for brides), in their migration trajectories (particularly moves to urban areas), and changes in the sphere of personal relationships (entering widowhood, ageing) are crucial in understanding marriage mobility.

INTRODUCTION

In the past, what did it mean when a person found a marriage partner from another social group? Given the dominant norms in a class-ridden society, we may surmise that such a couple had followed their own hearts and flouted the wishes of their parents. An increase in marriage mobility may thus herald the spread of "romantic love" and the demise of "traditional", "instrumental" marriage motives.[1] This interpretation of marriage mobility involves forces operating at different levels: the "micro" level (individuals and families), the "meso" level (local communities) and the "macro" level (society at large). Perhaps the couple's own life experience – a previous marriage, for example; geographical mobility, or occupational career – had made it easier for them to resist parental and community control.

Marriage mobility may, however, have had a different meaning in

* Department of Social Cultural Studies, Free University, Amsterdam, The Netherlands.
** International Institute of Social History, Amsterdam, The Netherlands.
1. E. Shorter, *The Making of the Modern Family* (New York, 1975).

different occupational and social groups. In some groups, such as farmers, social status and livelihood were inextricably tied to homogamy: a partner had to be found within the same group. For such groups, increasing heterogamy may point to structural changes in the economy which endangered social reproduction. Likewise, other social forces had an impact on courtship and marriage, and, eventually, on the meaning of social group differences. For instance, the spread of transport, communication, and leisure increased the number of contacts between people from different social backgrounds. Potentially even more important was the spread of secondary and higher education in improving individual resources and lessening the effect of one's social background.

Marriage mobility is an important topic of study, not just because it highlights social forces operating at the micro, meso, and macro levels, but also because it reveals their interconnectedness. On the one hand, shifting individual preferences and family strategies with regard to spouse selection result in changes at the aggregate "meso" and "macro" levels. On the other hand, local demographic changes and structural shifts in the economy change the "social landscape", forcing people to adjust their matrimonial ideals. The interplay between forces at the micro, meso, and macro levels forms the angle from which we will look at marriage mobility or "heterogamy".

The historiography of social mobility in the Netherlands has addressed overall national and regional patterns of mobility but does not provide us with a clear picture of the determinants of heterogamy. Most studies concentrate on one or several cities; very few include the countryside.[2] None of these studies systematically includes contextual demographic, cultural, or economic factors that affect the local marriage market. Only recently have techniques been applied that allow for the study of relative mobility. By controlling for group size, these log-linear models indicate whether society has become more open. The main conclusion is that, prior to World War II, Dutch society as a whole had not become more fluid.[3]

2. H. van Dijk, *Rotterdam 1810–1880. Aspecten van een stedelijke samenleving* (Schiedam, 1976); B. de Vries, *Electoraat en elite. Sociale structuur en sociale mobiliteit in Amsterdam 1850–1895* (n.p., 1986); O. Boonstra, *De waardij van eene vroege opleiding. Een onderzoek naar de implicaties van het alfabetisme op het leven van inwoners van Eindhoven en omliggende gemeenten, 1800–1920* (Wageningen, 1993); A. Janssens, *Family and Social Change: The Household as a Process in an Industrializing Community* (Cambridge, 1993); H. van Dijk, J. Visser, and E. Wolst, "Regional Differences in Social Mobility Patterns in the Netherlands between 1830 and 1940", *Journal of Social History*, 17 (1983–1984), pp. 435–452. For an overview, see O. Boonstra and K. Mandemakers, "'Ieder is het kind zijner eigene werken'. Sociale stratificatie en mobiliteit in Nederland in de achttiende en negentiende eeuw", in J. Dronkers and W.C. Ultee (eds), *Verschuivende ongelijkheid in Nederland. Sociale gelaagdheid en mobiliteit* (Assen, 1995), pp. 125–141.
3. M.H.D. van Leeuwen and I. Maas, "Groeiende openheid van de Nederlandse samenleving: een nieuw fenomeen of een lange trend? Intergenerationele, huwelijks- en carrièremobiliteit in

However, log-linear models tend to amalgamate experiences of people from all classes and widely different local contexts. In our view, it is vital to retain information on individual characteristics, as well as social position and local context, while controlling for group size in order to detect the determinants of social homogamy. A highly stimulating method using logistic regression has recently been proposed by Van de Putte in his analysis of partner choice in three nineteenth-century Flemish cities.[4]

In this article, we employ Van de Putte's method on an even larger scale, using all marriage certificates from the Dutch province of Zeeland for the period 1796–1922, covering both countryside and cities. Situated in the southwestern corner of the Netherlands, this province, consisting of islands, peninsulas, and part of the mainland, had been an important region of market-oriented agriculture and had played a significant part in industry and trade since the late Middle Ages. However, after the Spaniards conquered Antwerp at the end of the fifteenth century, the influential role of Zeeland's trade and industry dramatically declined. Economic development became characterized by a process of ruralization, making the province dependent on its commercialized agricultural sector, which specialized in the production of cash crops such as wheat, rape seed, flax, and madder, and – later in the nineteenth century – in the cultivation of potatoes, sugar beets, pulses, and onions as well.[5] Husbandry was of little importance: few cattle were kept and almost no milk and butter were produced. Two-thirds of the population lived in the countryside, which was dotted by many small communities.[6] In 1795, 33 per cent of the population lived in one of the cities; by 1909 this figure was actually lower – one-quarter.[7] On every island, a small town functioned as a trading centre in agricultural produce and provided services for the farming population, linking the town populations inextricably to agriculture. The only two cities were Middelburg, the capital, which hosted the provincial government, and Vlissingen (Flushing), a port and wharf city. Even in the twentieth century both were still provincial cities; in 1953 they had no more than 20,000 inhabitants.[8]

de provincie Utrecht, 1850–1940", *Mens en Maatschappij*, 70 (1995), pp. 321–333; *idem*, "Social Mobility in a Dutch Province, Utrecht 1850–1940", *Journal of Social History*, 30 (1997), pp. 619–644.

4. B. Van de Putte, "Het belang van de toegeschreven positie in een moderniserend wereld. Partnerkeuze in 19[de]-eeuwse Vlaamse steden (Leuven, Aalst en Gent)" (Ph.D., Catholic University of Leuven, 2003).

5. P. Priester, *Geschiedenis van de Zeeuwse landbouw circa 1600–1910* ('t Goy-Houten, 1998), pp. 54–55.

6. P.J. Bouman, *Geschiedenis van den Zeeuwschen landbouw in de negentiende en twintigste eeuw en van de Zeeuwsche landbouwmaatschappij 1843–1943* (Wageningen, 1946), p. 143.

7. Priester, *Geschiedenis van de Zeeuwse landbouw*, pp. 54–55.

8. P.J. Meertens, "Walcheren", in W. Banning (ed.), *Handboek Pastorale Sociologie. Deel I Zeeland, Zuid-Hollandse eilanden, Noord-Brabant en Limburg* (The Hague, 1953), p. 83.

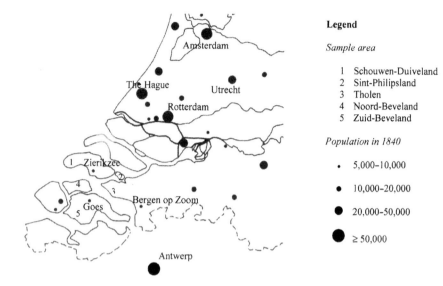

Figure 1. Zeeland islands and surrounding area (c.1840).
Source: Hans Knippenberg and Ben de Pater, *De eenwording van Nederland. Schaalvergroting en integratie sinds 1800* (Nijmegen, 1988), p. 39.

Many reports and studies on Zeeland have emphasized strong class-barrier differences. The social differentiation between the major groups in Zeeland, i.e. workers on the one hand and farmers and the middle classes on the other, appears to have been rigid, both in terms of living conditions and with regard to social-class relations. In the cities, the situation of the workers was plainly miserable. Around 1860 the physician Coronel described the apathy of the urban workers in Middelburg who waited idly in the streets every day for a temporary job as a porter. Because of malnutrition, most of them were too weak to do any heavy work.[9] The rural labouring population lived under conditions scarcely any better. In a provincial report drawn up after the subsistence crisis of the 1840s, it was noted that two-thirds to three-quarters of workers were unemployed in winter.[10]

The report stressed above all the isolation and mutual indifference in which the two groups lived. "In general there is little familiar association between the residents of the countryside [...]. They live, except for the

9. S. Sr. Coronel, *Middelburg voorheen en thans. Bijdrage tot de kennis van den voormaligen en tegenwoordigen toestand van het armwezen aldaar* (Middelburg, 1859), pp. 250–251.
10. *Rapport naar aanleiding van een ingesteld onderzoek omtrent den zedelijken en materiële toestand der arbeidende en dienstbare bevolking ten plattelande, uitgebragt op de Algemeene Vergadering der Zeeuwsche Maatschappij van Landbouw te Tholen, den 7ᵈᵉ juni 1849* (Middelburg, 1849), p. 6.

mutual obligatory assistance, which is always instigated by money, in complete dependence on themselves." According to the writers of the report, farmers paid scarcely any attention to the wellbeing of their labourers, and the labourers took no interest in their bosses either. This was clear from the indifference with which work was carried out and from the frequent changes of address of farmhands, even of those with permanent appointments.[11] This proletarianized and polarized social structure existed well into the twentieth century, as oral history interviews have shown. One rural labourer reminisced on the 1920s:

> On Saturday nights you saw the difference very clearly. Because then you went walking. To find a girl of course. But the labourers walked in School Street and the farmers and bourgeois youngsters walked around the Market. Completely divided. A labourer's boy with a farmer's daughter? Oh God no, they would have poisoned you![12]

Is the impression of strong social-class differences in Zeeland corroborated by the empirical facts on marriage mobility? Under what individual and family circumstances were the social barriers easier to cross? Was there a difference in this respect between localities, regions and time periods? Our research questions can be specified at the levels of the individual, the community, the region, and the province at large.

HYPOTHESES ON THE EFFECTS OF INDIVIDUAL, FAMILIAL, AND CONTEXTUAL CHARACTERISTICS

How did individual characteristics and family situation affect partner choice? We hypothesize that individual access to extended social networks is a crucial mechanism for heterogamy. It thus seems likely that migrants had lower chances of marrying outside their own group because they lacked access to local information channels and social gatherings that might have brought them into contact with other social groups. Was there a difference between migrants with a rural and those with an urban background? We also expect domestic servants among the brides to have been in contact with more diverse urban marriage markets, which would have heightened their chances of marrying outside their original social class. Age at marriage may also be of relevance. Did older persons have a more extended network and were they able to cross class boundaries more easily than younger people could?

Another factor is the extent of social control on courtship, by both parents and peer group. Strong social control will favour high levels of social-class homogamy. Individuals who were orphaned or half-orphaned

---

11. *Ibid.*, pp. 20–21.
12. K. Slager, *Landarbeiders. Verhalen om te onthouden* (Nijmegen, 1981), p. 23.

Figure 2. Two newly-wed farm-worker couples, walking from the village hall to the farmstead, island of Walcheren (Zeeland), c.1907.
Zeeland Documentation Centre

might have experienced less parental pressure to marry into their own social class. Moreover, they could rely less on their parents' resources to help them establish themselves in their own class. Also, if the bride had already borne a child before marriage, we may surmise that social control on courtship was weak. Was this associated with inter-group marriages? One's previous relational history is of interest as well. Was it the case, as has been argued, that widowed individuals could choose their new partners more freely, perhaps because communal pressure to marry into one's own social class had decreased? Divorce, on the other hand, carried a social stigma that may have induced downward mobility at remarriage.[13] Obviously, one's social-class background is a very important determinant in itself. Particularly those individuals originating from families that were characterized by location- and occupation-specific capital, and in which tacit knowledge was usually transferred from generation to generation (farmers, shop-owners, artisans), can be expected to have contracted homogamous marriages.

In determining the chances of inter-group marriage, the local context is equally relevant. As elsewhere, peer groups in Dutch communities tended

13. F. van Poppel, *Trouwen in Nederland. Een historisch-demografische studie van de 19ᵉ en vroeg-20ᵉ eeuw* (Wageningen, 1992), p. 540.

to ward off suitors from outside.[14] In very small or isolated localities this may have resulted in greater heterogamy, when the preference for a local partner overruled the preference for a socially equal one. Both population size and "isolation" (indicated by relative geographical mobility) will be included in the model. A similar mechanism may occur in municipalities with religious minorities; we may surmise that people will cross either geographical or social boundaries to marry a partner with the right creed.[15]

Zeeland mentality and culture were marked by strongly religious beliefs and church-going practices. In the nineteenth century, about 65 per cent of Zeeland's population was Dutch Reformed, one-quarter was Catholic and 15 per cent belonged to one of the many Orthodox-Calvinist denominations. Whatever their denomination, the Church played an important role in determining the norms and values by which most Zeelanders lived.[16] During the process of confessionally based vertical pluralism (*verzuiling*) in the last quarter of the nineteenth century and the beginning of the twentieth century, many Zeeland communities, especially those of mixed religion, experienced turbulent interconfessional relations.[17] In communities with large Catholic or Orthodox-Calvinist minorities and in religiously highly mixed communities, social intermarriage might have occurred more frequently as a result of a higher priority given to religiously homogamous marriages.

Local economic conditions will also have affected the process of partner selection. A rough indication is provided by migration surpluses. Clearly, municipalities with a large migration deficit fared worse than those that attracted newcomers. Moreover, communities with large migration surpluses might have stimulated heterogamy because the influx of newcomers made the atmosphere of a community more "modern" and "open" compared to places which were relatively isolated and closed-off. We include local marriage rates to see whether municipalities with depressed marriage prospects were also municipalities with less heterogamy.

Finally, the demographic and social aspects of the marriage market need to be discussed. Unfortunately, the censuses do not provide enough information on marital status by age. We cannot therefore include the sex ratios for nubile adolescents. However, we can measure the impact of the social composition of the marriage market by controlling for the relative

14. J.L. de Jager, *Volksgebruiken in Nederland. Een nieuwe kijk op tradities* (Utrecht [etc.] 1981), p. 45.

15. E. Beekink, A. Liefbroer, and F. van Poppel, "Changes in Choice of Spouse as an Indicator of a Society in a State of Transition: Woerden, 1830–1930", *Historical Social Research*, 23 (1998), pp. 231–253.

16. Bouman, *Geschiedenis van den Zeeuwschen landbouw*, p. 293.

17. M. Wintle, *Zeeland and the Churches: Religion and Society in the Province of Zeeland (Netherlands) in the Nineteenth Century* (Middelburg, 1988), pp. 145–153.

"supply" of fathers-in-law from particular social groups (see also the section on the multivariate analysis of marriage mobility).

In terms of systems of land-use, religion, and social differentiation, there were distinct regions within Zeeland, possibly resulting in regional intermarriage patterns.[18] The most southern region of Zeeuws-Vlaanderen belonged geographically to the mainland. It became part of France in 1795 and remained more strongly oriented towards Belgium than the islands did. The region was characterized by wheat-growing and large-scale farms.[19] Its eastern part (Oost-Zeeuws-Vlaanderen) was predominantly Catholic, while the western part (West-Zeeuws-Vlaanderen) contained communities with both substantial Catholic and Protestant populations. Walcheren was the most urbanized island, but its farms were relatively small-scale and sober, while more cattle-keeping and pastureland were found here than on the other islands. Most communities in Walcheren were Dutch Reformed or Orthodox Calvinist.[20]

Zuid-Beveland was one of the regions with the largest and most efficient farms in Zeeland.[21] In the beginning of the twentieth century, when population growth in other Zeeland regions stagnated, Zuid-Beveland was able to retain its population and even attract newcomers because of the diversification of its agricultural economy, with fruit-growing, fishing, and oyster-growing, and the development of trade and transportation hubs.[22] The southern part ("the pocket") contained a number of Catholic enclaves which increased in population over the nineteenth century. Furthermore, many communities also had substantial Orthodox-Calvinist minorities, and these were the site of religious conflict during the last quarter of the nineteenth century.

Noord-Beveland had even larger farms, with a number of them over 40 hectares. On this island the "farm aristocracy" wielded a lot of power, and the social difference between workers and farmers was very pronounced.[23] In comparison, Schouwen-Duiveland had more small- and medium-sized farms (especially in Duiveland). It was a typical area of out-migration: from the last quarter of the nineteenth century agricultural workers left in order to find work in one of the Dutch cities. However, in this region many workers were also able to start their own small farms when wages rose after the agricultural depression. As a consequence, the social distance between farmers and workers became less pronounced.[24] Finally, Tholen

18. J.'t Gilde et al., Zeeland met Goeree-Overflakkee (The Hague, 1993), p. 32.
19. Bouman, Geschiedenis van den Zeeuwschen landbouw, p. 255.
20. Meertens, "Walcheren", p. 76.
21. B. Breek, "Noord- en Zuid-Beveland", in Banning, Handboek Pastorale Sociologie, p. 47.
22. Ibid., p. 43.
23. Ibid., pp. 47, 63.
24. H. Cramer, J.M.T. Hefting, and M.G. Westerhof, "Schouwen-Duiveland", in Banning, Handboek Pastorale Sociologie, pp. 123, 125.

and Sint-Philipsland, the most northerly islands, which bordered on the Catholic province of Noord-Brabant, were marked by religious (Calvinist) orthodoxy. Farm size was relatively small, and the owner and his family were used to working in the fields themselves.[25]

In regions such as Tholen and Sint-Philipsland, Schouwen-Duiveland, and Walcheren, with smaller-sized farms and less social distance between farmers and workers, more heterogamy can be expected than in regions such as Noord-Beveland and Zuid-Beveland, where farms were bigger and social contrasts larger. Finally, in Zeeland, countryside and cities were separate worlds, particularly for the rural working classes. Farm workers who were born in the vicinity of Zeeland's cities in the beginning of the twentieth century declared that they hardly visited them.[26] These two cities allow us to test the hypothesis that urban life stimulates heterogamy through decreased social and parental control and a less traditional approach to human relations.[27]

Finally, our analysis of the temporal trends in social heterogamy will reveal influences at the level of the province. Over the period 1796–1922, ups and downs in the national and provincial economy influenced the likelihood of marriage mobility among cohorts of Zeelanders differently. The late 1840s were marked by a subsistence crisis, affecting the social situation of the poorest agricultural workers. The 1850s were relatively neutral years, while the 1860s and early 1870s were among the most prosperous years of the century. These "Champagne years" were followed by an agricultural depression between 1878 and 1895. A report from 1908 on the social and economic situation of the agricultural workers in Schouwen-Duiveland stated that "in the bad agricultural years, few marriages were contracted".[28] "For fear of poverty several men at an age above thirty years are still unmarried."[29]

During difficult economic periods marriages were postponed or not contracted at all. In addition, some people may have been forced to marry outside their original social group. The international agricultural depression of the last two decades of the nineteenth century and the ensuing mechanization and rationalization of farming practices led to a decline in employment opportunities in agriculture.[30] As a consequence, many

25. R.C. van Putten, "Tholen en St.-Philipsland", in Banning, *Handboek Pastorale Sociologie*, pp. 93–94.

26. J. Zwemer, *Een zekel om geit-eten te snieën. De geschiedenis van de landarbeiders op Walcheren 1900–1940* (Middelburg, 1987), p. 10.

27. Van de Putte, "Het belang van de toegeschreven positie", pp. 25–30.

28. "Verslag betreffende den toestand der landarbeiders in Zeeland", in *Verslagen betreffende den oeconomische toestand der landarbeiders in Nederland. II. Utrecht-Limburg* (The Hague, 1908), p. 252.

29. *Ibid.*, p. 255.

30. J.L. van Zanden, *De economische ontwikkeling van de Nederlandse landbouw in de negentiende eeuw, 1800–1914. A.A.G. Bijdragen 25* (Wageningen, 1985), pp. 69–70.

workers migrated to the cities and to the United States. On the other hand, the wages of those agricultural workers who remained rose, and more workers were able to hire or buy a small plot of land to be cultivated for their own use. Increased opportunities for education and work and easier opportunities to meet potential partners, due to public and private transport, will have stimulated greater openness and marriage mobility among the youngest marriage cohorts.

STRATIFICATION AND MOBILITY IN ZEELAND

Our analysis is based on data derived from an index of marriage certificates recently prepared for genealogical purposes.[31] The index covers 163,715 certificates of marriage from the province of Zeeland for the period 1811– 1922. The beginning of this period coincides with the start of civil registration, inaugurated by the Code Napoleon. In fact, the southern Zeeland region of Zeeuws-Vlaanderen had already been occupied by the French in 1795. Data are therefore available for this region from as early as 1796. The end of the period was dictated by privacy regulations. Unlike most other indexes, the Zeeland one is particularly rich in additional information on brides and grooms. Their occupations as well as those of their parents are given; there is information on the ages of bride and groom, their birthplaces, their previous marriages, and any premarital children born to the couple.

The municipality of marriage was the official place of residence of at least one of the spouses. However, we are primarily interested in the locality or area where the choice of partner had actually taken place. To what extent is the municipality of marriage helpful in this respect? An analysis of all marriage certificates in the database of the Historical Sample of the Netherlands shows that, between 1831 and 1922, 90.8 per cent of Zeeland brides actually resided in the place where they married (N = 946); for grooms this figure was lower, but still 72.7 per cent.[32] The difference was caused by the tendency of migrant women to return to their parents some time before the intended marriage and to marry in that locality. We therefore miss information on the place where they had found their husbands and to which they probably returned after marrying.[33] However,

31. The Zeeuws Archief in Middelburg granted special access to the marriage certificates database from the Civil Records of Zeeland 1796/1811–1922 for this research. The data were input by volunteers in the period 1997–2001. We would like to thank Leo Hollestelle for his kind advice.
32. On this database, see K. Mandemakers, "Historical Sample of the Netherlands", in P. Kelly Hall, R. McCaa, and G. Thorvaldsen (eds), *Handbook of International Historical Microdata for Population Research* (Minneapolis, MN, 2000), pp. 149–178.
33. We have controlled for this effect as much as possible by including whether the bride had been a domestic servant before her marriage. Since domestic servants were the quintessential

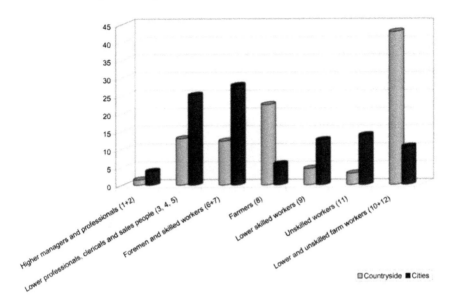

Figure 3. Social stratification in Zeeland province (by occupation of grooms' fathers), 1796–1922.

we feel that, on the whole, we can use the place of marriage as a proxy for the place of courtship.

In Figure 3 we take an initial look at the social landscape of Zeeland, using the HISCLASS classification by skill level.[34] For the countryside, Figure 3 presents a skewed picture: farm workers and farmers dominated the social landscape, while other groups of workers – clerical and sales people and managers – were relatively rare. In the cities, the occupational structure was more diversified; this was reflected by the large presence of managers of all types, and of skilled workers.

A first look at absolute levels of heterogamy over time (Figure 4 overleaf) shows few conspicuous developments. This reflects the stability of the social structure in Zeeland; throughout the period it remained a rural province with hardly any industrialization. Heterogamy was higher in the cities (Middelburg and Vlissingen) than in the countryside: almost 70 per cent of the fathers-in-law of urban grooms were in a group different from that of the grooms' fathers; the corresponding figure for rural grooms was about 45 to 50 per cent.

On closer inspection, however, we do find some interesting trends in

migratory female group, this variable is a proxy indicating, *inter alia*, those couples who might have met elsewhere, i.e. not in the locality of marriage.

34. M.H.D. van Leeuwen and I. Maas, "HISCLASS", paper presented at the 5th European Social Science History Conference (Berlin, 24–27 March 2004); I. Maas and M.H.D. van Leeuwen, "SPSS recode job from HISCO into HISCLASS", May 2004.

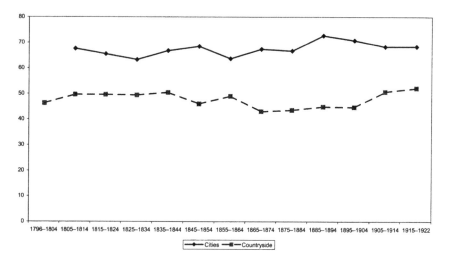

Figure 4. Development in heterogamy in Zeeland province, 1796–1922.

heterogamy. In the cities, we see a modest rise during the period 1885–
1894. This coincides with high levels of urban and interurban geographical
mobility.[35] In the countryside, on the other hand, the entire period 1865–
1904 seems to have been characterized by lower levels of heterogamy than
the first half of the nineteenth century. Only after 1905 do we find a clear
increase. How do we explain this? Zeeland had been hit hard by the
agrarian depression of the 1880s, which stimulated the mass emigration of
agrarian labourers to the Americas. Perhaps the changes we are observing
reflect the decline in the "supply" of farm workers, which caused the
number of mixed marriages to increase and thus "forced" increased
heterogamy among agricultural labourers. Or had Zeeland society as a
whole become more "open"? Was this "openness" also the reason for the
higher urban mobility rates? In our multivariate analysis we will try to
answer these questions.

Before we move on to this analysis, we will take a brief look at actual
mobility rates (Table 1). The highest levels of immobility, or homogamy,
are found among farm workers (70.1 per cent) and farmers (60.8 per cent).
In the countryside, it was virtually only through intermarriage between
children of farmers and farm workers that mobility could be brought
about. However, in Zeeland these groups were divided by strong class
barriers. Still, many ties must have existed, if only because sons of
impoverished farmers ended up as farm workers. Farm workers' daughters

35. J. Kok, "Choices and Constraints in the Migration of Families: The Central Netherlands,
1850–1940", *The History of the Family: An International Quarterly*, 9 (2004), pp. 137–158,
p. 144.

Table 1. *Marriage mobility in Zeeland province, 1796–1922: percentage distribution of social group of fathers-in-law by social group of fathers*

HISCLASS fathers	HISCLASS fathers-in-law								Total number
	1+2	3, 4, 5	6+7	8	9	11	10+12		
Higher managers and professionals (1+2)	30.8	32.3	13.7	14.3	3.8	1.2	4.0		826
Lower professionals, clerical and sales people (3, 4, 5)	3.7	29.9	17.8	12.8	7.6	5.7	22.4		7,041
Foremen and skilled workers (6+7)	1.4	20.3	24.9	16.3	8.8	6.6	21.7		6,559
Farmers (8)	1.2	8.5	8.4	60.8	2.9	1.8	16.5		10,126
Lower skilled workers (9)	1.4	19.4	21.2	11.5	9.9	8.1	28.4		2,659
Unskilled workers (11)	0.4	15.4	15.5	6.6	7.2	22.9	31.9		2,291
Lower and unskilled farm workers (10+12)	0.1	7.6	6.6	8.6	3.3	1.4	70.1		18,046
Total number	793	6,796	5,970	10,259	2,458	2,422	18,850		47,548

Source: Marriage certificates from the civil records of Zeeland 1796/1811–1922.

tended to work as servants in the households of farmers.[36] These manifold ties ensured that intermarriage was not entirely absent: 16.5 per cent of farmers' sons married a farm worker's daughter and 8.6 per cent of farm workers' sons married a farmer's daughter.

For the farmers themselves, homogamy was clearly related to their marriage strategies. For their children, Zeeland farmers actively sought partners who, with their inheritance either in cash or land, could counteract the divisive effect of equal inheritance. This is not to say that the farmers arranged the marriages of their children. For a month during the quiet winter period, older children would "go for a walk", that is, they left for short stays in the households of befriended or related farmers in roughly the same wealth position.[37] Although farm workers might have more actively sought to better their social position, marriage markets for farmers, farm workers, and the local middle class were highly segmented and the social barriers between them were rather closed. A former farm worker vividly painted the situation in the first few decades of the twentieth century as follows: "As an eighteen-year-old boy on the dance floor, you shouldn't try to dance with a shop owner's girl. That was not done. No, they didn't have anything either, those local shop owners, but we were only farm workers."[38] In reality therefore, homogamy was the norm – also for farm workers. Finally, small social groups, such as skilled workers and urban lower-skilled workers, tended to mingle more freely with adjacent classes. However, to interpret this mobility we need to take the relative group sizes into account.

MULTIVARIATE ANALYSIS OF MARRIAGE MOBILITY

Overall model (1796–1922)

We study marriage mobility by comparing the social groups of fathers of brides and grooms. Only fathers and fathers-in-law whose occupations were mentioned are included, which means that we select only those marriages where both fathers were still alive and neither retired nor unemployed. We take grooms as our point of departure, because we need to control for their own occupational mobility. Clearly, a groom who was himself (intergenerationally) mobile would have entered a new social environment that made him a likely candidate for a heterogamous marriage. Controlling for grooms' own mobility will allow us to observe more closely the degree to which class barriers were permeable.

36. H. Bras, *Zeeuwse meiden. Dienen in de levensloop van vrouwen* (Amsterdam, 2002).
37. This description pertains to the Zeeland region of West-Zeeuws-Vlaanderen in the early nineteenth century. See P. Van Cruyningen, *Behoudend maar buigzaam. Boeren in West-Zeeuws-Vlaanderen 1650–1850* (Wageningen, 2000).
38. Slager, *Landarbeiders*, p. 96.

In choosing their partners, people are subject to a number of influences. One is their preference for a partner from an appropriate social class. Other preferences include age, religion, and geographical origin. To isolate the social-class aspect, we need to control for all the other types of homogamy, but we can do so only for geographical origin and age.[39] The variable "endogamous marriage" controls for the preference for choosing a partner with the same birthplace. Similarly, the variable "same-age" marriage controls for age homogamy, and is defined as a marriage where the ages of the bride and groom differ by less than two years.

The larger one's own social group, the lower the chances of heterogamy. In order to control for "group size", that is for the "supply" of fathers-in-law, we have calculated the relative presence of the social groups of fathers-in-law within regional marriage markets for ten-yearly periods. This procedure is feasible because our database contains all marriages in the province. In Zeeland, marriage markets were bounded, since the province consists of various islands and an isolated area in the south.[40] For example, for sons of farm workers marrying in the Zeeuws-Vlaanderen region in the period 1785–1894 the variable "group size" is 48.6. This means that in the marriage certificates of this period and in this region 48.6 per cent of brides' fathers were described as farm workers.

Table 2 overleaf presents a logistic regression for the whole Zeeland dataset (1796–1922). In this method, the probability (p) of the dependent variable – in this case contracting a heterogamous marriage – being a yes or no is calculated in terms of *odds*, that is the probability of a "yes" divided by the probability of a "no" ($p/(1-p)$). The regression coefficients of the independent variables are the natural logarithms of the odds. By exponentiating them, we obtain *odds ratios*. These indicate the increase in the odds of the dependent variable being a yes resulting from an increase of one unit in the independent variable.[41] Table 2 shows that the inter-generational mobility of the groom himself was a very important factor: the odds ratio of marrying a woman from a different social group increased 154 per cent if the groom himself was already mobile. Similarly, group size is a critical factor. An increase of 1 per cent in the relative supply of fathers-in-law in the same group as one's own father decreased the odds ratios of marrying in a *different* group by 3.7 per cent. Both geographical and age homogamy were closely associated with social homogamy: partners of the same age (i.e. whose ages differed by no more than two years) and from the same birthplace tended to be from the same social group as well. Apart from these more or less expected results, we also found a host of other interesting effects.

39. Van de Putte, "Het belang van de toegeschreven positie", pp. 153–162.
40. See also J. Kok, "'Vrijt daar je zijt'; huwelijk en partnerkeuze in Zeeland tussen 1830 en 1950", *Zeeland*, 7 (1998), pp. 131–143.
41. S. Menard, *Applied Logistic Regression Analysis* (Thousand Oaks, CA [etc.], 1995).

Table 2. *Logistic regression of heterogamy of grooms (difference between social position of father and father-in-law), Zeeland 1796–1922 (odds ratios) (main model)*

	Odds ratio of contracting a heterogamous marriage
Age of groom	1.002
Age of bride	1.005
Groom is widower (first marriage=ref.)	1.040
Groom is divorced	1.216
Bride is widow (first marriage=ref.)	0.978
Bride is divorced	2.693
Groom's mother is deceased (still alive=ref.)	0.985
Bride's mother is deceased (still alive=ref.)	1.131***
Child legitimated	1.104
Endogamous marriage (exogamous=ref.)	0.832***
Groom is a rural migrant (born in the place of marriage=ref.)	0.896**
Groom is an urban migrant	0.851**
Bride is a rural migrant (born in the place of marriage=ref.)	0.931*
Bride is an urban migrant	1.223*
Older-husband marriage (same age=ref.)	1.072**
Older-wife marriage	1.093*
Group size (relative supply of father-in law's social group)	0.963***
Father higher manager/professional (HISCLASS 1&2)(HISCLASS 3,4&5 Lower managers and professionals, clerical and sales=ref.)	0.548***
Father foreman or skilled worker (HISCLASS 6&7)	1.624***
Father farmer or fisherman (HISCLASS 8)	0.343***
Father lower skilled worker (HISCLASS 9)	1.733***
Father unskilled worker (HISCLASS 11)	1.548***
Father lower or unskilled farm worker (HISCLASS 10&12)	0.658***
Groom intergenerationally mobile (not mobile=ref.)	2.541***
Bride is a (former) domestic servant	1.160***
1796–1804 (1815–1824=ref.)	0.974
1805–1814	1.147
1825–1834	1.088
1835–1844	1.154
1845–1854	1.006
1855–1864	1.000
1865–1874	0.875
1875–1884	0.901
1885–1895	1.082
1895–1904	1.039
1905–1914	1.170*
1915–1922	1.221**
Middelburg (Zuid-Beveland=ref.)	0.927
Vlissingen	0.847**
Noord-Beveland	0.776***

Table 2. *Continued*

	Odds ratio of contracting a heterogamous marriage
Schouwen-Duiveland	0.905**
Tholen	1.080
Walcheren	0.944
Oost-Zeeuws-Vlaanderen	0.901**
West-Zeeuws-Vlaanderen	0.748***
Constant	2.398***
N	46,889
Model Chi-square	11821,157
Nagelkerke R square	0,297

Source: Marriage certificates from the civil records of Zeeland 1796/1811–1922.
Note: * significance level p< 0.05; ** significance level p< 0.01; *** significance level p<0.001.

Overall, parental control on partner choice seems to have been ineffective in stimulating homogamy. At least, we found no increase in heterogamy with an increase in age at marriage; nor did we find more heterogamy among second marriages. The odds of heterogamy increased if the bride's mother was deceased. Was this related to diminished parental control? Or were girls from the middle classes simply less effective in maintaining their social position if their mother had died? This question can be answered in the next section where we look at heterogamy models per social group.

Migration had the effect of increasing the odds of marriage mobility, but only among urbanward-migrating women. For migrant men and for migrant women with a rural provenance, the odds of heterogamy were lower than for local residents. The social group differences were very strong and confirm the impression we gained from Table 1: the higher managers, farmers, and farm workers tended towards homogamy. The odds ratios of farmers' sons marrying heterogamously were thus 66 per cent lower than the reference group of the sons of lower managers and professionals. Interestingly, the odds of heterogamy increased (by 16 per cent) when the marriage certificate listed the occupation of the bride as "domestic servant". This may indicate that the experience of working in middle- or upper-class households had broadened the marriage horizon for servants.

We find no evidence of a linear increase in relative marriage mobility throughout the nineteenth century that would be consistent with the notion that "individualization" or "romantic love" was spreading. A significant rise in heterogamy is visible only from 1905 onwards. Can this be explained by a rise in "romantic love", in the sense of individual choice freed from community and parental control in towns and cities? For one thing, Zeeland's cities, once we control for occupational structure, were certainly not places of fluid class boundaries. In Vlissingen and Middelburg the odds ratios were lower than in the region of Zuid-Beveland. Even lower ratios were found in Noord-Beveland and Zeeuws-Vlaanderen, and particularly in the west of Zeeuws-Vlaanderen. These regional differences are more or less in line with the descriptions of the social divide between local farmers' "aristocracies" and the mass of propertyless workers. This divide was more pronounced in certain regions than in others.

Community contexts (1855–1922)

In what way did aspects of the community in which the marriage was contracted influence the groom's odds of intermarriage? Was it easier to marry someone from another social group in localities with many in-migrants? And in what way did the over-representation of certain religious groups in a community – especially during the process of confessionally based vertical pluralism – affect opportunities for heterogamy?

In Table 3 we estimate what were the effects on the groom's odds of contracting a heterogamous marriage of the population size, marriage rate, net migration rate, relative geographical mobility, and the relative proportion of Orthodox Protestants and Catholics residing in the marriage locality. The population size has been included for every municipality for each ten-year period. The local marriage rate gives the average yearly number of marriages per 1,000 of the population. Net migration is calculated as the net migration deficit for the municipality per ten-year period per 1,000 of the population. Relative geographical mobility totals in-migration and out-migration per ten-year period per 1,000 inhabitants. Finally, the proportion of Orthodox Protestants has been calculated by grouping the secessionist Orthodox churches in Zeeland. The variables were derived from the censuses, our set of marriage certificates, and the Historical Database of Dutch Municipalities.[42] However, information at community level is available only for the second half of the nineteenth century and the first few decades of the twentieth century. We therefore compare a model without context variables (model 1) and a full contextual model (model 2) only for this period. Here, we discuss simply the effects of the added community-level variables.

Table 3 (model 2) shows that the odds of grooms who married in either hamlets (less than 1,000 inhabitants) or larger villages and small towns

---

42. For a description, see E. Beekink, O. Boonstra, T. Engelen, and H. Knippenberg (eds), *Nederland in verandering. Maatschappelijke ontwikkelingen in kaart gebracht* (Amsterdam, 2003).

Table 3. *Logistic regression of heterogamy: the influence of community context during the period 1855–1922*

Covariates	Model 1: main model for period 1855–1922	Model 2 including municipal-level variables
Age of groom	1.002	1.002
Age of bride	1.002	1.001
Groom is widower (first marriage=ref.)	0.990	0.995
Groom is divorced	1.549	1.648
Bride is widow (first marriage=ref.)	0.981	0.989
Bride is divorced	2.670	2.812
Groom's mother is deceased (still alive=ref.)	0.994	0.981
Bride's mother is deceased (still alive=ref.)	1.107***	1.094**
Child legitimated	1.071	1.044
Geographically endogamous marriage (exogamous=ref.)	0.838***	0.834***
Groom is a rural migrant (born in the place of marriage=ref.)	0.873***	0.867***
Groom is an urban migrant	0.847*	0.833**
Bride is a rural migrant (born in the place of marriage=ref.)	0.924*	0.905**
Bride is an urban migrant	1.183	1.147
Older-husband marriage (same age=ref.)	1.082**	1.077**
Older-wife marriage	1.123*	1.124*
Group size (relative supply of father-in law's social group)	0.962***	0.962***
Father higher manager/professional (HISCLASS 1&2) (HISCLASS 3,4&5 Lower managers and professionals, clerical and sales=ref.)	0.658***	0.653***
Father foreman or skilled worker HISCLASS 6&7)	1.578***	1.585***
Father farmer or fisherman (HISCLASS 8)	0.343***	0.350***
Father lower skilled worker (HISCLASS 9)	1.871***	1.886***
Father unskilled worker (HISCLASS 11)	1.441***	1.425***
Father lower or unskilled farm worker (HISCLASS 10&12)	0.646***	0.647***
Groom intergenerationally mobile (not mobile=ref.)	2.576***	2.550***
Bride is a (former) domestic servant	1.161***	1.177***
1865–1874 (1855–1864=ref.)	0.876*	0.872*
1875–1884	0.902	0.875*
1885–1894	1.091	1.038
1895–1904	1.044	0.998
1905–1914	1.176**	1.145*
1915–1922	1.227***	1.212**
Middelburg (Zuid-Beveland=ref.)	0.931	0.823*
Vlissingen	0.843**	0.712**
Noord-Beveland	0.765***	0.834*

(Continued overleaf)

Table 3. *Continued*

Covariates	Model 1: main model for period 1855–1922	Model 2 including municipal-level variables
Schouwen-Duiveland	0.887**	0.909*
Tholen	1.067	1.141*
Walcheren	0.991	1.052
Oost-Zeeuws-Vlaanderen	0.890**	0.789***
West-Zeeuws-Vlaanderen	0.740***	0.702***
Population <1000 (1000–5000=ref)		0.839**
5000–20000		0.863**
>=20000		0.832
Marriage rate 0–5 (5–7=ref)		1.398
7–10		1.069*
>=10.		0.954
Unknown		1.271
Net migration −36 until −15 (−15 until −5=ref.)		0.970
−5 until 5		0.953
5 until 15		1.168*
15 until 53		1.159
Unknown		0.442*
Relative mobility 0–50 (50–100=ref.)		0.886
100–150		0.980
150–200		1.006
200–315		1.029
% Orthodox-reformed 12–18 (0–12=ref.)		1.071
18–23		1.032
23–32		0.962
>=32		0.957
% Catholic 10–20 (0–10=ref.)		1.018
20–60		1.121*
60–95		1.220**
95–100		1.340***
More than 10% orthodox-reformed and more than 10% Catholic		1.019
Constant	2.664***	3.153***
N	38,439	38,439
Model Chi-square (df)	10154.769 (39)	10265.225 (64)
Nagelkerke R Square	0.310	0.312

Source: Marriage certificates from the civil records of Zeeland 1796/1811–1922.
Note: * significance level $p < 0.05$; ** significance level $p < 0.01$; *** significance level $p < 0.001$.

(between 5,000 and 20,000 residents) contracting a heterogamous marriage decreased compared with the corresponding odds for grooms marrying in small rural villages (population between 1,000 and 5,000). Hamlets were unlikely to have much intermarriage anyway since they housed only farm workers and farmers. Why people in larger villages and small towns were

Figure 5. Farmer (right) and female farm workers (left) in the onion harvest on the island of Tholen (Zeeland), c.1932.
Zeeland Documentation Centre

less likely to marry heterogamously than those in small rural villages is hard to explain. Places with high marriage rates seem to have stimulated social intermarriage,[43] as did communities with high net migration rates (communities in which many new migrants settled). The same can be said for places with high relative geographical mobility, although the estimates are not significant. Perhaps the atmosphere of such "migratory" communities (as starting or stopping places for ferries and carriages to Holland, and as garrison towns) made it easier for individuals to cross social barriers.

The strongest determinant of heterogamy at community level was the proportion of Catholics.[44] The higher the proportion of Catholics, the larger the odds of the groom marrying outside his social group. Although Zeeland's Catholics were a minority, comprising just one-quarter of the population, they were well catered for by the dioceses of Breda and Haarlem. They had more religious personnel than either the predominant Dutch Reformed or Calvinist Orthodox groups. Catholic priests probably encouraged religiously homogamous marriages quite effectively, even when they were at the expense of socially mixed weddings.[45]

43. The effect of marriage rates is not, however, linear.
44. To avoid ecological fallacies, it would, of course, be preferable to also include individual-level indicators of the economic position of farmers and workers, and of the individual religious denominations.
45. Wintle, *Zeeland and the Churches*, pp. 70, 100.

MARRIAGE MOBILITY OF SPECIFIC SOCIAL GROUPS

So far, we have addressed the issue of intermarriage for all social groups together. However, the mechanisms for explaining whether and why individuals married outside their own group, and whether this was considered profitable or detrimental behaviour, varied across groups, depending on the respective economic and social resources at hand. Moreover, certain determinants could have had a particular effect on the odds of marriage mobility in one social group and not in another. Third, mapping out group-specific determinants also allows us to disentangle which social groups accounted for the most important general effects as observed in Table 2, for instance the increasing openness in the first two decades of the twentieth century. In Table 4, we investigate possible differences in the determinants of marriage mobility for the two most important groups in Zeeland's occupational hierarchy: farm workers and farmers. Together these groups comprised about 60 per cent of Zeeland's population. As we saw earlier, agricultural workers and farmers were also the most immobile social groups: 70 per cent of all farm workers and 60 per cent of all farmers married a bride originating from their own background.

To find out what then determined a mobile marriage in these major groups, and whether the determinants of a heterogamous marriage differed between them, we proceeded as follows. We first estimated a base model for farm workers and farmers together (results not reported). In order to detect whether class-specific differences played a role, we introduced in this model interaction terms which were constructed by multiplying the independent variables with a dummy for membership of the group of farm workers. In order to be parsimonious, we retained a model with only the significant interaction terms. Introducing these significant interactions improved the fit of the model from a Model Chi-Square (df) of 2477.867 (40) for the base model, to a Model Chi-Square (df) 3784.071 (55) for the model including interactions. In Table 4 we present the estimated coefficients for farm workers (column 2) and farmers (column 3).[46]

Before we start interpreting the results, it is important to stress the basic difference in what heterogamy actually meant for members of the two groups. If we assume that farm workers were at the bottom of the social hierarchy, heterogamy effectively meant upward mobility. For the sons of farming families, heterogamy could mean a change of social status either for better or worse. Most importantly, for farmers, homogamy – not heterogamy – was the ideal.

In both groups, the odds of marriage mobility for the groom were affected

---

46. For those variables for which an interaction term was significant, coefficients have been calculated for both groups separately: for farm workers, by multiplying the coefficients of the main effect and the interaction term; for farmers, by reporting the main effect.

by the couple's former life experiences. First, the odds of heterogamy increased with age. In a province where the rural population generally married quite early, marriages which were contracted at a later age were more prone to mobility. This might have been due to a weakening of parental control over partner choice as youngsters aged. But one can also imagine that the longer boys waited before marrying, the more time they would have had to get ahead in life by accumulating a working capital or raising the level of their income, which might have allowed them to attract women from a higher social group. This argument could have applied particularly to farm workers. For the son of a farmer, late marriage might also have indicated that he was in a difficult financial position: perhaps he had to wait until his father retired, or his older brothers and sisters had been settled, before he had enough money to be able to marry a farmer's daughter. Such a situation could have easily led to him marrying outside his own class.

When grooms married women older than themselves, they married heterogamously more often. Perhaps older women from the middle classes were forced to marry down because of their age. The relational biographies of the groom and bride prior to the marriage mattered as well. Especially among farm workers, widowed grooms who remarried had higher odds of marrying outside their original occupational group. Widowed workers might have been attractive partners on the marriage market because they had already been successful in securing a living. Labourers who legitimated a child on marriage married heterogamously less often, while farmers, on the other hand, had increased odds of intermarriage. This might be explained by the fact that, whether living in concubinage with the "legitimating" husband or not, the large majority of single mothers had a proletarian background.[47]

What exactly the groom and bride had "done" prior to their marriage in terms of migration and work experience determined the odds of inter-marriage in important ways. If a farm worker were a rural migrant (i.e. if he had migrated to the place of marriage from a rural community), his odds of marrying upward decreased. Marrying a bride who had migrated from a village also reduced the odds of a heterogamous marriage. Conversely, if his bride had migrated from a city, the odds of the farm worker marrying outside his social group (i.e. marrying upward) increased by no less than 640 per cent. But marrying a former servant decreased the odds of farm workers becoming socially mobile through marriage by one-third. In Zeeland, domestic servants mostly originated from families of unskilled agricultural workers.[48] Thus, marrying a domestic servant often meant a homogamous marriage.

47. J. Kok, *Langs verboden wegen. De achtergronden van buitenechtelijke geboorten in Noord-Holland 1812–1914* (Hilversum, 1991), pp. 100 ff.
48. H. Bras, "Social Change, The Institution of Service and Youth: The Case of Service in the Lives of Rural-Born Dutch Women, 1840–1940", *Continuity and Change*, 19 (2004), pp. 241–264, 247.

Table 4. *Logistic regression of marriage mobility of farm workers and farmers*

Covariates	Farm workers (HISCLASS 10 & 12)	Farmers (HISCLASS 8)
Age of groom	1.015***	1.015***
Age of bride	1.002	1.002
Groom is widower (first marriage=ref.)	*3.015***	*1.687***
Groom is divorced	2.861	2.861
Bride is widow (first marriage=ref.)	0.961	0.961
Bride is divorced	1.852	1.852
Groom's mother is deceased (still alive=ref.)	*0.900**	*1.087*
Bride's mother is deceased (still alive=ref.)	*1.301**	*1.086*
Child legitimated	*0.744***	*2.818***
Geographically endogamous marriage (exogamous=ref.)	*0.830*	*1.015*
Groom is a rural migrant (born in the place of marriage=ref.)	*0.996*	*0.837**
Groom is an urban migrant	1.135	1.135
Bride is a rural migrant (born in the place of marriage=ref.)	*0.755**	*0.957*
Bride is an urban migrant	*7.402***	*2.039**
Older-husband marriage (same age=ref.)	1.057	1.057
Older-wife marriage	1.127*	1.127*
Group size (relative supply of father-in law's social group)	0.966***	0.966***
Father farm worker (father farmer=ref.)	3.624***	0
Groom intergenerationally mobile (not mobile=ref.)	3.097***	3.097***
Bride is a (former) domestic servant	*0.638***	*3.624***
1796–1804 (1815–1824=ref.)	0.852	0.852
1805–1814	1.092	1.092
1825–1834	1.054	1.054
1835–1844	1.218	1.218
1845–1854	0.993	0.993
1855–1864	0.995	0.995
1865–1874	0.872	0.872
1875–1884	0.784*	0.784*
1885–1894	0.969	0.969
1895–1904	0.904	0.904
1905–1914	*0.860***	*1.578***
1915–1922	*0.779***	*1.905***
Middelburg (Zuid-Beveland=ref.)	1.015	1.015
Vlissingen	1.132	1.132
Noord-Beveland	*0.850**	*0.562***
Schouwen-Duiveland	*0.745***	*1.588***
Tholen	*0.932**	*1.249**
Walcheren	0.998	0.998
Oost-Zeeuws-Vlaanderen	0.950	0.950

(*Continued*)

Covariates	Farm workers (HISCLASS 10 & 12)	Farmers (HISCLASS 8)
West-Zeeuws-Vlaanderen	*0.612***	*0.989*
Constant	0.319***	
N	27,862	
Model Chi-square (df)	3784.071	
Nagelkerke R Square	0.176	

Source: Marriage certificates from the civil records of Zeeland 1796/1811–1922.
Note: * significance level p< 0.05; **significance level p< 0.01; ***significance level p<0.001.
Significant differential effects in italics (see text for explanation of method).

For the group of farmers, rural migration decreased the odds of intermarriage too, which meant that rural migration allowed farmers' sons to remain in their class. Farmers' sons who married migratory brides of urban descent had 104 per cent higher odds of intermarriage than those who married a woman born in the place where they married. Likewise, a farmer's son who married a former domestic servant had 262 per cent higher odds of marrying heterogamously. As we have already noted, servants were mostly the daughters of agricultural workers; a farmer's son marrying a maid thus resulted in downward mobility. To sum up: the bride's migration and work experience is essential in understanding heterogamy in rural Zeeland.

Apart from the relational, migration, and work histories of individuals, their parental backgrounds also mattered in explaining marriage mobility. The odds of farm workers marrying upward were augmented when they married a bride whose mother was already deceased. As suggested earlier, middle-class women were thus less effective in securing their social position if their mother had died. Both the absence of the social capital of the mother and the possible pressure related to the introduction of a stepmother into the broken household may have limited opportunities for an advantageous marriage. We can explain in the same vein our finding that if a worker's mother had already died, his odds of marrying upward decreased. In contrast, the presence or death of the parents of bride and groom did not significantly affect the odds of heterogamy among farmers.

Finally, macro-structural characteristics made a difference as well. During the agricultural depression (1878–1895) the marriage mobility of both farmers and farm workers decreased. In depressed economic times opportunities for intermingling diminished. Contrasting with the generally increasing social fluidity since the turn of the twentieth century (illustrated in Table 2) were the decreasing odds of heterogamy among agricultural workers in the 1910s. On the other hand, the odds of heterogamy among farmers increased significantly in the first two decades of the twentieth century. Because of the restructuring of Zeeland's agriculture after the agricultural depression it became increasingly difficult for farmers to survive, and many of them had to switch to other occupations. Moreover, with the increase in education, farmers' children were able to choose other livelihoods outside farming. The general increase in the "openness of society" observed in the first few decades of the twentieth century (Table 2) can thus largely be accounted for by the rise in heterogamy among farmers.

There were also regional differences. In Noord-Beveland and the western part of Zeeuws-Vlaanderen, regions with large farms and rigidly polarized social structures, both farm workers and farmers married more often in their own class. On the islands of Schouwen-Duiveland and Tholen, however, the odds of intermarriage among farm workers and farmers diverged. In these areas farm workers were less likely to intermarry, while the farmers on these islands were increasingly forced to leave their occupation on marriage. As noted earlier, the farms on these particular islands were relatively modest; the smaller potential inheritance for grooms might have made it difficult for them to remain in farming, and they might increasingly have been forced to marry a woman from another social group.

CONCLUSION

In this article, we have investigated developments in and determinants of socially mixed marriage in a Dutch province (Zeeland) during the long nineteenth century by taking into account forces at the level of previous individual and family histories, characteristics of communities, and temporal influences and trends at the macro level of society. We have focused particularly on how these forces interacted within different social groups, in particular within the groups of agricultural workers and farmers, as they were the most important social classes in the rural social hierarchy of Zeeland. In the Zeeland countryside farmers and workers lived "in indifference together", as a report from the 1850s put it. Aside from work, these groups seem to have had little contact and few ties. The social barrier between them showed up in their high levels of homogamy: 70 per cent of all farm workers and 60 per cent of all farmers married into their own social group.

For farmers, homogamous marriage was the ideal, as they strived to hand down their farms and land to the next generation. Conversely, while Zeeland's workers might not have actively avoided socially mixed marriage, they often had so few social and financial resources that they were severely hampered in ascending the social ladder. From the perspective of nineteenth-century social reporters, workers had become "apathetic" and "indifferent" as a consequence. In fact, the indifference and isolation observed by social reporters was due to contradictory ideals with regard to life in general, and marriage in particular. However, the picture was not as grim and static as that painted by contemporaries. Our evidence shows that mutual ties leading to intermarriage were not entirely absent: 30 to 40 per cent of these rural residents married outside their original social class. About 17 per cent of farmers' sons actually married the daughter of a worker, while 8 per cent of workers' sons married the daughter of a farmer. Uncovering the antecedents of these "deviant" mixed marriages is instructive as they explain how social group differences worked in the nineteenth century.

Of course, general social and economic changes and trends influenced the process of intermarriage in rural Zeeland, both for workers' and farmers' sons. In economically depressed times, opportunities for workers to find a bride from a higher social group decreased, while for farmers regional agricultural schemes and acreage influenced the extent to which they could re-establish themselves as farmers. At the beginning of the twentieth century, possibly as a consequence of a differential increase in education, the odds of heterogamy among workers generally decreased while those among farmers increased. However, as our analyses showed, socially mobile marriages were caused first and foremost by the shape of the previous individual and family histories of the groom and bride.

For the sons of farmers, the options with regard to occupation and place of residence during their youth were crucial in this respect. Obviously, farmers' sons who chose an occupation other than their fathers' often married into another social class. But marrying a bride who had herself worked in another occupation, especially as a domestic servant, also resulted in a heterogamous marriage. The bride's urban descent too meant that often the ideal of social reproduction was not reached. One's previous relational history played a significant role in a similar way: having legitimated a child, being a widower, or being elderly hampered one's prospects of joining the farming class. In a social-group context where homogamy was very strong and actively strived for, the personal histories of the groom and bride were thus important factors in explaining whether they could achieve this ideal. Those who "had" to marry heterogamously were tainted by certain deviations in their own or their family's previous life course which made them less desirable partners in the farmers' marriage market.

In the case of agricultural workers who might have strived, more or less consciously, for social ascendance, previous life histories were just as important, although the meaning of both mixed marriage and the life leading to it was often the reverse of that of his age peers from farm families. If a farm worker wanted to escape his social class, it was advantageous for his bride to have spent her youth in an urban environment if he married relatively late or was already widowed. In contrast to farmers, in the case of farm workers the previous migration and familial careers of the groom – and especially his bride – increased his odds of escaping his lot. It is hard to say of course whether previous choices with regard to occupation, geographical mobility, and personal relations were the cause or consequence of one's initial social position. The fact is that these individual characteristics were inextricably linked through the life course, leading to an accumulation of disadvantage or advantage later in life, in this case specifically in relation to marriage outside one's original social group.

In the literature on social stratification and mobility, an overwhelming degree of attention has been devoted to the structural and temporal causes of mobility and heterogamy, often to such an extent that the mechanisms by which heterogamy, or for that matter homogamy, came about remain hidden or are only very generally explained. By laying bare differences in determinants between social groups and by offering group-specific explanations, we have shown the importance of forces at the level of individual and family life courses in shaping a phenomenon such as socially mobile marriage. This is not to say that general trends and macro-structural forces did not play a role. They "trickled down", however, through specific social groups to families with specific histories, to influence specific individual lives.

IRSH 50 (2005), Supplement, pp. 275-295 DOI: 10.1017/S0020859005002142

Total and Relative Endogamy by Social Origin: A First International Comparison of Changes in Marriage Choices during the Nineteenth Century

INEKE MAAS AND MARCO H.D. VAN LEEUWEN

INTRODUCTION

The introductory chapter to this volume presented a number of theories and hypotheses on the determinants of endogamy; the following chapters described endogamy in different historical settings and tested some of those hypotheses. The tests looked especially at the effects of individual characteristics of spouses, and sometimes of their parents. Results relating to changes in macro characteristics over time and their effect on the likelihood of endogamy were presented. Because all these chapters refer to only one country or region, regional comparisons are seldom made (there are some exceptions: Bras and Kok on differences between parts of the province of Zeeland; Pélissier *et al.* on differences between rural and urban areas, and Van de Putte *et al.* on differences between several Belgian cities and villages).

The aim of the present chapter is to shed some light on differences in endogamy between countries, regions, and periods.[1] We start by describing the steps that were taken to increase the comparability of the results. The first was the decision to opt for marriage registers as a source of data on endogamy. The second was the decision to classify occupations using HISCO. Thirdly, based on HISCO, HISCLASS was used as a taxonomy of class. We will refrain from describing the datasets, but refer instead to the preceding chapters in this volume for this information. We then proceed by describing total and relative endogamy in the regions and countries covered in this volume. We ask how large the differences in endogamy were between countries and regions, between rural and urban areas within countries, and to what extent endogamy changed over time within regions.

MARRIAGE RECORDS

The contributions in this volume have used marriage records as a source, which greatly facilitates comparisons. Marriage records are not the only

---

1. We would like to thank the authors of the individual chapters for kindly providing us with endogamy tables.

source of historical information on endogamy according to class of social origin, however. One could use other sources, such as marital contracts drawn up by notaries or censuses listing all people, whether married or not. Globally, however, marriage records are probably the most ubiquitous source. Furthermore, they cover a very high proportion of the population and are relatively easy to use. They are not entirely flawless, though. Not all partners marry; not all marriage certificates have the required occupational information for both the father of the bride and the father of the groom; and the occupational information is imperfect and must first be processed using a comparative historical class scheme.

Although, in the past, geographical and temporal variations existed in the proportion of people that ever married, the overwhelming majority of the world's population did marry. In Europe, more people remained unmarried than in many other parts of the world – as Hajnal's discovery of a European marriage pattern confirms – but, until recently, even in Europe the overwhelming majority of the population married.[2] Long-lasting relationships outside marriage did exist – the article by Holt, which looks at a slave society in Brazil, gives one example – and could in some instances encompass a sizeable proportion of the population, but until recently consensual unions were the exception.[3] This implies that marriage records offer information on long-lasting, intimate contacts of a very high proportion of the population, perhaps more so than any other single source.

This is not to say that the information they do not give, and the individuals and social contexts they do not cover, are uninteresting. One thing this source cannot clarify is the process of choosing between marrying (and, if need be, marrying downward socially) and staying single – the topic of Arrizabalaga's contribution to this volume, where, using marriage records in combination with other sources, she discusses the various options open to men and women. Furthermore, it is often difficult to trace migrants, and thus to illuminate the even more complex choice between marrying, staying single locally, or migrating – but it is certainly not impossible, as the article by Pélissier *et al.* makes clear.

To study the processes of class formation, one needs to have an indication of the social class of origin of bride and groom, in a way which is

2. J. Hajnal, "European Marriage Patterns in Perspective", in D.V. Glass and D.E.C. Eversley (eds), *Population in History: Essays in Historical Demography* (London, 1965), pp. 101–143; J. Hajnal, "Two Kinds of Pre-industrial Household Formation Systems", in R. Wall, J. Robin, and P. Laslett (eds), *Family Forms in Historic Europe* (Cambridge, 1983), pp. 65–104.
3. Stockholm offers an example of a city with a high proportion of consensual unions in the nineteenth century. See Margareta R. Matovic, "The Stockholm Marriage: Extra-Legal Family Formation in Stockholm 1860–1890", *Continuity and Change*, 1 (1986), pp. 385–413. Precisely because they were consensual rather than officially registered, it is not easy to know what proportion of the population was in such unions.

similar for all the regions and periods one would like to compare. Without this, one can never be sure whether the differences in social endogamy observed are merely artefacts – a consequence of non-comparable ways of allocating occupational titles from different languages, regions and periods into a class scheme. The same problem arises in comparative intergenerational research, and there it has been noted that even in many contemporary studies:

> [...] there is invariably a passage in which methodological problems and, in particular, problems of comparability of cross-national data are discussed and acknowledged to be grave. But then, this ritual having been completed, the analysis of the data goes ahead, even with a variety of *caveats*. The possibility that seems not to be contemplated, however, is that the degree of unreliability in the data is such that analyses should simply *not* be undertaken; that rather than such analyses being of some value as "preliminary" studies, which may subsequently be improved upon, they are in fact no more likely to have some approximate validity than they are to give results that point entirely in the wrong direction.[4]

Clearly, comparisons of important historical structures and processes would be less problematic if the occupational codings were comparable. In this volume we try to achieve comparability of results by first coding all occupational titles into the same fine-grained comparative historical coding scheme (HISCO) and then regrouping these codes into twelve social classes (HISCLASS), which for present purposes are collapsed into seven.

HISCO

HISCO is an occupational classification system that is both international and historical, and simultaneously links to existing classifications used for present-day purposes.[5] It did not emerge from nothing, but is a historicized version of a system with proven comparative credentials: the International Labour Organization's International Standard Classification of Occupations (ISCO). Both HISCO and the 1968 version of ISCO upon which it was based have ten major groups; these are divided into minor groups, which are subdivided into unit groups. HISCO has some 1,600 of these unit groups and is thus a detailed coding system. To give an example,

4. J.H. Goldthorpe, "On Economic Development and Social Mobility", *British Journal of Sociology*, 36 (1985), pp. 549–573, quotation on p. 554. The same point was made by H. Kaelble, *Historical Research on Social Mobility: Western Europe and the USA in the Nineteenth and Twentieth Centuries* (London, 1981), and *idem*, *Social Mobility in the 19th and 20th Centuries: Europe and America in Comparative Perspective* (Leamington Spa, 1985).

5. Marco H.D. van Leeuwen, Ineke Maas, and Andrew Miles, *HISCO: Historical International Standard Classification of Occupations* (Leuven, 2002); *idem*, "Creating a Historical International Standard Classification of Occupations: An Exercise in Multinational, Interdisciplinary Cooperation", *Historical Methods*, 37 (2004), pp. 186–197.

codes 6–xx.xx refer to the primary sector of the economy, with codes 6–2x.xx identifying various types of agricultural and animal husbandry workers. This last group includes codes 6–22.xx for field crop and vegetable farm workers and these, in turn, include several more specific occupational categories: general field crop farm workers (6–22.10), vegetable farm workers (6–22.20), wheat farm workers (6–22.30), cotton farm workers (6–22.40), rice farm workers (6–22.50) and sugar-cane farm workers (6–22.60).

The tasks and duties of each unit group are described, and occupational titles are coded into the unit group that matches the work its bearer does, the work as defined by the tasks and duties. In addition to the 1,600 five-digit codes, HISCO has three additional variables (status, relation and product) which are used to store information on social and employment status and product – information often found in historical records. Of these variables, status is of most interest here, since it contains information that may be used to code an occupation into its corresponding social class. The status variable distinguishes between types of ownership, stages in an artisan career, principals and subordinates, levels of education of persons still in the educational system, and indications of "pure" status, such as nobility.

Before discussing the transition from code to class, it is useful to know that the coding of occupational titles worldwide is ongoing; the progress so far can be seen on the History of Work website of the International Institute of Social History.[6] At present the website contains occupational titles coded into HISCO from the following countries: Belgium, Brazil, Canada (Quebec), England, Finland, France, Germany, Greece, The Netherlands, Norway, Portugal, Spain, Sweden, and Switzerland. Work on coding occupations in other countries, such as India, Italy, Russia, and the Philippines, is currently underway.[7]

HISCLASS

How does one transform 1,600 occupational unit groups into a convenient number of social classes? We cannot go into too much detail here, but we will briefly sketch this process. First, however, we would like to acknowledge the influence of the pioneering work of Gérard Bouchard.[8]

---

6. See www.iisg.nl.

7. See also V. Vladimirov (ed.), *Istoricheskor professiovedenie. Sbornik nauchnikh statie* (Barnaul, 2004).

8. G. Bouchard, *Tous les métiers du monde. Le traitement des données professionelles en histoire sociale* (Quebec, 1996). There are, of course, differences between HISCLASS and Bouchard's class scheme, which, in large measure, follow from the fact that we needed a scheme for comparisons not just between time-periods but also between territorial units. Thus we used the international HISCO as a starting point, and asked a group of historians from various countries to test the social-class scheme.

Like him, we wanted a historical social-class scheme that is both theoretically grounded – in identifying and closely following the underlying dimensions of social class in the past – and firmly tied to an empirical body of knowledge on these dimensions. To transform occupations into classes, a set of fixed criteria was necessary; these had to be as simple as possible. Ad hoc decisions were permissible, and sometimes unavoidable, but they could not form the basis of a social-class scheme. We did not want to classify occupations using just our historical intuition, although the intuition of a good specialist historian has sometimes proven to be rather good.[9] A theoretically, empirically and procedurally grounded class scheme has the advantage that all the cards are on the table, so to speak. Each step is documented, and can be questioned by the community of scholars: they may propose changes, test them, and see what difference these make. Thus a social-class scheme becomes a clear proposition regarding the social structure of past societies; one that can be questioned, rejected, or refined and, over the years, modified to take account of its flaws.

Our position on the virtues and flaws of any social class scheme is echoed in the following remarks by W.A. Armstrong:

> Any process of grouping, whether by age, birthplace, or in this case occupation, inevitably occasions some loss of detail. There are historians who instinctively object to the blanketing effect of all general schemes of classification, and on very much more reasonable grounds, those who prefer to use simple groupings of occupations, which are neither strictly hierarchical (social ranking) nor yet industrial groupings [...]. They are likely to point to the difficulties of deciding what are the criteria of social classes (and the shortage of information on some of the relevant variables) and to the various practical difficulties involved. To such historians, there might seem to be virtue in simply considering individual occupations as such, unaffected or uncontaminated by modern systems of classification, and they may well be suspicious of what look like rigid and inflexible general schemes, conjured up without mature consideration.
>
> We would not wish to claim that the schemes put forward later are fully comprehensive, entirely logical or perfectly suited to every scholar's purpose. Objections may very well be raised to the effect that this or that occupation ought "obviously" to have been placed in an alternative group or social class. Nevertheless it would be widely agreed that if research is conducted with some

---

9. Several studies have shown that there are both high correlations among expert historians as well as between historical intuition and contemporary rankings based on income, education, or social prestige. See T. Hershberg, M. Katz, S. Blumin *et al.*, "Occupation and Ethnicity in Five Nineteenth-Century Cities: A Collaborative Enquiry", *Historical Methods Newsletter*, 7 (1974), pp. 174–216; D.J. Treiman, "A Standard Occupational Prestige Scale of Use with Historical Data", *Journal of Interdisciplinary History*, 7 (1976), pp. 283–304; R.M. Hauser, "Occupational Status in the Nineteenth and Twentieth Centuries", *Historical Methods*, 15 (1982), pp. 111–126; Matthew Sobek, "Work, Status and Income. Men in the American Occupational Structure since the Late Nineteenth Century", *Social Science History*, 20 (1996), pp. 186–207.

common basis of classification, order and uniformity could be introduced in the field [...]. By following the schemes suggested here, no one need feel that his hands are tied. There is no reason why particular occupations could not be singled out for special analysis where appropriate, and alternative schemes can and should be applied according to individual interest. At the same time, if all would consider using these schemes *alongside* their own, their findings could be tabulated in forms which would be meaningful to other workers in the field. Anarchy might be avoided.[10]

A social class, it can be said, is a set of persons with the same life-chances. Historians working with self-construed local class schemes seem to agree that the main dimensions of social class are the manual–non-manual divide, skill level, the degree to which one supervises others, and the economic sector.[11] A felicitous characteristic of a social-class scheme constructed along these lines is that it results in social classes familiar to historians. It thus seems to conform to the way historians have generally seen society and, as a consequence, it can draw on the existing literature. Table 1 specifies how the twelve social classes in HISCLASS are derived (in a slightly stylized way) from the main dimensions of class. In order to avoid very small numbers in some classes, and thus a high volatility due to random factors, the studies in this volume have not used the full scheme but instead a version of HISCLASS condensed into seven classes: 1+2 higher managers and professionals; 3+4+5 lower managers and professionals, clerical and sales personnel; 6+7 foremen and skilled workers; 8 farmers and fishermen; 9 lower-skilled workers; 11 unskilled workers; 10+12 lower-skilled and unskilled farm workers.

It is one thing to specify the main dimensions of social class; it is quite another thing to allocate occupations to the appropriate class in a systematic way. This task is now far easier than ever before, however, because much of the work has already been done by the HISCO coding scheme, which reduces the world of work worldwide into some 1,600 basic

---

10. W.A. Armstrong, "The Use of Information about Occupation", in E.A. Wrigley (ed.), *Nineteenth Century Society: Essays in the Use of Quantitative Methods for the Study of Social Data* (Cambridge, 1972), pp. 191–310, quotation on p. 197.

11. See the review by Bouchard, *Tous les métiers du monde*, pp. 33–60, of major historical and sociological studies. See also the social-class scheme developed by a team of German historians (Federspiel, von Hippel, Hubbard, Kaelble, Kocka, Lundgreen, Mocker, Schraut, and Schüren) in R. Schüren, *Soziale Mobilität: Muster, Veränderungen und Bedingungen im 19. und 20. Jahrhundert* (St Katharinen, 1989). To the list of main dimensions of class could be added employment status, in the sense of being employed, an employer, or a working proprietor. Employment status is, however, often not given in historical datasets. This severely limits the scope for close matching with the current sociological EGP classification. This is regrettable since this classification is often used today to make international and temporal comparisons. See R. Erikson and J.H. Goldthorpe, *The Constant Flux: A Study of Class Mobility in Industrial Societies* (Oxford, 1992). The HISCLASS taxonomy will not, however, look entirely strange to users of EGP.

Table 1. *Dimensions of social class in HISCLASS*

Manual/ non-manual	Skill	Supervision	Sector	Class labels	Number
Non-manual	higher-skilled	yes	other	Higher managers	1
			primary		
		no	other	Higher professionals	2
			primary		
	medium-skilled	yes	other	Lower managers	3
			primary		
		no	other	Lower professionals, clerical and sales personnel	4
			primary		
	lower-skilled	yes	other		
			primary		
		no	other	Lower clerical and sales personnel	5
			primary		
	unskilled	yes	other		
			primary		
		no	other		
			primary		
Manual	higher-skilled	yes	other		
			primary		
		no	other		
			primary		
	medium-skilled	yes	other	Foremen	6
			primary		
		no	other	Medium-skilled workers	7
			primary	Farmers and fishermen	8
	lower-skilled	yes	other		
			primary		
		no	other	Lower-skilled workers	9
			primary	Lower-skilled farm workers	10
	unskilled	yes	other		
			primary		
		no	other	Unskilled workers	11
			primary	Unskilled farm workers	12

categories (and some auxiliary variables), in line with present-day schemes. To allocate the HISCO codes to a social-class scheme we processed information from the *Dictionary of Occupational Titles (DOT)*.

Research for the *DOT* was initiated in 1934 by the United States Employment Service "for the use of public employment offices and related vocational services".[12] Prior to that, the various employment offices had their own systems of classifying occupations, and no common scheme existed. In addition, the various local schemes were incomplete. This made it impossible to describe the world of work in general – i.e. to compile national employment and unemployment statistics – and made it more difficult to find jobs for the unemployed:

> [...] getting qualified workers into appropriate jobs is a task that can be done most adequately when the transaction is based on a thorough knowledge of both worker and job. [...] Thus, it becomes part of the duties of public employment offices to learn as much as possible about jobs and workers in order to be able to act as an effective placement agency. If a foundry superintendent wants the public employment office to send him a cupola tender, the office must know enough about the work and worker to be able to refer a registered applicant who has previously been classified as qualified and capable of doing the work.[13]

To obtain this knowledge, occupational analysts – employees from the US Employment Service – went to plants and businesses all over the country to observe men and women at work. They collected information on tasks performed, knowledge required, machine equipment and materials used, physical demands and working conditions, and required worker characteristics. The third edition of the *DOT*, for example, was based on over 75,000 job observations relating to over 45,000 job studies.[14]

The first edition of the *DOT* was published in 1939, the second in 1949, the third in 1965 and the fourth in 1977. In addition, several supplements or revisions to the entire corpus were prepared and published. A much revised edition of the fourth edition was published in 1991, for example, as the "fourth edition, revised 1991". The coverage of the dictionary in terms of the number of occupations and the information per occupational category grew over time, and both the structure and the information were modified to accommodate changes in the American economy.

The third edition, issued in 1965, was the first systematically to list information on the nature of the work (working conditions, work performed, and industry), but also on the demands made by the work on the workers in terms of training time, aptitudes, interests, temperaments, physical demands. This information extended and replaced the

---

12. US Department of Labor, *The Dictionary of Occupational Titles*, 2 vols (Washington, DC, 1939), vol.1, p. iii.
13. *Ibid.*, p. xi.
14. *Ibid.*, p. ix.

previous classification into skilled, semiskilled, and unskilled occupations. The completeness of the information contained in the third edition makes it appealing to use this edition rather than previous editions for HISCO purposes. Of course, it remains to be seen to what extent information from the world of work in the USA in the mid-twentieth century can be used to characterize the worlds of work earlier or elsewhere. This very same problem makes the fourth edition of the *DOT* – which basically contains the same sort of information – a less suitable starting point for our purposes.

The problem of anachronism remains when using the 1965 *DOT* to characterize earlier societies, but from the start it was clear that the problem was not insurmountable. This was evident from Bouchard's successful attempt to use information from the French-Canadian *DOT* to characterize occupational terms from vital registers from the Saguenay region in French Canada in the nineteenth and twentieth centuries, and to classify these occupational terms systematically into a small number of classes. Bouchard's book is extremely well documented and contains a systematic and detailed discussion of the various problems that he encountered, the solutions he chose, and their reliability.[15]

Briefly, we first matched each of the 1,600 HISCO categories to one of the over 10,000 *DOT* categories. We did this not on the basis of name similarity, but by carefully comparing the description of the tasks and duties of a particular HISCO unit with that of a specific *DOT* category. Once the match had been made, we used the numeric information that *DOT* gives for each category on the dimensions in the HISCLASS scheme.[16] Having completed this operation, we wanted to test the validity of the scheme by making systematic use of expert knowledge. We therefore consulted a small group of historians with a working knowledge of the world of work.[17] We asked them to score HISCO groups on the dimensions that HISCLASS uses (manual/non-manual, skill level, supervision, sector) and to classify HISCO groups directly according to the twelve social classes of the class scheme. Where a majority of these experts disagreed with the results derived from our *DOT* exercise, we re-examined the data and, by and large, concurred with the experts. Usually, we understood the root of the problem, and this use of expert judgement should, we feel, have removed the worst flaws in *DOT*, in our matching

---

15. Bouchard, *Tous les métiers du monde*.
16. It is documented in M.H.D. van Leeuwen and I. Maas, "HISCLASS", paper presented at the 5th European Social Science History Conference (Berlin, 24–27 March 2004), and it will be the subject of a future publication.
17. The experts were Marie-Pierre Arrizabalaga, Hans Henrik Bull, Gordon Darroch, Sören Edvinsson, Georg Fertig, Matts Hayen, and Jan Kok. It goes without saying that we are extremely grateful for their collaboration.

procedure, and in applying *DOT* to a historical context. One result, we feel, is that anachronistic use of *DOT* has been greatly reduced.

As it stands, we certainly do not believe that HISCLASS is beyond criticism. We do think, however, that it is a historical social-class scheme that can be used to compare social structures and mobility in different parts of the world, in the sense expressed by Armstrong.[18] There is one flaw we would like to mention here. In historical populations a large proportion of the population ends up in the farming class (see Figure 1, which shows the proportion of grooms from the rural classes in the studies in this volume). This is not a HISCO problem, as HISCO has various categories of farmer, both according to specialization and to the nature of their activity, varying from cotter status to manager of a large estate. Nor is it a HISCLASS problem either, because these two groups end up in categories other than that of the average "farmer" (they are placed among the rural labourers and the managers respectively). The problem is one of the vagueness and incomparability of the sources. In many cases the historical source gives just "farmer" without any further qualification. In other cases there is extra information, but this varies by time and place to such an extent that no common ground could be found for distinguishing subcategories. If, however, a subdivision is necessary for a certain type of analysis and the source gives the necessary information, the historian is of course at liberty to make it.

DIFFERENCES AND CHANGES IN TOTAL ENDOGAMY

Now that comparable data exist on the class distributions of the fathers of brides and grooms in a number of regions and periods, we want to present what is the first truly comparative analysis of endogamy by social origin. The most commonly used measure of social endogamy is the percentage of couples both of whom originate from the same social class, i.e. those couples who can be found on the diagonal of an endogamy table. Figure 2 shows these percentages for the countries and regions studied. Five periods are distinguished: all years before 1800; 1800–1833; 1834–1866; 1867–1900; and all years after 1900. These periods are necessarily broad because some of the datasets are rather small and preclude any further temporal subdivision. To facilitate comparisons between regions we chose to use the same periods for all regions.[19] At first sight it appears that, compared with

18. Some results on its use across cultures will be discussed at the next European Social Science History Conference in Amsterdam, in the spring of 2006.
19. It would have been preferable to have used shorter time-periods and to have avoided the open-ended start and end periods which are used in most of the articles in this volume. For comparative reasons, it would also have been preferable to have territorial units of more or less equal size.

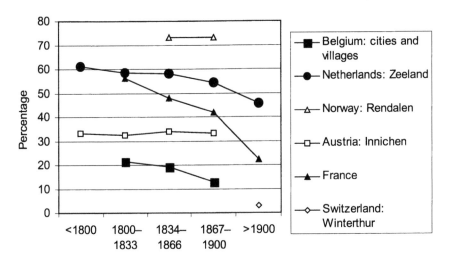

Figure 1. Proportion of grooms from the rural classes, by country and period.

regional differences, endogamy changed little over time. The largest change over time occurred in the Rendalen region (Norway), where the percentage of socially endogamous marriages decreased from 76 per cent in the period before 1800 to 61 per cent in the period 1867 to 1900. In rural areas of France, endogamy decreased by 11 percentage points between 1867–1900 and the period after 1900. In all other regions and countries the within-country changes never exceeded 10 percentage points over the whole period.

If we take a closer look at changes in endogamy over time, it also becomes clear that the nineteenth century was not especially characterized by decreasing endogamy. Clear increases in endogamy are visible in the Belgian villages and in Innichen between 1800–1833 and 1834–1866, in the Scanian parishes in Sweden between 1834–1866 and 1867–1900, and in urban France between 1867–1900 and the period thereafter. The largest decreases in endogamy occurred in the period before 1800 (in the Norwegian region of Rendalen and in the Austrian town of Innichen) and in the period after 1900 (in rural France and the Dutch province of Zeeland). There are no indications of a decrease in endogamy at all between the first and second part of the nineteenth century. Between the second and third part of the nineteenth century endogamy decreased in rural Belgium and urban France.

There were large differences between countries and regions. The highest rate of endogamy (76 per cent) was found in Rendalen (Norway) in the years before 1800, the lowest (29 per cent) in Winterthur (Switzerland) in the period after 1900. Regional differences between rural and urban areas

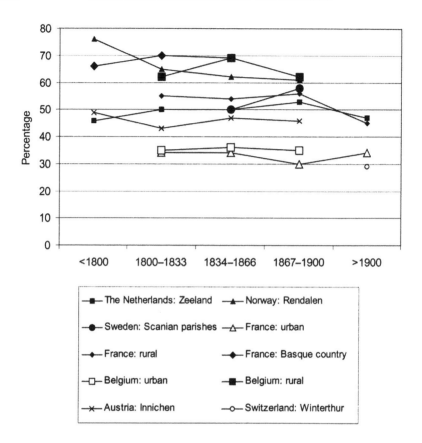

Figure 2. Total endogamy by region and period.

were especially large. Four of the regions in our study can be classified as rural: the Basque country (France), Zeeland (the Netherlands), Rendalen (Norway), and the Scanian parishes (Sweden). They were all characterized by high percentages of endogamous marriages (on average around 68 per cent, 50 per cent, 65 per cent, and 54 per cent respectively). For France and Belgium we can distinguish between urban and rural regions. Within the French countryside around 50 per cent of all marriages were endogamous; within Belgium's villages the corresponding figure was 65 per cent. In contrast to these high endogamy rates in rural areas, rates in urban areas of France, Belgium, and Winterthur (Switzerland) were much lower, at 32 per cent, 35 per cent, and 29 per cent respectively overall. Whether Innichen (Austria) should be regarded as urban or rural is a matter of debate. Earlier, we showed that the proportion of grooms from the rural classes exceeded 30 per cent in Innichen and was clearly higher than in the Belgian cities and Winterthur. Consistent with its intermediate level of urbanization,

Innichen shows percentages of endogamous marriages that are in between those of the urban and rural regions in our study.

As was shown in several of the preceding chapters, the percentage of endogamous marriages is strongly affected by the class structure. Large classes generally have higher endogamy rates than small classes. Further, rural classes are characterized by high endogamy. More or less by definition, rural areas and periods were characterized by an uneven class distribution in which two classes (farmers and farm labourers) were much larger than the other classes.

The dissimilarity index is a measure of how much the class structure of a given society deviates from a situation in which all classes are of the same size.[20] We calculated the dissimilarity index for the class distribution of the fathers of the groom for all regions and periods presented in Figure 2. The highest dissimilarity index was found for Rendalen (Norway) in the period before 1800. It was as high as 71 per cent, indicating that 71 per cent of the fathers of all grooms would have had to change class for there to have been a class distribution in which all classes were of the same size. The lowest dissimilarity indices were found in the Belgian cities and in urban parts of France (between 19 per cent and 22 per cent). The dissimilarity index correlates highly (0.88) with the percentage of fathers in the rural classes (HISCLASS 8 and 10+12). More importantly, the correlation between the dissimilarity index and the percentage of endogamous marriages is 0.86 and the correlation between the percentage of fathers in the rural classes and endogamy is even higher (0.90). These high correlations confirm our conclusion based on Figure 2, namely that the percentage of endogamous marriages was principally a function of the extent to which the class structure was dominated by the rural classes.

In the next section we will investigate what differences in endogamy between regions and periods remain if we take the effects of the class distribution into account.

DIFFERENCES AND CHANGES IN RELATIVE ENDOGAMY

In research on mobility and endogamy a range of models has been developed to analyse the association in a cross-tabulation (for example, of the social origin of the groom and the social origin of the bride) which remains after the effects of the marginal distributions (the class structure of the fathers of the groom and the bride) are taken into account. This residual association is called "relative endogamy". We estimated a model which calculates one measure for the amount of endogamy for each class (i.e. one parameter for each diagonal cell of the table, which we will refer to

---

20. The dissimilarity index is calculated as $0.5 * \Sigma_i |(\text{Percentage in class}_i - 100/i)|$ in which i is the number of classes.

as relative endogamy), one measure for the strength of the association between class of origin of bride and groom under the condition that they do not marry endogamously (i.e. one parameter for all the non-diagonal cells, which we will refer to as relative exogamy), and measures for the relative distances between the classes. Classes whose members are very unlikely to marry one another are thought to be further apart in social reality than classes whose members are likely to marry each other. Unfortunately, the endogamy tables for Rendalen (Norway), the Scanian parishes (Sweden), the Basque country (France), and Innichen (Austria) had to be omitted from these analyses because some of the HISCLASSes were not present in these regions at all.[21]

The first result of this model is thus the relative distances between the HISCLASSes.[22] These distances are shown in Table 2. Higher managers and professionals and lower-skilled and unskilled farm workers are at the extreme ends of the estimated continuum. This means that the sons of higher managers and professionals were very unlikely to marry the daughters of lower-skilled and unskilled farm workers, and vice versa. The remaining classes occupy positions in between which are comparable to the positions they would occupy on a status scale. The likelihood of sons of foremen and skilled workers marrying daughters of a higher manager or professional was higher than the corresponding likelihood for sons of lower-skilled workers and clearly higher than the corresponding likelihood for sons of unskilled workers. The class of farmers and fishermen occupies a position in the middle, indicating that their children could marry either upward into the other propertied classes or downward, by marrying children from the other rural class. A final interesting finding is the relatively large distance between the two classes at the top. If the children of higher managers and professionals married outside their own class, it was very likely that they did so with children of lower managers, professionals, clerical and sales people. However, the relatively large distance between these two classes indicates that this was not a very common phenomenon.

The second result of the model gives us the class-specific relative endogamy parameters for the region and period that we chose as the

---

21. The model estimated is the so called Row and Column Effects (II) model. See Leo A. Goodman, "Simple Models for the Analysis of Association in Cross-Classifications Having Ordered Categories", *Journal of the American Statistical Association*, 74 (1979), pp. 537–552. We used the lEM program to estimate the model. See Jeroen K. Vermunt, *Log-linear Event History Analysis: A General Approach with Missing Data, Latent Variables, and Unobserved Heterogeneity* (Tilburg, 1996).

22. We assumed that the distances are equal for fathers of the bride and fathers of the groom, which is not unlikely, and equal for all periods and regions, which will be a topic of future research. Compare for example the distances estimated for Winterthur in the chapter by Schumacher and Lorenzetti, pp. 65–91.

Table 2. *Estimated distances between the social classes with respect to the likelihood of intermarriage, and class-specific relative endogamy in Belgian cities 1800–1833*

HISCLASS		Relative position	Class-specific relative endogamy, Belgian cities 1800–1833
1+2	Higher managers and professionals	−2.07	−2.88
3+4+5	Lower managers, professionals, clerical and sales people	−0.12	0.40
6+7	Foremen and skilled workers	0.18	0.30
8	Farmers and fishermen	0.20	1.95
9	Lower-skilled workers	0.40	0.38
11	Unskilled workers	0.68	1.14
10+12	Lower-skilled and unskilled farm workers	0.73	1.34

"reference category". In our case these are the Belgian cities in the period 1800–1833. These parameters are also shown in Table 2. The higher the estimated parameter value, the greater the likelihood of brides and grooms marrying within their own class. Belgian brides and grooms originating from the two rural classes showed a high likelihood of endogamy. In the first few decades of the nineteenth century the likelihood of young men and women from Belgian cities escaping their class of origin by marrying upward were rather small if they originated from the unskilled working class. At the other extreme of the social continuum, however, the children of higher professionals and managers were relatively likely to marry outside their own class. Note, however, that this is after taking into account the relatively large distance between this class and the other classes, as discussed above. We could interpret these findings as indicating that at the beginning of the nineteenth century the sons and daughters of higher managers and professionals in Belgian cities were more likely to marry outside their own class than one would have expected on the basis of the distance between this class and other classes, as estimated using information from all regions and all periods.

More interesting than the relative endogamy parameters in the Belgian cities in a specific period are the differences in relative endogamy between regions and periods. To facilitate the interpretation of the results, we estimated the extent to which all classes in a certain period or region were more (or less) likely to marry within their own class than in another period or region.[23] The results are presented in Figure 3. The Belgian cities between 1800 and 1833 are the reference category. As one can see from the graph, the relative endogamy value for this reference category is

1. A value above 1 for a certain period and region indicates that brides and grooms from all classes there and then were on average more likely to marry within their own class than brides and grooms in the Belgian cities between 1800 and 1833. A value below 1 indicates a lower likelihood of doing so.

At first sight it is clear that the distinction between rural and urban areas that we found for total endogamy is not applicable to relative endogamy. For example, after taking the different class distributions into account, we found that brides and grooms from Belgian villages married less endogamously than brides and grooms from Belgian cities. Relative endogamy in French rural and urban areas was similar during most of the period under investigation. Only between 1867 and 1900 were brides and grooms from French rural areas more likely to marry within their own class than brides and grooms from French urban areas. Winterthur (Switzerland) had the lowest rate of relative endogamy; the Dutch province of Zeeland the highest, at least for the period 1834–1900.

With respect to changes over time in class-specific relative endogamy we can conclude that the six regions do not show a single consistent pattern of change. Whereas the likelihood of marrying within one's own class of origin increased during the nineteenth century in Zeeland (the Netherlands), it decreased in urban regions in France and remained stable in the Belgian cities. In Belgian villages brides and grooms were more likely to marry within their own class in the middle of the nineteenth century than at the beginning or the end; in rural France the opposite was the case.

Finally, the model estimated provides us with information on the strength of the association between class of origin of the bride and class of origin of the groom where they did not marry endogamously (thus in the non-diagonal cells of the endogamy table). We refer to this measure as relative exogamy, with a high level of association implying a low likelihood of exogamy.[24] Data on relative exogamy in the different periods and regions are presented in Figure 4.

The figure for the rural villages in Belgium is striking. Whereas all other regions show a slow upward or downward change in relative exogamy, in the Belgian rural villages the association between the class of origin of the bride and that of the groom drops strongly from almost eleven to a little below four.[25] This means that if the Belgian rural population married outside their class of origin in the first three decades of the nineteenth

23. For details on these "uniform-change" models see Yu Xie, "The Log-Multiplicative Layer Effect Model for Comparing Mobility Tables", *American Sociological Review*, 57 (1992), pp. 380–395.

24. The same terminological confusion exists in mobility research, in which this association is referred to as "relative mobility" or "social fluidity".

25. This measure of association can be interpreted as an odds ratio weighed by the estimated distances between the classes.

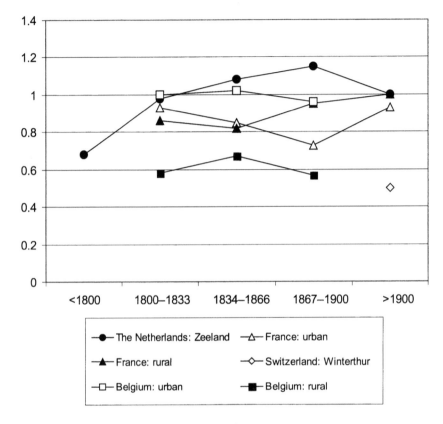

Figure 3. Relative endogamy by region and period.
Note: Relative endogamy parameters describe uniform differences in all seven class-specific endogamy parameters between countries and regions. Belgian cities in 1800–1833 are the reference category.

century, they were likely to marry into a neighbouring class. Later in the nineteenth century, the likelihood of marrying more distant classes increased strongly.

The changes in relative exogamy in the other countries, and the relative positions of these countries compared to each other, are rather similar to the changes and relative positions with respect to relative endogamy. The Dutch province of Zeeland shows an increase in the likelihood of endogamous marriage and in the likelihood of marrying over a short social distance until at least the mid-nineteenth century, with a modest decrease thereafter. The Swiss city of Winterthur shows a relatively low likelihood of endogamy and a high likelihood of marrying exogamously over a larger social distance. The urban and rural regions of France differ little on both criteria, and in both cases the pattern in the Belgian cities is closest to that of the province of Zeeland (the Netherlands) too.

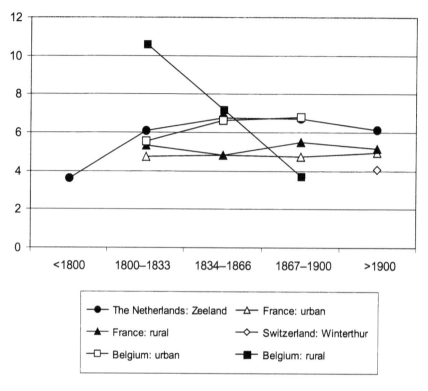

Figure 4. Relative exogamy by region and period.
Note: Relative exogamy parameters describe the association between social origin of the bride and social origin of the groom outside of the diagonal of the endogamy table. They are odds ratios scaled by the relative distances between the social classes.

CONCLUSION

This chapter presented the first truly comparative figures on endogamy by social origin in several regions and for periods before the twentieth century. This comparison was possible due to the development of an international classification of occupations, HISCO, and a standard procedure to group occupations into social classes (HISCLASS). As a result, we can begin to discern what was general and what was unique to regional variations and to temporal patterns before the twentieth century (and indeed how unique the twentieth century was compared with previous centuries).

Based on the regions and periods included in this study, three preliminary conclusions can be drawn. First, total endogamy was strongly related to the proportion of the population originating from the rural classes. In societies dominated by one or two rural classes, endogamy was much higher than in societies whose populations were more or less evenly distributed across all the seven classes that we distinguished. Although not shown in this chapter, this first conclusion leads to a second, namely that with modernization and the accompanying shift in the class distribution total endogamy decreased over time. Thirdly, relative endogamy and relative exogamy did not change uniformly over time and seemed unrelated to the level of urbanization in the regions.

Although we would very much like to give explanations for the variations in endogamy we found, at present it is not easy to test systematically and statistically the hypotheses presented in the opening chapter of this volume. The search for comparable indicators of the determinants of endogamy is seriously hampered by the large differences in size of the regions being studied here. What seems a reasonable indicator for a town (whether, for example, there is a factory or a railway station) does not make much sense for a country, and vice versa. Another problem is the broad periods that are distinguished. The effects of historical events that are relatively short (war, for instance) are therefore hard to detect. A further problem is the small number of cases. All in all, there are only twenty data points for six countries. This makes it difficult to detect regularities.

Some of the theoretical hypotheses in the opening chapter are, however, supported by the results presented in various chapters in this volume. Van de Putte, Oris, Neven, and Matthijs demonstrate the significant effect of group size in general on social homogamy, while also showing that a distinct ethnic cleavage – between the native French-speaking population of Walloon cities and the Dutch-speaking immigrants – reduced the scope for native Wallonians to enter into socially endogamous marriages. But was this ethnic divide stronger than that between the French-speaking natives in the industrial centre of Winterthur and the German-speaking rural migrants of which Schumacher and Lorenzetti write?

If a man was upwardly mobile, this influenced his ability to marry outside his social class, both in the Dutch province of Zeeland, as discussed by Bras and Kok, and in France, as borne out by Pélissier, Rébaudo, Van Leeuwen, and Maas. But did it matter more in France than in the Netherlands? And did it matter as much in the Brazilian plantation society described by Holt? Sweden's 1734 Marriage Act stipulated that no one could be forced into marriage, but it also stipulated that marriage required consent. In the case of women, this would normally have been given by the father. As is apparent from the contribution by Dribe and Lundh, there was no age limit either: regardless of her age, an unmarried woman had to obtain consent in order to marry. Dribe and Lundh also write that fathers often forced daughters to marry against their will. Parental pressure was also apparent in the Norwegian valley studied by Bull. There, opportunities to meet were also regulated by means of night-courting, a phenomenon that served to subject the choice of partner of young men and women to the scrutiny not only of their peers but also of their parents. Bull also stresses the effect of inheritance laws on those farmers who had something to bequeath – an effect different for the eldest son than for his siblings. Fathers pushed sons to marry endogamously, he concludes; thus, if the father died prematurely the eldest son would be more likely to marry exogamously. While we know that parental pressure in various forms, including bundling, existed in both Nordic countries, we do not know if the existence of bundling, in addition to other forms of pressure, gave parents in Sweden and Norway more control over their children's destiny than in other countries.

To investigate to what extent these results for single countries also hold for other countries, two requirements have to be met. First, we need additional data on endogamy in more regions and periods, to increase the number of cases at the macro level. We hope that more and more historical marriage registers will become available for comparative research, especially those covering regions (notably outside Europe) not included in this volume. We also hope that even more occupational titles will be coded using HISCO and HISCLASS and become available for comparative research into the history of work through the History of Work website.[26] The regions studied and the time blocks into which the data were divided in this conclusion are, in a sense, gifts of chance. If more regions and countries could be covered, the global similarities and divergences would become more apparent, and the time horizon could extend beyond the nineteenth century (the focus of many of the studies in this volume) while the time blocks could be narrowed, even for the nineteenth century. This would allow us to see more detail, and make it easier to explain what we can see.

Secondly, comparable data on the macro characteristics of these regions and periods need to be compiled. For this, we hope, good use can be made of ethnographical, anthropological, and qualitative historical material. In his survey of social mobility studies, some twenty years ago, Kaelble remarked that:

> Two theatres of the history of social mobility have none of the actors and very few of their spectators in common. Sociologists mostly do not know the historical studies, since they often regard them as too limited, too crude in their statistical methods, too narrow minded in their analytical approach, too far removed from the long term view of present trends. Historians usually take little interest in sociological studies since they are regarded as not taking account of

---

26. The website also contains photographs and other images of the world of work, an as yet small dictionary of occupations, and other information. It is hoped that, with the help of those interested in the world of work, this website will continue to grow.

social history in its entirety, as being too difficult to interpret because of the quantitative techniques employed, as remaining too general and vague in their conclusions.[27]

This volume will, we hope, serve as a bridge between this era and a new one: an era which sees interdisciplinary collaboration, a stretching of historical and current time, and in which social endogamy across the globe (and processes of social inequality and mobility more generally) is compared and explained.[28]

27. Kaelble, *Historical Research on Social Mobility*, p. 114.
28. We have already commenced a more ambitious project to analyse endogamy according to social class in a large number of regions and time periods. This project will also gather more comparable information on macro characteristics to explain differences in total and relative endogamy. This research is part of the HISMA (Historical International Social Mobility Analysis) project. Using occupations and measures of social class and prestige as indicators, HISMA tries to promote research into social inequality and mobility, through the study of marriage according to social class in the past, the historical study of careers, and the study of intergenerational social mobility. A session of the next International Economic History Association Conference (to be held in Helsinki in the summer of 2006) will be devoted to this topic.

www.ingramcontent.com/pod-product-compliance
Ingram Content Group UK Ltd.
Pitfield, Milton Keynes, MK11 3LW, UK
UKHW020451010325
455719UK00015B/530